S0-EAU-290

Turning Points

broadview
press

Turning Points

*Decisions Shaping
the Evolution of
the International
Political Economy*

BY MARK R.
BRAWLEY

Copyright © 1998 Mark R. Brawley

All rights reserved. The use of this publication reproduced, transmitted in any form or by any means, electronic, mechanical, photocopying, recording, or otherwise, or stored in a retrieval system, without prior written consent of the publisher – or in the case of photocopying, a licence from CANCOPY (Canadian Copyright Licensing Agency) 6 Adelaide Street E., Suite 900, Toronto, Ontario M5C 1H6 – is an infringement of the copyright law.

CANADIAN CATALOGUING IN PUBLICATION DATA

Brawley, Mark R. (Mark Randal), 1960–
    Turning points: decisions shaping the international political economy

Includes bibliographical references and index.
ISBN 1-55111-152-7

1. International economic relations – History.
I. Title.

HF1359.B72 1998   337'.09   C98-930786-7

BROADVIEW PRESS, LTD.
is an independent, international publishing house, incorporated in 1985.

North America
Post Office Box 1243, Peterborough, Ontario, Canada K9J 7H5
3576 California Road, Orchard Park, New York, USA 14127
TEL (705) 743-8990; FAX (705) 743-8353; E-MAIL 75322.44@compuserve.com

United Kingdom and Europe
Turpin Distribution Services, Ltd., Blackhorse Rd., Letchworth, Hertfordshire, SG6 1HN
TEL (1462) 672555; FAX (1462) 480947; E-MAIL turpin@rsc.org

Australia
St. Clair Press, Post Office Box 287, Rozelle, NSW 2039
TEL (612) 818-1942; FAX (612) 418-1923

www.broadviewpress.com

Broadview Press gratefully acknowledges the support of the Ontario Arts Council, and the Ministry of Canadian Heritage. We acknowledge the financial support of the Government of Canada through the Book Publishing Industry Development Program for our publishing activities.

This book was designed and readied for the press by Zack Taylor, Black Eye Design.

Printed in Canada

10 9 8 7 6 5 4 3 2 1

For Adèle

Contents

Acknowledgements

....

I wish to thank Mike Lusztig and Charles Lipson, who, perhaps without knowing it, encouraged me to undertake this project. I especially want to thank Michael Harrison of Broadview Press for offering me the opportunity to write this text and for ensuring that things moved ahead smoothly. Three anonymous reviewers gave me excellent criticisms, and if the themes and arguments in the text run tightly together, it is partly through their efforts as well as mine.

More broadly, the contents reflect my own training; I therefore owe a great debt to Jeff Frieden, David Lake, and Art Stein. I also wish to thank my colleagues at McGill, but especially my partners in the McGill/ Université de Montréal Joint Research Group in International Security. They created the atmosphere in which I could spend time reflecting on the broader issues in international relations and international political economy. I should also thank McGill University and the Political Science Department more directly, for I wrote much of this book while on sabbatical.

Special thanks also go to Donna Aronson, who ably proofread the early versions of this text and assisted in research. Much of the credit for this must be shared with her, though any faults would be due to my judgement. Richard Tallman, the copy editor, corrected as many of the remaining mistakes as he could locate, and I thank him for his efforts. Most of all, I want to thank Annette and Adèle, for being patient with me while I spent time on this, and for making sure I remember what matters most in life.

Mark R. Brawley
MCGILL UNIVERSITY

Note to Instructors

This textbook was designed with certain goals in mind—thus I find it important to remark on what is and is not included here. Much of this reflects my own beliefs on the different tasks that texts, lectures, and discussions serve. While some may argue that students need to be given only a small amount of information, and that same information should be presented to them as many times as possible and in as many forms as possible, I do not agree. In my view, a textbook should provide a guide, which, along with lectures, provides a coherent framework for a wider array of materials and exercises. Additional readings should provide further information that students can digest in terms of the text and lectures. Thus, this book has a limited set of aims.

First, in terms of the chapters on theories and paradigms in Part 1, this text is intended to serve as an introductory text for international relations. That is, the concepts and arguments presented in these first chapters are not specific to international political economy. Most of the examples presented in these chapters are those explored in the original works laying out particular paradigms or arguments—thus they are often not examples from international political economy (IPE) at all. To illustrate how these same arguments hold for IPE, however, one must provide examples in lectures.

The cases in Part III are drawn from a variety of time periods and from all three issue-areas. They are presented in chronological order, but need not be presented that way. For instance, Chapters 10, 11, 12, 14, and 19 consider decisions regarding shifts in trade policy. Within that set, two chapters (12 and 14) consider shifts to protectionism. Chapters 13, 15, 17, 20, and 21 examine decisions regarding international monetary policy. Within that group, two chapters (13 and 17) examine what happens when a national money is used as the key currency and a currency overhang develops. As such, these chapters also reflect some of the consequences of international investment on the source country; the receivers' point of view can be found in Chapter 18 and, to a lesser extent, in Chapter 16. Chapters 16 and 18 look more closely at the causes and consequences of different development strategies. These cases can also be structured in ways that stress different theoretical purposes, depending on the instructor's goals.

The cases end with comments about the consequences of the decisions taken for the evolution of the international political economy. The case summaries provide a context in which to place the case. They do not provide a summary evaluating the theories applied in the cases. Most of the time, the results are left fairly open. Since there is room for interpretation and debate about the relative importance of each argument, such issues are best left for discussion in conferences, though lectures, too, could draw some conclusions. Moreover, each of the historical cases only draws on a limited set of sources—not all the sources available. Again, this was a conscious decision. The Suggested Readings at the end of each chapter are normally (but not always) additional, in the sense that their points of view are not well represented in the case material here. These lists are an excellent source for extra reading assignments to complement this text. The contrasting points of view can then be explored in lectures and discussions.

Introduction

This is a book first and foremost about international relations. It is designed for students who have no prior experience with theories of international relations, let alone international political economy. It is intended to illustrate how political scientists theorize about international relations. The cases discussed in Part III are drawn from international political economy. The book therefore introduces the core issues of international political economy, to illustrate how *theories* from *international relations* deal with the particular problems posed by the study of the politics of international economic relations. [Note: Terms appearing in *italics* can be found in the glossary.] As an introductory text, it does not explore every angle of *international political economy*, but rather attempts to provide students a set of concepts and analytical tools they can build on in later classes.

Why Study International Relations?

Many different events occur at the international level, that we wish to understand. Whether we are concerned with extremely hostile actions (such as the outbreak of wars, or the issuance of military threats) or with examples of co-operation or mutual benefit (such as an agreement to lower barriers to trade between two countries, or the formation of an alliance), we try to understand these events in terms of patterns of activity. As a pair of theorists put it, "the facts do not speak for themselves … what we know depends on how we go about organizing all the events and trends to which we attach significance."[1] More importantly, we want to understand the world in terms of causal patterns. We want answers to many different questions: why will one thing happen rather than another? when will it happen? how will other actors react? The list of possible questions is endless.

Our task as political scientists in the field of international relations is to make sense of these events. The first major point for students to understand is that we use theories or models to simplify things. The world is a complex place, and international relations is no different—it is very complicated. All sorts of factors shape the international political economy or the actions of particular states. As political scientists, our objective is to understand international relations, by selecting and focusing on the most important forces influencing events. Why? Because we are concerned with the future. We want to take some control over our future. That means the theories or issues we will consider in this book are causal theories. We will be focusing on explaining why certain things happened in the past, to establish causal patterns, which we hope will provide some guidelines as to how to act in the future. Without some understanding of how things happen, we have little guidance for action. Without an understanding of what causes war, what brings about a trade agreement or some other type of event, how will we know what to do to prevent something undesirable from occurring, or what to do to bring about something positive? How else can we choose from several possible plans for action?

Of course, we can never have a perfectly accurate predictive model of the future because one can never anticipate how the future may differ from the past; this is especially true when one tries to predict human behaviour. Predicting human behaviour is very difficult; political science is not a pure science, but social in nature. As in the other social sciences, political scientists will always have trouble making perfect predictions. The future may be quite different from the past in innumerable ways, so there is always the possibility, even the likelihood, that any predictions we make based on models of past behaviour will be somewhat inaccurate. But just because we cannot predict the future with total certainty does not mean we should forgo any planning, or likewise forgo any attempt to make educated or informed analyses of the possibilities (or probabilities) of something happening.

In fact, in the field of international relations, there are usually all sorts of people making recommendations about the foreign policies of states. People are always ready and willing to give advice on what to do, usually without giving us the causal model they are basing their arguments on. Journalists make policy recommendations in their editorials, suggesting that one particular policy will produce a set of particular outcomes, while a different policy would lead to an alternative outcome—they therefore have a causal theory implicit in their argument. The same can be said for politicians. Historians frequently describe past events in causal terms—they, too, often use causal theories, usually implicitly. Simply by emphasizing one aspect of a story over another, they are implicitly supporting one theory over another. Why else would we need to know this information? The news media, by stressing particular bits of information and ignoring an infinite amount of other pieces of information, are using certain types of implicit models of causality, otherwise the bits of information they give you would not be relevant to your lives, and neither they nor you would bother with them.

A Theoretical Approach to International Relations and International Political Economy

One of the most important characteristics differentiating political science from history or journalism is its emphasis on constructing causal theories. Though we discuss the same events as historians or journalists, our efforts are much more self-consciously an effort in theory-construction, and this requires us to lay out the logic of our arguments in an explicit form.[2] We seek to understand the linkage between cause and effect, and clarify that linkage through comparisons of various past events.[3] We are searching for connections we can generalize; historians, on the other hand, are experts on the specific. A good political scientist should also stress a sense of humility and awe in theory-construction, recognizing the limits of his or her own knowledge and the limited range of our probabilistic statements.[4] While we use the same evidence as our basic building blocks, the results of our construction look rather different.

What Is a Theory?

Since theories are the central theme throughout this book, you need to understand more specifically what we mean when we use this term. I follow the definition Kenneth Waltz uses in his book, *Theory of International Politics*. He discusses both "laws" and "theories." He defines a *law* as ways of establishing relationships between variables, as facts of observation.[5] Of course, the most interesting associations are those relating a cause and an effect.

We use the term *variable* to refer to the forces or factors of both cause and effect, because when we take repeated observations of a relationship we are trying to locate changes in each side of the equation (i.e., we want to see how both the cause and the effect vary). For example, we may think that good grades are the result of studying. We would therefore want to take observations of students who do varying degrees of studying. We would expect to see that as a student does more of the assigned reading for a course, the grade he or she receives will rise—the variation in grades depends on the variation in completing the readings. In more technical language, the effect is referred to as the *dependent variable*, because we are expecting changes in it to depend on changes in the value of the causal variables. The causal variables will presumably also change in value, but since we are only concerned with explaining one thing at a time, we do not worry about why they vary in value; thus, we refer to them as *independent variables* (i.e., their values will change independently of other parts of our theory).[6] A theory can have more than one independent variable. For instance, grades are not merely a function of reading all the assigned texts—attending lectures, participating in discussion groups, prior experience in a similar course, and a host of other factors presumably affect grades as well. A more complex theory would elaborate the relationship between a variety of independent variables and the dependent variable.

In this text, in terms of the effects, we will be concerned with variations in the behaviour of states (foreign economic policy, to be specific) or the behaviour of other actors (such as corporations, political parties, bureaucracies, or individuals) as one side of the equation. The separate fields within social science reflect different interests in the subject we are trying to explain. International relations is primarily about describing and predicting the variation in state policies towards other states, or towards international organizations or foreigners, though increasingly we try to describe and predict the behaviour of non-state actors. Comparative politics is primarily about describing and predicting the variation in state policies within states, and it, too, is now focusing on describing and predicting the behaviour of non-state actors.

Laws are connections between variables of which we have repeated observations of such strength and number that we can safely expect the relations to continue into the future. Laws are few and far between in the social sciences, though, precisely because so little fits this definition. A *theory*, on the other hand, Waltz defines as a speculative process for explaining observed relationships between variables.[7] Causality is therefore an important aspect of any theory, since we are speculating that changes in the independent variables have some sort of impact on the dependent variables. Probability is another important facet of our understanding of a theory, however, since by Waltz's definition we are not certain about the relationship between the variables. (If we were certain, we would have a law.) Because we are not certain about the relationship between the variables, and because there are an infinite number of possible variables to consider, it is quite possible to have more than one causal theory consistent with the same facts. Since we lack definitive causal relationships (which we would label laws), and several different causal relationships seem possible, political science is rife with debates about which theories are more persuasive—and that is where the main thrust of this text lies, in the debates between specialists in international relations over the persuasiveness of various theories as explanations for changes in foreign economic policies.

Some people point out that our ability to make predictions will never be very good. These pessimists go on to argue that any attempt to predict or, even worse, to prescribe policies based on a prediction would be unwise and risky. I would argue that simply because we cannot be certain in our predictions does not mean we should give up on building theories; it means we should try harder, but be wary of the fact that perfect predictions are unattainable. The pessimists must not only criticize the endeavours here, but offer an alternative. If we wish to take control over the future, how should we do so? If we don't develop prescriptions through the creation, criticism, and refinement of theories that attempt to explain causal relationships, how then are we to develop policy prescriptions?[8] More importantly, how do we convince others to try one prescription rather than another?

Since theories are statements of probability, and since theories are used within political or policy debates, how should one go about comparing theories? There are several important factors to keep in mind. Obviously we can compare theories in terms of the accuracy of their predictions or descriptions of past events, but *accuracy* is in fact only one point of comparison among several. We can compare specific qualities of theories in terms of the tasks theories are intended to perform.[9]

The Qualities of Theories

Our theories or models are simplifications of reality, so of course many things are lost in the process of constructing models or theories. As stated above, predictive theories are probability statements. That means one of the qualities of a theory we can always talk about is *accuracy*. No theory will be right 100 per cent of the time, but we can compare theories that are right half of the time to theories that are right a third of the time. Of course, because theories are simplifications of reality, they focus on some independent variables at the expense of others. The theories do not work perfectly because all these other variables come into play, so there are always excuses for the theory's failure to provide accurate predictions or descriptions. (Theorists expect a certain amount of inaccuracy, and therefore often cover themselves by including the statement that their theoretical predictions will hold ceteris paribus, or "all other things being equal.") Sometimes the theorist creates so many caveats that the theory is difficult to pin down and test with any facts!

Besides accuracy, two other important aspects of theories are traditionally used as bases of comparison: *generalizability* and *parsimony*. Generalizability means "how broadly can I apply this theory?" "For how many cases will this theory be useful?" Since we want to understand causality across several different cases, and may want to use our theory in future situations, generalizability is important. As noted above, this emphasis on generalizable arguments is one of the characteristics differentiating political scientists from historians.

Parsimony refers to the degree of simplicity. Is the theory simpler than other theories that attempt to explain the same phenomenon? Is the theory "cleaner" or "neater"?[10] Parsimony reflects the ability to explain much of the variation in the dependent variable with as little information or theory as possible. It serves as a proxy measure for efficiency—how much "mileage," in terms of explanation, can you get out of a little bit of theory and a little bit of evidence. More recently, some scholars have begun to use the term *leverage* to refer to much the same idea: according to Gary King, Robert Keohane, and Sidney Verba, leverage is the ability to explain as much as possible with as little as possible.[11]

Yet another quality of theories we can identify for the purposes of comparison is *falsifiability*.[12] Essentially, philosophers of science have warned us to keep a perspective on what we consider as an explanation. In the natural sciences, different explanations for the transit of the sun across the earth's sky have been accepted as fact. But with new information, new scientific techniques, and new models or theories, these explanations have evolved. In hindsight, what was accepted as the explanation at one point in the past looks ridiculous to us today; our understanding today will perhaps look just as ridiculous to our grandchildren. Thomas Kuhn explored some of these developments in the evolution of the hard sciences in his work, *The Structure of Scientific Revolutions*, which drew examples from the development of physics. The conclusion of Kuhn, Imre Lakatos, and other scholars who study science and the pursuit of knowledge is that we can never know anything for sure—our explanations are never certain. Something else could be going on that we have yet to grasp or understand. We can be certain, however, of the incorrectness of our theories. Thus, our goal should not be to prove something correct, since that would be impossible, but rather to put our best explanations constantly to the test by trying to disprove them. That is where the notion of falsifiablity comes in; we need to construct our theories in such a way that we can test them and disprove them—we should make explicit the grounds for rejecting our theories as incorrect, though we can never know for certain that they are correct![13]

Kuhn's work on the development of physics is also appreciated for its ability to illustrate how much scientists internalize the paradigm they are applying. His examples laid out how much a well-established paradigm or set of theories had to be questioned and criticized before the scientists were willing to abandon the theory and turn to an alternative. Kuhn therefore discussed such shifts in thinking in terms unlike those one might expect—

he compares them to changes in faith, or psychological dramas, rather than the result of cool calculation. While we might promote more rational decisions in our own search for theories in international relations, we should be aware of how difficult it is for these shifts in thinking to take place.

The tricky thing when comparing theories is to balance out considerations of these various properties. An accurate theory or model, one that fits reality closely, is often quite complicated and takes many different factors into account. This means tailoring a theory to a specific case. That gain in accuracy could mean a loss in generalizability and/or parsimony. Making a generalizable theory often means dropping out details, so you tend to lose accuracy. One thing to note once we examine specific theories is the manner in which different types of theories embody these trade-offs. We should also be sensitive to the fact that theories do different things—and that clearly affects how we should evaluate theories in terms of accuracy or generalizability.

We must also remember that more than one theory can fit the evidence. Philosophers and historians of science have pointed this fact out over and over again.[14] In the specific examples considered in the later chapters, historical events may often be overdetermined. (That is, several theories may provide explanations that are entirely consistent with each other as well as with the historical record. One way to deal with overdetermination, however, is to explore the details of how events unfolded in such a way that one explanation appears to be more consistent with the facts than another.)

Given what these last few paragraphs say about comparing theories, how does one ultimately resolve choices between theories? Well, for starters, theories can be compared along one dimension: accuracy in prediction, perhaps. But is a very good description of the past more important than a good prediction? Is parsimony more important than generalizability? Those are questions of taste. Two rational people, interested in the scientific pursuit of knowledge, can disagree about those issues.[15] Only when one theory can do just as well as another theory in all categories, but also better in one or more, can we clearly judge the first to be preferable.

The Tasks of Theory

What do theories do? They serve us in several ways. We've been discussing how we use theories to *predict*, but that isn't all they can do for us. We may also use theories to *describe* the world of today or to help us understand the past. That means they tell us about the past and the present. They hopefully tell us something about the future, so they may be used to predict as well. Theories can also be used to *prescribe* policies—that is, they should also tell us about how to take control over the future. Sometimes, theories also offer a *normative goal*, that is, they provide us with a vision of the way things ought to be.

A good example of a theory that performs all four of these tasks (description, prediction, prescription, and a normative goal) fairly evenly would be Marxism. Karl Marx developed a view of the world based on an analysis of historical development (description), arguing that capitalism would create all sorts of social and political problems because of its inherent contradictions (prediction), but that such problems could be solved through a world socialist revolution (prescription), which would deliver mankind to a socialist utopia (the normative goal). *The Communist Manifesto*, a rather short document, presents Marx's theory performing each of these tasks.

Since theories or models are simplifications or representations of reality, a theory begins with a set of things assumed to be true. These *assumptions* are useful for eliminating some of the confusion of the real world. As things assumed to be true, and as simplifications, assumptions are bound to be false some of the time (if not quite often). The value of an assumption is determined not by seeing if it passes a true-false test, but by examining how it shapes the theory. Is the assumption logically consistent with the theory? Does the assumption make the theory more accurate, or parsimonious, or generalizable? Those are the appropriate questions to ask about an assumption. Try to remember that as political scientists, we are building models of reality, not reconstructing reality itself. A model airplane is rather different from the real thing. One is merely a representation of the other. Assumptions are elements of abstract thinking, to help us create these representations by eliminating parts of reality.

Grouping Theories Together

Theories that share assumptions can be gathered into groups; the theories constructed in a similar fashion tend to share similar qualities. Hence, people who construct theories in a similar fashion are usually referred to under a single title. (The group may then be referred to as a "school of thought," or practitioners of a "paradigm" or "approach.") The debates that exist in international relations between these different groups usually come down to disagreements in the evaluation of different assumptions. Building theories on different assumptions usually leads to very different predictions (and therefore different policy prescriptions). Through the comparison of theories' abilities to carry out the tasks discussed above, in terms of the qualities listed earlier, we try to settle disputes between schools of thought.

One of the earliest groups of theorists to form in modern times shared the belief (or rather, the theories they constructed shared the assumption) that people were basically good—or at least that laws and institutions could bring out the goodness in people. This group came to be known as the idealists. They were referred to as *idealists* because their assumption about human nature made it possible for them to build theories that prescribed paths to achieving an ideal world, a world of peace, love, and understanding. There were different theories within this group, but because of their underlying assumptions, the link to their normative goals was strong.

Those more cynical about mankind put stock in a different set of assumptions, and constructed theories by first assuming that people are selfish and desire domination over others. To highlight their distinction from the idealists, they were known as the *realists*. These two groups, plus the *radicals* who stand outside these two groups (and who are often from a *Marxist* tradition), are the three main groups of theorists in international relations[16] (although we will also be discussing many others, such as *liberalism, constructivism,* and *institutionalism* as well as other ways to organize theories into different groupings). We often refer to such groupings of assumptions as *paradigms*. A paradigm is an example, but in political science the term is used to refer to an example that others copy and employ as well. The set of core assumptions that define a grouping of theories is what separates one paradigm from another.[17] Because the assumptions can be grouped in several different ways, discussions of paradigms can be a bit confusing. We will be employing two different organizing principles when grouping theories together. First, we will look at variants of idealism, realism, Marxism, liberalism, and other popular approaches in international political economy. Second, we will try to organize the same theories in a different fashion, on the *levels of analysis*.

The original split between realists and idealists was over assumptions about human nature. But that is not the only assumption one might make; a Marxist or a constructivist might not worry about human nature at all when making assumptions to create a theory. So another way of grouping theories would be to look at some key defining characteristic, such as the type of actor assumed to be the most important. This approach was once one of the most popular methods for organizing theories into groups, and is known as grouping theories by the levels of analysis.[18] What one finds in the social sciences is that people understand human activity as the result either of the characteristics of individual units within the society (i.e., people, households, or business firms) or of characteristics of the social organization itself. In economics, for instance, we find this in the distinction made between macro- and micro-economics.

In the study of foreign policies, or foreign economic policies, things are a bit more complex. We have a number of different divisions to make, since we are talking about the behaviour or action of states and how citizens from different countries interact to create international outcomes. So we find two levels of explanation or analysis right away. Some explanations focus on the characteristics of the state itself, which we will call *state-level* or *national-level* theories, and others focus on the society of states or the international *system level*.

As an example of each type of explanation, consider Canada's membership in NATO. How do we understand Canada's decision to enter this organization? A system-level explanation would focus on the characteristics of the international system to understand this event: Canada belongs to NATO because in the 1950s there were two superpowers, and to be safe a country had to join one of the alliances led by each superpower. The existence of the two superpowers is critical for understanding Canada's decision in this theory. What about state-level explanations? Well, these would focus on Canada's domestic characteristics to explain the decision. In this sort of theory, the cultural, social, and political aspects of Canada drove it to join NATO.

We can come up with other levels of analysis by considering the composition of states. States are made up of government bodies, social classes, interest groups, etc., and each of these in turn is composed of individuals. It is possible to explain the policies of states as the result of the characteristics of groups or individuals within states. We get several other levels: *societal*, *bureaucratic*, and *individual*. When Canada signs a treaty with another country, is it the result of all Canada acting together? Or is it the result of some specific subset of Canadians determining the outcome? Or can it only be understood as the result of the actions or thoughts of a particular person, perhaps an influential leader or negotiator? Each of these levels will become clearer as you spend some time thinking about them and handling them. And remember, each of these represents a group of theories, not simply one theory.

We refer to them as the levels of analysis, because they can be stacked hierarchically (see Figure 1), with the narrowest form of social organization at the bottom (the individual) and the broadest at the top (the international system).

FIGURE I: THE LEVELS OF ANALYSIS

System level
State level
National Characteristics
Domestic Politics
Bureaucratic Politics
Individual Idiosyncrasies

In Chapter 1, we will begin with a discussion of the evolution of the various paradigms, beginning with the debate between the realists and the idealists. In Chapter 2 we take a different tack, and arrange theories by the levels of analysis. If you look closely at the definitions of the paradigms discussed below, you will see that each paradigm can usually be placed on a different level of analysis. Realists focus on the state as the primary actor, and their arguments are about states interacting—thus they fall into the systemic level. Idealists tend to focus on individuals, so their theories can often be grouped on that level. Marxists focus on classes as the primary actor, and classes interact within societies, so that is where they tend to be found. Some modifications of Marxism have come to focus on characteristics of capitalist states (i.e., on the state level), and on how states organize the international economy (i.e., on the system level). As you can see from this simple discussion, the various ways to organize theories can overlap, although often these fits are imperfect.

In Part II, we examine three issue-areas in international political economy. These three issue-areas (trade, international investment, and international monetary relations) cover the most important aspects of the international economy, though they are not completely comprehensive. Each chapter in Part II will discuss some of the relevant economic theories on the subject, but will especially explore the political ramifications of economic activity in these areas. The goal is to establish a critical understanding of the interaction of political and economic issues concerning the international economy. In Part III, particular examples of regime change or foreign economic policy behaviour are examined. Each case offers us an opportunity to test out various theories. By viewing the theories as they are applied and comparing their abilities to describe and explain events, the reader has a possibility to evaluate various groups of theories. Moreover, each case is a pivotal change, a turning point in the evolution of the international political economy. Finally, in Part IV, questions concerning the refinement of theories are engaged, and the overall evolution of the international political economy is discussed in brief.

Notes

1   James R. Rosenau and Mary Durfee, *Thinking Theory Thoroughly* (Boulder, Colo.: Westview Press, 1995), 57.

2   Or at least we should make our theories explicit; see the recommendations made, ibid., 5.

3   It is possible to use "thought-experiments" (or counterfactuals) as well as the historical record, though one must take special care in how this is executed. For more on counterfactuals, see Robert Keohane, Gary King, and Sidney Verba, *Designing Social Inquiry* (Princeton, NJ: Princeton University Press, 1994).

4   Rosenau and Durfee, *Thinking Theory Thoroughly*, 2.

5   Kenneth Waltz, *Theory of International Politics* (Reading, Mass.: Addison-Wesley, 1979), 1.

6   Sometimes we will be interested in understanding why the independent variable changes, of course, but that may require us to create a whole separate theory.

7   Waltz, *Theory of International Politics*, 6.

8   The one possible counter to this argument is that one can make such decisions based on faith rather than logic.

9   Kenneth Waltz talks about explanatory power, predictive power, and elegance. See *Theory of International Politics*, 69-70. The sorts of qualities I will discuss below appear in Thomas Kuhn's *The Structure of Scientific Revolutions* (Chicago: University of Chicago Press, 1962). The same ideas also appear in Adam Pzerworski and Henry Teune, *The Logic of Comparative Social Inquiry* (New York: Wiley, 1970).

10 See Kuhn's thoughts in *The Structure of Scientific Revolutions*, 155. This is similar to the term "elegance" that Waltz uses.

11 Keohane, King, and Verba, *Designing Social Inquiry*, 29-31.

12 See Imre Lakatos, "Falsification and the Methodology of Scientific Research Programmes," in Lakatos and Alan Musgrave, eds., *Criticism and the Growth of Knowledge* (New York: Cambridge University Press, 1970), 91-196. Lakatos is building on the ideas of Karl Popper, who discussed falsifiability in *The Logic of Scientific Discovery* (New York: Basic Books, 1959).

13 For a discussion of how Kuhn's views of falsifiability differ from Popper's, see the interpretation offered by Lakatos in the article cited above. Lakatos develops the notion of "sophisticated methodological falsificationism," which stresses, among other things, that disproof is not the same thing as rejection of a theory, and the need to test sets of theories rather than just a single theory. In other words, finding out that a theory doesn't work all the time doesn't disprove it so much as show its level of accuracy. However, there are certain instances where a theory must be accurate if it is to be viable at all; falsifiability is about establishing the grounds for rejecting a theory (or set of theories).

14 See Kuhn, *The Structure of Scientific Revolutions*, 76.

15 For a broader discussion of such issues, see ibid., 199-201; also see Kuhn's comments on p. 262 in "Reflections on my Critics," in Lakatos and Musgrave, eds., *Criticism and the Growth of Knowledge* (New York: Cambridge University Press, 1970), 231-78.

16 See, for instance, Robert Gilpin, *U.S. Power and the Multinational Corporation* (New York: Basic Books, 1975), 26-33.

17 See the discussion in John A. Vasquez, *The Power of Power Politics: A Critique* (New Brunswick, NJ: Rutgers University Press, 1983), ch. 1, esp. 2-5.

18 One of the first articles to discuss this technique was John David Singer, "The Level-of-Analysis Problem in International Relations," in Klaus Knorr and Sidney Verba, eds., *The International System: Theoretical Essays* (Princeton, NJ: Princeton University Press, 1961), 77-92 (published in *World Politics* that year as well). A later exposition of this method for organizing theories can be found in S.J. Andriole, "The Levels of Analysis Problems and the Study of Foreign, International, and Global Affairs: A Review Critique, and Another Final Solution," *International Interactions* 5, 2/3 (1978), 113-33.

Part One

APPROACHES TO
INTERNATIONAL RELATIONS

One

....

DEBATES AND THE EVOLUTION OF PARADIGMS

The Origin of the Study of International Relations

The origin of international relations as a field within political science is commonly traced to the psychological, political, and emotional impact of World War I. While earlier scholars wrote about international relations, the form of the study of international relations as we now practise it only began after World War I. Prior to that time, the study of international relations had been haphazard and unscientific, because up to 1918 the study of international relations was primarily the study of diplomatic history, with some current events and international law mixed in. The emphasis was on practical knowledge for those working in the field of diplomacy. Students would have learned such things as who was who in current international political circles, which diplomats were posted where and what the contents of recent treaties contained—things we might still study—and occasionally there were informal attempts to understand causality via analyses of cases from diplomatic history. These analyses, however, were inconsistent.

The carnage of World War I produced the first real impetus to understand international relations via more scientific methods. The world was shocked by the enormous human and monetary costs of the war. To make sense of these costs, and perhaps to justify such expenditures, an effort was made to see World War I as "the war to end all wars." For their part, scholars began to do all they could to prevent another such war from occurring. They stressed the need to reach some understanding of why this war had occurred in the first place. So the modern study of international relations began with an emphasis on developing predictive and prescriptive theories.

The Realist-Idealist Debate

Initially, one group of theorists, the *idealists*, would build on the public revulsion from the carnage of World War 1 to dominate the field of international relations; yet, a set of rival views was already in the background, and within twenty years a great debate arose. This would only prove to be the first of several that have gripped the field. This first major debate was between two camps, one of which traced its lineage to the previous study of diplomatic history, the other being predominantly drawn from those who had previously studied international law. Both sides were concerned with the possibility of another major war. Those who drew on legal studies approached the task of preventing future wars by emphasizing the importance and utility of international law. Why are laws useful in domestic society? Because they influence the way people act. Without laws in place, people would behave differently. Change the laws and people do behave differently. Laws guide behaviour, and are used to make humans interact in ways considered more desirable by those who write the laws. Laws, in that sense, create better citizens. Those who stressed the potential for international law to create a more peaceful society of states became known as the *utopians*, or idealists, because they stressed the possibility of perfecting the behaviour of man and thus perfecting the actions of states.

THE CORE ASSUMPTIONS OF CLASSICAL IDEALISM

1. Humans are perfectible.
2. There exists a harmony of interests between people and between nations.
3. Therefore, war is never an appropriate way to solve disputes; instead, the underlying harmony of interests should be uncovered and emphasized.
4. The correct laws and institutions can guide behaviour, and thus bring out the good in humans (i.e., expose the harmony of interests between people and between states).

The idealists stressed choice, rationality, and the potential or actual existence of a harmony of interests between individuals and, therefore, also between states. As they might have put it, "couldn't any rational person see how futile war was, how stupid the whole affair of World War 1 had been, and therefore couldn't we all agree not to do it again?" They argued that there were ways in which the international system could be perfected, in which it could be brought to different standards of state behaviour. Thus, idealism has always been very teleological (goal-oriented), and has always emphasized the normative goal of international peace.

Those who focused on historical patterns took a different stand. For them, war was something to be expected—it was a traditional way in which states had resolved their most important disputes. *Realists*, as these scholars became known, stressed the importance of power in international relations, if not in all social interactions. They stressed continuity in states' behaviour, especially in the willingness to use power to resolve differences. They considered the utopians to be idealistic and unrealistic (note the pejorative connotations associated with those words today). In contrast to the assumptions made by the idealists that humans were perfectible through the creation and application of law, realists assumed that humans were basically selfish, greedy, and interested in dominating each other. By drawing on diplomatic history, the Realists stressed how humans had been evil to each other much more often than they had been nice. (It is important to stress that this was a debate over assumptions, not facts—realists have no special claim to reality.)[1] Whereas the idealists could work with the broad public impressions flowing from the results of World War 1, realists took more time to develop their ideas. Indeed, it took the work of one realist, E.H.Carr, to show how realism was developing as the counterpoint to idealism.[2]

The Failure of the League of Nations and World War II

Carr is remembered as one of the earliest proponents of realism. His observations of the international situation in the late 1930s reflected a sober assessment of idealism, but a careful reading of his work also yields insights into the problems of *classical realism*. Carr argued that idealism was flawed by being overly optimistic about the ability of scholarship to change the world. Idealism stressed prescriptions and normative goals over developing an understanding of how things actually worked. As such it was doomed to fail. Of course, Carr pointed out how realism—as a foil to idealism—therefore had its own weaknesses. Most important among these, according to Carr, would be realism's failure to develop a finite goal, as well as its inability to develop an emotional appeal to the public, and to render moral judgements—all of which would ultimately undermine realism's ability to provide grounds for actions.[3]

Carr was writing in 1939; his assessment was based on some of the events he had already observed, such as the failure of legalistic attempts to prevent war in the 1930s. (The League of Nations had been created with the express purpose of implementing international law to punish aggression, yet it seemed impotent in the face of fascism.) The advent of World War II merely proved his point even more strongly. The war gave the realists control over the agenda of the field of international relations. Yet as Carr also recognized, much of the earliest realist writings were merely arguments against idealism; realism did not begin with a coherent set of logical arguments but was merely anti-idealism.

Early realists focused their arguments on human nature and the sorts of assumptions one should make about what drives human interactions. Reinhold Niebuhr, for instance, drew upon Christianity to argue that man was tainted by sin and thus was not perfectible; like other realists such as Hans Morgenthau, Niebuhr also argued that man had a will to live, which drove humans to want to dominate their environment and each other.[4] Morgenthau rooted his version of realism in human nature and the desire for power.[5] The will to survive becomes a will to power. These same assumptions could then be translated into the affairs of states. The realists gained ground in their debates with idealists by arguing that morality played no role in the foreign policies of other states (such as Nazi Germany or the Soviet Union) and therefore the foreign policy of the U.S. or other Western democracies should be just as amoral when facing these threats. Much of this debate swirled around the real-world issues of foreign policy in the late 1940s and early 1950s. In the minds of these early realists, moral objectives were luxuries the Western states could rarely afford in those days.[6]

THE CORE ASSUMPTIONS OF CLASSICAL REALISM

1. Humans have a will to survive, which makes them selfish.
2. The will to survive means a will to dominate the environment, including other humans.
3. Since this creates competition to dominate, the will to survive creates a search for power.

Realism also changed as time went on. While realists maintain dominance today, they do not now have, nor have they ever had, universal appeal. Idealism fell out of favour in the early post-World War II era, but later paradigms took up some of the core arguments from idealism. Realism's dominance did not prevent a variety of other approaches from arising. These other paradigms often challenged realism directly. Indeed, some of the rivals to realism are currently flourishing but, in the 1950s and 1960s, realism clearly held sway.

Realism and the Cold War

In many ways, the decades of the 1950s and the 1960s were not merely the time when realism seemed most dominant, they were the golden years of security studies.[7] Because the United States and other Western powers were locked in an ideological struggle and an arms race with the Soviet Union, there were constant demands from governments for informed analyses of military and diplomatic strategies. These demands stimulated theoretical analyses of security affairs, and many of the brightest minds were drawn into the field.

Realism changed during this time in some of the ways which Carr's assessment had predicted. Without the rival idealists offering a strong alternative, realists began to question the utility of their own assumptions. Kenneth Waltz argued in *Man, the State, and War* that human nature was not such an important factor on which to base theories.[8] Indeed, he argued that human nature was not set, therefore it was not useful to make any assumptions about human nature—humans were capable of acting for either good or evil purposes. Moreover, states could be thought of in the same way; they too were capable of acting for either good or evil purposes. Waltz's underlying argument was that the particularities of situations influenced how humans (or states) behaved. Waltz therefore proposed that it did not matter whether one assumed human nature to be basically good or basically evil; in certain situations, good people (or good states) acted the same as evil people (or evil states). Though it took some time for these ideas to gel into a coherent set of assumptions, realism was changing.

Another Great Debate: Behaviouralism and Realism Transformed

The second great debate in international relations was fought primarily among realists. This concerned the research methods one should employ.[9] The debate occurred primarily in the 1960s and 1970s, though factions persist on both sides to this day.[10] Scholars disagreed over the best ways to uncover causality, the best methods for interpreting evidence, and the best ways to go about asking questions. On one side were the *traditionalists*, who argued for a continued emphasis on history and the study of particular historical episodes as unique events. On the other side, *behaviouralists* stressed the need to aggregate information in order to apply methods of data analysis (statistics) to interpret the evidence. This sort of debate still goes on in political science overall as well as in other social sciences such as history (where the arguments are just beginning).

One of the most important aspects of realism as it developed was its emphasis on the notion of *sovereignty*, the concept that states exercise the ultimate legitimate political authority. States enforce laws and do not have to answer to other political authorities, only to themselves. For realists, the fact that states respect no higher authority and exercise political authority over other actors (whether individuals or groups) makes states the most important actors in international relations. When two sovereign actors have a dispute, how do they resolve it? If each respects no higher authority, they must settle the dispute between themselves. Each state can act as judge, jury and executioner. And that means to survive, or to achieve goals beyond mere survival, states have to have power to deal with other states.

These are some of the basic building blocks of realist theories. States, as sovereign entities, are seen as the primary actors in international relations, and are therefore assumed to be *rational* and unitary (in other words, the state acts as a coherent, single entity).[11] The international system, because it lacks an authority above the individual units (states), is anarchic. Realists use the term "anarchy" not in the sense of chaos but in that there is no sense of government superior to the actors in question. In such a system, states are under constant threat and must do what they can to defend their own interests, and hence must maximize power. Note that in this version of realism, there is no need to make an assumption about human nature.

Kenneth Waltz, in *Theory of International Politics*, lays out the basic points of realism in a slightly different way, showing how realism has continued to move away from its original focus on human nature.[12] Waltz says we can understand states' policies by understanding the system in which they operate. The key concept for Waltz is *structure*. Structure is a way of depicting the relations of the units, or the composition of the system. As he puts it, "units differently juxtaposed and combined, behave differently and in interacting produce different outcomes."[13] This thinking can be easily portrayed in a diagram.

FIGURE 2:
WALTZ'S VIEW OF CAUSALITY IN INTERNATIONAL POLITICS

change in structure

LEADS TO

change in state interactions

LEADS TO

a new outcome

According to Waltz, structure has three characteristics: an ordering principle, the differentiation of the parts, and the distribution of capabilities. The ordering principle refers to whether the system is hierarchical or anarchic. Domestic politics is characterized as hierarchical—the national government is usually dominant, with lower levels of government exercising authority over a specific range of topics and answerable to the authorities above. Realists such as Waltz assume the international system to be anarchic. Differentiation of the units refers to the similarity in functions that actors perform. For instance, in domestic politics, different levels of government perform different tasks; one level maintains roads, another level the health care system, another national defence, and so on. Typically, different levels of government perform different tasks (though there can be some overlap). Waltz's point is that at the international level, states perform very similar functions (they each provide legal systems, defence, monetary systems, public infrastructure, etc.). The units are alike in that sense. They are rivals in providing these services and do not rely on each other. Units do differ in their capabilities to perform such activities or functions well. Some states have greater capabilities than others.

Waltz's assessment of these three characteristics of the international system are meant to hold true for the modern period. Since it is useful to understand each element of his definition of structure in order to know how people use structural realism, as his approach is known, we should remember that the international system did not always have these same specific characteristics. The Peace of Westphalia, in 1648, with its numerous treaties, first recognized all states as sovereign and as the ultimate actors in international politics (at least in the treaties). Prior to that, political units were organized in different ways. Many political units were linked hierarchically in two ways. First, units were linked through the old feudal system; there were kings, dukes, princes, barons, etc., with the king exercising authority over the dukes, the dukes over princes, and so on down the line. At the same time, much of Europe was also administered through the Catholic Church, along hierarchical lines. The Catholic Church has its own power structure, and this method of organization existed alongside and within the same set of political bodies, for there were political entities attached to the Church. Bishops and abbots also ruled territory in those days, so they exercised religious authority but also civil authority.

The Peace of Westphalia began the recognition of a shift away from these dual hierarchical forms of international organization towards a more anarchic situation. Each state was soon considered equal and sovereign, rather than an element in a hierarchic structure. More interestingly, prior to 1648, sovereignty did not inhere to a political unit; rather, it was characteristic of a person. This can still be seen in one of the meanings of the word *sovereign* in English: supreme ruler. Before the Peace of Westphalia, sovereign actors were kings, princes, bishops, and the like. It was only in the peace settlement reached in 1648 that sovereignty was attached to the state. One should not, therefore, expect Waltz's specific assessment of the characteristics of the international system to fit pre-modern periods, because his assumptions would not be appropriate.

The first two aspects of structure, according to Waltz's definition, haven't changed that much since 1648. But in terms of the third trait, the distribution of capabilities, there has been tremendous change. The distribution of power is therefore the key variable on the causal side in structural realism and is a characteristic of the system of states. To make the point another way, the distribution of power can only be understood through an examination of the units together, as a set, not by studying a single state. Many present-day realists no longer talk much about human nature, but instead they focus on systemic factors and how these constrain the behaviour of states.[14]

THE CORE ASSUMPTIONS OF STRUCTURAL REALISM

1. States are the most important actors in international relations (but not the only actors).
2. States are unitary, rational actors.[15]
3. The international system is anarchic.
4. States, to protect their own interests in this environment, will seek to maximize their power.

A basic notion we will see surfacing again and again in realism is the *security dilemma*, a concept used to describe relations between sovereign states in the context of international anarchy.[16] The fear of being dominated by one's neighbour causes each state to treat its neighbours as the potential source of threats. As a consequence of the anarchic environment, each state prepares to meet potential threats to its security or interests. One state's attempts to enhance its security via power maximization, however, threatens other states. This creates a chain reaction. The irony is that all states make great efforts to ensure their security, but in the end they remain essentially insecure.

At the same time, definitions of security or national interest have always been controversial.[17] Because it was so difficult to come to any particular agreement on what national interest means, realists tried to evade this question by assuming that the goal of survival comes before all other goals; since power was necessary for survival, power was the most important goal. Others argued that power could be translated into other goals. Some realists, however, have softened their emphasis on states' desire for power. These scholars have modified realism in a different direction, to recognize how citizens demand much more from their governments than merely national defence. Citizens expect their states to provide a smoothly functioning economy with full employment, for instance. A list of other expectations placed on the modern state would be quite long. Power is not always very useful for attaining these goals, so some realists (often called neo-realists) began to think of security (or survival) as only a minimal goal.[18] Once survival was ensured, other goals become important. Thus, instead of assuming that states maximized power, they assumed that states maximized utility. Utility is an open concept, which the neo-realists could consider past state actions helped to define (look to what the state had spent money and effort to attain, for instance), or they simply could leave the concept vague.

THE CORE ASSUMPTIONS OF NEO-REALISM

1. States are the most important actors in international relations (but not the only actors).
2. States are unitary, rational actors.
3. The international system is anarchic.
4. States will seek to maximize their utility.

Some of the Rivals to Realism

There are other definitions of systems besides the one Waltz developed into structural realism. Hedley Bull, for instance, worked within the realist tradition but developed a set of arguments based on different assumptions.[19] Bull defines a system as being in existence when a group of states see themselves bound by a common set of rules governing their relations (such as international law, diplomacy, international organizations, rules of war, etc.). It is important to appreciate how Bull is bringing in notions of community and interaction into this definition, which makes it quite different from Waltz's. Anarchy can reign, while other features of society continue to play a role and constrain actors' behaviour.

The system-level does not only belong to the realists. Radicals have their own views and their own theories, which often operate in a similar fashion to realism. Helen Milner, for instance, has criticized some of Waltz's assumptions.[20] Milner does not completely disagree with Waltz's approach, as she, too, stresses the importance of the international system. Milner, however, disagrees with some of Waltz's assessment of the characteristics of the international structure. She highlights the differences in her views by elaborating arguments made by more radical theorists. For instance, Milner considers Waltz's assumption that states are functionally undifferentiated; this assumption may not be very useful if one is interested in questions of international political economy. Radicals, such as Marxists, may agree with Waltz that, politically, all states claim to perform the same functions, but in the international economy there is a great degree of specialization and therefore of differentiation. Whenever trade is taking place, there is a division of labour; that is, different states provide different goods and services to the international economy. The Marxist critique of the *division of labour* in the domestic economy is that this creates class divisions. Classes are not arrayed anarchically—they are functionally different and organized hierarchically. So

modern Marxists may look at Waltz's definition of the system and argue that
the assumptions should be quite different, which of course leads to rather
different theories.

In *classical Marxism*, the theory developed in the nineteenth century by
Karl Marx and Friedrich Engels, states were certainly not perceived to be the
most important actors. One of Marx's most profound contributions to the
social sciences was his emphasis on social classes. Classical Marxists argue that
social classes are the most important actors in domestic or international politics. Writing at the time of the Industrial Revolution, Marx was interested
in how economic changes affected society. He observed how economic
changes defined or redefined social hierarchies and he argued that classes act
in their own material interests. Most importantly, he believed that all economic output was ultimately produced by the labour of workers. Since
workers did not enjoy all the earnings from their output (entrepreneurs,
middlemen, and bosses kept large portions of any economic gains), some of
the rightful earnings of the working class were being taken from them via
market transactions. In fact, Marx was primarily criticizing the Liberal analysis (the different versions of Liberalism will be discussed below).

THE CORE ASSUMPTIONS OF CLASSICAL MARXISM

1. Social classes are the most important actors in politics.
2. Classes act in their own material interest.
3. The expropriation of surplus value is exploitation.

Classical Marxism was developed primarily as a model of the domestic
political economy. It was not designed to explain or predict state behaviour.[21] It was created as an alternative to liberalism, another paradigm established to model the domestic political economy. These two paradigms,
liberalism and Marxism, actually have older roots than realism (though
defenders of realism would say that examples of realist thinking have existed
for millennia.)[22] Liberalism and Marxism spawned theories of international
relations, and these compete with the various versions of realism.

Just as realism has changed over time, so, too, has Marxism. For our purposes, we should begin with the two variants of Marxism most often used
in international relations. The first was developed by writers in the late nineteenth century. These scholars were concerned with explaining European
imperialism. Marx himself would have probably argued that members of the
same class shared so much in common that their class interests overrode their
national differences—a banker from England and a banker from France had
more in common with each other than with the working class from their
own countries. Yet Marx and Marxists also believed that states acted in the
interest of their capitalist class. When states competed against each other for

territory in their imperialist policies of the late nineteenth century, Marxists explained this competition in terms of the states acting in the interests of each country's capitalists against capitalists from other countries. This version of Marxism was made prominent by V.I. Lenin (who developed his theory as the basis for political action, which he then implemented by successfully leading the Russian Revolution), hence it was once termed Leninist, but now is more often referred to as *instrumental Marxism.*

THE CORE ASSUMPTIONS OF INSTRUMENTAL MARXISM

1. Social classes are the most important actors in politics.
2. Classes act in their own material interest.
3. The expropriation of surplus value is exploitation.
4. States act in the interest of their national capitalist class.

In many ways, then, this version of Marxism resembles realism, since it depicted states in conflict with other states. In this version of Marxism, however, states are interested in maximizing the economic benefits of their own capitalists, not maximizing national power. The consequences of changing this assumption are enormous, as we shall see in some of the cases.

Over time, however, there seemed to be problems with this version of Marxism. States began to develop and execute policies that did not seem to follow a program of profit maximization. The capitalists within these states did not seem to be gaining any direct benefits from the policies being pursued. States taxed capitalists and instituted welfare policies to alleviate some of the problems workers faced. States carried out expensive policies internationally that did not seem to have any economic pay-off, such as the U.S. involvement in Vietnam. Economically, Vietnam was not very valuable— yet the U.S. was willing to expend extensive resources to prosecute a war defending South Vietnam against communism. The obvious solution for Marxists to resolve these shortcomings in their theories was to alter their assumptions slightly. Instead of seeing states acting in the interests of their own national capital class (and therefore against other capitalists from other countries), some Marxists began to assume that states acted in the interests of their own capitalists by acting to protect the workings of capitalism— which sometimes meant doing things against the immediate interests of the capitalists themselves in order to protect the overall capitalist system. This became known as *structural Marxism*, since it emphasized how states acted politically to maintain the overall political economic structure of capitalism.[23]

THE CORE ASSUMPTIONS OF STRUCTURAL MARXISM

1. Social classes are the most important actors in politics.
2. Classes act in their own material interest.
3. The expropriation of surplus value is exploitation.
4. states act to maintain capitalism, which may be against the interests of capitalists in the short run.

More recently, another form of analysis has sprung from Marxism. This approach mixes together different kinds of actors, for it retains an emphasis on classes but perhaps stresses the role of states even more. It is also rooted in the work of historians and sociologists. It is called *modern world-systems analysis*, because it analyses the coaction of the international political and international economic systems in the modern capitalist era.

The Modern World-Systems Approach

The main arguments of Immanuel Wallerstein (who is often considered the originator of the concept of world-systems analysis) stress how the emergence of capitalism required the creation of an international economy; the development of this international economy, in turn, had profound consequences for the evolution of domestic political economies.[24] Wallerstein, of course, was not working alone. He was building on similar types of analysis done by a group of historians in France led by Fernand Braudel (the Annales school) and by other Marxists, such as Theotonio Dos Santos and André Gunder Frank, who were interested in the consequences of imperialism and international trade.[25]

Wallerstein's work is a blend of history, sociology, and political science. It does not purport to develop an explicit theory of international relations that will perform the tasks of theory as laid out in the earlier sections of this text. Instead, Wallerstein's arguments are really about the historical development of the international political economy. As such, the arguments provide a framework other theorists have used to develop a number of specific theories. Generalizable arguments have been made to illustrate how some patterns of activity recur.[26]

THE CORE ASSUMPTIONS OF MODERN WORLD-SYSTEMS ANALYSIS

1. The world is a structural whole, and is the appropriate unit of analysis.
2. The various parts of the system are functionally related, via the international division of labour.
3. States and markets are the products of underlying social (i.e., class) dynamics.

The practitioners of this approach depict the international system as a hierarchical structure. At the top of this hierarchy are the core states, characterized by a combination of political and economic power. They are the most economically developed states with the highest concentration of capital. Being economically developed, and therefore also rich, they are able to generate the most political power. They then use this political power to shape the international political economy in ways that enhance their political and economic dominance. Again, there are numerous similarities to the types of arguments realists make. These similarities have been perceived by some as a weakness. Some Marxists have been highly critical of the modern world-systems approach.[27] Their criticisms spring from the ways in which the arguments made have diluted Marxism's traditional assumptions. Are classes still the most important actors? Does economic change drive political change? For these reasons, Marxist critics are often harsher on this approach than non-Marxists.

Marxism's Original Rival: Liberalism

Marx developed his arguments to criticize *classical liberalism*. In the mid-nineteenth century, liberalism was at its height, claiming that everyone would benefit from participation in markets. Economic advancement would spread to everyone—something Marx did not believe. Marx saw the impact of the Industrial Revolution, especially the creation of an industrial working class, and did not think the working class was benefiting from the economic changes Europe was then undergoing.

Liberalism had its own start in international political economy in the late eighteenth century as a challenger to absolutism. Under absolutism, the monarch had claimed absolute powers over the individual, in either the political or economic realm. At the international level, absolutism had produced mercantilist policies. Mercantilism generated tremendous tax revenues for the state, but only by inhibiting the development of the international political economy. Liberalism developed different notions of how to think about the proper functioning of the national and international economy. Instead of emphasizing the role of the state and the importance of a positive balance of payments (as mercantilism had), liberalism aimed to free the individual both politically and economically from the state. It also promised that national wealth would be increased if individuals were free to compete against each other, as opposed to having the state interfere with the market. This was true at the domestic and international level, according to the classical liberals.

Among the most important classical liberals were Adam Smith and David Ricardo, though there were many others. Smith and Ricardo developed theories about international trade to illustrate mathematically that trade would normally benefit both sides in an exchange. These arguments will be explored in the later chapters on international political economy. What is important to note at this point is that these economic arguments were used as a basis for a variety of political theories. The basic assumptions of classical liberalism highlight the differences between this approach and the mercantilism of the absolutist monarchies that had come before, but they also underscore the emphasis liberalism has always placed on economic gain (as opposed to idealism, though there is obviously overlap between the two).

THE CORE ASSUMPTIONS OF CLASSICAL LIBERALISM

1. Individuals (plus households or firms) are the most important actors.
2. Individuals are rational (and obviously unitary) actors.
3. Individuals maximize their utility.
4. Everything is tradeable.
5. Individuals' indifference curves can be aggregated into social indifference curves.[28]

Because it was engaging mercantilism, liberalism always had both a domestic and an international aspect. Later theorists and policy-makers began to elaborate variants of liberalism focused much more on international political economy. Richard Cobden, a British politician in the mid-nineteenth century, developed a version of liberalism intended to show that if international economic relations were guided by liberalism, political benefits would result. *Commercial liberalism*, as this view is known, argued that free trade was not only beneficial to individuals in an economic sense, and therefore economically beneficial to states since states are merely agglomerations of individuals, but also provided positive spin-offs to the international system. If all states participated in free trade, they would learn to meet their desires through exchange. Trade would benefit all sides and therefore undercut the sources of conflict between states. In short, free trade was the route to international peace.

These ideas so infused the thinking of British policy-makers in the early nineteenth century that the British government was seriously considering how to devolve the British Empire. While the Empire was not dismantled then, the thinking remained. Commercial liberalism resurfaced several times later. Sir Norman Angell made precisely these same sorts of arguments just prior to World War I.[29] The same concepts can be found in the writings and practices of Cordell Hull. Hull, a Congressman in the U.S. House of Representatives, and later Secretary of State in Franklin D. Roosevelt's administration in the 1930s, observed the economic blocs created by Nazi

Germany and Imperial Japan, and understood that the erection of barriers between economies would eventually lead to war. If countries were trying to create industrial economies that could survive without trade altogether, these economies would need a variety of resources. How could an industrial state survive without such resources as oil, minerals, and ores? Germany and Japan seemed to be pursuing these raw materials through military conquest rather than through trade. In Hull's view, a smoothly functioning international economy based on liberal principles was a clear alternative to wars between the major powers.

THE CORE ASSUMPTIONS OF COMMERCIAL LIBERALISM

1. Individuals (plus households or firms) are the most important actors.
2. Individuals are rational (and obviously unitary) actors.
3. Individuals maximize their utility.
4. Everything is tradeable.
5. Therefore trade is the route to cooperation and peace.

Republican Liberalism

A rival view of liberalism had always existed alongside the classical and commercial versions. Classical and commercial liberalism had been founded on economic theories. These other theories placed greater emphasis on political liberalism. Though Woodrow Wilson is the most famous modern proponent of *republican liberalism*, the roots lie in the writings of Immanuel Kant. Kant theorized about the foreign relations of republics over 200 years ago; at that time there were no true democracies and only a small number of republics. Kant's arguments emphasized that republican states behaved differently towards each other.

What is important in the development of national policies according to republican liberalism is having political liberalism within countries. Where individuals have a say in the formulation of national policy, national policy will be peaceful and will pursue the creation of wealth. This characteristic behaviour is tempered by the demands of national security whenever a republic confronts a non-republican state. When two or more republics interact, they create an international community. Such ideas are mirrored in the works of many scholars. The idea that democratic states behave differently in their own interactions is quite popular because modern democratic states have rarely if ever engaged in wars against each other. Today's arguments stress how democratic states practise particular norms. These norms constrain the ways in which these states behave.

1. Individuals are the most important actors.
2. Individuals are rational (and obviously unitary) actors.
3. Individuals maximize their utility.
4. National self determination, where individuals can express their preferences, is the route to international peace and understanding.

Another reason these ideas have recently gone through a great resurgence is that democratic practices are much more widespread than ever before. First, many countries have gone through dramatic changes of government since the early 1980s. Developing countries and former members of the Soviet bloc have transformed themselves into democracies. They have also, by and large, liberalized their domestic economies. Based on the theories of how democracies behave and the growth in the number of democracies in the system, several scholars and policy-makers expect the future to be extremely peaceful.[30] The current popularity of such arguments clearly illustrates that alternatives to realism are alive and strong.[31]

The Successors to the Idealists—Complex Interdependence

It is worth noting that idealism never disappeared entirely. Just as realism evolved over time, so did idealism. The successors to idealism also have something to say about system-level theories. They would argue that the international system is characterized by a high degree of interdependence. This point is extremely important when we consider the integration of economies. Whereas realists use the notion of sovereignty to divide states into separate entities, the idealists have always seen linkages between states and between the people within states. An important reason for the advent of these linkages is the nature of technological advance. As technology improves, the world becomes "smaller" in the sense that we know more about other peoples, other cultures, and political events elsewhere. This flow of information and communication is important to the modern idealists (or transnationalists, as they are also referred to), for it helps connect issues. Also, as a national economy becomes more advanced, it builds greater linkages with other economies. These linkages mean that events in one country or one economy have an effect on events elsewhere. *Interdependence* can be defined as a situation in which changes or events in any single part produce some reaction or have a significant consequence in other parts of the system. Others have defined interdependence as the mutual contingency of policies; as linkages increase, interdependence increases, so states therefore have to communicate with each other more often to co-ordinate their actions.[32]

The notion of interdependence was used by the idealists to challenge realists' ideas respecting the security dilemma, since they were really saying that state A's welfare depended on state B's welfare and vice versa. Threatening another state was only threatening one's own interests. This was a reassertion of the notion of the "harmony of interests." Theories of technological advance and interdependence quickly became more than just a system-level approach, however, because they suggested the importance of other actors besides states. Governments might co-ordinate their activities through international organizations; these intergovernmental organizations (or IGOs, such as the UN) might take on a life of their own. Groups mattered at the domestic level because they influenced government policy and might develop international linkages of their own, independent of governments. Some groups might coalesce into their own organizations. These non-governmental organizations (or NGOs, such as Greenpeace) have grown in number and power in recent years. Firms mattered because they were increasingly using technology (in terms of transportation and communication) to become multinational firms. Moreover, these other actors often became transnational or multinational because they wanted to evade government policy, or they sought to change government policy through new political manoeuvres. So while some transnationalists focused on the level of state interaction (because they were still interested in explaining state policy), they increasingly moved beyond that. Realists, on the other hand, have remained focused on states and the system-level of analysis. The central difference between the two comes down to their different assumptions about the degree of importance of a whole range of actors.

THE CORE ASSUMPTIONS OF COMPLEX INTERDEPENDENCE

1. States are not always the most important actors in international relations.
2. States are not rational unitary actors, but are composed of many different groups, bureaucracies, individuals, and firms.
3. States are under pressure to do much more than ensure survival of the country—so they have many different goals, and power may not be the most important.

Complex interdependence has the obvious advantage that it can incorporate a vast array of different actors as causal forces.[33] This breadth is both a strength and a weakness. By including so many possible actors and allowing for states to have so many different goals, complex interdependence provides little guidance to theorists. Which actors are the most important to consider? Which can be safely ignored? Does one need to look at all actors of all types? The complex interdependence model serves an important purpose in criticizing structural realism, but it is unclear in how it offers a rival theory. Complex interdependence is open to interpretation—perhaps too open.

The Blossoming of International Political Economy

The politics behind international economic relations had already been studied by economists (e.g., Smith, Ricardo) and by political activists (e.g., Hobson, Lenin), but mainstream international relations had in fact left these issues chiefly to the economists in the decades after World War II. This mirrored the separation of economics and political science in academia, but it also reflected the everyday functioning of the real world. When people in the industrialized Western countries began to ask why some policies turned out the way they did or wanted to offer policy prescriptions about economic relations, they normally engaged in debates completely within an economic framework. Such debates were often devoid of political issues. Economists' predictions were adequate for many questions, even in the absence of an analysis of the politics of the questions posed.[34]

Eventually, however, some of the predictions became less accurate. Models that had performed well in the past began to lose their efficacy. Monetary affairs were thrown into disarray by pressures on the U.S. dollar. The value of currencies had been fixed under the Bretton Woods accords; yet the relationships between currencies (and between each currency and the reserves held to support its value) no longer made sense. Market forces and government policies now clashed. The fixed exchange rates could no longer be maintained—what should happen? Should rates merely be fixed at new levels, or should currency markets set the rates? Economists were divided. National interests were divided, too.

Direct political interferences in the international economy also emerged. The Organization of Petroleum Exporting Countries (OPEC) embargoed the sale of oil. By limiting the amount of oil available, the OPEC members achieved two goals: they increased the price of oil (and thus their own revenues), and they showed their support for the Arab states in their political confrontation with Israel. This was a clear example that politics could enter into the functioning of the international economy. A much broader political challenge to the international economy was mounted in the 1970s as well, drawing from the more radical perspectives. Some mainstream economists, such as Raoul Prebisch, had endeavoured to show how an international economy based on liberal markets tended to leave the economically developing countries further and further behind the industrialized nations. Prebisch advocated greater management of international economic affairs as a corrective to the workings of the market. Marxists extended the argument in dependency theory. They argued that such markets were clearly exploitive, and therefore the less economically advanced countries should withdraw from them; political challenges to the capitalist international economy were necessary. Fuelled by such analyses, representatives from less economically developed countries gathered together and, working though the various agencies and bodies of the United Nations, used their numbers to vote for changes in the ways the international economy works. Their demands ranged from calls for increased foreign aid from the industrial states to rearranging global trade relations.[35]

Such changes in the real world and the re-evaluation of theories and models forced scholars to appreciate the role politics had always played in the workings of the international economy. Many began to think about how certain U.S. foreign policies had created an environment where the economic relations between the Western countries could operate largely without political interference. As political scientists had always understood about the domestic economy, a seemingly apolitical economy is the result of rigorous political construction. The apparently apolitical domestic economy of the U.S. or Canada can only exist if there are contracts (enforced by courts and police), if there is a currency (which must be managed) to allow for smooth market transactions and for savings and investments to take place, if there is an infrastructure to support the communication and transportation networks, and so on. Some of these same political functions were necessary for the apparently apolitical post-World War II international economic relations between the Western powers. When the U.S. seemed unable or unwilling to provide the necessary leadership in providing the political underpinnings the international economy required, the international economy failed to function as well as it had.

In short, the rapid changes in the world not only raised new questions for scholars but also undercut our faith in existing models and theories. In this environment, the subfield of international political economy (IPE) blossomed. IPE developed to confront these very questions that were largely outside the realm of mainstream international relations. To answer these new questions, international political economists began to incorporate more analytical techniques from economics and explored the connections between international relations and other fields in political science (particularly comparative politics) more deeply than ever before.

This is not to say that security studies died or even withered away. In the 1980s, security studies (perhaps sparked by the ideas and methodologies so prominent in international political economy) experienced a renaissance. In the 1990s, now that the Cold War has ended and new subjects are rising to confront specialists in international relations, we have seen greater recognition of the interaction between economic and security affairs. Economic factors seem so prominent in many different events today ranging from explanations of the Soviet Union's collapse to the political integration of Europe.

In the 1970s, though, the key questions challenging the new subfield of IPE all had to do with characteristics of the international economy. To describe the characteristics of the international political economy, scholars developed the concept of *international regime.*[36] An international regime can be defined as a set of "principles, rules, norms and decision-making procedures around which actors' expectations converge."[37] In short, a regime is a set of prescriptions and proscriptions for state behaviour. Regimes can vary considerably. Sometimes the rules are implicit; at other times they are laid out in explicit detail in a treaty. Sometimes regimes cover a very narrow subject; in other instances they are quite broad. The concept is an extremely useful one not only because it is flexible, but also because it gives us a method for describing practices in the international political economy. Not everyone finds the concept equally useful; dependency theorists had always focused more explicitly on the international division of labour, for instance, and many scholars still preferred theories aimed at explaining the individual state's policies rather than traits of the international political economy.

In the early 1970s, the regimes in the international political economy seemed to be in flux. The rules and practices governing monetary relations had already given way—but to what? What new rules were likely to emerge? How much would the rules governing trade change? Would the developing countries succeed in their efforts to alter several economic regimes in some fundamental way? Scholars and policy-makers alike were unsure. The efforts to address these questions resulted in a new paradigm, one based primarily in IPE: *institutionalism.*

Explaining Changes in International Regimes: Institutionalism

Institutionalism was inspired by the observations and arguments made by scholars of IPE in their work on international regimes. Realists had always explained the creation and persistence of international rules and practices as an outcome of the exercise of power. The realist belief was that it took the concentration of power in the hands of a single actor to create some semblance of order in the international system. (These arguments fall under the rubric of *hegemonic stability theory*, to be discussed later.) According to realists, once power becomes decentralized that semblance of order is lost. In the early 1970s, economic order seemed to be breaking down as the U.S. fell in power relative to West Germany, France, and Japan. Realists expected more international practices to become increasingly disordered as time went on.

By the early 1980s, it was clear that even though the U.S. continued to decline economically relative to other states and was certainly weaker than it had been a decade before, few international regimes had fallen apart. This sparked opponents of the realism paradigm to develop rival explanations. Robert Keohane drew on the literature on domestic institutions to argue that regimes that served useful purposes would be maintained by the participants—without the sanctioning of a hegemonic power.[38] As long as the regimes delivered benefits to the participants, the participants would have reasons to maintain those regimes. There would be no need for a hegemonic leader, according to Keohane. From these arguments, originally formulated to explain why regimes persisted despite changes in the distribution of power, institutionalists were able to create theories explaining other examples of co-ordination and co-operation. They soon turned their focus to questions concerning the emergence of international regimes.

Institutionalism based on the rationalist perspective (or *rationalist institutionalism*) explains the creation and persistence of international institutions by viewing institutions as mechanisms for actors (most often states) to ensure that their joint activity leads to outcomes they prefer.[39] Art Stein analysed such actions as two sorts of problems: dilemmas of common interest and dilemmas of common aversion. An example of a dilemma of common interest is a collective good and requires the actors involved to engage in collaboration. Collaboration is required because the actors are interested in reaching a specific preferred outcome. Dilemmas of common aversion, such as the avoidance of an accident, require the interested actors to co-ordinate their activities—that is, they simply want to avoid one outcome (an accident) out of many possible.[40] Institutions matter because they help actors achieve their joint interests.

THE CORE ASSUMPTIONS OF RATIONALIST INSTITUTIONALISM

1. Actors are self-interested, rational utility maximizers.
2. International regimes can facilitate the making of agreements by actors.
3. Actors are interested in the pursuit of goals that are not always zero-sum in nature.

Keohane himself has pointed out how this early institutionalism was based on rational calculation, but a second form of institutionalism, a "reflective" approach, also exists. This second approach (also referred to as a "sociological approach") emphasizes the importance of subjectivity and the embeddedness of existing international institutions and regimes.[41] Rationality is always contextual, and the structural realists sometimes assume too much to be already established and fixed. Existing institutions and norms shape the ways in which preferences—including the desire for power itself—are defined. The institutionalists using a reflectivist approach stress that regimes are rarely the product of purely rational design, "but rather emerge slowly through a less deliberative process, and that they are frequently taken for granted by the people who are affected by them." In their view, utility maximization is not such a clear-cut issue when international institutions or international regimes are forming.[42] *Reflectivist institutionalism*, therefore, poses a more straightforward challenge to realist thinking.

One realist scholar, Joseph Grieco, has engaged the institutionalists in a debate. Grieco has provided a sketch of the basic assumptions of institutionalism. In short, he identifies assumptions reminiscent of those at the core of complex interdependence: states are not the single most important actors in the international system; states are not unitary actors, but rather are agglomerations of different agencies and actors each exercising a different form of authority; furthermore, power is not the ultimate goal for states, since other forms of interaction may matter more in the modern world and because states are expected to do much more than simply defend the national territory and interests.[43] This set of assumptions is compatible with more than one argument.

Keohane himself has sketched out the most important assumptions of rationalist institutionalism in his journal articles and in *After Hegemony*.[44] Instead of emphasizing non-state actors, Keohane continues to assume that states are the key actors. Often Keohane even continues to assume states to be self-interested, unitary actors. Moreover, he is also assuming that the international system is anarchic. Because power is not the only goal of state action, however, the interaction of states can take on forms quite unexpected from the structural realist perspective. Power is relative. When one state has more, another has less; thus, we refer to this type of situation as "zero-sum." Any increases in one side's power must involve decreases in the other's, so that the changes cancel each other out (i.e., the sum of the changes is zero). But when other goals are at stake, such as wealth, the situation could be quite different. Trade involves voluntary exchanges where each side intends to gain; hence, the interaction is positive-sum. Co-operation is not only possible but is likely whenever these egoistic actors see potential joint gains from co-operation. As Keohane puts it, "regimes are valuable to governments where, in their absence, certain mutually beneficial agreements would be impossible to consummate."[45] Regimes are created in this perspective, not as exercises of power, but as devices to further co-ordination (as noted above), and hence can be constructed voluntarily by their participants.

Both versions of institutionalism therefore provide a framework for developing hypotheses about strategic interaction and seek to explain examples of co-operation as well as competition. These hypotheses attempt to explain systemic outcomes, not the specific foreign policy of a state. The debate between structural realists and most institutionalists has therefore centred on which has a better explanation for how international institutions or regimes have evolved.

Another "Reflective" Paradigm: Constructivism

Institutionalists have had a harder time producing a plausible explanation for the creation of regimes, which is why the reflectivist approach has garnered more attention of late. The logic of regime persistence should also fit for regime creation, yet when one looks more closely at the historical record it is hard to separate out the role of state power; Keohane was careful to make his specific arguments about the evolution of international regimes after hegemony had ended, though he hoped to use that information to make inferences about regime creation. Yet other rivals of structural realism have emerged that look more intensely at the creation of norms and practices at the heart of regimes. These theories, generally referred to as *constructivism*, come from a similar "reflective" background to that of institutionalism. Constructivism also incorporates the role of ideas as a causal factor in a way completely unlike other paradigms.[46]

Just as institutionalism was a reaction to realism, so, too, is constructivism. Structural realism intentionally makes an abstract simplification by separating structure and process. In structural realism, process flows from structure. Constructivists pose questions about the blurring of structure and process. Is process only the outcome of structural constraints, or is structure affected by process? The clearest way to illustrate this problem would be to discuss alliances. Structure is determined by the distribution of capabilities, which influences the way states act: perhaps to form new alliances. The new alliances create a new distribution of power. Structure has therefore changed, if only in a minor way.[47]

Constructivism is potentially a quite powerful concept. According to Alexander Wendt, the principles of self-help and power politics identified by realists were socially constructed. They are institutions that have evolved, not essential features of an anarchic situation.[48] In other words, Wendt offers a different way for understanding realism and thus for explaining outcomes consistent with realism. Yet constructivism offers to do much more. Key concepts such as interests have no meaning, argue the constructivists, until the actor's identity has been established. Interests can never be assumed devoid of social context. Constructivism represents a broad assault on theories and paradigms based on assumptions intended to cover many types of situations. Constructivists therefore do not aim to create theories as generalizable as those created by realists, for instance. This doesn't mean the constructivists have an easy task ahead of them. Constructivists seek to understand the co-determination of structures (or institutions) and process. Perhaps for this reason the analyses of empirical examples using this approach are as yet underdeveloped.[49]

THE CORE ASSUMPTIONS OF CONSTRUCTIVISM

1. Interests and preferences are socially constructed, and hence are flexible rather than enduring.
2. Ideas are important as forces shaping preferences, identity, etc.
3. Rationality is always contextual.

In some senses constructivism is merely harkening back to some of the beliefs of the early idealists. By emphasizing how the structure of the international system and even the nature of the actors themselves are malleable, constructivists provide a picture of the future with many possibilities. By using education, by introducing new ideas or new points of view, they believe the interests of social actors can be redefined and behaviour changed.

International Relations and the End of the Cold War

This is an exciting time to be creating and refining theories of international relations. The world has recently changed in unanticipated and interesting ways, not unlike the early 1970s. Policy-makers and theorists alike confront new questions as well as old enduring ones.[50] Among theorists, some continue to argue that nothing has really changed while others believe the world order has changed fundamentally.[51] Either way, international political economy will play a fundamental role in how the field of international relations develops in the near future. IPE was the source of much innovative work in the past two decades and has also had a tremendous impact more broadly. It has infused security studies with new and interesting ideas.[52] It has played an important role in the current debates over definitions of security. It has become intertwined with comparative politics.

FIGURE 3: THE EVOLUTION OF PARADIGMS

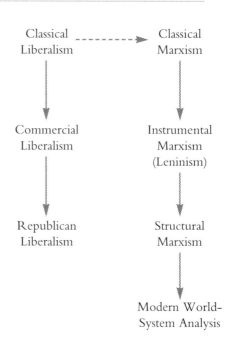

Broken lines denote negative relationships (where a paradigm is spawned in opposition to another), solid lines denote positive relationships (where one is an evolution of another).

The sorts of questions we confront fall into two broad categories. On the one hand, specialists in IPE have always been interested in the ways in which international regimes persist, evolve, or fall apart. What causes an international regime to change? Why do some change at a faster pace than others? Why do some seem to perform well, while others do not? Our paradigms have largely been constructed to answer these sorts of questions. Another set of questions pertains to how individual states behave. Why does a state choose to change its foreign economic policies? Why would it change its policies at one point in time rather than another? While these sorts of questions are related to those above (for any international regime worth talking about guides state behaviour in some fashion, and a change in the behaviour of a single state often produces changes in an international regime), they remain different. In addressing such questions, we can associate particular qualities of theories with models or theories from different levels of analysis, as detailed in the next chapter.

Suggested Readings

David Baldwin, "Power Analysis and World Politics," *World Politics* 31, 2 (January 1979), 161-94.

Hedley Bull, *The Anarchical Society: A Study of Order in World Politics*. London: Macmillan, 1977.

Edward H. Carr, *The Twenty Years Crisis, 1919-1939*. New York: Harper & Row, 1964.

David Dessler, "What's at Stake in the Agent-Structure Debate?" *International Organization* 43, 3 (Summer 1989), 441-73.

Michael Doyle, "Thucydidean Realism," *Review of International Studies* 16 (July 1990), 223-37.

Morton A. Kaplan, *System and Process in International Politics*. Huntington, NY: Robert Krieger, 1975.

Robert Keohane, ed., *Neorealism and Its Critics*. New York: Columbia University Press, 1986.

Robert Keohane and Joseph Nye, *Power and Interdependence*. Boston: Little, Brown, 1978.

Thomas Kuhn, *The Structure of Scientific Revolutions*. New York: Cambridge University Press, 1962.

Hans J. Morgenthau, *Politics Among Nations*. New York: Knopf, 1978.

Immanuel Wallerstein, *The Modern World-System 1*. San Francisco: Academic Press, 1979.

Kenneth Waltz, *Man, the State, and War*. New York: Columbia University Press, 1954.

Kenneth Waltz, *Theory of International Politics*. Reading, Mass.: Addison-Wesley, 1979.

Alexander Wendt, "Anarchy is What States Make of It," *International Organization* 46, 2 (Spring 1992), 391-425.

Notes

1   On this point, see Martin Griffiths, *Realism, Idealism, and International Politics: A Reinterpretation* (New York: Routledge, 1992).

2   E.H. Carr, *The Twenty Years' Crisis, 1919-1939* (New York: Harper, 1964, originally published in 1939).

3   Ibid., 89.

4   Michael Doyle has referred to this as Fundamentalism—where human beings' psychological and material needs create a drive for power, and power is both a means to goals and an important goal in itself. See "Thucydidean Realism," *Review of International Studies* 16 (July 1990), 223-37.

5   Hans Morgenthau, *Scientific Man vs. Power Politics* (Chicago: University of Chicago Press, 1946).

6   Moreover, many of these early realists (such as Morgenthau or Carr) would have seen moral goals in international affairs as mere smokescreens for actual material or power interests.

7   See the contribution of Peter Katzenstein in "The Role of Theory in Comparative Politics: A Symposium," *World Politics* 48, 1 (October 1995), 1-49. For a recent brief discussion of "great debates" in international relations, see pp. 10-15.

8   Kenneth Waltz, *Man, the State, and War* (New York: Columbia University Press, 1954).

9   Morton A. Kaplan, "The New Great Debate: Traditionalism versus Science in International Relations," *World Politics* 19, 1 (1966), 1-20.

10 One of the recent versions of this argument has centred on the correct method for analysing deterrence success and failure. See Christopher Achen and Duncan Snidal, "Rational Deterrence Theory and Comparative Case Studies," *World Politics* 41 (January 1989), 143-69.

11 The assumption of rationality contains three conditions: first, the actor is assumed to have perfect information—it is assumed the actor knows all its options and all the costs and benefits (the ramifications) associated with each option; second, the actor must understand the causal effect of each possible choice; third, the actor must be able to rank its choices, which requires that it be able to relate what it values into some sort of schedule of preferences.

12 Waltz, *Theory of International Politics*.

13 Ibid., 81.

14 See Doyle, "Thucydidean Realism."

15 All rational actor models assume that choices are made beginning with perfect information (that the actor knows all its possible choices, as well as all the costs and benefits associated with each), that the actor then assesses all the costs and benefits involved with each choice, that it knows its own preferences, and that it can then select the proper choice for attaining its highest preference. Assumptions of rationality are critical for all models that treat actors as purposive.

16 See Glenn H. Snyder, "'Prisoner's Dilemma' and 'Chicken' Models in International Politics," *International Studies Quarterly* 15 (March 1971), 66-103; Robert Jervis, "Cooperation under the Security Dilemma," *World Politics* 30 (January 1978), 167-214.

17 The best discussion of this problem can be found in Arnold Wolfers, "National Interest as an Ambiguous Symbol," in *Discord and Collaboration* (Baltimore: Johns Hopkins University Press, 1962), 147-65; originally published in *Political Science Quarterly* 67, 4 (December 1952).

18 For a broad discussion of the possible meanings of the term "neo-realism," see Robert Keohane, ed., *Neorealism and Its Critics* (New York: Columbia University Press, 1986).

19 Hedley Bull, *The Anarchical Society* (London: Macmillan, 1977).

20 Helen Milner, "A Critique of Anarchy," in Robert Art and Robert Jervis, eds., *International Politics: Enduring Concepts and Contemporary Issues* (New York: HarperCollins, 1996), 70-80; originally published as "The Assumption of Anarchy in International Relations," *Review of International Studies* (1991).

21 For instance, Marx himself wrote very little about one of the most important aspects of international politics in his time: imperialism. His thoughts on imperialism are primarily found in letters and his accounts of British imperialism in India, which were written for the *New York Daily Tribune*. It remains clear that he thought of class as superseding nation-state; one only has to look at his address to the First International in October 1864.

22 Many realists cite the works of Hobbes, Machiavelli, and even Thucydides to support this position.

23 A well-known offshoot of this approach is dependency theory, which will be discussed in later chapters.

24 See Immanuel Wallerstein, *The Modern World-System*, 3 vols. (New York: Academic Press, 1974, 1980, 1989); Robert Gilpin, *The Political Economy of International Relations* (Princeton, NJ: Princeton University Press, 1987), 67-72.

25 Braudel's most important works include *Civilization and Capitalism, 15th-18th Century*, 3 vols. (New York: Harper & Row, 1979, 1982, 1984); Dos Santos wrote a pioneering article on dependency, "The Structure of Dependence," *American Economic Review* 60, 2 (May 1970), 231-36; and Frank wrote a large book exploring dependency in the Americas, *World Accumulation, 1492-1789* (New York: Monthly Review Press, 1978).

26 See, for instance, the works of Christopher Chase-Dunn, Albert Bergesen, and Terence Hopkins. A helpful overview can be found in Christopher Chase-Dunn, "Comparative Research on World-System Characteristics," *International Studies Quarterly* 23, 4 (December 1979), 601-23.

27 Most notable has been Robert Brenner's "The Origins of Capitalist Development: A Critique of Neo-Smithian Marxism," *New Left Review* (1977). See Robert A. Denemark and Kenneth P. Thomas, "The Brenner-Wallerstein Debate," *International Studies Quarterly* 32, 1 (March 1988), 47-65.

28 Social indifference curves refer to an indifference curve representing society as a whole. As such, this assumption essentially eliminates the problems of moving from numerous individuals' wants to those of a society—even though there are many different ways to do this, which in fact alters the results, as comparative politics shows.

29 See Norman Angell, *The Great Illusion* (New York: Putnam's, 1910). Angell argued that war between industrialized nations was obsolete due to economic interdependence. Specifically, he tried to show that war "did not pay" and that perceived economic gains from victory in past wars were quite illusory. His works were widely read in the years after World War 1, so much so that in 1933 he received the Nobel Peace Prize.

30 See the recent work of Bruce Russett and several collaborators, *Grasping the Democratic Peace*, (Princeton, NJ: Princeton University Press, 1993); and also Francis Fukuyama, "The End of History?" *National Interest* (Summer 1989), 3-18.

31 See the recent review article by Steve Chan, "In Search of the Democratic Peace: Problems and Promise," *Mershon International Studies Review* 41, 1 (May 1997), 59-91.

32 Robert Keohane and Joseph Nye, *Power and Interdependence* (Boston: Little, Brown, 1977).

33 Complex interdependence was initially developed by Robert Keohane and Joseph Nye in "The Role of Transnational Forces," *International Organization* 25 (Summer 1971), 721-48.

34 Economists had not solved all their questions, of course. Explanations for patterns of trade and investment among the most economically developed countries remain a matter of contention to this day. See the discussion in the chapter on trade.

35 For the response of one American realist to these challenges, see Stephen Krasner, *Structural Conflict: The Third World Against Global Liberalism* (Berkeley: University of California Press, 1985).

36 There have always been other ways to discuss the characteristics of the international political economy, such as the international division of labour.

37 Stephen Krasner, *International Regimes* (Ithaca, NY: Cornell University Press, 1983), 1.

38 See Robert Keohane, *After Hegemony* (Princeton, NJ: Princeton University Press, 1984).

39 See the description in Lisa Martin, "An Institutionalist View: International Institutions and State Strategies," in John A. Hall and T.V. Paul, eds., *International Order in the Twenty-first Century*, forthcoming.

40 Arthur A. Stein, *Why Nations Cooperate* (Ithaca, NY: Cornell University Press, 1990).

41 Interestingly, John A. Hall, a sociologist, has noted that the rationalist versus reflectivist debate now going on in political science has had its parallel in sociology in the competition between the "idealist" and "materialist" approaches. See Hall, "Ideas and the Social Sciences," in Judith Goldstein and Robert Keohane, eds., *Ideas and Foreign Policy* (Ithaca, NY: Cornell University Press, 1993), 32.

42 Robert Keohane, "International Institutions: Two Approaches," *International Studies Quarterly* 32 (December 1988), 389.

43 Grieco uses the term "neo-liberal," but since the only liberal aspects are in the normative goals this approach seems to contain, I will abandon the "neo-liberal" reference. See Joseph Grieco, *Cooperation Among Nations* (Ithaca, NY: Cornell University Press, 1990), 4-6.

44 The most important article would be Robert Keohane, "The Demand for International Regimes," *International Organization* 36, 2 (Spring 1982), 141-71.

45 Ibid., 150.

46 For a recent volume exploring the role of ideas as causal factors, see Goldstein and Keohane, eds., *Ideas and Foreign Policy*.

47 David Dessler, "What's at Stake in the Agent-Structure Debate?" *International Organization* 43, 3 (Summer 1989), 462.

48 Alexander Wendt, "Anarchy Is What States Make of It," *International Organization* 46, 2 (Spring 1992), 395.

49 One of the main efforts to provide such an empirical basis for constructivism was the special issue of *International Organization* 46, 1 (1992). More empirical analyses using constructivism should be available soon.

50 See David A. Baldwin, "Security Studies and the End of the Cold War," *World Politics* 48, 1 (October 1995), 117-41.

51 For one proponent of the view that nothing has changed, see John Mearsheimer, "Back to the Future: Instability in Europe after the Cold War," *International Security* 15 (1990), 5-56.

52 For example, see Jonathan Kirshner, *Currency and Coercion* (Princeton, NJ: Princeton University Press, 1995); Joanne Gowa, *Allies, Adversaries, and International Trade* (Princeton, NJ: Princeton University Press, 1994); Edward D. Mansfield, *Power, Trade and War* (Princeton, NJ: Princeton University Press, 1994).

Two

THE LEVELS OF ANALYSIS—
SYSTEM–LEVEL ARGUMENTS

Introduction: Grouping Theories by Levels of Analysis

Different levels of analysis are most suited for particular types of questions. Why would a state suddenly change its policies? What explains why new policies mirror or diverge from past policies? Theories that address these sorts of questions are most easily organized in terms of levels of analysis, which requires a special emphasis on one aspect of the theories' assumptions: the most important actor. At each level, one actor is assumed to be more important than other possible actors.[1]

System-Level Theories and the Concept of Power

Systemic level theories concentrate on characteristics of the system, and most often on the system's structure, to explain state behaviour. Structural realism is an excellent example of this sort of argument. More specifically, realists explain state behaviour by using the distribution of power as their key causal variable. Different distributions of power among the sovereign states in an anarchic environment drive them to act differently.

Before examining the impact of the distribution of power in the system, we should first consider the meaning of the notion *power*. Power is a central concept in all political science, but it is often poorly defined. Jeffrey Hart has identified three different definitions of power: (1) power over other actors, (2) power over resources, (3) power over events and outcomes.[2] Hart considers the third definition to be the most useful because, ultimately, it encompasses the other two definitions. It is general enough to capture examples of coercion, where one state may exercise power over other actors or expend resources, but it also includes examples of co-operation. This definition of power in international politics as power over outcomes is useful for describing past events, but how useful is it for building predictive theories? For our most pressing task—creating predictive theories—this definition of power will not be of much help because we cannot recognize power, defined along these lines, until after the event has already occurred.

Robert Dahl has given political science one of its oldest and most durable definitions of power. Power, according to Dahl, is control over actors.[3] This control appears in three ways: (1) control over actions (getting an actor to do something he/she otherwise wouldn't do, which clearly is a limited definition since it only pertains to coercion); (2) control over the agenda (that is, control over which issues are debated, which decisions will be taken, and when); and (3) control over preferences (the ability to influence what other actors desire—as through advertisements and propaganda; this has also been referred to as ideological or cultural power). Here, too, we can usually only recognize power after it has been used.

The problem with each of these examples and with most other definitions of power is that they tend to be descriptive and cannot be easily applied if we are interested in including power as an element in a predictive theory. That is, we are usually asking questions such as "how much power is necessary to control another state's actions?" This question underscores an obvious point, yet one deserving important consideration: power is relative. A measure of power only takes on meaning when placed in a framework of comparison. Is Iraq powerful? Against Kuwait, the answer is yes; against an alliance combining Kuwait, the United States, Britain, France, Canada, and Kuwait's other allies, the answer is no. Of course, even here we get into problems of comparison, because measurements of power are often like comparing apples and oranges. Before the war in the Persian Gulf, some experts described Iraq as powerful because that country had a large, experienced military equipped with thousands of tanks, hundreds of aircraft, etc. As it turned out, one Iraqi plane wasn't equal to one British, Canadian, or American plane. The same was true for other weapons, such as tanks and artillery, and also for comparing military units as a whole. Numbers alone do not tell the whole story.

This problem of measurement is complicated by intangible aspects of power other than the quality of resources. Ray Cline tried to develop a formula to measure potential power that captured the easily measured factors but also introduced the intangible aspects of power.[4] He argued that potential power (Pp) equalled the critical mass of population and territory (c), plus economic capabilities (E), plus military power (M), multiplied by the country's strategy and will to use power (s and w). The resulting formula looked like this: $Pp = (c + E + M) \times (s + w)$. This formula is an interesting attempt to incorporate tangibles and intangibles in the same equation. It is not clear how one would measure the intangibles (other than in an arbitrary fashion), but the formula was meant to capture such situations as the Vietnam War, where the seemingly more powerful country lost. Cline would argue that the strategy and will (i.e., s + w) of the U.S. were so low as to approach zero, and therefore nullify any advantage in quantifiable resources. But again, we can only assign weights to these variables representing strategy and will after the fact, so this may not be any better than the definitions of power presented earlier. Simply put, it is hard for political scientists to escape this fundamental problem of defining power.

Power and Structure

As mentioned above and in Chapter 1, structural realists often look at the distribution of power, however poorly defined, to create theories about how states will behave. In a situation where states are sovereign actors in an anarchic environment, the stronger powers will be able to enforce their wishes on the weaker ones—but how, then, will the major powers behave? What does this mean for our traditional concern about the risk of war between major powers? What does this mean for structural realists' theories about the operation of the international political economy?

When realists talk about the system level, especially when they are employing structural realism and therefore want to talk about how structure shapes behaviour, they define structure in terms of the distribution of capabilities. The simplest way to do that is to identify the number of major powers or poles in the system. The various sorts of structures are easily imagined: first, a *unipolar* distribution is possible—a system with a single major power. In such a system, according to the realists' jaded view, that one powerful actor would simply eliminate its rival states. While we have never seen such a structure before, we can use these realist assumptions to construct a theory about what we would expect to occur. We can even loosen up this argument a bit to consider a system with one state that has greater capabilities than the others but not so much more power that it could actually eliminate the other states. Such a structure is described as *hegemonic*, that is, dominated by a single actor. This single actor may not be able to take complete control over the other states, but it would certainly be able to express its will and influence events towards its own desires. This is a more practical version of the structure with a single pole, and some scholars consider the current distribution of power to be hegemonic, with the U.S. as the only pole.

A second possible distribution of power would be *bipolar*, where there were two poles, or two strong states, or even two strong alliances. We can find such distributions occurring at different times in history. Such a system may have existed among the Greek city-states, when Athens and Sparta each led powerful alliances. Prior to World War 1, two alliances faced off against each other (the Triple Entente, composed of France, Russia, and Britain, versus the Triple Alliance made up of Germany, Austria-Hungary, and Italy). A more recent example of a bipolar system occurred after World War 11, when the U.S. and the Soviet Union combined scientific knowledge, technology, industrialized economies, and continental resources to emerge as superpowers and become the leaders of rival alliances (NATO and the Warsaw Pact).

A third possible distribution of power would be *tripolar*—where three states hold considerably more power than the other members of the international system. Since analysts disagree over measurements of power, some see tripolar distributions when others see bipolar distributions of power. Some argued that in the 1970s the system could be characterized as tripolar, given the rise of the People's Republic of China as an independent actor with nuclear capabilities. Others argued that this was not the case, since the Chinese could not project their power very far. (They had nuclear missiles, but they could not send their troops any distance because of their limited supply system and weak navy.) Nevertheless, as long as China could threaten the Soviet Union, we could say that the structure was indeed tripolar.

After tripolarity, we begin to talk of *multipolar* structures, systems characterized by many poles. We can thus talk about several different structures and about changes from one to another (as when states in a multipolar situation line up into two separate alliances). Realists take this information about structure, combine it with their assumptions, and create theories about how states will behave differently in the different structures. This will become clearer if we consider a practical application. The most obvious application would be to return to the main question separating the realists and idealists—how do we prevent another major war from occurring? Instead of turning to international law and international institutions (such as the United Nations), the realists said the answer to finding a stable peace had to be found in the distribution of power. That meant elaborating some theories about which of these various types of systems were more peaceful and stable.

Waltz argued in the 1960s that bipolarity produced a stable and peaceful system because states are rational, power-maximizing units, and since power is relative, states will do their best to match any increases in their neighbours' power in order to lessen possible threats.[5] In a bipolar system, each of the major powers has only one other state to fear and therefore has only one country to focus on in this competition. A balance of power will occur, and both states will strive to maintain this balance. In such a situation, each of the major powers will also be able to control and constrain its allies (who by definition are all weaker than either superpower). This element of control, added to the element of competition, led Waltz (in 1964) to predict that a bipolar distribution of power would create much verbal jousting and posturing, arms races between the two top powers, and other forms of competition, but with little chance of war actually breaking out.

Richard Rosecrance, on the other hand, argued that bipolarity was dangerous.[6] According to Rosecrance, bipolarity made international affairs a zero-sum situation for the two major powers. Since power is relative, any gain by one of the major powers automatically means a loss for the other. This situation is dangerous because every possible source of power is contested, no matter how small. Conflicts are likely to erupt over the most minor of issues. In a multipolar world, by comparison, alliances are constantly shifting, and each of the major powers is unsure which of the others poses a threat; conflicts therefore spring only from large issues. In a multipolar world, small changes in potential sources of power don't matter very much, but in a bipolar world every issue is contested.

Rosecrance reached these conclusions largely through an *inductive* approach—that is, through historical analysis of past distributions of power. He studied the diplomatic results of different distributions of power from 1740 to 1960. He noticed that the international system had experienced quite a number of different distributions of power. In previous periods characterized by bipolarity, such as the one that developed from 1890 to 1914, the distribution of power apparently created rivalries that eventually led to war. On the other hand, Rosecrance found that peace and stability were associated with other distributions of power, particularly multipolar ones. Before we debate the various merits of the theories developed by Rosecrance and Waltz, remember what theories are supposed to do for us. Not only should they provide descriptions and make predictions, they should also guide our policy prescriptions. Consider the utility of their theories in terms of advising policy. Is it practical to say peace will come through a multipolar system? How can statesmen end bipolarity? Is it possible to follow a policy prescription that suggests the distribution of power should be altered? Perhaps, for American statesmen may have opened up diplomatic relations with the People's Republic of China in the 1970s for precisely this reason.

Theories can be based on other characteristics of the international system or structure besides the distribution of power. For instance, Rosecrance developed another notion, that of a *regulator* or coping mechanism.[7] His insight is derived from the manner in which some engines operate. A regulator is a device that maintains the smooth operation of the engine. An example would be the valve on a steam engine, which allows enough of the pressure to escape, thereby preventing the boiler from exploding. In terms of the international system, a regulator is a device or resource that keeps the system on track. Rosecrance found that diplomats had different sorts of devices for keeping the system peaceful and stable at different times. In the pre-World War I period, the most important regulator was the use of non-European regions as pools for compensating the European powers. Rivalry among the European states was contained because whenever a European state made gains within Europe, its rivals could be sated by granting compensation in the form of territory in Africa or Asia. Thus, no one state was terribly unhappy, and no one state could get an enormous advantage on the others. This regulator worked as long as there was plenty of colonial territory available (i.e., tracts of land unclaimed by one of the major powers). When almost all of Africa and Asia had been divided among the European powers, compensation became more difficult, and thus the nature of European competition changed. Alliances were created, and the multipolar situation moved to bipolarity as two armed camps formed.

The distribution of power can also be used to explain particular outcomes in international political economy. If power is shared among many countries, the problems of competition in an anarchic environment might well cause them to pursue protectionist trade policies, since each would fear falling behind the others. If there were two powerful states or alliances and power was distributed roughly equally between the two, then we might find a parallel division in the international economy, since we might expect to find economic competition mirroring political competition. A unipolar distribution of power would mean that the single powerful state (or alliance) would have the ability to structure international economic relations in the way it desires.[8]

Economics and Power: The Concept of Power Transition

When Waltz discussed the nature of bipolarity, he noted that the two poles could try to match each other's power through two different strategies: one internal and the other external. Developing power through internal activity requires the dedication of greater economic resources or wealth to the realization of power and/or influence in the international sphere. This usually requires a lengthy period of time, and was not always possible in the days when all economies were based on agricultural activity. Economies were slow to change then, so internal sources of power were difficult to modify. Another method, tapping into external resources, is to form alliances. Bringing together a group of states into an alliance, so that their individual powers are united as a single force, can change the distribution of power quite rapidly. Of course, under special circumstances, internal measures can develop a country's power just as rapidly. When a country undergoes industrialization for the first time, its ability to convert resources into power changes dramatically.

During different historical periods, the appeal of these strategies for maximizing one's power has changed. When the Industrial Revolution occurred in Britain, it enabled that country to convert its internal resources more rapidly into military power. This meant Britain was able to dominate some of its rivals in terms of power—at least until these other powers began to industrialize, too. When rapid internally driven change in a country's strength alters the systemic distribution of power, we get what A.F.K. Organski labelled a *power transition*.[9]

Organski argued that as the "power gap" between two states narrows, war becomes more likely since the newly stronger state will try to alter the old relationship between the two countries. This illustrates an important aspect of realist thinking, for one can infer from this logic that in a power disequilibrium the more powerful country will also be more satisfied with the status quo. The weaker state is assumed to be less satisfied. As the weaker state gains power, it is able to voice its dissatisfaction with the situation. Organski's ideas develop several other themes, but here we are only interested in his views on the consequences of different distributions of power in the system. Organski argued that as the distribution of power neared a balance, war would become more likely.

The Many Meanings of Balance of Power

The term *balance of power* has meant a lot of different things to different people. Ernst Haas, in a survey of the literature in international relations, uncovered eight separate meanings. On the one hand, it can mean (1) any distribution of power (it doesn't matter if power is evenly distributed or not). Others use the term to mean (2) an exact equilibrium, or perfectly even distribution of power. Some have used the phrase to mean (3) hegemony or dominance, or the attempt to gain a position of dominance. Still others have employed the term to mean (4) stability in the distribution of power (i.e., that there have been no changes in how power is distributed among countries). Some even take "balance of power" to imply a concert among the major actors.

Haas found that still others used "balance of power" to refer to the opposite, that is, (5) that the balance of power results in instability and war. Some used the phrase to refer more generally to (6) power politics, or to (7) a universal law of history (that in international relations a balance of power will be attained), while others refer to "balance of power" as (8) a plan of action or policy prescription for decision-makers. Some of Waltz's ideas are covered by the seventh definition, for Waltz believes that sovereign states in a situation of anarchy will attempt to balance power as the means for individual states to survive. This does not mean that Waltz always expects balances to be achieved, but rather that he expects states to strive constantly to create a balance of power.

Waltz and others have used this idea to talk about why the system's structure has remained so similar over time, except for changes in the distribution of power. States would only surrender their sovereignty if forced to—as in a unipolar system. Yet we have never seen a truly unipolar system in modern times. Waltz and others have argued that this is because whenever one state strives to attain a position of unipolarity or dominance over all others in the system, the other states have banded together to balance the power of the potentially dominating state and thereby thwart that state's ambitions.[10] In such situations, countries with few common interests will form alliances to deal with this common threat. As long as the states in the system value their autonomy and sovereignty, domination by a single state seems very unlikely.

While Waltz argues that sovereign states in an anarchic environment will produce balances of power, he cannot tell you how that balancing will take place. Will states seek to create alliances, or will they attempt to increase their power through internal measures? To underscore this point, let us consider how this theory makes trade-offs between the various qualities of theories. At first glance, the theory seems precise in its predictions and descriptions of state behaviour; it is clearly generalizable, for it is meant to be applied to all states in the modern period; it is quite vague, on the other hand, when one tries to understand just what is or is not "balancing." This makes it difficult to ever falsify the theory; moreover, there is no clear time reference—how long does it take a state to recognize the need to balance? Several different forms of behaviour would fit this prediction, from forming alliances to building up one's own military in isolation. Even though Waltz's thesis may be logical and generally correct, it does not give very solid predictions about what states will actually do in terms of policy.

Thinking of International Politics as a System

Morton Kaplan, writing in the late 1950s, analyzed international relations in terms of a mechanical system and in so doing developed a prescription for action to stabilize the international system.[11] Kaplan developed six recommendations for maintaining a balance of power: (1) build up your power, but prefer negotiations over fighting; (2) fight rather than surrender to rivals; (3) stop fighting before you eliminate a major power; (4) oppose any state that tries to dominate the system (a state that strives to attain unipolarity); (5) oppose any state or ideology that seeks to subordinate the nation-state; and (6) Accept any partner into your alliance (even recent enemies) and allow defeated powers to re-enter the circle of major powers. Such a system may be stable, but it would not be peaceful. Kaplan's model mixed together descriptions and policy prescriptions.

What we find in Kaplan's work, but don't have in the writings of Waltz, is some notion that policy choices shape the use of balance of power to maintain or manage the system. Kaplan based his model on theoretical conjectures but also on prior diplomatic practices. Between the 1700s and World War 1, multipolar systems appear to have been more stable, though not always peaceful. In the eighteenth century there were numerous wars, but these were limited affairs. Kaplan looked at the diplomatic practices prevalent in those days and found that major states did not try to eliminate other major states. There was clearly a gathering of alliances to prevent the domination of Europe by a single power (Napoleonic France), and then a widespread agreement among statesmen and diplomats of the day that a five-power system was more stable and better for each country's own security. Defeated powers were allowed to recover quickly and to re-enter the diplomatic scene.

The treatment given defeated powers was very deliberate. After the twenty years of warfare associated with the French Revolution and Napoleon, the statesmen (such as Castlereagh, Talleyrand, and Metternich) who would rebuild Europe did so around a set of principles specifically designed to create a stable, peaceful system. The management of the system was to be through a conscious, co-ordinated effort, known as the *Concert of the Great Powers*. Formal negotiations were held to compensate actors, and efforts were made to deal with threats before they became vital issues. Non-systemic factors also appear to have been important. All five major powers were concerned with peaceful domestic governance and feared revolutions in their own countries, and all five were satisfied with the international status quo.

The consensus of the great powers broke down when some became less satisfied with their position in the international system. For example, Prussia's unification of Germany created a strong power with accordingly strong ambitions. Bismarck, the statesman guiding the new country's foreign affairs, directed Germany's original policies to isolate Germany's most feared opponent: France. Thus, through secret treaties, Germany was actually able to create not a balance of power but a secret coalition of four states opposing France (the four being Germany plus Italy, Austria-Hungary, and Russia). This distribution of power lasted until Bismarck was removed from office (1890) and his replacements began to simplify Germany's relationships. Where Bismarck had created relationships giving Germany a free hand, his replacements alienated Russia, giving France the option of building a rival alliance.

The bipolar post-Bismarck European system proved dangerous because bipolarity heightened the competition between the two sides. Each side feared losing allies, which would mean a gain in the strength of the other side. When Germany's most important ally, Austria-Hungary, decided to augment its power by asserting control over Bosnia, Austria-Hungary's policy clashed with that of Serbia, an ally of Russia. In the ensuing crisis, each weak power was able to ask for and receive support from stronger allies. Serbia asked Russia for help, which Russia felt it had to give or risk losing an ally; the Germans similarly felt compelled to give Austria-Hungary help against the Russians; otherwise, they would lose one of their important allies. The French became involved as well, for they could not afford to lose their most important ally, Russia. Bipolarity meant that each alliance was reluctant to see any alliance member weakened. Since everyone knew the various linkages, as soon as the Austrians decided upon war with Serbia, the Germans attacked France. Clearly, what had been set up as a peaceful, stable system a century before with the Concert of the Great Powers, had developed into a very unstable and dangerous system. World War 1 was the result.

One way of modelling the relationship between the distribution of power and war is to think about the conclusions drawn from these different theorists and historical examples, and display them graphically. There may be a high chance of war if there are two major powers, but this lowers with tripolarity and then goes back up when the international power system is multipolar. In the strictest terms, from the eighteenth century to the late nineteenth century, Europe could best be described as multipolar, for power was distributed among four to seven states during this time. Yet because of the attitudes or policies of statesmen, the results were quite different from one period to the next. In the eighteenth century, something like a balance of power described by Kaplan occurred. Wars were frequent but of a limited nature. Napoleon tried to form a unipolar system but was blocked by a coalition of the other major powers. The Concert of Europe established after the defeat of Napoleon was a very different situation from the 1700s, for very few wars occurred. The Bismarckian period saw the creation of an unbalanced coalition aimed at France, which then turned into a more balanced bipolar system via alliance-creation. But note that the structure of the system, as defined by Waltz, did not change very much, save for the rise of a united Germany in the late 1800s. So what else did change?

Status Inconsistency

What we might want to add to the purely structural discussion is a notion of whether states support or accept the status quo. As mentioned earlier, structural realism suggests that the strong states get what they want and the weak do not; the distribution of power is used to define both states' capabilities and their interests. Yet sometimes strong states appear to be dissatisfied with the international system. Another way of looking at this question is through *status inconsistency*. Sociologists have used this notion to argue that expectations are formed by individuals about their roles in society in one facet of life, but often this fails to match up with other parts of life. When this happens individuals can respond with frustration, unhappiness, and even violence or aggression. One excellent example of status inconsistency is a member of the clergy. As a person holding a position of clear ethical standing, a member of the clergy is normally given great respect by other members of the community. At the same time, members of the clergy normally do not earn large salaries and thus typically face economic hardships. Social status and economic status in this instance are quite inconsistent, and this inconsistency can lead to emotional distress or difficulty in relations with other people.

This argument has been transferred to the international level to refer to states that have gained in power but not in status. Historians write about the "German problem" prior to World War I.[12] Germany was newly powerful but lacked the recognition due a great power—Germany wanted all the trappings of a nineteenth-century imperial power, including colonies, a navy, and so on. In an effort to attain such things, Germany disrupted the affairs of other states and challenged the international status quo. Similar arguments were made about the Soviet Union, especially in the late 1960s and early 1970s, when the Soviets were building up their navy, getting much more involved in Africa, trying to insert themselves into the Middle East peace process, and so on. It might not be such a threat to peace to have states with status but no power, but it is perhaps quite dangerous to have the opposite mix, for such states would have the willingness and the ability to use force to alter the situation. Stability and peace can then only be ensured through negotiation or deterrence.

Balancing versus Bandwagoning

Perhaps the balance-of-power approach is flawed or needs something added. We have covered definitions of the balance of power and different arguments as to why and how balances occur, but what actually happens in balancing? When a state feels threatened it joins other individually weak states in an alliance to strengthen its own position and side with enough power to face down the threat. The threatened state is supposed to gather together other threatened states, each weak individually, and unite them in an alliance with enough power to defend themselves as a group. In practice, however, weak states sometimes do the opposite. Waltz says balancing occurs in the international system since states are trying to keep their security and independence, yet we have also seen states joining the stronger side.

This is referred to as "bandwagoning," because a similar practice is found in domestic politics. Before an election, political parties select a leader; during the leadership competition, the various candidates compete against each other quite fiercely, then once one begins to emerge as the likely winner, the losers are said "to jump on the election bandwagon" because they want their side to win in the election and they wish to play a role in the future government. Keep in mind, however, that this describes a different kind of political situation than international relations.

Stephen Walt, who first gave bandwagoning serious analysis, agrees with Waltz that some states balance power to ensure their security. But Walt goes on to add that some very weak states may find bandwagoning much more attractive because, if a very weak state were to join the weaker side, it might not tip the scales in the balance of power between the two sides.[13] If the actions of this very weak state might not make any difference for determining which side would win, joining the weaker side would simply mean joining the losers. Why join the side that is likely to lose? A very weak state might be better off joining the stronger side and thereby at least be included among the victors.

Walt's notion of bandwagoning is a good example of a system-level argument, because it illuminates the conditions under which states will balance, or when they will bandwagon. The key factors in a state's decision or strategy are the relative strengths of the two sides, and its own strength. (Notice how this is all drawing on the distribution of capabilities.) What is perhaps missing in Walt's analysis, which Kenneth Waltz would be quick to point out, is that when a weak state joins a powerful alliance, it is giving up its freedom of action—other members of the alliance are unlikely to listen to it, and the stronger members will be able to compel the weak state to be involved whether it truly wishes to be or not. The bandwagoner may be thrusting itself into a situation of dependence, a concept that will be developed later.

Hegemony

Another theoretical interpretation of the necessary systemic ingredients for peace argues that peace and stability occur in hegemonic or dominated systems. Theorists ranging from Robert Gilpin and George Modelski to Immanuel Wallerstein have written that imbalances of power lead to peace, because when there is a recognizably dominant power it can provide order via the issuance of threats or the promises of benefits.[14] (If the hegemonic power is truly strong, it doesn't have to resort to war to achieve its goals, since no weak power would be foolish enough to resist.) As balancing occurs, other states have the possibility of combating the hegemonic country's demands, challenges are made, and major power wars result. When a hegemonic power exists, it can dominate the scene and create international relationships to its liking.

This may sound antithetical to the balance-of-power school, especially when we see that these hegemonic theorists cite the same historical evidence (though they will obviously be giving it a different twist). Britain provided international order in the 1800s, and the unfortunate rise of Germany led to Germany's naval arms race with Britain and, eventually, to World War I. After World War I international relations were chaotic because no leading country emerged, though the United States might have had the capabilities if it had asserted itself. After World War II, when the U.S. finally did assert its power, it was able to provide order at least to the Western countries.

This theory has an economic bias to it, in that it has been used to describe order in economic relations. In security terms, it is not clear that there has ever been a period when the international system could be described as hegemonic. In economic terms, however, there have been occasions, such as when Britain went through the Industrial Revolution or when the U.S. emerged from World War II, when one country has commanded a huge economic lead over all other states. In economic terms, then, we can identify hegemonic states. The relationship between hegemonic states and international regimes will be one of the key system-level themes to be explored below.

As for the relationship between the distribution of power and major power war, the real disagreement comes down to how one interprets certainty and uncertainty. How should we consider the way states deal with risk? There is a logical plausibility to rather opposite views. Where a balance of power exists, there is uncertainty as to whose threats are more potent. If a state is averse to taking risks, it will not endanger itself by fighting a war it is unsure of winning. If, on the other hand, running risks is acceptable, then war settles the issue of which state is actually stronger and determines which should back down in a dispute. Where one side has a clear advantage (i.e., if an imbalance exists), a risk-averse weak state will obviously back down. War involves more risk for the weaker power and thus is a less rational course of action for that power unless it is very risk-acceptant. Would certainty make threats more effective? Does certainty therefore reduce the possibility of war, or does it encourage states into taking risks? Even states identified as possible hegemonic powers have not always won the wars they fought. The example of the U.S. in Vietnam stands out—as noted previously, intangibles do matter, such as the willingness to pay the costs of victory. In any war, no nation-state can know with complete certainty which side is going to win.[15]

As will be detailed later, hegemonic distributions of power are often related to certain developments in the international political economy. Free trade and stable monetary orders appear to occur when capabilities are concentrated in the hands of a single powerful state. Realists would argue that such stable relations are the result of the actions and interests of the single hegemonic state. (*Hegemonic stability theory*, as this realist argument is known, will be discussed in more detail in Chapters 7 and 8.) Thus systemic characteristics such as anarchy or distributions of power matter for how one might explain changes in the international political economy.

The Security Dilemma

The notion that equal distributions of power are dangerous, because they make all states insecure, brings us back to the notion of the security dilemma (see the earlier discussion in Chapter 1). In an anarchic environment, where a country cannot be sure who its friends are (or will be), one state's attempts to enhance its security via power maximization becomes threatening to other states. This in turn causes states to increase their own power. Such actions create a continuous chain reaction as all states strive to outdo the others. Though all states make great efforts to attain security, they remain essentially insecure.

We can model the security dilemma using game theory. Two states, A and B, have a choice, to arm or not to arm; their combination of choices make for four possible outcomes, and we can rank each state's preferences for one outcome versus the others. The final outcome is determined by the decisions each actor makes. In this case, each actor has a dominant strategy—that is, each actor is better off making the decision to arm regardless of the decision of the other actor. Consider the boxes in the diagram. If A decides to arm, but B is unarmed, then A receives its highest preference (and $4 > 3$, the result for A if it had chosen to be unarmed as well). If B decides to arm, then A would at least avoid its worst outcome (where it would be unarmed, but B armed; in this case, $2 > 1$).

FIGURE 4: THE SECURITY DILEMMA

A's hierarchy of preferences:

highest	=	to be armed, but have B unarmed (4)
next highest	=	both unarmed (3)
low	=	both armed (2)
lowest	=	to be unarmed, when B is armed (1)

B's hierarchy of preferences:

highest	=	to be armed, but have A unarmed (4)
next highest	=	both unarmed (3)
low	=	both armed (2)
lowest	=	to be unarmed, when A is armed (1)

$$B$$

		DISARM	ARM
	DISARM	3 , 3	1 , 4
A	ARM	4 , 1	2 , 2

Game theory is useful because it vividly illustrates how outcomes are the result of joint decision-making; the results are from the strategic interaction of the two sides. It in this case represents the *prisoner's dilemma*, an example of the failure of two actors to recognize their harmony of interests. In this particular game, the dominant strategy drives each actor to make a decision that leaves them jointly worse off than they could otherwise be. In the security dilemma interpretation, a player always attains a higher preference by arming, regardless of the actions of the other player. In the prisoner's dilemma game, the result of both players' choices leaves them worse off than if they could co-ordinate their activities. With co-ordination, the two players could presumably reach the outcome where both are unarmed—which they would both prefer to the outcome where they are both armed. Realists use this game to underscore how situations can drive actors to socially sub-optimal outcomes.

Factors Influencing the Security Dilemma

The security dilemma may be a bit of an oversimplification. After all, desires to raise defence levels may not threaten one's neighbours. Country A may simply build extensive fortifications, for instance, which do not enhance its ability to assault country B. This has led some scholars to try to categorize different kinds of weapons and weapon systems, to sort out offensive and defensive weapons. Advances in technology or changes in the style of warfare can tilt military abilities in favour of the offence or the defence, which can make the security dilemma more urgent or less urgent.[16]

According to Robert Jervis a variety of factors may influence military capabilities, including technology, geography, military doctrines, and strategies. When these factors make offence dominant, it is easy for attacking forces to defeat defensive forces; in such a situation, the risks of the security dilemma are doubly apparent. Each state is vulnerable to attack. When the best defence is a good offence, it makes sense for each side to want to attack first whenever there is a dispute, because whoever attacks first has the better chance of winning.[17]

In a system where defences are more powerful than offences, attacking forces are unlikely to achieve victory. States are more secure. Going to war is less likely to achieve positive gains, so states will resort to war less frequently. Such a situation is likely to be more stable and peaceful. The difficulty, of course, lies in recognizing whether the current situation favours offence or defence. Which weapons are dominant? Which weapons are offensive and which are defensive? A fort is usually considered defensive, since it is immobile; so is a gun permanently installed in a fort. Being immobile makes it an easy target so most guns are no longer placed in forts but are either wheeled or placed on tracks. Are mobile artillery pieces offensive or defensive? Iraqi tanks were offensive when they were driven into Kuwait, but defensive once they were dug into bunkers. Any assessment of today's military hardware depends not on the qualities of the weapons themselves but rather on their use.

Historically, it is hard to find a period when offence or defence was truly dominant. There is always some mix. What may be more important is which one people believe to be dominant. This creates an opening for the role of ideas. As Jervis discusses, where weapons are easily identifiable as offensive or defensive, and when one type of weapon does dominate, it has important consequences for the security dilemma.[18]

TABLE I: OFFENCE, DEFENCE, AND THE SECURITY DILEMMA

	OFFENSE DOMINATES	DEFENSE DOMINATES
POSTURES NOT DISTINGUISHABLE	Twice as dangerous	Security dilemma exists, but it is solvable
POSTURES DISTINGUISHABLE	Security dilemma exists but aggression possible	Twice as stable

Geopolitics

Related to the notions of offence and defence are questions about geography. Some states are blessed with features that naturally enhance their security. Island countries like Britain and Japan could rely on their natural barriers, plus a navy, to stay aloof from other powers—what the British called "splendid isolation." The Japanese were able to cut themselves off from outside contact for several centuries. Other forms of terrain matter, too, for defence. Mountainous areas are more easily defended, so the Swiss, for instance, have adopted a "porcupine" strategy. Rather than enter into alliances, the Swiss have tried to stay neutral for most of the last two centuries. This neutrality has been based on military training for a large part of the population but also relies on the mountainous topography. The Swiss have taken the attitude that if others choose to invade, the Swiss will simply resist so fiercely that the aggressors would never benefit. Many say the terrain of the former Yugoslavia fosters the same kind of defence, thereby explaining the reluctance of the UN to entertain a ground role in Bosnia.

Other countries may have geographic weaknesses that heighten their security dilemma. Israel, because it is small, fears that an offensive action by one of its neighbours could harm it disastrously, and therefore has been more likely to engage in pre-emptive strikes against any perceived threats; Israel has also adopted an offensive strategy to ensure that any fighting is done within its neighbours' territories rather than its own. Located in the middle of Europe, Germany has found itself with too many threatening neighbours at times. To avoid fighting a war on two fronts, Germany has adopted particularly aggressive strategies such as the Schlieffen Plan in 1914. Climate might be another factor to consider; after all, bad weather saved the Russians from Napoleon in 1812, and then again from Hitler in 1942.

Geopolitical arguments have died out to a great extent in the last forty years because technology has changed, and as technology changes it affects the way we view geography, especially the way geography interacts with military issues. Originally, Alfred T. Mahan argued that the strongest countries would be those with the most powerful navies.[19] In the late 1800s, when Mahan was writing, naval force was the fastest way to project power around the globe. Then, however, as railroads were being extended and developed, land transportation became as rapid as ocean vessels. Eventually it became clear that it was faster to move troops by rail from Asia to Europe (or vice versa) rather than by ship, because the ships had to go much longer distances, and Mahan's ideas fell out of favour.

This change in technology sparked Halford Mackinder to theorize that the most important area of the world geopolitically was what he termed the *Heartland* of Eurasia.[20] Whoever controlled this area (spanning from Central Europe right across Siberia) would not only control resources, but via railroads would be able to deploy military forces rapidly and thereby threaten and/or control all the rest of Europe and Asia. Mackinder argued that other states must prevent a single power from dominating the Heartland. This point of view was challenged after World War II by an American, Nicholas Spykman. Spykman argued that it was the *Rimland* around the edge of the Eurasian land mass that was most important, not because of lines of transportation and communication (which now seemed less important because of the advent of air transport and missile technology), but because economic activity happened to be concentrated there (i.e., in Britain, France, Italy,

Germany, Japan).[21] In the context of the 1940s, Spykman argued that the U.S. needed to ensure that potential enemies (the Soviets, Nazis, or others) did not dominate the Rimland.

The overall point is that geopolitics seems to matter less as technology improves. Technology affects our ability to overcome physical barriers and therefore alters the implications of geography. The advent of aircraft ended Britain's splendid isolation. But the creation of new weapons brings us back to some questions about offence and defence, for offensive weapons have ranges—they can project power different distances. When transportation technology was poor, it was difficult to apply force long distances away. For instance, if the British wanted to send troops into Afghanistan in the nineteenth century, they had to ship the men from Britain to India (with the ship stopping to take on coal, water, and other supplies at several points along the way, and each stop had to be manned), then land them in India, put them on trains up to the Northwest Frontier (the trains having to be supplied and protected as well), at which point the troops then marched through the Khyber Pass and had to be kept in constant supply via a chain of stations and forts. It might take thousands of soldiers and sailors to get 100 infantrymen from Britain into Afghanistan.

Kenneth Boulding tried to model this situation with his idea of a "loss of strength gradient." The notion was that due to the limits of technology, a country's ability to project power fell the further it moved away from home territory.[22]

FIGURE 5: BOULDING'S LOSS OF STRENGTH GRADIENT

DISTANCE FROM TERRITORY

But as technology improves, how does this gradient change? The slope of the line depends on the level of technology. If technology improves, this line will flatten out. Advances in sea transport, aviation, ground transportation, and communications all serve to smooth out this strength gradient.

In a similar vein, Rosecrance has argued that states make a choice in how to pursue gains in the international arena.[23] They may try to attain benefits from other states via coercion, or they may try economic exchange. Improvements in technology have radically altered that choice in recent decades, according to Rosecrance. Instead of finding it easy to seize and occupy territory militarily, even the most powerful countries have difficulty holding land where the populace resists. Meanwhile, in regard to economic transactions, improved communication and transport mean that gains from trade are higher and higher. Wise states, in this view, will abandon the use of coercion and instead pursue international economic competition. In short, the same logic applies to both security and international political economic issues.

Interdependence as a Systemic Concept

Theories can be built around other conceptualizations of the system and systemic characteristics, as noted in Chapter 1. The above discussion has been largely focused on realists' views of the system. Liberals and institutionalists point out that the system must have other characteristics besides those the realists speak of, because states act in ways that realists would not expect. Realists do not expect states to rely on each other unless they must, yet states do rely on each other, especially if we consider their economic relations.

The theorists of complex interdependence argue that the world has been transformed in recent decades. As a result of various economic, political, and societal changes, international relations are different because, even though states may make claims to sovereignty, they are largely penetrated by actors that reside and move among many different states. These actors vary from multinational corporations to international non-governmental organizations (NGOs) such as Greenpeace. Today, when states develop policies, they must take into account the variety of actors and forces exerting pressure on them—and such actors and pressures are more than just other states seeking to maximize power.

This highlights another area of dispute among theorists exploring systemic-level explanations, a dispute that was first raised in a serious fashion by those arguing that complex interdependence was a better characterization of the international system than classical realism: states have many other goals besides simply maximizing power. Proponents of complex interdependence suggested that states often placed other goals above power maximization—states may spend a large part of their budgets on defence, but that's not the only thing they spend money on. In fact, defence is not even the fastest growing portion of most countries' budgets, and everyone understands that citizens demand much more from their governments than ever before. Compared to the turn of the century (when defence was one of the state's primary goals), most citizens expect their state to provide a stable, growing economy, promote certain types of social improvement (be it in the areas of health care, education, equality of living standards, or whatever), regulate the environment, and so on.

One response among theorists has been to examine how security is being redefined. Another has been to modify some of the core assumptions in structural realism; as we saw in Chapter 1, neo-realists simply adjusted their assumption about the goals of state activity in a way that would allow them to talk about security but also about other aims. Yet another response has been to discuss how these other priorities are set, and this often means exploring non-systemic factors, perhaps most especially differences in the ways interests become organized and express themselves politically within different domestic political institutions. In short, such criticisms of structural realism have forced many theorists to take a closer look at non-systemic arguments.

Marxist Conceptions of the System— the Modern World-System

Another point of criticism made by the complex interdependence theorists has been to question the realists' assumption about anarchy. Not all realists have assumed that international relations lack any sort of organization,[24] but for the most part they have stressed that states perform similar functions and are independent and sovereign actors. Interdependence, on the other hand, is a concept borrowed from economics; it is often used to describe relationships resulting from specialization in economic activity. In other words, interdependence comes from different actors performing very different tasks but integrating their activity in such a way that the results are more profitable than they otherwise would be. This sort of thinking lies at the heart of economists' understanding of how international trade is undertaken.

Since the proponents of complex interdependence were largely drawing from a traditional economics background, they tended to consider such specialization to be a trade-off between increasing vulnerability (since each actor came to rely on others) and benefits (since greater economic output was the result). Marxists and other radical theorists, on the other hand, used this same criticism to challenge the realists, but put a much more negative spin on the resulting economic relationships. According to Marxists, not only was the international system characterized by states performing different functions, these functions reflected a division of labour organized in a hierarchic fashion, similar to the way one would conceptualize the relations between classes within society. On the top are the richest states, with the most autonomy and the most power; below are middle-level states with less range to manoeuvre, and more vulnerability; and then at the bottom are the states that are largely exploited economically by the other states and the most vulnerable.

Summary: The Qualities of Systemic-Level Theories

Finally, we need to consider the qualities of theories and evaluate the characteristics of systemic theories. Are they accurate? Some are, relatively; some aren't—we will have to reserve judgement until we take into consideration specific theories. But certainly we can say that system-level theories are very generalizable (that is, they can be applied to a wide variety of cases since they are meant to apply to the behaviour of all states). And system-level theories tend to be parsimonious—they tend to be simple and short but assert many predictions. So whether or not they are accurate, we can say that as a group, system-level theories are parsimonious and generalizable.

Also, remember that system-level explanations can be built together, so that perhaps some notion of the structure taken from Waltz can be complemented by the existence (or lack thereof) of a regulator (taken from Rosecrance) or of international regimes, or of some notion of a state's satisfaction with the status quo, in order to explain why some systems are stable and peaceful when compared to others. Remember, too, that we have spent most of our time discussing realist theories at the system level, but others were mentioned: radicals look at economic connections and some idealists or liberals talk about affection, community, or morality playing a role at the systemic level.

One way of thinking about the limitations of system-level theories is to find two states located in similar structures and see if they are acting similarly. This was precisely the tactic taken by Peter Katzenstein[25] when he edited a set of articles comparing how each of the industrialized states responded to the Arab oil embargo. While they all responded with the same general goal in mind (all tried to secure sources of energy), they chose very different policies to attain this goal. France and Japan invested heavily in government nuclear programs, other states tried to be friendlier to the Arab states, while some (most notably the U.S.) became more hostile to OPEC. System-level arguments may tell us that each state will want more secure sources of energy, but such arguments may not indicate how different states go about pursuing their goals. For more detailed arguments and explanations, we may need to turn to the lower levels of analysis.

Suggested Readings

Hedley Bull, *The Anarchical Society: A Study of Order in World Politics*. London: Macmillan, 1977.

Robert Gilpin, *U.S. Power and the Multinational Corporation*. New York: Basic Books, 1975.

Robert Gilpin, *War and Change in World Politics*. Cambridge: Cambridge University Press, 1981.

Robert Keohane and Joseph Nye, *Power and Interdependence*. Boston: Little, Brown, 1977.

David Lake, "International Economic Structures and American Foreign Economic Policy, 1887-1934," *World Politics* 35, 4 (July 1983), 517-43.

Hans Morgenthau, *Politics Among Nations: The Struggle for Power and Peace*. New York: Knopf, 1978.

Notes

1   It is worth noting, however, that the systemic and state levels may both focus on the state as the key actor, though the systemic level considers how states are arranged.

2   Jeffrey Hart, "Three Approaches to the Measurement of Power in International Relations," *International Organization* 30, 2 (Spring 1976), 289-305.

3   Robert Dahl, "The Concept of Power," *Behavioral Science* 2, 3 (July 1957), 202.

4   Ray Cline, *World Power Assessment* (Boulder, Colo.: Westview, 1977).

5   Kenneth Waltz, "The Stability of a Bipolar World," *Daedalus* 93 (Summer 1964), 881-909.

6   Richard Rosecrance, *Action and Reaction in World Politics* (Boston: Little, Brown, 1963).

7   Ibid., 220-21.

8   See a similar discussion in Stephen Krasner, "State Power and the Structure of International Trade," *World Politics* 28, 3 (April 1976), 317-47.

9   A.F.K. Organski, "The Power Transition," in Organski, *World Politics* (New York: Knopf, 1958).

10 This thinking is laid out most clearly and in most detail in Charles Doran, *The Politics of Assimilation: Hegemony and Its Aftermath* (Baltimore: Johns Hopkins University Press, 1971). The same thinking emerges in analysis using the modern world-systems approach; see Christopher Chase-Dunn, "Interstate System and Capitalist World-Economy: One Logic or Two?" *International Studies Quarterly* 25 (March 1981), 19-42.

11 Morton A. Kaplan, *System and Process in International Politics* (Huntington, NY: Robert Krieger, 1957).

12 David Calleo, a political scientist, reviewed this and several other explanations for Germany's foreign policy prior to World War 1. See Calleo, *The German Problem Reconsidered* (New York: Cambridge University Press, 1978).

13 Stephen M. Walt, *The Origins of Alliances* (Ithaca, NY: Cornell University Press, 1987).

14 Gilpin has discussed hegemony in two books: *U.S. Power and the Multinational Corporation* (New York: Basic Books, 1975), and *War and Change in World Politics* (Cambridge: Cambridge University Press, 1981); Modelski's arguments were laid out in most detail in *Long Cycles in World Politics* (Seattle: University of Washington Press, 1987); Wallerstein's arguments appeared in the three volumes of *The Modern World-System* (New York: Academic Press, 1974, 1980, 1989).

15 This does not preclude states from initiating wars they are unlikely to win. Leaders may wish to gamble, even when the odds are against them; defeat in war may appear preferable to surrender without a contest; limited goals may also be at stake, so that the definition of winning is not clear. For an in-depth analysis of such issues, see T.V. Paul, *Asymmetric Conflicts: War Initiation by Weaker Powers* (Cambridge: Cambridge University Press, 1994).

16 See George Quester, *Offense and Defense in the International System* (New York: John Wiley & Sons, 1977); Robert Jervis, "Cooperation under the Security Dilemma," *World Politics* 30, 2 (January 1978), 186-214.

17 As an example, the geographic position of Israel and the speed of modern military equipment have combined to encourage Israel to strike first on more than one occasion.

18 Jervis, "Cooperation under the Security Dilemma."

19 Alfred T. Mahan, *The Influence of Seapower on History, 1660-1783* (Boston: Little, Brown, 1897).

20 Halford Mackinder, "The Geographical Pivot of History," *Geographical Journal* 23 (April 1904); Mackinder, *Democratic Ideals and Reality* (New York: Norton, 1962).

21 Nicholas Spykman, *America's Strategy in World Politics* (New York: Harcourt Brace Jovanovich, 1942); Spykman, "Geography and Foreign Policy, 1," *American Political Science Review* 32 (February 1938), 213-36.

22 Kenneth Boulding, *Conflict and Defense* (New York: Harper & Row, 1963).

23 Richard Rosecrance, *The Rise of the Trading State* (New York: Basic Books, 1986).

24 See, in particular, Hedley Bull, *The Anarchical Society: A Study of Order in World Politics* (London: Macmillan, 1977).

25 Peter Katzenstein, ed., *Between Power and Plenty* (Madison: University of Wisconsin Press, 1978).

Three

THEORIES FROM
THE NATIONAL OR
DOMESTIC LEVEL

Some critics of system-level analysis argue that they "black-box" the state; that is, system-level theories consider all governments to have the same goals and to think and act in the same manner. Those assumptions serve to clarify situations and to reduce complexity. As such, they promote abstract theorizing, but some theorists consider them oversimplifications. The latter have argued that a theory of domestic politics is needed to compensate for two things that systemic theories tend to lack: (1) an elaboration of social purposes—what it is that states are trying to do besides simply survive; (2) a better understanding of why different states react differently to similar stimuli (as explored in Katzenstein's *Between Power and Plenty*).

The Variety of Theories at the National or Domestic Level

These domestic-level or national-level arguments can be lumped into various categories, with emphases on very different factors: (1) political culture (e.g., is a nation-state imbued with a militaristic culture? is it peaceful? tolerant?); (2) regime type (the most popular of which at the moment is that democracies don't fight each other; another one might be that dictatorships are more likely to be aggressive); (3) ideology (do Communist states have different goals than other states? do Islamic republics such as Iran or the Sudan behave differently from other states?); (4) domestic political stability (when a society is unstable at home, do leaders have an interest in fomenting trouble abroad to distract the public? or does instability at home weaken a state and paralyse its foreign policy?). In addition, a wide variety of theories build on (5) the economic characteristics of countries. (Are capitalist countries more imperialistic than non-capitalist countries? Are high-technology countries more demanding of their neighbours in terms of what they need, and therefore do they engage in greater trade?) While this list is hardly exhaustive of domestic-level theories, most examples could be placed in one of these subcategories.

Culture and History

If we start at the top of the list, recognizing that the subcategories are in an arbitrary order, consider *culture* as a possible causal factor. Culture is a difficult concept to make use of, especially if one is interested in constructing predictive theories.[1] On the one hand, most people agree culture exists; it is passed on from generation to generation within a society, and it definitely has meaning across individuals and across time. In the past, however, theories that used cultural factors to explain foreign policies merely promoted stereotypes. Any meaningful argument using culture as a causal variable must be wary of these dangers. At the same time, cultures differ, peoples from different lands may have very different values, and they may have different perspectives on many issues (including foreign policy).

One example of a culturally based theory would be the argument that the United States lost the war in Vietnam because Americans valued life more than the Vietnamese. When the war escalated and casualties on both sides increased rapidly, the Americans conceded they could not win. This argument is bolstered by some pieces of evidence. For instance, the North Vietnamese lost a much higher proportion of their population in battle than just about any other example for which accurate figures exist—perhaps up to 4 per cent of the pre-war population of the North. During the war, General Giap of North Vietnam was supposed to have said that "life and death don't matter." Yet this particular example hardly makes sense, since it isn't placing life and death in perspective with other values. It may not have been so much that the Vietnamese didn't value life as much as Americans, but rather that the Vietnamese valued other things more highly than the Americans (e.g., the political future of Vietnam) and therefore were willing to make sacrifices the Americans weren't prepared to match.

Another problem plaguing cultural theories is the slow manner in which culture changes. Since foreign policy is constantly changing, it is difficult if not impossible to use cultural arguments to explain these rapid changes in behaviour. Culture can only be appealing for developing explanations of consistent behaviour. Due to this weakness and the inherent susceptibility of such theories to slip into stereotyping, cultural theories are no longer employed very often. That said, it is still important for the successful conduct of diplomacy to understand how culture shapes values from one country to another. If one state wants to threaten another, but misunderstands what that other state or society values, then the threat could easily be misdirected. The same holds for delivering rewards. If we do not understand what the other state values, it may be difficult to structure positive incentives to bring the other side to behave as wished. While cultural theories are no longer used often by political scientists, being sensitive to cultural differences may be important for making any theory or policy more effective.

The Ideological Characteristics of States

In a similar vein, we can examine how *ideology* can be an important factor in explaining or predicting state behaviour. As a professor, Henry Kissinger developed arguments based on ideology in order to develop a theory binding together the goals of foreign policy with other typical characteristics.[2] Kissinger identified three functions of ideology. He linked each function to specific aims, then theorized about the foreign policies that would be generated. First, ideologies provide images of what the world should look like. When different countries have different ideals, Kissinger reasoned, they are more likely to get into conflict. Kissinger argued that this effect was proportionate—when the countries were very distant ideologically, their conflict would be greater. Second, ideologies provide conceptual frameworks for understanding the world. This means ideologies may colour the analysis of decision-makers. Ideology provides the lens through which the actions of other states are interpreted. Third, since ideologies provide positive goals for nation-states, they establish the ideals that states work towards, thereby establishing the goals of foreign policy beyond mere survival.

By viewing states along these lines, Kissinger could group them into three broad categories. The first category contained the democratic, economically advanced states we generally label the West. This group consists of Western Europe, Canada, the U.S., and Japan. In these states the leadership is very pragmatic and highly bureaucratized. The leadership approaches foreign policy as a set of problems to be managed. Foreign policy is seen as a series of problematic episodes with rational solutions. This means they are more likely to fit our notions of rational, unitary actors as developed by system-level theorists.

A second category of states, however, would act very differently according to Kissinger. This second set consisted then of the Soviet bloc. The leaders of these countries were guided by Marxist-Leninist ideology and analyses. According to these analyses, objective factors were the guiding forces in the development of mankind—with a world socialist revolution at the end, of course. These states' policies were very goal-oriented and very much focused on achieving the end of global revolution. The third category of states Kissinger called the charismatic revolutionary countries, because at the time he was writing many Third World countries were ruled by popular nationalists. The popularity of such leaders was often due to the critical role these particular individuals played in the country's political formation or independence. These countries were considered revolutionary, though, because they tended to challenge the international status quo.

This approach provides a simple way to think about the manner in which different countries formulate and pursue foreign policy goals. This approach also provides a better sense of what it is that states might fight over, beyond merely survival. Moreover, the information deduced from Kissinger's arguments can be used to create new arguments. For instance, this framework could be used to reach a better understanding of why some states form alliances with one another. Kissinger used it to build more sophisticated theories about how states from the three groups interact. The bureaucratic/pragmatic states are obviously oriented to the status quo and managerial. That also means they are primarily reacting to other states' policies rather than seizing the initiative. The other states have the advantage, therefore, in that they set the agenda through their own actions. The results worried Kissinger, for it meant that the issues confronting states, and the time at which such issues arise, would be determined not by the West but by either the charismatic revolutionary states, which hoped to alter the status quo, or by the Marxist-Leninist states, which were potentially pursuing a coherent and comprehensive plan to incite world revolution.

Theories of "Lateral Pressure"

Other state-level or society-level arguments are based on the variations in the economic attributes of states. Like Kissinger's arguments raised above, these factors can be used to deduce variation in states' goals. Robert North created such an argument by looking at three characteristics of states.[3] First, North said that states with larger populations require greater volumes of resources to satisfy their needs. Likewise, states that are economically advanced and possess advanced technology consume more resources. These states need to extract greater amounts of resources from other countries. A simple assessment allows one to identify which states place the highest demands for resources on the international system.

TABLE 2: POPULATION, TECHNOLOGY, AND
THE LEVEL OF DEMAND FOR EXTERNAL INPUTS

| | | *Population* | |
		HIGH	LOW
Technology	HIGH	High demands	Medium demands
	LOW	Medium demands	Low demands

While this simple framework helps to establish the sorts of demands states or societies have, to understand how this influences their foreign policy we must introduce a third factor: their domestic supply of resources. Some states, such as Brazil, Canada, Australia, Russia, and the U.S., possess vast resources at home. Even though they may have technologically advanced economies and large populations, they are able to meet many of their own needs. Countries with high needs and very few or limited domestic resources, on the other hand, will have to look internationally to satisfy their demands. North argued that these countries have the potential to be troublemakers in the international system.

As an example, we could examine the role Japan has played in the international system in the last century. Japan is very densely populated, its economy is very advanced and industrialized, but it is not very rich in resources. Japan thus fits the case of a potential disruptive member of the international system according to North's analysis, for the country should have intense needs for foreign resources. What this particular state-level analysis doesn't tell us, however, is how Japan will go about filling its requirements. North's argument simply states that Japan's international relations will be important for that country's economic survival. Trade is one route for meeting these needs. When trade fails, though, as it did in the 1930s (when other countries placed barriers against imports and/or joined exclusive trade blocs), a country with high resource needs such as Japan may be driven to imperialism to satisfy its demands. What we need, then, to complete this picture is a sense of the international economic environment.

The Domestic Economic Sources of Imperialism

Another more well-known argument based on domestic economic factors was developed by J.A. Hobson and Lenin, at the beginning of this century.[4] Hobson, Lenin and others wished to explain the resurgence of European imperialism in the late nineteenth century. Both Hobson and Lenin based their arguments on the development of capitalism within Europe. They and others argued that capitalism could only survive by paying workers extremely low wages. If the workers weren't exploited, businesses would collapse, causing the capitalist economy to crumble. Using Marxist economic theories, they believed this exploitation was reaching its maximum. As technology progressed, workers' wages declined. Machinery did more work, labour less. But firms rely on the exploitation of labour for their profits in Marxist analyses, so when labour's input fell, firms could not exploit labour as much. The Marxists expected firms' profits to fall over time, and in fact profits did decline in the economic downturn of the 1870s. In response to this, firms formed monopolies or cartels to control and reduce competition. Even though such actions bolstered profits somewhat, the Marxists expected such processes to continue. As the firms reduced workers' wages further, the workers' ability to buy goods had to fall. This in turn would put further downward pressure on profits. Firms then respond by looking for export markets. After developing markets abroad they may even begin international investments. Firms will be especially interested in economically underdeveloped areas, where the capital invested won't face very high competition and will therefore make high profits. But investments in such areas need protection, so the capitalists will urge their own governments to seize political control of these other territories. Thus, according to Hobson and Lenin, capitalist countries were being driven by their own domestic economic failures to engage in *imperialism*.

Hobson's version was produced earlier, and Lenin apparently borrowed much of Hobson's reasoning. Lenin went on to add a few more critical steps. Lenin asked "what happens when capitalist imperialism covers the globe? How would the capitalist countries deal with their problems then?" They could only gain new markets or new areas for investment by taking them away from other imperialist powers. Of course, critics of Lenin's views have developed numerous counter arguments, and Lenin's evidence has largely been contradicted over time: underconsumption is not such a problem since most people in industrialized countries live better than ever before; investment has been concentrated in the other economically developed countries, not the economically underdeveloped ones; and also, one can see that the places that received many investments were not necessarily colonies but were often other major powers. None the less, Lenin's argument has been extremely popular ever since it was written some eighty years ago.

It is important to note that Lenin and Hobson both assumed that the state is dominated by the capitalist class. (See the difference between instrumental and structural Marxism in Chapter 1.) Capitalists of one country were in competition with capitalists from other countries; workers, on the other hand, shared interests with other workers, no matter what country they were from. (Thus the authors retained their belief in that final recommendation of the *Communist Manifesto*: "Workers of the world unite!") Today, we have many reasons to question these assumptions, since capitalism may turn out to be very cosmopolitan (via multinational companies) and workers very nationalistic. These examples illustrate how theories of international relations can be based on the economic characteristics of states, while the understanding of those characteristics can vary widely—not simply just among Marxist theories, but among different types of non-Marxist economics as well.

Theories Based on Regime Type

Rather than classify a state on the basis of its economic traits (and consider the consequences of the economy for the formulation and pursuit of goals), we can execute the same sort of argument but emphasize states' political characteristics instead. A simple version of this type of argument bases its understanding of states' foreign policies on the form of regime. These theories have a long tradition. Some people have argued that authoritarian regimes are dangerous, for instance, because they use coercion at home and therefore have a propensity to use violence in all situations. Democratic regimes, on the other hand, have domestic politics characterized by tolerance, diversity, pluralism and compromise. These same attitudes and policies may carry over to democratic regimes' behaviour in the international realm. Totalitarian regimes are the opposite—they tolerate no rival viewpoints and never compromise. If those attitudes are carried over into the international realm, conflict between states is more likely.

Theories about the behaviour of totalitarian states focus on that defining feature: the state totally controls the flow of information, of education, of social life, etc.[5] A totalitarian state whose society is penetrated by ideas or information from a neighbouring state may seek to maintain its monopoly over information and ideas by lashing out to knock out the external source of rival views. This may be the only way for the state to defend its total control over domestic society. (An example might be the concerns expressed in Soviet policies towards the states along its southern borders after the Islamic revolution in Iran; the threat of a similar revolution occurring elsewhere and spilling over into the Soviet Central Asian Republics may have inspired the invasion of Afghanistan.)

In contrast, classical theorists such as Immanuel Kant have argued that democracies are more peaceful, or at least they are more peaceful among themselves, because they have greater respect for law and compromise and more tolerance.[6] Other scholars have noticed how peaceful democracies are with each other but argue that the key difference is that democratic institutions constrain decision-making by political leaders. Democratic governments must do things that are popular with their citizens. The majority must be convinced that a policy is worthwhile if it is to be pursued with any success. Those who actually do the fighting and dying—the citizens—are more likely to resist war as a way to resolve disputes if they are given a say in the decisions.

Liberalism and Theories of the Behaviour of Democratic States

The belief that democracies are more peaceful than other sorts of states has surfaced a number of times, most notably with Woodrow Wilson's diplomacy during World War 1 and then later during the Cold War. In the last two decades, statistical studies have produced a startling confirmation of these ideas: given strict definitions of democracy and war, no two democracies have ever engaged in a war against each other.[7] Since the number of democratic regimes rose rapidly in the late 1980s and early 1990s thanks to the debt crisis (which discredited so many authoritarian regimes in the developing world) and the breakdown of the Soviet bloc, these issues suddenly became of terrific import. At least one writer heralded these changes as "the end of history" since all the major powers were adopting democratic institutions.[8] In a world of liberal democracies, war would be unlikely; ideological conflict was also disappearing.

The current fascination with "the democratic peace," as it is now referred to, is actually a qualified version of earlier arguments. Originally, arguments were made claiming all democracies were peaceful towards all other states. (The statistics, however, show that democracies engage in warfare as often as other types of regimes, they just refrain from engaging in war with each other.) Woodrow Wilson spoke of "making the world safe for democracy," since he believed it was other states that started wars. In his thinking, the best way to achieve worldwide peace would be to convert all states to democratic practices.[9]

On the other hand, one theorist, Theodore Lowi, has turned this statement on its head.[10] Lowi argued that democracies were actually more dangerous to their neighbours than were other states. Lowi based this argument on his observations of democratic practices and how such patterns might affect the formulation and execution of foreign policy. Leaders in democracies have to persuade their public of the efficacy of policies. In order to get approval, they often oversell their policies. Because it is difficult to get public support and construct a majority, leaders in democracies often take a small event and blow it out of proportion—they may create an international crisis. This kind of overselling, especially of threats, can be found in the foreign policies of many democracies but was most apparent in U.S. foreign policy during the Cold War. The Reagan administration spoke of the Sandinistas in Nicaragua as a threat to the U.S.; while one may not have approved of what the Sandinistas were doing, they hardly posed a threat to the security of the United States.

An example with greater consequences would be the incident that led the U.S. Congress to pass the Gulf of Tonkin resolution. U.S. naval forces were patrolling off the coast of North Vietnam in 1965, trying to intimidate North Vietnam into ending its support of the Viet Cong in the South. During one dark night, the U.S. forces believed they were under attack. President Lyndon Johnson used this incident to persuade Congress to support his administration's desire to send more forces to Vietnam and to engage the North Vietnamese and Viet Cong more directly. Congress approved the use of force in response. It has never been clear whether the U.S. forces were actually attacked or whether the sailors were simply nervous and misinterpreted the situation, but Johnson was able to use this event to build support for the use of military force.

Lowi argued that this tendency to oversell policies drives democracies to take extreme positions. During wars, for instance, democracies tend to ask their enemies for unconditional terms. They often engage in crusading wars, where they aim not simply to win but rather to convert their opponent into a democracy (which usually means the opposing leadership has to be eliminated). Lowi notes that totalitarian regimes don't have to engage in overselling since they can change public opinion more rapidly and easily. Also, such regimes can move without the support of the majority; they have a greater ability to ignore public opinion, or at least to block access to information and therefore reduce criticism of their policies.

Lowi also pointed out that the policies of democracies could be difficult for other types of states to anticipate since democracies do not act consistently. Lowi identifies how one particular aspect of democracies—internal political competition—may confuse other countries' decision-makers. Overcoming such internal divisions takes time, as does the construction of a solid consensus behind a specific policy; democracies simply move slowly. When a non-democratic country is engaged in diplomacy with a democracy and sees the democracy racked with internal divisions and likewise slow to act, the non-democratic country may believe that if it acts quickly and decisively to achieve a limited goal the democracy opposes, it might succeed before the democracy can muster a reaction.

Many people believe this is exactly the sort of interaction and calculation that went on in the Iraqi decision to invade Kuwait. The Iraqis may have thought they could seize Kuwait with impunity before the U.S. responded. The miscalculation comes in the failure to recognize that democracies can also move quickly once a crisis begins. Normally, democracies move slowly and must contend with domestic rifts, but in a crisis the *rally-round-the-flag effect* may result. All people are asked to pull together and fulfil their patriotic duty, and therefore fall in behind their leaders. (Naturally, some leaders may try to create this effect by engineering international crises via overselling.) This inconsistency (slowness in everyday decision-making, but speed during crises) means that other states miscalculate and get themselves into conflicts with democracies that they did not intend.

Liberalism in International Relations: The Importance of State-Society Relations

An important aspect of these arguments, which is perhaps more subtle but also more useful, is to consider how state-society relations vary. We have many notions of the state in political science and of how it is constrained by or linked to society. On one extreme we can think of the state as being totally dominated by certain social actors. Lenin and some other Marxists would contend that the state was merely the instrument of the capitalist class. The theory of totalitarian states discussed earlier assumed that the state was largely independent of society and could do pretty much as it pleased.

These two positions are extremes, and if we imagine them as end points on a spectrum, most states fall somewhere in between. This affords us some ways to identify differences among democracies, for instance, since some states are stronger versus other social actors while others are weaker. Stephen Krasner talks of how insulated the key decision-makers are from societal pressures as one way to identify stronger or weaker states.[11] The U.S. is an example of a state that is weak against its society, because the U.S. government is open to pressure from societal actors at many points—special interest groups can lobby Congress, the President, and his advisers, take action in the courts, battle for public opinion directly, and so on.[12]

Many theorists of American politics view the U.S. government as a broker between these interest groups, trying to please as many interests as possible. Policy reflects the struggles between various interest group pressures. Other democratic governments are not so penetrated by societal actors. A country like Japan has a state composed of rather insulated decision-makers—many policies are set by bureaucrats unaffected by elections or public opinion. If few groups have access to these key bureaucratic decision-makers, the decision-makers can come up with policies and pursue them in a more consistent manner. We would expect those policies to have a single goal since they wouldn't reflect the views of a wide variety of groups (as U.S. policy does). We can also examine some of the variation in policy instruments that different democracies wield: Canada and the U.S. rely on macroeconomic policy to guide the economy, which means treating actors the same way (i.e., everyone faces the same changes of interest rates in the market), whereas in other countries such as France and Japan the governments don't have to work with such broad instruments (i.e., they can more selectively affect interest rates so that one company may be able to borrow money at much cheaper rates than another).

Regime Tools and Policy Instruments

Katzenstein's edited volume *Between Power and Plenty* explored these differences in policy instruments as part of a possible alternative to system-level theories. The authors each took an industrialized country that appeared to be similarly located in the international system and examined how each reacted to a similar problem (the OPEC oil embargo). The variation in policy responses illustrated differences in the states' strength vis-à-vis their societies and illuminated the different policy instruments each state had at its disposal. Faced with the international oil shortage, each country needed more energy; yet each responded to this problem in a distinct way.

Those states with governments considered relatively strong versus their own societies, France and Japan, acted quickly, decisively, and with a single-minded purpose. They sought a new form of energy that would be under the state's own control, so they both embarked on massive programs to build nuclear power plants. This was meant to free them from the threat of future embargoes. In the U.S. case, where the state is relatively weak compared to its society, the state's response was much slower and much more muddled; all kinds of interest groups lobbied the government (ranging from environmentalists to oil companies), each arguing for a particular solution. When the government tried to satisfy every group, the policy became a mish-mash that culminated in very limited results.

To show this variation in response, Katzenstein developed a grid, mapping out the relationship between the relative strengths of the state and society and the policy response selected. Where the state is strong and society weak, policy reflects the state's wishes, and where it is the other way around policy reflects society's wishes.[13]

TABLE 3: THE INTERACTION OF STATE
AND SOCIETAL CENTRALIZATION

		State Centralization	
		HIGH	LOW
Societal Centralization	HIGH	Japan	Germany & Italy
	LOW	France & Britain	U.S.

It is important to note that the policy instruments available to the state provide only half the information in this calculation. Societal inputs are also used. This mix of state characteristics and societal inputs is probably the most common form of model or theory in international political economy.

Because societal splits caused by economic issues are easily identified (thanks to elaborate models developed in economics that we can easily borrow), political scientists can use this information to discuss political competition over foreign economic policy. Information on the governmental structure is then needed, for domestic political institutions frame the political competition between groups.

FIGURE 6: A TYPICAL DOMESTIC-LEVEL ARGUMENT
IN INTERNATIONAL POLITICAL ECONOMY

societal groups→organization→domestic politics→state institutions→policy

It is safe to say that such theories are much more common in international political economy than in security studies precisely because of the nature of the issues at stake. Economic policy creates divisions within societies that are more clearly observed. The cleavages within societies created by security issues, on the other hand, are much more difficult to predict or explain.

Foreign Policy Consequences of Domestic Disturbances

Another important national-level argument looks at domestic society's stability as a determinant of the likelihood the state will adopt an aggressive foreign policy. In this view, war is the result of policy decisions made by élites, who may be responding to either international pressures or domestic social pressures. This view is interesting in that it seeks to understand state policy not in terms of "national interest" but the interest of the élite. Élite decision-makers may choose one policy over another to satisfy their own needs, regardless of the interests of the rest of society or the state as a whole. After all, if a weak state is told by a strong society what to do, who tells a strong state what to do? If an élite is concerned with its own interests, then it may be worried about its own position within the domestic political system. From this starting point, two logical but opposing theories emerge.

The first is known as *externalization*. Externalization occurs when a society is becoming unstable and, in order to reconsolidate their control, élite policy-makers instigate an international incident, crisis, or conflict to divert the population from domestic problems or domestic differences.[14] By identifying an external enemy, the élites hope to create greater domestic cohesion—the rally-round-the flag effect. The logic of the other theory relating domestic turmoil and foreign policy runs in the opposite direction. Whereas externalization theories argue that domestic instability may drive élites to adopt more active foreign policies (leading to more foreign engagements), an opposite view also exists: in countries with domestic instabilities, the élite may be so preoccupied with settling internal problems that its members are unable to manage foreign affairs effectively. Instead of becoming more externally oriented, this theory suggests that domestic turmoil can lead a state to reduce its foreign relations. A good example might be the Soviet Union in the 1920s, when it was preoccupied with the attempt to transform its economy. Another would be the U.S. in the 1930s, when the Great Depression forced the government to concentrate its efforts on domestic issues. As a consequence, the U.S. largely ignored international developments such as the rise of Hitler in Germany or Japanese aggression in Asia.

These two theories present the connection between domestic instability and international policy or conflict rather differently. The key question seems to be whether or not one believes engaging in international conflict will lead to more domestic cohesion and stability. The evidence is quite mixed. In 1870, Bismarck used a war between France and Prussia to get Prussia's German allies to agree to unify and create a single country. In 1905, the Russians hoped that war with Japan would reduce pressures for political reform and consolidate the Czar's control. Instead, the war put so much pressure on the economy and society that appeals for political reform were accelerated.

In more recent times, the Vietnam conflict clearly split the American society quite deeply—the scars are still visible. But in the Gulf War, President George Bush got the highest approval ratings any president has ever received since they started taking polls, and this was definitely caused by the rally-round-the-flag effect since his approval rating dropped afterwards. So even in the same country within a short span of time, the relationship between domestic politics and the identification of external enemies isn't clear or consistent. Success in the crisis or conflict may be a key factor, of course—quick, decisive actions seem to pay off.

Summary: Evaluating National-Level Theories

When evaluating the state- or national-level of analysis, we find a wide variety of theories. Each builds on specific characteristics of states or societies to predict variation across states' policies. In contrast, systemic-level theories suggest similarity between foreign policies when states are placed in similar situations. System-level theories also tend to assert uniformity in states' goals. Domestic-level theories lead us to expect to see more variation in policy because different kinds of states want different things. State-level theories pick up on more details, and they tend to make more specific descriptions and predictions than system-level theories.

At the same time, this specificity comes at a cost. Because state-level theories typically employ more information than system-level theories, they have different characteristics than system-level theories. State-level theories make use of more details and hence tend to be more descriptive. They may seem more accurate in analysing historical situations, but that doesn't necessarily mean they provide better predictions—that would involve comparing specific theories.

More important for our considerations, state-level theories are not as generalizable as systemic theories. Systemic theories are meant to work for all states. We could use theories on balancing or bandwagoning to make a prediction about any state's foreign policy, but we could not do the same thing with most state-level theories—an argument about capitalist countries engaging in imperialism would not be applicable to Vietnam's invasion of Cambodia or the Soviet Union's invasion of Afghanistan. We simply wouldn't be able to apply them to those cases. And many state-level theories include details that make them useful only for a specific, limited subset of cases.

If we turn to the last characteristic of theories, parsimony, we find that systemic theories are fairly parsimonious compared to state-level theories. The trade-off is that system-level theories usually provide somewhat vague predictions. More information is required for state-level theories, but hopefully what is lost in parsimony is gained in accuracy. Again, some specific theories may have to be considered to evaluate how such a trade-off is made.

Suggested Readings

Peter Gourevitch, "The Second Image Reversed," *International Organization* 32, 4 (Autumn 1978), 881-912.

Peter Katzenstein, ed., *Between Power and Plenty*. Madison: University of Wisconsin Press, 1978.

Helen Milner, "Trading Places: Industries for Free Trade," *World Politics* 40, 3 (April 1988), 350-76.

Ronald Rogowski, *Commerce and Coalitions*. Princeton, NJ: Princeton University Press, 1989.

Notes

1   John A. Hall, however, points out that many of the past uses of culture can now be found in our use of the concept of ideas or beliefs as a causal factor. See "Ideas and the Social Sciences," in Judith Goldstein and Robert Keohane, eds., *Ideas and Foreign Policy* (Ithaca, NY.: Cornell University Press, 1993), 43-48.

2   Henry Kissinger, *American Foreign Policy* (New York: W.W. Norton, 1969).

3   Robert C. North, "Towards a Framework for the Analysis of Scarcity and Conflict," *International Studies Quarterly* 21 (December 1977), 569-91.

4   Excerpts from both Hobson's "The Theory of Underconsumption" (1894) and his larger work *Imperialism: A Study* (1902), as well as from Lenin's *Imperialism* (1916), have been reprinted in numerous texts. One set can be found in D.K. Fieldhouse, *The Theory of Capitalist Imperialism* (London: Longmans, 1967), which also contains other contemporary writings.

5   For example, see Ivo K. Feierabend, "Expansionist and Isolationist Tendencies of Totalitarian Political Systems: A Theoretical Note," *Journal of Politics* 24 (November 1962), 733-42.

6   Immanuel Kant, *Perpetual Peace* (New York: Columbia University Press, 1939).

7   For some of these early findings, see Steve Chan, "Mirror, Mirror on the Wall ... Are the Freer Countries More Pacific?" *Journal of Conflict Resolution* 28, 4, (1984), 617-48; Michael Doyle, "Liberalism and World Politics," *American Political Science Review* 80, 4 (1986), 1151-61; and Erich Weede, "Democracy and War Involvement," *Journal of Conflict Resolution* 28, 4 (1984), 649-64. There was an explosion of such work in the early 1990s.

8   Francis Fukuyama, "The End of History?" *National Interest* (Summer 1989), 3-18.

9   See Ray S. Baker, ed., *Woodrow Wilson and World Settlement* (Garden City, NJ: Doubleday, Page & Co., 1922).

10 Theodore Lowi, "Making Democracy Safe for the World: National Politics and Foreign Policy," in James N. Rosenau, ed., *Domestic Sources of Foreign Policy* (New York: Free Press, 1967), 295-331.

11 Stephen Krasner, *Defending the National Interest* (Princeton, NJ: Princeton University Press, 1978), 55-61.

12 For this point, see ibid., 61-70.

13 Peter Katzenstein, "Conclusion: Domestic Structures and Strategies of Foreign Economic Policy," in Katzenstein, ed., *Between Power and Plenty* (Madison: University of Wisconsin Press, 1978), Table 111, 324.

14 For example, see Arno Mayer, "Internal Causes and Purposes of War in Europe, 1870-1956," *Journal of Modern History* 41 (September 1969), 291-303.

Four

BUREAUCRATIC
POLITICS

Once we drop down another step in the levels of analysis, we begin to examine theories emphasizing individuals as the key actors in international relations. There are two very different ways of thinking about individuals and foreign policy decision-making. One is to treat each individual as a unique entity, so that any foreign policy decision could only be understood or predicted if we knew how the particular decision-makers thought or behaved. That would be focusing on idiosyncratic features of individuals, and those theories will be examined in this chapter. Another way to consider the role of individuals, however, is to view them as actors strongly affected by the positions they hold. Their positions on policy are formed by the roles they play within domestic politics. The models we are building are actually about positions, roles, or offices rather than the particular characteristics of any one individual.

The Importance of Role

These theories are based on the assumption that duty and responsibility—defined by the role one plays—determine how individuals behave and therefore shape how individuals formulate and execute foreign policy. This level of analysis was developed after analysts experienced frustrations with system-level arguments. Since realist system-level arguments assume states are unitary actors, a single state's policies should be rational as a package—the entire range of policies should be coherent and aimed at similar goals. Yet when we look at any one country's policies, we often see contradictory schemes conducted at the same time. Such contradictory actions cannot be understood or explained using a theory that assumes all policies to be the decisions of a single rational actor. Some of the best examples can be found in domestic affairs; consider how the U.S. government handles cigarettes.

The government subsidizes the production of tobacco, then turns around and spends money to dissuade people from smoking![1]

Foreign policies often have the same element of irrationality when one considers the entire range of policies a country pursues at any one point in time. To understand this confusing mix of policies, practitioners of the bureaucratic politics approach drop the assumption that the state is a unitary actor and replace it with one that says the state is composed of disparate groups or organizations. It is assumed that each of these organizations has its own set of goals and determines a portion of policy output. The sum of these varied goals and policies may work well, or the various policies may simply undermine each other. Some of the best examples come in the area of defence procurement, such as the U.S. military's purchasing of aircraft.

From an overall point of view, a single rational decision-maker might be able to establish the specific number of aircraft necessary to defend the U.S. This number would undoubtedly be lower than the actual number of planes and helicopters the U.S. military actually operates. The result must be somewhat wasteful of scarce resources, since the government could spend the money in other ways. To understand why, we can apply the bureaucratic politics model; such an approach focuses on who decides which aircraft (and how many) to buy. The U.S. military is not a monolithic organization but is made up of four services or branches: the Air Force, the Navy, the Army and the Marines. So who decides how many aircraft to procure? One might think it would be the Air Force, since the Air Force should be responsible for military applications of aircraft. But that is hardly the end—the Navy has its own planes and helicopters, and not just for attacking other naval forces but for attacking targets on land, too. And even though the Marines are really part of the Navy, they purchase and operate their own planes and helicopters as well. Which of these branches has traditionally operated the most helicopters? None of the three mentioned so far, but rather the U.S. Army. The Army wants to operate its own air support under its direct command. Since the Army isn't allowed to buy planes (that is done by the Air Force), it procures helicopters—even though helicopters may not perform as well as fixed-wing aircraft and require much higher maintenance.

The results are an overabundance of some types of weaponry and overlapping responsibilities. From an overall perspective, it is wasteful and inefficient. Yet this is the outcome of the decisions made within the Pentagon. The heads of each branch of the military are not necessarily thinking about what is best for the country, but rather are thinking in terms of what is best for their particular branches of the service: the head of the Navy argues strongly for everything the Navy wants, and so on. The individual's goals in this model are established by the role each plays, by the office he or she might hold.[2]

This sort of thinking was first developed by Graham Allison in his analysis of the Cuban missile crisis.[3] Allison set out three rival models for interpreting how the crisis unfolded. (This is the same sort of practice we will be employing in the cases, in Part III.) Allison labelled the three prototypes Models I through III. Model I was a standard systemic level argument (assuming the state to be a single, unitary, and rational actor), which Allison felt didn't work well. His Model III is better known today as *bureaucratic politics*. Model III worked better in Allison's estimation because it saw policy as the result of internal bargaining among bureaucrats within each government—foreign policy was the result of different actors (each with his or her own goals in mind) fighting among themselves over their country's foreign policy.

Theorists using the bureaucratic politics approach point out that particular decision-makers see the problems of foreign policy differently, depending on their responsibilities and goals. They therefore are likely to offer different solutions to problems or suggest alternative policies. A good example of this point might come from American decisions regarding the possible development of an anti-ballistic missile (ABM) system in the 1960s.[4] It was rumoured the Russians were already well along in creating such a system, and the U.S. President at the time, Lyndon Johnson, saw this as a problem. He didn't particularly see it as a threat to the U.S., but he saw it as a problem for himself. As president, he believed his re-election hopes hinged on the public's belief in his ability to handle foreign policy. He needed to appear to be doing something about the Russian competition. Johnson didn't really require that a substantial effort be made to match the Russians, but he needed some sort of symbolic effort. Johnson therefore handed the issue over to his staff.

His advisers viewed the problem quite differently. They were concerned that any new arms program would upset U.S.-Soviet relations. The foreign policy officials didn't want the Russians to feel threatened. Due to such worries, the foreign policy staff in the White House suggested that any American ABM system be limited, and perhaps even imperfect. A vast missile defence system operating with high levels of efficiency would negate the Russians' ability to threaten the U.S. In so doing it would undermine the Russians' ability to deter the U.S. from launching its own first strike. The end result would be to make the Russians very nervous. These advisers therefore wanted a system that would protect U.S. missiles from a Soviet attack, thereby ensuring the U.S. held a potent retaliatory force and enhancing America's deterrence of a possible Russian attack. But this meant building a small ABM system which would defend missile bases rather than American cities—what would the voters think?

And, of course, other actors were involved as well. Each of the armed services wanted in on any new large defence program, so they were engaged in a fight over who would operate the ABM system. If the system was to protect cities, the Army argued the project fell within its domain. The Air Force said missiles were its responsibility, so it should man the new defences. Congress viewed things through a completely different lens, and was concerned not simply with who would operate the system but which private contractors would be hired to build it, how much it would cost, and so on. In short, each of the prominent decision-makers envisioned a very different ABM system. (In the end, no ABM system was ever constructed, though testing was undertaken.)

Bureaucratic Goals

The example illustrates how each of these individuals—the President, his advisers, the head of the Army, the head of the Navy, the congressmen—were acting rationally, but each was pursuing a goal specific to his or her job. Since this model focuses on organizations or bureaucracies as the key actors, one must turn to these bodies to identify the goals identified with a particular role. In an important book expounding on the bureaucratic politics approach, Morton Halperin and Arnold Kanter identify five goals of organizations.[5] The first is to defend the bureaucracy's essential mission or purpose. One must continually prove to others that one's organization has important responsibilities and deserves to exist in the future. The second goal refers to defending and/or extending the organization's domain or bureaucratic "turf." This means decision-makers must not only be proving their bureaucracy plays an important role, but that no other bureaucracy can do the job as well. Much time and energy are spent defending one's area of responsibility from encroachment by others. The third goal is maintaining the organization's autonomy—defending its independence, ensuring no one else gains dominance over the organization. The fourth goal is maintaining morale within the organization (which is important for making sure the organization functions well). The fifth goal is, of course, making sure the organization's budget grows.

Information is required for any bureaucratic politics argument to work well. One must know who the key decision-makers are and which interests they are reflecting. This is important, for not all governments are organized in the same way. The Canadian military, for example, is much more unified than the American military, so we might expect it to reach different policy decisions. In fact, Kim Nossal has argued that the bureaucratic politics model doesn't work very well for Canada, or probably for many other countries, because it was developed in the U.S. and reflects the divided and bureaucratic nature of the government there.

One should also remember that the organization of government can be changed. Different presidents in the U.S. organize their cabinets differently. If policy outcomes are to be changed, what in fact does the bureaucratic politics model prescribe? Changing the bureaucratic structure will produce different policy. In the U.S., for example, there used to be a cabinet position titled the Secretary of Health, Education, and Welfare. But to show a greater effort aimed at education, a separate Department of Education with its own secretary was created, and the rest of Health and Welfare was renamed Health and Human Services. When Ronald Reagan wanted to deregulate the production of energy, he dismantled the Department of Energy. The intention was to decrease the role of government to allow the market to determine energy policy instead.

When a brand new bureaucracy is set up, it must fight to establish its own turf. When it was argued that the U.S. could do more to support arms control efforts, it was decided that a separate arms control agency should be created. If an organization within the executive branch was pushing for arms control measures, so the argument went, results would follow. But a big fight ensued over whether this agency would belong to the State Department or the Department of Defence. A similar struggle occurred when the U.S. decided to create a high-level trade negotiator—would the post be assigned to the State Department or the Department of Commerce? That position, the Special Trade Representative, wound up belonging to neither. Shifting posts, reassigning duties, and creating and dismantling agencies and offices are all signs that someone believes that bureaucratic structures do make a difference for policy outcomes.

Bureaucratic Organizations and the Execution of Policy

These examples illuminate how the bureaucratic politics or "*role*" approach works (in explanation, description and prescription). In particular, this approach is good for explaining events and outcomes with which systemic-level arguments have great difficulty, especially those situations where a country's foreign policy seems to have competing elements. The key insight is that the policy is the result of differing viewpoints: even when the policies fit together, they may not seem rational from an overall viewpoint, which can only be understood as the result of pushing and pulling among different decision-makers.

Bureaucracies and organizations matter in another aspect of foreign policy; we have already seen how roles affect decision-making, but even after decisions have been made the characteristics of organizations and bureaucracies determine how foreign policy is executed. This was another key insight Allison uncovered in his analysis of the Cuban missile crisis. Organizations played a significant role in that crisis when it came to the conduct of foreign policy. The only way Allison could make sense of how well messages were sent and received, and therefore assess the ability of the two sides to communicate and to interact, was to disentangle the effect of *organizational processes*. Here again we have a way to explain why policy did not appear to be driven by a single rational actor. The point here, however, is that policy may be rationally formulated by those in charge of foreign policy (in this case, the President and his advisers), but then bureaucracies and organizations may not be able to carry out that policy as originally intended.

One of Allison's best examples of the impact of organizational process concerns the way in which the missile crisis began. The Soviets did their best to transfer missiles to Cuba undetected. In order to threaten the U.S. with more missiles, the Soviets were interested in shipping their medium-range missiles to bases where they could reach their targets. But the Soviets understood the provocative nature of their actions. To avoid an American response before the threat was in place, the Soviets made great efforts to move the missiles into Cuba, construct the bases, and make the missile bases operational before the U.S. could detect anything. They knew that if the U.S. discovered the missiles before they were ready to fire, the Americans might launch air strikes. The missiles would be highly vulnerable to an air attack. Yet American intelligence services found the preparations before they were finished.

Since this was a secret mission, the Soviets took very special precautions. They very carefully loaded their troops and equipment on regular freighters and ordered all the troops to stay below decks for the entire voyage from the Soviet Union to Cuba. The troops and their equipment were unloaded at night and only moved about in secrecy. All of this was done without U.S. knowledge. When the Soviets went about setting up their missile sites, however, the U.S. knew exactly what they were doing. The missile sites were laid out in a very distinctive pattern that American intelligence analysts recognized immediately. The analysts had seen exactly the same patterns in aerial photographs taken over Eastern Europe and the Soviet Union. The Soviet engineers had done nothing differently! When the Soviet missile troops got to Cuba, they simply took out their manuals, which told them how to assemble a missile battery, and followed the manual's instructions. Despite all the efforts to maintain secrecy, organizational practice blew the operation and a major crisis resulted.

The point to take from this example is that organizational routines (the kinds of things these groups practise over and over again, the way the members of the organization are trained, and so on) constrain the ability of organizations to act. Even if the perfect plan can be formulated, even if decision-making is quite rational, organizational traits such as *standard operating procedures* (SOPS) can still intrude. These constraints can easily cause a policy to fail or at least to appear as irrational.

Allison also found evidence of such problems in the execution of American policy in the Cuban missile crisis. While U.S. intelligence had identified the missile sites early, it was far from perfect. Allison uncovered evidence of a bitter turf war between the Air Force and the CIA. The President wanted more air reconnaissance photos of Cuba. Which agency should provide these photos, the Air Force or the CIA? The CIA had the right kind of spy planes (U-2s, which flew higher than missiles could reach in those days), so it claimed it should do the job. The Air Force countered that it was better suited to perform this mission—what would the world think if a U-2 was shot down or crashed? Wouldn't it be much better if there was a man in uniform on board, rather than a civilian? After all, in 1960 a U-2 spy plane flown by Francis Gary Powers, a CIA pilot, had developed a problem and was at a lower altitude over the Soviet Union when it was shot down by the Russians, and this had led to serious diplomatic crisis and embarrassment. While the two sides argued, precious time was lost and no photos were taken. Finally, the situation was resolved by training Air Force pilots to fly the CIA's planes, but this took more time.

All these examples are invaluable for illustrating how, in practice, the formulation and execution of foreign policy are affected by internal decisions. The process of decision-making shapes how policy is decided, and the range of choices decision-makers select from are limited by what the state's bureaucratic organizations are capable of doing. This also shows how choices made rationally may get implemented in a different way, so that policy doesn't appear to be rational in the end.

Is Bureaucratic Politics a Phenomenon Specific to U.S. Policy-Making?

Many of the examples provided so far have drawn from U.S. foreign policy. Moreover, many of the applications of bureaucratic politics have been focused on the security relations between the U.S. and the Soviet Union. Some Canadian researchers believe that this approach suits analysis of U.S. foreign policy but is less well adapted for applications to other countries. Countries with parliamentary systems, such as Canada, appear to have fewer of the internal differences spawned by the American system of checks and balances. The bureaucratic politics approach can be applied successfully elsewhere, but it is worth noting some of the difficulties researchers confront when doing so. Detailed information is needed. One must know who is invited to participate in decision-making and which bureaucracies they represent.

It was always somewhat difficult to create bureaucratic politics arguments about the former Soviet Union's foreign policy because we didn't have enough information about just who was making which decisions. We could guess that the Soviets also suffered from some of the signs of bureaucratic politics, such as overspending on their military. Yet it was hard to develop any detailed predictions because we didn't know who was involved in which decisions, or often who was even running particular bureaucracies. It was a major part of the analysis simply to identify who was holding what job or who was involved in policy-making circles. A whole new field developed: "Kremlinology." Kremlinologists were experts who analysed photos or other information coming from the Soviet Union, gleaning whatever possible insights they could by learning who was standing next to whom at the last parade or funeral. It was always easier to apply this approach to the U.S. and especially to past policy decisions, because that information was so much easier to attain. Now that the Cold War has ended, we can go back and examine past Soviet policy in much greater detail.[6] For instance, the inability to establish just how many nuclear weapons the Soviets constructed reflects how the various branches of the Soviet military struggled to have nuclear weapons included in their bureaucratic turf. The information requirements simply make it difficult to apply the bureaucratic politics approach to countries with closed governments.[7]

It is astounding what kind of information is required to answer questions such as: Who is important? Which organizations matter? How do organizations compete? And, more importantly, how is competition resolved? In Japan in the 1930s, the civilian government had been ousted. The military ran things, but the military was divided between the Army and the Navy. The Army thought Japan's true interest lay in invading China, which would mean being able to obtain necessary material resources for the Japanese economy. This policy also naturally handed the most important responsibilities to the Army. The Navy, on the other hand, was worried about oil supplies for its fleet, so it wanted Japan to occupy much of southeast Asia, including Indonesia. This policy gave the highest responsibilities to the Navy. How did they resolve this difference? At one point, the Navy was certain it was going to be attacked by the Army, so all Navy offices were protected by sandbags and armed guards. As it turns out, the Japanese decided to pursue both policies: conquer China and also attack to the South. The policy results were not very rational since Japan chose to launch a large-scale ground war and take on the world's foremost naval power at the same time. Success in either effort alone would have been unlikely, but by attempting to do both Japan was doomed to defeat.

In this particular example, as in some of the others mentioned above, policy was decided on simply by letting each organization do what it wanted. Sometimes compromises do occur (as when Air Force pilots operated CIA planes in the Cuban missile crisis) and the end result can be fairly close to what we might expect if a country really did act in a unitary and rational manner. A major weakness of the bureaucratic politics approach is the inability to predict how these disputes will turn out. The approach gives us tremendous insight into what the different actors are likely to be arguing about, but how will the negotiations be resolved? If we work backwards and use this approach to provide descriptions of past events, the model is strong—it incorporates so many details and the interpretations are quite persuasive. But for predictions we have some serious problems. Moreover, the informational requirements mentioned earlier make the model less than parsimonious. Once a model specific to one country has been created, it may not be of much use for examining decision-making elsewhere since decision-making structures vary widely. These are the strengths and weaknesses of the approach.

Bureaucratic Politics and International Political Economy

Most examples of bureaucratic politics are drawn from the realm of security affairs. The approach seems to have little favour in IPE, though there are major exceptions.[8] This is partly because so many of the key questions confronting scholars in IPE concern the development of the international political economy as a whole rather than a particular country's policy decision (though these two are related matters). Also, scholars in international political economy have powerful alternative arguments at the state level. Whereas security specialists may look at bureaucratic actors who have rather amorphous constituencies, scholars in IPE draw on the vast array of economic models that identify rather specific interest groups within society. It might be more useful to draw on both sets of arguments.

As an example of a more balanced approach, one could consider how international monetary policy is typically made. Responsibilities for such policies usually rest with two separate bureaucracies: a central bank and a treasury (a finance ministry). A central bank is normally given a measure of independence and has the responsibility for managing the national currency. A treasury usually has to worry about financing the government's budget—though it may also have powers to regulate and manage the country's financial system. Since these two agencies have overlapping jurisdictions but different bureaucratic missions, the way they interact can therefore have a powerful impact on the way policy is formulated. Moreover, while a minister of finance is usually dependent on public support to remain in office, a central bank only maintains its independence because other public authorities have conceded it—so there are ample opportunities for domestic interest groups to exert pressure on these bureaucratic actors.[9]

Challenges to the Bureaucratic Politics Paradigm: The Individual versus the Role

If we can answer the necessary questions regarding the participants in decision-making, the bureaucratic politics approach usually provides a powerful description of the policy selection. But how about prediction? This approach can be used to say that foreign policy is not likely to reflect the rational calculation of a single actor, but then what will it look like? We would have to be able to predict who will be involved in the next decision, as well as what point of view they will have. Robert Art wonders whether this can be done consistently—he claims adherents of the bureaucratic politics approach waffle on this point.[10] Art questions whether one can separate idiosyncratic factors from those that derive from the role a person plays. The bureaucratic politics model says that all Canadian external affairs ministers should act the same because their positions in the bureaucracy are the same. But how do things like experience, attitude, or personality fit into the equation? Put differently, Art wonders whether someone does something because of the position or because of who he/she is as a person, and argues that the theories applied in this area should specify evidence differentiating the two. The alternative is to argue that the individual's experiences and personality shape decision-making more than the constraints imposed by the role. To understand more of these alternative views, we next examine the idiosyncratic features of individuals and their potential impact on decision-making.

Suggested Reading

Graham Allison, *The Essence of Decision: Explaining the Cuban Missile Crisis.* Boston: Little, Brown, 1971.

Jonathon Bendor and Thomas Hammond, "Rethinking Allison's Models," *American Political Science Review* 86, 2 (June 1992), 301-22.

Jack Levy, "Organizational Routines and the Causes of War," *International Studies Quarterly* 30, 2 (June 1986), 193-222.

David A. Welch, "The Organizational Process and Bureaucratic Politics Paradigms: Retrospect and Prospect," *International Security* 17, 2 (Fall 1992), 112-46.

Notes

1   The assumption of rationality contains three conditions: first, the actor is assumed to have perfect information—it is assumed the actor knows all its options and all the costs and benefits (the ramifications) associated with each option; second, the actor must understand the causal effect of each possible choice; third, the actor must be able to rank its choices, which requires that it be able to relate what it values into some sort of schedule of preferences. In this instance, the evidence suggests an inability to rank preferences.

2   It is interesting to note that Canada has attempted to integrate its armed forces, in part to overcome some of the inter-service rivalries that plague most militaries. The degree of success Canada has achieved is debatable, however.

3   Graham Allison, "Conceptual Models and the Cuban Missile Crisis," *American Political Science Review* 63 (September 1969), 689-718; also in Allison, *The Essence of Decision* (Boston: Little, Brown, 1971).

4   Morton H. Halperin, "The Decision to Deploy the ABM: Bureaucratic and Domestic Politics in the Johnson Administration," *World Politics* 25, 1 (October 1975), 62-95.

5   Morton H. Halperin and Arnold Kanter, *Readings in Foreign Policy: A Bureaucratic Perspective* (Boston: Little, Brown, 1973).

6   In fact, one of the most interesting aspects of such research was a gathering together of the surviving participants from each side in diplomatic wrangling over the Cuban missile crisis.

7   See Matthew Evangelista, *Innovation and Arms Races: How the United States and the Soviet Union Develop New Military Technologies* (Ithaca, NY: Cornell University Press, 1988).

8   The works of I.M. Destler (and his later collaborations with C. Randall Henning) provide excellent examples of just how powerful the approach can be. See Destler, *Making Foreign Economic Policy* (Washington: Brookings Institution, 1980).

9   This sort of argument—mixing bureaucratic politics with sectoral interests—is laid out in Mark R. Brawley, *Afterglow or Adjustment?* (forthcoming).

10 Robert Art, "Bureaucratic Politics and American Foreign Policy—A Critique," *Policy Sciences* 4 (1973), 467-90.

Five

THEORIES BASED ON THE IDIOSYNCRATIC CHARACTERISTICS OF INDIVIDUALS

Whereas theories of bureaucratic politics were based on the assumption that foreign policy is the result of decisions made by individuals whose actions can be understood by examining their responsibilities or duties, the individual level of analysis more commonly builds causal theories by exploring decision-makers' idiosyncratic features. That is, instead of focusing on the positions of foreign policy decision-makers to understand what ideas or policies the individuals will put forth and support, practitioners of the individual level usually focus on attributes specific to the individual.

The notion here is that while role or other constraints derived from bureaucratic structures matter for some part of the explanation (especially in specifying who is worth analysing, since it explains who should be involved in foreign policy decision-making), other factors influence what those decision-makers are likely to do. Naturally, the Prime Minister and the Minister for External Affairs are likely to have the most say about foreign policy, but why should we assume that all executives or cabinet members think alike? Perhaps their idiosyncratic features, their individual personalities, their beliefs, their psychological make-up, their experiences, or a host of other potential factors influence their decisions much more than their roles.

Perception and Misperception

An interesting point with which to begin our discussion involves the different ways people perceive events. In each of the other theories drawn from other levels of analysis we have assumed an objective reality, discernible to all relevant parties, with which decision-makers interact. Yet in real life, different people may look at the same event or incident and perceive it quite differently. Since a single stimulus can be interpreted or perceived differently, we would naturally expect variations in the way people react to the stimulus.

FIGURE 7: MODELLING THE ROLE OF PERCEPTIONS

stimulus → perception / interpretation → decision

This thinking questions the utility of the assumption about rational calculations because, instead of assuming that individuals objectively identify all possible responses to the stimulus and evaluate them objectively, this approach will assume that individuals have predilections for certain kinds of responses. By examining those predilections, scholars hope to be able to explain and/or predict the way individuals would react to similar stimuli at other points in time.

Rejection of the assumption of rational calculation is not without reason. For truly rational calculation to occur, several conditions must hold. The decision-makers are assumed to have perfect information—they are assumed to know all their options and to know all the costs and benefits (the ramifications) associated with each option. That also means they must understand the causal effect of their choices. Neither of these conditions are ever met in reality. The assumptions could still be of value, however. (Remember how we evaluate assumptions: not by a true/false test, but rather by their consequences for the quality of our theory.) A third condition for the rational actor model is that actors must be able to rank their choices, for they must be able to relate what they value into some sort of schedule of preferences. This is an easy task in and of itself, but can only be achieved if the prior two steps are fulfilled accurately. If the first two conditions are not met, then neither can the third, except by accident. Since decision-makers are unlikely ever to conduct rational calculation under these conditions, the proponents of the individual level of analysis argue that other factors shape decision-making. These other factors are usually components of personality or decision-making styles that provide the individual with short-cuts for reaching conclusions in policy-making.

Belief Systems

The proponents of individual-level analysis argue that there are valuable alternatives to the assumption that actors are truly rational. Their most persuasive argument is to pose the question: do decision-makers seem to be taking the steps necessary for rational calculation? One way of examining these predilections to respond in a non-rational manner would be to explore the *belief systems* leaders have. Decision-makers often hold sets of beliefs (sometimes grounded in ideology, sometimes grounded in personal experience) that force them to interpret or perceive other countries' actions in particular ways. These belief systems may cover things such as how foreign policy is supposed to be conducted, what the proper goals of foreign policy should be, what is considered diplomatic and tactful (as well as what isn't), what is peaceful and what is aggressive, and so on.

Decision-makers rely on belief systems when confronting problems associated with the failure to achieve the conditions necessary to execute rational decision-making, as well as when dealing with stress.[1] If it is difficult to live up to the standards of the rational action model in practice—because there is always some uncertainty or lack of information about some options or the consequences of certain actions—belief systems offer a short-cut in decision-making. Stress, caused by fear, guilt, shame, or some other emotion, can also cause confusion, reduce the evaluation of alternative policies, or terminate the search for information.

Alexander George developed the idea of *value-complexity* to describe situations where policies may entail trade-offs in values the decision-maker would rather not face.[2] Instead of making a tough decision, one that would leave the decision-maker with a certain sense of failure, a decision-maker can respond to these difficulties in a variety of ways, often determined at least partially by his or her belief system. When faced with value-complexity or lack of information, decision-makers may make a complex picture simpler by discounting information they don't want to deal with, ignoring some information altogether, or forgetting previous bits of information that were confusing. The number of techniques found in real-life examples is endless, but the point is always the same: to alter the perception of reality in such a way as to negate the difficult decision. Some of the best examples of this sort of behaviour come from the actions of John Foster Dulles, who served as the American Secretary of State in the Eisenhower administration. Dulles thought the Soviet Union presented a threat to the U.S. due to the evils inherent in Communist ideology.

Dulles's beliefs drove him to perceive and interpret Soviet foreign policy as rooted in evil. As such, Soviet policies were a constant threat to the U.S. and its allies.[3] Whenever friction with the Soviet Union developed, Dulles tended to assume the worst. He would portray a random Soviet act as the beginning of (or perhaps merely an integral element of) some sinister Soviet plot. If intelligence came in with photos showing a large ship under construction in a Russian port, Dulles would immediately declare he saw a warship being built, even though, rationally speaking, there wasn't enough detail to determine whether the vessel in question was a warship or just a freighter. Other American analysts would try to give a more accurate assessment of the same information and thus a debate would start.

In these debates, disagreements get resolved by the group only if they can reach a consensual understanding or interpretation of the information they have received. Anyone entertaining a different viewpoint would bring in whatever supporting evidence he could muster. But Dulles would ignore any evidence that undermined his predetermined conclusions, or at least he would attack its credibility. Sometimes he would even reinterpret evidence to put his own spin on it. Therefore, even when the Soviets would do something apparently unprovocative, Dulles would question the Soviets' intention—perhaps they're only being nice because they want to lull the U.S. into letting its guard down. Vigilance was never required more than when the Soviets were supposedly quietly minding their own business. You can see how this sort of belief system could have played a role in generating (and then maintaining) the Cold War.

Responding to Uncertainty

Uncertainty can also undermine rational calculation. When uncertainty becomes a problem, there are several ways to deal with it. Procrastination can occur as a result of calculation (that is, leaders can decide that the best thing to do is to wait for more information to come in before making any decision), but it can also be what we call *defensive procrastination*. Defensive procrastination can occur when people refuse to deal with a problem in the hopes that the problem will resolve itself. The decision-maker weighs the alternatives, doesn't make up his or her mind, doesn't act, but instead hopes the problem will simply go away.

Another concept about decision-making we often use is *bolstering*. Bolstering occurs when decision-makers stop engaging in the broad search for information and, instead of exploring the full range of policy options, merely search for information that supports the choice they have already made. Someone like Dulles would not look at all the information available to him but would order aerial reconnaissance or send out spies to look for the evidence he wanted to find. This kind of activity is called bolstering because it is done to support a position already determined.

How Do Individuals Behave in a Crisis?

There is another angle to consider when thinking about how individual-level factors may lead foreign policy to deviate from expectations derived from a system-level analysis. This focuses on how situations affect decision-makers and their decisions. *Crises* have an impact on the decision-making process, and this change in the process affects the final results. There are several ways to define a crisis, but most definitions include (1) a high threat to something the decision-makers value; (2) surprise—are decision-makers caught off guard?; (3) the need for a quick response—do decision-makers have a limited time-frame in which to react?; and some authors and scholars include (4) fatigue as a key factor in the crisis, too (though this may be quite secondary).[4]

Again, the main point is that these factors cause decision-makers to act in ways that pull them away from rational decision-making. Their actions would thus be inconsistent with the expectations generated by arguments based on the assumption of rational action. Decision-makers under stress (which is caused by the high threat or the need to act quickly) tend to limit their choices unnecessarily. They don't give full consideration to the complete range of choices they actually have. They also often exhibit increased cognitive rigidity; they tend to rely on that which they believe to be true without questioning whether or not this is the case in this particular instance. They become less tolerant, less creative, and rely much more on previous historical examples or stereotypes.

Crises that exhibit high threat, surprise, and the need for a quick response can also cause decision-makers to be myopic—the decision-makers think only about short-run consequences and only focus on one or two issues. Consider the way George Bush and his advisers dealt with the Gulf War. They were so focused on the diplomatic and military effort to compel the Iraqis to leave Kuwait that they never adequately thought through the ramifications of their policy if it actually was successful. What should happen if the allies decisively defeat the Iraqi army? The Bush administration handled things well (at least from their viewpoint) up to the end of the conflict, but then they were unprepared for the next stages.

Finally, researchers have observed that some decision-makers in a crisis will deny their own control over events, and instead shift full responsibility to their opponent in the crisis. These decision-makers may believe their own hands are tied (that their own choices are extremely limited) whereas their opponents have a full range of choices. For all these reasons, scholars have seen that the assumptions made by the rational-actor, system-level theories concerning foreign policy decisions are not representative of decision-making practices during a crisis.

Some of the popularity of individual-level theories hearkens back to the 1940s and early 1950s. It was difficult for most people to understand the outbreak of World War II without discussing the particular personalities of the leaders of certain countries.[5] Would World War II have occurred if Germany had been led by someone other than Adolf Hitler? Because Hitler was mentally unbalanced, German foreign policy in the late 1930s was unbalanced, too. To understand German foreign policy, theorists and historians argued, one had to understand how Hitler thought and acted. Similar arguments were made about Soviet foreign policy in the 1940s and 1950s, with the beginning of the Cold War. If Stalin determined Soviet foreign policy and Stalin was not rational, then what motivated Stalin's actions? How did he think? If one believed Stalin was paranoid, would Soviet foreign policy reflect his paranoia? To enter debates about the sources of Soviet foreign policy, one had to understand Stalin and his personality.

Typically, we view the foreign policy of a totalitarian or even an authoritarian state as an extension of the leader's personality. Since the society of such a state appears to be dominated by the particular individual who leads the state (think of recent examples, such as Iraq or Libya), it is easy to see why the country's foreign policy would be shaped by the leader's personality as well. Moreover, we often see patterns in the personalities of the leaders themselves. To have placed oneself in a position of control over an entire country, the leaders (people like Saddam Hussein or Khaddafi) had to be willing, we believe, to use brute force to eliminate their domestic rivals. Such attitudes could well be transferred to the international arena; therefore, these states could be likely to pursue policies exhibiting intolerance and violence against external enemies.

There are potential problems with this sort of approach, however. One challenge comes from explaining changes in foreign policy. If we say the reason Iraq has a belligerent foreign policy is because Iraq's leader is belligerent, but the leader has been in power many years, why is Iraq belligerent only part of the time?[6] Personalities are usually considered to be fairly fixed—they take long to form and do not suddenly switch in the span of a day or two. Yet foreign policies can change quite rapidly. How, then, are the two related? If one considers the differences in the rate of change in the causal variable and the rate of change in the dependent variable, then the relationship between the two may not be as strong as initially suspected.

More commonly, the problem with focusing on personalities as a causal factor behind foreign policy is that the argument becomes circular because it becomes impossible to separate cause and effect. Just how does such a problem arise? Someone argues that a certain leader is overly aggressive, and uses this to explain why a particularly aggressive foreign policy was chosen. What is the evidence that this leader is overly aggressive? The policy itself. Circular arguments are impossible to falsify. If they can never be proven wrong, the theorist has a problem.

FIGURE 8: A CIRCULAR ARGUMENT

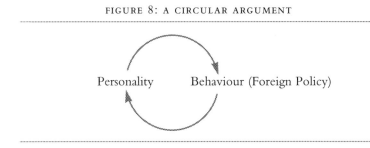

Personality   Behaviour (Foreign Policy)

The natural response for theorists has been to introduce further steps into the equation as evidence of behaviour in other areas or as sources of the personality traits. If the theorist can understand how a leader's personality is shaped in the first place, then these factors can be seen as the underlying cause of the foreign policy; the evidence of the impact these forces have could hopefully be seen in other facets of the individual's life, not just in foreign policy. The sorts of information that theorists have brought into play range from minute factors developed by psychologists to quite broadly defined life experiences.

Lest one get the impression that this approach would only be applicable to the study of decisions made by leaders of totalitarian countries or ones that we suspect have an apparent psychological disorder, we should remember that this approach is intended to be a full rival to those already presented. We should be able to look at the leaders of any state and employ these arguments to examine any kind of behaviour. In fact, some of the best early work on the personalities of leaders and how they related to foreign policy outcomes was done on Woodrow Wilson.[7] As U.S. President during World War I, Wilson played an important role in the diplomacy of the war and in the peace deliberations once the war was over. Wilson had his peculiarities, so he was a good candidate for this kind of study. The work focuses on his childhood and how his upbringing shaped his adult personality, which in turn affected how he handled foreign policy in this crucial period of history. The analysis therefore hangs on debates surrounding the roots of his personality.

Wilson's parents were very strict. His mother, in particular, was very protective of him as well as being strict. She wouldn't let her son go to public school and mix with other children until his later teens, so his early schooling was completed at home. His father was a clergyman. Both parents were apparently very righteous—dead certain about their beliefs—and they transferred this rigid attitude to their son. Also, because he was kept away from other children, Wilson didn't necessarily learn to interact and to share, or to learn to compromise. None the less, Woodrow Wilson was very smart and a great orator; he was successful at Princeton University (where he served as a professor and then later president of the university).

From there he entered politics, and again he was very successful, eventually being elected President. But as President, those aspects of his personality formed by his childhood and his relationships with his parents came back to haunt him. As part of U.S. foreign policy, he wanted to remake the world; World War I gave him the opportunity to make changes.[8] He helped shape the Treaty of Versailles, which established such notions as the right to national self-determination and the need to spread democracy. But then it came time for countries to ratify the agreements, which included joining Wilson's most ambitious project: the League of Nations. Although

Wilson had been chief architect of this international institution, many Americans were not interested in having the U.S. become a member. Americans who were bitter over the role the country had played in World War I were reluctant to support an organization that proposed to tell states what they could or could not do. Eventually, after debates in the U.S. Senate (which must ratify all treaties under the U.S. system of government), it was apparent to all that the Senate was willing to agree to join the League of Nations only with certain reservations in effect. Wilson, however, refused to accept the compromise that had emerged, as we might have predicted given his personality. As a result, the League of Nations began without the dominant economic power of the day as a member.

Similar analyses have been done on other leaders, focusing on relationships with parents, childhood factors such as illness (it has been argued that weak or sickly boys grow up to be men who overcompensate for their physical problems with "macho" personalities), and so on. For most theories found in psychology, an application or case can be found in foreign policy analysis. Another way of examining the sources of personality, or certainly of examining the sources of belief systems, is to explore the relationship between life experiences and behaviour. More interestingly, we can explore how big events shaped the experiences of an entire group or generation, and therefore shape how that generation perceives foreign policy issues.

Generational Arguments

Many journalists implicitly executed this sort of analysis when Bill Clinton was first elected President. He was, after all, the first "baby boomer" in the White House, and journalists attempted to use that information to predict how his administration would differ from those of his immediate predecessors. The previous presidents, from Bush right back to Kennedy and Eisenhower, were men who as young adults had seen the U.S. rise from the Great Depression of the 1930s, be attacked at Pearl Harbor, and then emerge from World War II as a world power. The U.S. had swung from isolationism to engagement in foreign affairs on a global basis in the span of two decades. The experiences these men faced in their late teens and early twenties were largely linked to military service. They (and many of their advisers) had witnessed momentous changes in the world. They had confronted Nazism, seen their country become the victim of a surprise attack, and survived a world war in which many lost close friends and family members. All these things shaped this generation's view of external affairs and, in particular, of the proper U.S. foreign policy.

Presidents from this generation rejected isolationism as short-sighted. In the 1920s and 1930s, the U.S. had turned its back on the world's many problems and instead focused on domestic problems. Yet the world's problems grew larger and larger until they arrived at America's own doorstep. This generation could only view isolationism as a mistake. Likewise, they believed that appeasement of totalitarian dictatorships was wrong—in the 1930s, when Hitler said he only wanted the German-speaking parts of Czechoslovakia and Austria, Britain and France had not resisted. Instead, they thought that conceding to such demands would satisfy Hitler. After Hitler launched his real war, the lesson this generation drew was that appeasement only fuelled the appetites of totalitarian dictators. They would not engage in appeasement. When these leaders faced the Soviet Union, they resisted any and every move the Soviets made and conceded nothing.

The impact of World War II made these leaders focus much more of their attention on the potential threat from totalitarian dictatorships and, of course, on the danger of another world war starting. World war was something painfully real. But how does this compare with the "baby boomers" now in the White House? They grew up thinking of the U.S. as a world power. Their most powerful political experience concerning international affairs would be watching their country divided and frustrated over the war in Vietnam. Instead of seeing a world remade by the U.S. and its allies, they saw a world unravelling despite U.S. power. Rather than seeing a U.S. that surged ahead of other powers militarily and economically, they saw one losing its lead or perhaps even falling behind economic and political rivals. They grew up not with world war, but with the risk of wars such as those fought in Korea or Vietnam.

We can do a similar generational analysis of the last Soviet leaders—some analysts believe a generational shift was the key change that caused the breakup of the Soviet Union.[9] The former leaders were those who had lived through the Revolution and the Russian Civil War, or at least through the Nazi invasion and World War II. Their perspective was of a hostile outside world, ready to attack the Soviets whenever the country was vulnerable. Eventually, a younger generation, people like Gorbachev, took the reins of power. These individuals had only dim memories of World War II. Instead, their belief systems were shaped not only by the period of Soviet military power but by economic stagnation. Their view was of a country striving to succeed in the foreign affairs realm at the cost of driving the society into the ground. A similar but perhaps even more persuasive analysis could be done on the generational shifts in the leadership in China, where some of the original revolutionaries have held power for a very long time.

At least one scholar, Michael Roskin, has used this sort of generational analysis to explain the cyclical nature of American foreign policy.[10] One generation pursues a very active foreign policy, but the generation just coming of age at that time sees the problems associated with such active engagement. Once that second generation assumes positions of power, it turns its back on the world. The problems created by isolationism, in turn, affect the third generation, encouraging this generation to pursue a more active foreign policy once they take power. Woodrow Wilson got the U.S. involved in World War I, but the next generation chose to be isolationist. Isolationism did not prevent American involvement in World War II, so the next generation became much more outwardly oriented, trying to take a proactive policy stance. This global involvement brought on the Cold War, plus the Korean and Vietnam Wars. Roskin expects this cycle to continue. The journalists writing in 1992 made much the same sort of argument about Clinton and the "baby boomers." They expected the Clinton administration to turn its back on the world and become more isolationist.

The glaring weakness of this argument is that not everyone in a generation has the same experiences. All the members of a generation do not think alike. Moreover, all the foreign policy decision-makers in one country are rarely of the same generation at any given time—generations do not follow neatly one after another.

Interpersonal Generalization Theory

Another way to introduce other evidence about decision-makers' personalities is known as interpersonal generalization theory. In this theory, an individual's interpersonal relations are analysed to provide insight into how the individual is likely to handle his or her country's relations with other states. Someone studying Lyndon Johnson would discover that he was very hard on his advisers and his administrative staff. He excelled in Congress because he was good at mixing bullying tactics with appeals to get people to agree with his point of view. He used to call in his staff individually and berate them as a way to get them to work harder and to defend their points of view. So we can see how someone could model his personality based on how he treated the people around him and use that to build an argument about how he would conduct foreign policy.

Franklin Roosevelt exhibited quite different interpersonal relations. He was a master at engineering compromises, which enabled him to guide legislation successfully through Congress. He brought some of these same interpersonal skills with him when he engaged in diplomacy. Indeed, many theorists and historians have argued that a number of the problems of the post-World War II era in Eastern Europe resulted from the mismatch of Roosevelt's interpersonal skills with Stalin's. In the negotiations between the two men, Roosevelt kept offering concessions regarding the postwar Soviet role in Eastern Europe in order to create compromises. Stalin, on the other hand, was not known for his ability to compromise or to make concessions, and he did little of either in the Yalta negotiations.

Summary: Appreciating the Differences in Individuals

What are the strengths and weaknesses of the individual level theories that focus on personality or psychological make-up? Well, as was previously mentioned with respect to the generational arguments, identifying the generation being referred to can be difficult. Moreover, it is usually incorrect to assume that everyone from one generation will think alike. Leadership does not shift in smooth patterns with one generation succeeding another, either. Any analysis of a generation's viewpoint will depend on who within that generation becomes the focus of attention.

A similar set of problems may weaken theories about how personality drives an individual's foreign-policy decision-making. Case selection can be a problem, as well as establishing consistency across cases.[11] The danger with many of these theories is that they are inductive, which requires greater care in case selection. Because the cases are often not viewed systematically, one leader's childhood is often not compared with others. To a large extent, these theories are only as convincing as the underlying arguments about personality, which are usually drawn from disciplines far removed from political science. When working at this level, one must be careful to construct theories that can be properly tested with a wide selection of cases. Any theory based on idiosyncratic characteristics of individuals should stand up to the other qualities we expect theories to have: they should exhibit generalizability, consistency across cases, and they should be falsifiable. If the theory is unable to meet these criteria, we will never be able to move away from mere description and make the theory clearly predictive.

At least the policy prescriptions that flow from this type of theory are clear—do not allow certain personality types to hold positions of leadership. That means perhaps screening candidates for leadership, or in the case of another country's leadership, the theories could lead to the recommendation that, in order to change that country's policy, it will first have to have a new leader. Another question to ponder is: are these theories rivals to the others already discussed, or complements? For example, bureaucratic politics arguments are good for explaining foreign policy events that are inexplicable from the perspective of systemic theories. Those two theories are based on such different assumptions that they can only be seen as rivals. The same could probably be said about individual level theories and bureaucratic politics. Similarly, some of these individual-level theories might be good for making sense of something totally unexpected and seemingly irrational (such as why a weak country would attack a stronger one). Some of these individual-level theories might actually need rational actor, systemic-level theories as the first step in their analysis; the individual-level theories then fill in some of the blanks on why policy looked the way it did. Often, individual-level theorists are engaging in this sort of analysis implicitly; they require other information to work. This is something to remember when we apply theories from this level in the cases in Part III.

Suggested Readings

Michael Brecher, *Decisions in Crises*. Berkeley: University of California Press, 1980.

Alexander George, "The Causal Nexus between Cognitive Beliefs and Decision-Making Behavior: The 'Operational Code' Belief System," in Lawrence S. Falkowski, ed., *Psychological Models in International Politics*. Boulder, Colo.: Westview Press, 1979, 95-124.

Alexander George, "Ideology and International Relations: A Conceptual Analysis," *Jerusalem Journal of International Relations* 9, 1 (March 1987), 1-21.

Jack Levy, "An Introduction to Prospect Theory," *Political Psychology* 13, 2 (June 1992), 171-86.

Notes

1   Alexander George, "The 'Operational Code': A Neglected Approach to the Study of Political Leaders and Decision-Making," *International Studies Quarterly* 13 (June 1969), 190-222; George, "The Causal Nexus between Cognitive Beliefs and Decision-Making Behavior: The 'Operational Code' Belief System," in Lawrence S. Falkowski, ed., *Psychological Models in International Politics* (Boulder, Colo.: Westview Press, 1979), 95-124.

2   Ibid.

3   For more on Dulles, see Ronald W. Preussen, *John Foster Dulles: The Road to Power* (New York, 1982).

4   Michael Brecher's list includes a high threat to something valued, a time constraint, but also the probability that the situation will end in some sort of military exchange before it is resolved. See Brecher, "State Behavior in International Crisis," *Journal of Conflict Resolution* 23, 3 (September 1979), 446-80, as well as Brecher's works with Jonathan Wilkenfeld. Also see Glenn Snyder and Paul Diesing, *Conflict Among Nations* (Princeton, NJ: Princeton University Press, 1977), 7. This specific list is from Richard Ned Lebow, *Between Peace and War* (Baltimore: Johns Hopkins University Press, 1981).

5   A prime example would be Alan Bullock, *Hitler: A Study in Tyranny* (New York: Harper & Row, 1964).

6   This problem appears in several arguments constructed inductively.

7   Alexander L. George and Juliette L. George, *Woodrow Wilson and Colonel House* (New York: John Day, 1956). Then see Edwin A. Weinstein, James William Anderson, and Arthur S. Link, "Woodrow Wilson's Political Personality: A Reappraisal," *Political Science Quarterly* 93 (Winter 1978), 585-98; Alexander L. George and Juliette L. George, "Woodrow Wilson and Colonel House: A Reply to Weinstein, Anderson, and Link," *Political Science Quarterly* 96 (Winter 1981-82), 641-65.

8   John Stoessinger counts Wilson as the first of his "crusaders" in American foreign policy. See Stoessinger, *Crusaders and Pragmatists* (New York: W.W. Norton, 1979).

9   For a view of Soviet generations, see the discussion in Richard Ned Lebow, "Generational Learning and Conflict Management," *International Journal* 40, 4 (Autumn 1985), 555-85.

10 Michael Roskin, "From Pearl Harbor to Vietnam: Shifting Generational Paradigms," *Political Science Quarterly* 89, 3 (Fall 1974), 563-88.

11 Blema Steinberg's *Shame and Humiliation* (Montreal: McGill-Queen's University Press, 1996) is an example of the correct way to compare cases. By illustrating Eisenhower's ability to assess his own skills objectively, she can compare his personality with those of the other presidents who were less objective in evaluating their own abilities. These self-images shaped how the different presidents dealt with advice.

Six

IDEAS AS
CAUSAL FACTORS

In recent years, scholars in international relations and international political economy in particular have become fascinated with the way ideas shape the behaviour of states. The selection of policy seems to be powerfully influenced by the popularity of particular policies. Currently, liberal trade policies are favoured, for instance. Some ideas seem to be in vogue at some points in time and not others—these things can surely affect the selection of one policy over another.

The three most obvious ways that ideas can influence policy have been laid out by Judith Goldstein and Robert Keohane in the introduction to a volume on the subject. According to Goldstein and Keohane, "ideas influence policy when the principled or causal beliefs they embody provide road maps that increase actors' clarity about goals or ends-means relationships, when they affect outcomes of strategic situations in which there is no unique equilibrium, and when they become embedded in political institutions."[1]

The ways in which ideas influence policy choices may be more obvious in international political economy than in other parts of international relations, because policy options are often specified by our understanding of how the economy works. Economic models change. Different economic models stress different economic and political variables. When new variables are added to our economic models or old variables are dropped, new policy options are instantly created or old policy options are immediately eliminated. Ideas could clearly play a role in how policies are selected.

An Example of the Power of Ideas: Keynesianism and the Great Depression

The potential influence of ideas may be most evident in the wake of an economic crisis. In the early 1930s high unemployment and falling economic output racked each of the industrialized countries. Things weren't working as expected; predictions weren't coming true; policies to rectify the situation weren't eliciting the proper responses. Existing economic models offered little in the way of policy recommendations that might work. A dramatic economic crisis such as this encourages economists and policy-makers to challenge existing models and propose alternatives.

Specifically, in the early 1930s the dominant view among theorists was that the economy would right itself. Government needed to sit patiently on the sidelines while the market resolved its own problems. Yet as the government stood aside, economic problems worsened. Eventually, policy-makers ignored the economists and began to try pretty much anything that might offer relief. Through practice, decision-makers discovered that some of their old theories simply did not hold true. They had believed that the most important rule in domestic monetary affairs was simply to maintain the stability of the value of money. This was done by fixing the value of currencies in terms of gold. The gold standard sacrificed domestic monetary goals (and autonomy in monetary policy) to an external goal: convincing foreigners that the money was worth retaining. The domestic repercussions to these practices were generally positive, since the money supply was held stable and inflation was avoided. (Sometimes deflation occurred, however.) Yet the French experience of the 1920s, when that country had accidentally undervalued its currency, proved that a country's exports could be boosted artificially. Britain's experience at the same time, when the belief was that sterling had to be kept at a stable value, had been to place sterling back at the value (in terms of gold) it had been at for nearly the previous century. This was an overvaluation and made it difficult to sell British goods abroad. The unintended undervaluation of French currency helped stimulate that country's exports, which in turn raised employment higher than it otherwise would have been. In Britain, the overvaluation of the currency worsened the economic problems of the period.

Once the gold standard came apart in 1931, countries soon drew on these experiences. One of the lessons they thought they had learned was that they could manipulate their money supplies to undervalue their currencies, thereby promoting exports. While the sum of these actions proved disastrous (since many countries tried to do the same thing at the same time, undercutting each other's efforts), the point was that old ideas no longer held sway. New policies were attempted. Just by abandoning the old thinking, many new policies were possible.

Of course, some economists had already been thinking about dropping the old gold standard/laissez-faire conceptions and were pondering ways that government could play a more positive role in the economy. The economists soon developed models of the new situation. By introducing variables to represent government policy options (particularly noting how the government could use fiscal policy as well as monetary policy in a discretionary manner to stimulate economic activity), the British economist and civil servant John Maynard Keynes made sense out of the different policies being tried. His models presented these new variables as possible policy levers governments could use to manage the economy. His vision of the economy changed the way government officials in many countries approached economic policy—including foreign economic policy—after the Great Depression.

Ideas, Theories, and Models as Constraints on Decision-Making

More than anyone else, social scientists should realize the power that a social science model can exercise on the way decisions are made. Again, international political economy is an area where we can appreciate this point, perhaps due to the technical nature of economic matters. The hard sciences often exhibit similar characteristics. A single framework or paradigm becomes dominant, and this paradigm (just like the examples from international relations described in Chapter 1) provides practitioners in the field with a way to understand the world and operate in it.

Peter Hall speaks of *policy paradigms* and of the impact of ideas:

> In technically complex fields of policy, such as macroeconomic policy-making, decision-makers are often guided by an overarching set of ideas that specify how the problems facing them are to be perceived, which goals might be attained through policy and what sorts of techniques can be used to reach those goals. Ideas about each of these matters interlock to form a relatively coherent whole that might be described as a policy paradigm. Like a gestalt, it structures the very way in which policy-makers see the world and their role in it.[2]

Hall's concept is quite useful. It is a way of identifying sets of ideas that shape the way decisions get made.

Goldstein and Keohane discuss three different types of beliefs, which can be thought of as the causal pathways through which ideas affect policy.[3] The first is a world-view. This broad concept covers everything from an actor's self-image to the beliefs an actor has of what is and is not possible. World-views are provided by religion and/or ideology. These beliefs are perhaps the most important, for they are the deepest—they shape identities and goals. The second category is labelled principled beliefs and denotes normative convictions concerning what is right (just) from what is wrong (unjust).

While these principled beliefs tend to be grounded in a world-view, most world-views are broad enough to capture competing principled beliefs. (Goldstein and Keohane point to the example of slavery. Christianity was used first to justify slavery, then to condemn it.) The last type they identify is causal beliefs. These are convictions about cause and effect. Such beliefs are grounded in consensus among élites or experts. Causal beliefs are important, for they identify which policies or strategies are considered most effective.

Tracking the Influence of Ideas

In international political economy we can see certain ideas come to prominence and spread among the nations of the world. The tracking of economic models illustrates this point quite nicely. Whole economic frameworks come and go. As mentioned above, prior to 1920, the gold standard dominated economic thinking. The gold standard gave participating governments little discretion when enacting monetary policy. Government and central bank policies were aimed at meeting external objectives: maintaining currency stability. It was widely believed that markets would stabilize themselves, if only governments would allow them to operate without interference.

When things went awry in the late 1920s and early 1930s, the ideas inherent in the gold standard were challenged. New models and theories emerged. As mentioned above, John Maynard Keynes created a model to capture the degree of government intervention in the economy. From this model, Keynes was able to illustrate how governments could take action in the domestic economy to stimulate production and employment. *Keynesianism*, as these policies of intervention were soon labelled, involved demand management through the government's fiscal and monetary policies. Government expenditures were no longer viewed simply as what the government had to pay to provide services but rather as a tool for provoking economic activity. Keynesianism was adopted in most countries in the West (though there were many experiments with socialism and fascism, as well). It seemed to provide a good understanding of how economies worked and offered policy solutions to most problems in a way that was easy to understand.

Politicians and decision-makers used the Keynesian approach for several decades before new vexing problems arose. In the 1960s, but even more so in the 1970s, predictions based on Keynesian models seemed to be breaking down. Relationships between variables were coming apart. The best example was with the relationship between unemployment and inflation. In the 1930s, when unemployment was high, discretionary use of fiscal and monetary policy had used inflation to stimulate the economy. This led one economist, A.W. Phillips, to posit a relationship between inflation and unemployment. When one rose the other fell. This did not hold true completely, for as the rate of unemployment approached zero, no amount of stimulation could rid the unemployment problem completely. (Unemployment would drop to what economists refer to as the natural rate of unemployment; there would always be some people in between jobs simply because they had moved from one city to another or desired a career change, for example, creating a "natural" or "normal" level of unemployment.) The relationship between the two variables was a curve, which came to be known as the *Phillips curve*.

FIGURE 9: THE PHILLIPS CURVE

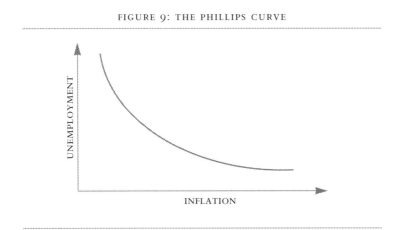

Policy-makers were supposed to decide where on this curve they wanted to place the country's economy and then select the appropriate policies to shift the country along the curve. At one point in the 1970s, however, odd things began to happen. The relationship changed; Keynesian models didn't anticipate this or other changes. In the case of the Phillips curve, inflation went up, and unemployment didn't fall. A whole new economic term was coined to capture the sense that we now had an economy with stagnant rates of growth but high inflation, too: *stagflation*. Clearly, this outcome did not make people very happy, and policy recommendations didn't seem to help. Stimulating the economy would make inflation worse; dealing with inflation would make unemployment worse. As economic policies failed to deal with the emerging problems, policy-makers and economists began searching for alternative ideas.

Among the alternatives available, one hearkened back to the old gold standard concept, which was popular among some academics. This approach said that the gold standard had worked well since it provided individuals with predictability. What governments needed to do was provide that same predictability—especially in the monetary realm, since the big problem in the 1970s was inflation. Economists argued that people's expectations of inflation had been raised by the government's constant use of policy to stimulate economic growth. These expectations needed to be broken. Otherwise, people's expectations of inflation would ensure that inflation would continue in the future. (This was because a rational individual, expecting prices to rise, will charge higher prices on his or her own services and output; if everyone acts rationally in the expectation of inflation, prices will be increased.) The economists knew it made little sense to argue that the money supply should be fixed by a country's gold reserves; history had proven why this was problematic.[4] Instead, the economists argued that the government should simply limit the growth of the money supply. By publicly announcing low targets for growth of the money supply and sticking to these targets, government policy would be believed. People's expectation of future inflation would be reduced. When they stopped planning on inflation, inflationary pressures would lessen. These economists became known as *monetarists*, because their models identified changes in the money supply as the key policy variable. While monetarists' ideas drove much of the policy decisions in the 1980s, the debates between Keynesians and monetarists continue to be played out.

Which Matters More, Ideas, Individuals, or Institutions?

One of the difficult aspects of using ideas as a causal variable is our inability to separate their impact from the impact of other variables. Historically, we often associate specific ideas with the individuals who promote them. France signed a trade agreement opening up its economy to British goods in 1860, for instance (see Chapter 10); the treaty was proposed by Michel Chevalier, at the behest of Emperor Napoleon 111. We know from his writings that Chevalier was a strong proponent of classical liberalism. What this case illustrates is the difficulty in separating the impact of the idea of liberalism from the impact of the individual—would a different person promoting the treaty have pushed for a different result? We have no way of knowing, since both variables are present in this case.

Other efforts to illustrate the power of ideas stress other types of actors as the carriers of the ideas. One popular approach examines the role of *epistemic communities*. An epistemic community is defined as a group of experts whose consensus on what constitutes knowledge creates a shared view on an issue.[5] As Albert Yee has noted, the emphasis on epistemic communities as a reference point conflates the role of experts with the role of ideas. Epistemic communities may have power independent of ideas, or the ideas prevalent at one point in time may help explain the existence of the epistemic community in the first place. The real difficulty is in identifying the characteristics that make one idea more persuasive than another.[6] "Newness" isn't enough, for some ideas circulate for many years before becoming dominant.[7] One possible angle could be to explore the connections between crises and ideas.[8] By definition, a widespread crisis provides the necessary conditions for a collapse in the credibility of an idea or policy paradigm. It is not clear how a new policy paradigm gets selected, however.

The same sort of problem can occur with other potential causal factors. For instance, Goldstein and others have tried to show how institutions and ideas both have an impact. In fact, on closer examination, one sees the impact of ideas, institutions and crises; as Goldstein and Keohane put it, "ideas embedded in institutions specify policy in the absence of innovation."[9] In this view, institutions mediate between ideas and policy. Institutions are formed at a point in time and embody the causal and principled beliefs prevalent at that time.

Yee is critical of how Goldstein tries to show the independent impact of ideas, because it is difficult to separate out the impact of institutions from the influence of ideas.[10] Thus for Yee, Goldstein's evidence is not simply illustrating the power of ideas in American foreign policy—rather, the evidence indicates the strength of both institutions and ideas in that area.[11] Since the institutions embody many of the ideas, it may simply be impossible to find cases that could illustrate the impact of one of these factors without the other.

One way around this problem is to pose the role of ideas in a slightly different light. Geoffrey Garrett and Barry Weingast talk about ideas as focal points for joint action.[12] In other words, shared beliefs affect how actors come together for interaction. They point out that most problems of arranging effective co-ordination or co-operation can be solved in a number of ways. How do we understand which solution is likely to emerge? They point to the importance of shared beliefs in their explanation for the emergence of strategies for solving co-ordination problems.[13] Their work stresses the importance of shared culture, history, or prior institutions, among other things. By backing up and considering strategies for actors' interaction, they offer an explanation for why some institutions are created in the first place. This, in turn, may provide more insight into why and when institutional change takes place.

There are still those who doubt the importance of ideas in answering our most important questions. Some theorists have tried to depict the debate about the role of ideas as idea-based theories versus interest-based theories.[14] This may be an overstatement, however, since most theorists using ideas as causal factors have aimed only to explain a limited range of outcomes and often rely on a mix of variables, where ideas are one component of the cause-effect equation. Often, an outsider looking in on these debates notices how the two sides are merely engaged in a dispute over which came first, the chicken or the egg. Ideas may matter, especially when they limit the range of policy choices given serious consideration; yet material interests may be the source for innovation in ideas. We may need a greater understanding of innovation in ideas, in institutional change, and in the evolution of ideas before we can sort out this discussion and reach more solid conclusions.

Summary: Ideas Are Important, But How Should We Study Them?

The impact of ideas on foreign policy has only recently been given serious study. Attempts to compare the strength of ideas versus rival causal factors have only been undertaken in a systematic fashion in a few instances.[15] As Goldstein and Keohane note, "reflectivist scholars have been slow to articulate or test hypotheses," though their edited volume is a step in this direction.[16] Further research in this area is called for, but it must address the criticisms identified above.

Anyone who believes strongly that this is a variable whose strength is underestimated must pay careful attention to research design. On the one hand, it is easy to make a purely theoretical argument in favour of the power of ideas. Abstractly, the constructivists who have proposed such a point of view are very persuasive. Yet it remains less obvious that their analyses of empirical results will answer those questions that other theories fail to answer. Where are the anomalies to structural realism or liberalism, and what sort of evidence could constructivists or the proponents of the power of ideas (or norms) bring to bear on those issues?[17]

Conclusions on the Levels of Analysis

Levels of analysis organize theories along one dimension: what assumption is made about the dominant actor? Is the key actor supposed to be a state, or a group within a state? Is it an individual acting out a role, or is it an intangible force, such as an idea or norm? The range goes beyond the groupings identified here.[18] The key point to remember is that each specific theory can usually be placed within a paradigm (as discussed in the previous chapter) or a level of analysis. These are two separate ways of sorting out theories for comparison.

Paradigmatic debates tend to swirl around different questions from the debate over the utility of one level of analysis versus another. The levels of analysis debate has generally been about which types of theory best answer questions about the behaviour of a particular state in a particular circumstance. Why did the U.S. choose to break the link between gold reserves and the dollar in 1971? Paradigms more often compete in their ability to answer questions about broader changes in the international realm. Why did an international regime, such as the Bretton Woods monetary regime, fall apart? In some ways these may not be so different—when a state decides to act in a particular way, it has consequences for the rest of the international system. In this case, the American decision to break the link between gold and the U.S. dollar was the turning point in the story of the Bretton Woods regime. The cases we examine in Part III will all be examples of states making decisions that have proven to be turning points for the development of the international political economy. First, however, it is necessary to delve into the key issues dominating the research agenda of international political economy.

Suggested Readings

Judith Goldstein, *Ideas, Interests and American Trade Policy*. Ithaca, NY: Cornell University Press, 1993.

Judith Goldstein and Robert Keohane, eds., *Ideas and Foreign Policy: Beliefs, Institutions and Political Change*. Ithaca, NY: Cornell University Press, 1993.

Ethan Kapstein, "Resolving the Regulator's Dilemma: International Coordination of Banking Regulations," *International Organization* 43, 2 (Spring 1989), 323-47.

Albert S. Yee, "The Causal Effects of Ideas on Policies," *International Organization* 50, 1 (Winter 1996), 69-108.

Notes

1   Judith Goldstein and Robert Keohane, "Ideas and Foreign Policy: An Analytical Framework," in Goldstein and Keohane, eds., *Ideas and Foreign Policy* (Ithaca, NY: Cornell University Press, 1993), 3.

2   Peter Hall, "The Movement from Keynesianism to Monetarism: Institutional Analysis and British Economic Policy in the 1970s," in Sven Steinmo, Kathleen Thelen, and Frank Longstreth, eds., *Structuring Politics* (New York: Cambridge University Press, 1992), 91-92.

3   Goldstein and Keohane, "Ideas and Foreign Policy," 8-10.

4   Moreover, the two countries with the largest new supplies of gold were South Africa and the Soviet Union—and no one wanted to give either of these countries leverage over the international economy.

5   See the special volume of *International Organization* 46, 1 (1992), especially the introduction by Peter M. Haas, "Epistemic Communities and International Policy Coordination," 1-36.

6   Albert S. Yee, "The Causal Effects of Ideas on Policies," *International Organization* 50, 1 (Winter 1996), 86-87.

7   There is a lovely quote from Keynes's *The General Theory of Employment, Interest, and Money* (1936) to be found in the preface to John Odell's *U.S. International Monetary Policy* (Princeton, NJ: Princeton University Press, 1982).

8   The sort of work to emulate would be that of John Odell, especially "From London to Bretton Woods: Sources of Change in Bargaining Strategies and Outcomes," *Journal of Public Policy* 8, 3/4 (1988), 287-315.

9   Goldstein and Keohane, "Ideas and Foreign Policy," 13.

10 Yee, "The Causal Effects of Ideas on Policies," 88-91.

11 Ibid., speaking of Goldstein's book, *Ideas, Interests and American Trade Policy* (Ithaca, NY: Cornell University Press, 1993).

12 See Geoffrey Garrett and Barry Weingast, "Ideas, Interests, and Institutions: Constructing the European Community's Internal Market," in Goldstein and Keohane, eds., *Ideas and Foreign Policy*, 176.

13 Ibid., 182.

14 Stephen Krasner's contribution to the Goldstein and Keohane volume comes close to this; see "Westphalia and All That," in Goldstein and Keohane, eds., *Ideas and Foreign Policy*, 235-64.

15 One of the first was John Odell's *U.S. International Monetary Policy* (Princeton, NJ: Princeton University Press, 1982).

16 Goldstein and Keohane, "Ideas and Foreign Policy," 6.

17 This question is not meant to be negative; ongoing research is aimed to do exactly this sort of task. For instance, T.V. Paul is currently examining why some states have chosen not to develop nuclear weapons, even though they possessed the requisite technology. His work suggests that international norms can have an effect on state policies, even in such crucial areas of security policy. His work is a direct challenge to realist thinking.

18 Some of the most popular texts identify as many as eight levels, though these often exhibit overlap. In *World Politics: The Menu for Choice*, 4th ed. (New York: Freeman, 1992), Bruce Russett and Harvey Starr discuss the merits of six distinct levels of analysis.

Part Two

THE POLITICIZATION
OF INTERNATIONAL
ECONOMIC ISSUES

Introduction

THE INTERPLAY OF
POWER AND WEALTH

The discipline of international relations is often divided into two main sub-fields: security studies and international political economy. The examples examined in the rest of this book are drawn from international political economy. The cases were selected because they represent turning points in the evolution of the international political economy. What exactly do we mean by the *international political economy*? The term "international" is fairly straightforward and should be a familiar concept to students. But what about "political economy"? The methods and subject matter of political economy can be defined. According to Jeffry Frieden, regardless of the paradigm one employs, modern political economy "studies how self-interested actors combine within or outside existing institutional settings to affect social outcomes." In terms of the methods typically employed, analysis is done through four steps: (1) defining actors and their goals; (2) specifying actors' policy preferences; (3) determining how actors will unite into groups for political action; and (4) following their interactions through and with social institutions.[1]

Frieden's definition is perhaps a bit broad; more narrowly defined, political economy is the analysis of the interaction of power and the processes of wealth creation. The subject matter could thus be described as the distribution of wealth and power. Political economy combines techniques, subjects, and theories from a variety of fields. Obviously, political economy draws heavily from economics and political science, but it is not unusual to find much material from sociology, anthropology, and many of the other social sciences.

From political science, political economy borrows an emphasis on power. Power is the central concept in political science. Political science asks such questions as "where does power come from?" and "how is power used?" As we saw in Chapter 1, the major drawback for political scientists is their inability to define power. We may know power when we see it, but can we identify power before it has been exercised?

The Roles of Power and Wealth in International Political Economy

The difficulties in defining power are compounded when we turn from security issues and look more intensely at the politics associated with economic relations. How important is military power for understanding the development of free trade? As we shall see in the case studies, a realist would argue that it is very important. Most realists believe that certain types of power are fungible, which simply means these forms of power can be exercised in different issue-areas. A realist would believe that military power can be used for defending one's territory or it can be used to compel other countries into making trade concessions. Other forms of power might simply be issue-specific rather than fungible, which means these other assets are useful only within a specific issue-area. Having a large supply of timber may give a country power only within negotiations concerning the international trade in wood products. That supply of timber does not, however, translate into power in very many other issue-areas.

Since specific questions in international political economy often come down to questions of policy within a single issue-area, the difficulties inherent in defining power and in dealing with doubts over the fungibility of power combine to make it difficult to apply many of our theories. Whenever power is a key factor, these questions arise. Consider a dispute over fishing. Which countries should a realist focus on when describing the distribution of power in this issue-area? Those with large fishing fleets or those possessing large armed naval forces? (How does one measure size of fishing fleets, anyway? By number of ships? Total tonnage? Ability to take fish out of the sea?) As noted in Chapter 1, these problems may hinder our ability to construct and refine theories.

Economists have had an easier time of it, for the central concept upon which most of their models are constructed is wealth. Economics is concerned with the creation and distribution of wealth. Unlike power, wealth in monetized market economies can be measured quite easily. All one has to do is discover the price—how much does it cost? A dollar figure can be established for just about everything. (Of course, for assessing the economic status of a society, economic indicators are not always precise either.) As a result of this ability to specify their central concept, economists have developed their discipline into a more precise, scientific, and mathematical field. As such, political scientists often envy the progress economists have apparently achieved in the last few decades.

At the same time, a student of political economy should be wary of the ways in which both the terms "power" and "wealth" are used. Both concepts are considerably more "slippery" (or "woolly," as Susan Strange might put it!) in reality than they are in textbooks. The economists' definition of wealth often misses elements of the total concept they are trying to grasp. The more important idea behind their notion of wealth might be that wealth is anything that enhances "quality of life." Since markets do not exist for everything (examples range from a healthy ozone layer to national defence), economists can only estimate the market value of such things.

Political economy goes beyond either political science or economics by focusing on the relationship between power and wealth. At one time, these two concepts were considered so interrelated that it would have been nearly impossible to think of studying one without the other. Many of the great thinkers of the late eighteenth and early nineteenth centuries (such as Adam Smith and John Stuart Mill) were known as political economists for this very reason. The separation of political science and economics into two distinct disciplines only began some 100 years ago. Some universities maintained departments of political economy as recently as the 1960s. This split developed after liberal economists began to construct more abstract and mathematical theories. Because the liberals discounted a role for government in the economy, they left the role of politics (and power) outside their models. Since these abstract theories seemed to work powerfully without the role of power explicitly introduced, economics was able to develop apart from questions of the creation and intentional exercise of power.[2]

The liberal background of most economists of the period when this split between politics and economics began meant that they viewed the use of power to resolve disputes between individuals or states as illegitimate or even unnatural. Political scientists tended to see power and its use or abuse as a fact, and something to be studied in its own right. This showed up in international relations in the debate between idealists and realists; the genesis of realism was based in the belief that one should set aside one's normative goals and study the world as it exists.

Despite their faith in the ability of markets to allocate resources efficiently and fairly, classical liberals discovered several situations where markets did not deliver the best outcomes for society as a whole. Modern liberals recognize these situations as examples where politics should play a role in the economy.[3] Public goods constitute the first and most significant of these situations. A *public good* has certain characteristics. The first of these is non-excludability—no one can be excluded from enjoying this good. An example of this might be clean air or, better yet, a lighthouse. A lighthouse provides a service by shining a light out to sea to tell passing ships where land is. But any ship can see the lighthouse—you can't shine the light on some ships and not others. The second characteristic of a collective good is non-rivalness. Non-rivalness means one person's consumption doesn't prevent someone else's consumption. Again, using the lighthouse example, when one ship sees the lighthouse, it doesn't absorb the light, it doesn't prevent other ships from seeing the lighthouse, too.

What is the result of the combination of non-rivalness and non-excludability? Who would build a lighthouse? If you owned a ship you might want one. But if you built one for your own personal use, everybody else could use it. Could you ever charge anyone? And how could you ever tell if people were using it? Private lighthouses are rarely built. Instead, all shipowners have to help pay for the lighthouse, through the government taxing all users.

We can model this as an example of market failure—that is, as a mechanism for delivering this sort of good, markets typically fail. (This situation can be illustrated by the prisoners' dilemma, discussed earlier, though public goods provision and the prisoners' dilemma are not necessarily synonymous.) This is an example where rational utility-maximizing individuals pursuing their own interests fail to achieve a situation where everyone is made better off. This is a paradox for classical liberals, since freely trading individuals making rational choices arrive at a suboptimal outcome; it illustrates a market failure, where even liberals now agree the government should step in.

A second major exception to liberalism's faith in markets comes from *externalities*. Externalities are situations where the market fails to cover the entire set of costs and benefits associated with a particular transaction. As by-products of a market transaction, externalities can be either positive or negative. Pollution is a good example of a negative externality.[4] A consumer orders something from a producer; the producer's factory makes the item in question, but in the process spews out smoke and soot that lands on the surrounding neighbourhoods. Everybody else in the neighbourhood is made worse off by the pollution, and the resulting losses total far more than it would cost the factory to put filters on its smokestacks. From the point of view of society as a whole, it would be worth it to install the filters. From the point of view of the factory, the costs of the pollution are external to the factory, whereas the cost of the filters would be directly on it—so the factory owners choose not to put the filters on. The recourse for everyone else is to get the government involved, to force the factory to make the smokestack improvements. Again, there is a role for government. Of course, when we combine this with the fact that internationally there is no legitimate political body wielding authority over sovereign states, then we find no real solution to the problem—a good example would be acid rain or depletion of the ozone layer.

An economist, Ronald Coase, developed the *Coase theorem* to describe possible situations where problems with externalities can be overcome in the absence of any government, thus shedding insight into typical situations we might find in international relations. The Coase theorem states that if (1) there is a legal framework to establish liabilities; (2) there is perfect information (and also each party understands its own preferences), and (3) there are zero negotiating costs (i.e., it doesn't cost anybody anything to sit down and engage in talks), externalities can be resolved through deal-making. Of course, in reality there are always some costs to negotiating, and in the international economy there is no supergovernment that can clearly establish liabilities in a firm way, and perfect information is unattainable, so this theorem should only be used to suggest ways in which externalities can be reduced.

Robert Keohane has used the Coase theorem to examine the international economy. Keohane employed Coase's insights to explain why international economic relations are governed by international regimes.[5] As noted earlier, international regimes are defined as principles, rules, norms of behaviour, and procedures around which actors' expectations converge.[6] This definition is designed to convey a complex idea. The easiest way to understand is to think of regimes as agreed upon types or standards of behaviour. There are proper ways to act and improper ways to act. There may or may not be any penalties for acting improperly, but there are usually benefits for acting properly. Regimes exist to reduce negotiating costs, to provide stability, and to assess blame or responsibility—in short, they help to approximate the conditions Coase identified would help resolve externalities in the absence of government. Regimes are the main way we conceptualize systems of interaction at the international level, and are not the exclusive property of any one approach.

The third and final major exception found in classical liberalism is in situations where the market is characterized by *monopoly* or *oligopoly*. Most of liberalism's conclusions on the benefits of markets apply only when there is perfect competition. Whenever there is oligopoly (where several large producers dominate the market) or monopoly (where one producer controls the market), the market may produce socially suboptimal outcomes. Monopolists and oligopolists are able to maximize their profits and hurt everyone else. They are able to make themselves better off at everyone else's expense. Since the market does not guarantee a beneficial outcome for everyone, there is again a role for government to play—in this instance the government regulates the economy.

So to summarize, classical liberals circumscribed the role for politics because they failed to anticipate how numerous situations might arise where everyone could not simultaneously make themselves better off through trade. Modern political economists have discovered at least three examples where the market is unable to guarantee those results; these are points of debate in political economics, since they are the most significant instances where modern liberals see a role for politics.[7] Liberalism (and neoclassical economics) still has a highly normative character to it: the market is the preferred allocator of resources and wealth, and in general politics just messes things up. Only in the cases where the market has failed is there a plausible excuse for government to get involved in the economy.

The distinction between the two fields was exacerbated by many of these normative differences, which have become deeply ingrained. The differences may have been temporarily reduced in the 1930s and 1940s, but they resurfaced in the 1950s and 1960s. It was precisely in the post-World War 11 period that economic models became much more mathematical and sophisticated. These new models showed how well the economy could work in the absence of power.

In international affairs after World War 11, the establishment of the international economy on liberal principles reinforced this division of studies. Because their models gave reasonably good answers to their most important questions, and their predictions were useful, the economists didn't need to consider what political scientists had to say about the role of power. Trade and economic development could be fostered in the absence of political interference. With the benefit of hindsight, politics were very important for the success of the neoclassical economists' models. Power played an important role in the workings of the international economy, but this role was largely masked. The postwar liberal trading system worked well because the United States was willing to provide a particular set of political structures and American allies largely accepted this situation. As soon as disputes arose in the early 1970s over how the liberal international economic system should be managed, the links between politics and economics reappeared. The political and economic turmoil of that time illustrated that political power could be used to manipulate markets, that markets would not necessarily function well in the absence of political order, and that market power could be translated into political ends. Scholars and policy-makers regained an interest in studying political economy in international relations. People realized that the separation between international economics and international politics had been artificial.

At roughly the same time, political scientists had begun to emulate many of the analytical techniques employed by economists. In what has been referred to as the Behavioural Revolution, which swept through several of the social sciences in the 1960s, social scientists began to seek the objective bases of human behaviour. Behavioural models in political science were constructed on similar assumptions and theoretical formulations as models created in other social sciences. Many political science models began to look and sound much like the models used in economics; the logic employed in both disciplines became quite similar. When the problems of the early 1970s occurred and people responded by returning their attention to the links between economics and political science, the participants in the two fields were in a better position to consult with each other. The similarities in analytical techniques allowed for political economy to re-emerge as a significant field of study in a very short time.

One of the political scientists destined to lead this re-emergence of international political economy in the 1970s was Robert Gilpin. Gilpin identified the central subject of study in international political economy as the tension between the state and markets. He discusses states as territorial units, requiring loyalty, with exclusivity, and having a monopoly on the legitimate use of force. Markets, on the other hand, stress functional integration, contractual relationships, and expanding interdependence between buyers and sellers. On many separate points, states have desires and powers that create friction with the operation of markets. This tension Gilpin describes can only be addressed through political economic analysis. It highlights the cracks left by the separation of political science and economics, for this tension results from the collision of the processes of wealth-creation and the exercise of power.

The Substantive Issue-Areas Ahead: Trade, Investment, and Monetary Relations

International political economy covers a wide range of topics.[8] These different issue-areas can be organized in many different fashions. We will use the broadest definitions here and only examine three main areas: international trade, international investments, and international monetary relations. Trade is obviously important—when one thinks of the politics associated with the international economy, trade disputes immediately come to mind. Trade qualifies as a topic in this field precisely because it is a method for creating and distributing wealth. Since states control levels of trade and periods of relatively free trade have been quite rare, it is safe to assume that the interaction of states has shaped the characteristics of trade over time. International investments also affect the levels of economic activity within countries. Jobs are created or lost and levels of industrial or agricultural output rise or fall as a result of decisions concerning where to locate production. It is worth noting that in recent years international capital flows have increased in value to the point that they involve much more wealth than trade flows. Monetary relations are also an area where political decisions can have enormous repercussions on how wealth is created and distributed—both within and among countries. Changing a country's exchange rate will have immediate ramifications for trade, by adjusting the relative prices of goods coming and going from the country in question. Trade may be unnecessary if international investments mean products are produced locally rather than being shipped abroad. Shifts in exchange rate may make it profitable to invest capital in another country, or they could possibly wipe out any profits earned from those investments in a flash. Thus, not only are these three issue-areas quite broad, but what occurs in one will have consequences for activities in the other two. Taken together, they should give students the depth and breadth of understanding necessary to engage in further study in international political economy.

Suggested Readings

David Baldwin, "Power Analysis and World Politics: New Trends versus Old Tendencies," *World Politics* 31 (January 1979), 161-94.

Peter M. Blau, *Exchange and Power in Social Life*. New York: John Wiley & Sons, 1964.

Robert Dahl, "The Concept of Power," *Behavioural Science* 2 (July 1957), 201-15.

Christer Jönssen, "Bargaining Power: Notes on an Elusive Concept," *Cooperation and Conflict* 16 (December 1981), 249-57.

Klaus Knorr, *The Power of Nations: The Political Economy of International Relations*. New York: Basic Books, 1975.

Harold Lasswell and Abraham Kaplan, *Power and Society*. New Haven: Yale University Press, 1950.

James G. March, "An Introduction to the Theory and Measurement of Influence," *American Political Science Review* 49 (June 1955), 431-51.

Herbert A. Simon, "Notes on the Observation and Measurement of Political Power," *Journal of Politics* 15 (November 1953), 500-16.

Notes

1 Jeffry Frieden, *Debt, Development, and Democracy: Modern Political Economy and Latin America, 1965-1985* (Princeton, NJ: Princeton University Press, 1991), 16. These typical methods apply for those theoretical approaches that assume actors behave rationally.

2 Alfred Marshall is a good example of someone who led this split. Marshall argued that the workings of the economy were based on natural laws and argued that these natural laws could be discerned through logic and observation. But more importantly, these laws worked despite the intentions of individuals. Results came from the workings of the market. With this kind of approach, one could easily build models and theories that abstracted away from the acts of irrational human beings. This allowed economists to conceptualize the economy as a separate entity. There were no necessary roles for the government or power. Instead, the government becomes something exogenous, a force outside the economy, which merely steps in occasionally, usually upsetting the predictions of the nice models the economists constructed.

3 We should remember that classical liberals' assumptions drove them to expect that rational individuals could attain their interests through some sort of trading.

4 One can easily think of some sort of positive externality as well. For instance, when a new expensive building is constructed, it may change the way others regard neighbouring property. In this instance, the by-product has driven up the value of others' assets.

5 See Robert Keohane, "The Demand for International Regimes," in Stephen Krasner, ed., *International Regimes* (Ithaca, NY: Cornell University Press, 1983), 141-71.

6 See Krasner, ed., *International Regimes*.

7 Most liberals have always seen a role for other services by the state: defining and enforcing property rights and providing for defence from outside aggression, for instance. The latter can be seen as a public good, of course.

8 Some of the questions posed in the introduction of one textbook, Thomas D. Lairson and David Skidmore, *International Political Economy: The Struggle for Power and Wealth* (New York: Harcourt Brace, 1993), 9, include: How do governments and domestic interests affect foreign economic policy? How do we understand the different ways political leaders and institutions are entangled in managing and conditioning market outcomes? What is the role of political power and international institutions in shaping the terms of trade flows and capital transfers? How do a nation's economic growth and technological prowess affect its international influence?

Seven

THE POLITICS
OF TRADE

The politics of trade are characterized by distributional questions. Which countries benefit from trade? Does it matter whether one country benefits more than another? Who gains from trade within each country? Who is hurt by trade? By answering these questions concerning the distributional consequences of trade, we can gain a better grasp of the related political issues. How do states determine their trade policies? Which matters more in trade policy decisions, domestic pressures, the international environment, or ideas? We shall begin with one of the most basic questions: why does trade take place?

The Reasons for Conducting Trade: Comparative Advantage

Economists use the concept of *comparative advantage* to explain why trade takes place, as well as to make the claim that free trade is mutually beneficial. This argument was initially described by Adam Smith. Years later David Ricardo expanded on the idea and developed a more elaborate mathematical and graphical interpretation.[1] Comparative advantage refers to an actor's ability to produce a good or service more efficiently than other actors. Since we are interested in explaining international trade, the actors in this case are countries. If one country can manufacture paper more efficiently (that is, use fewer inputs such as capital and labour to produce a unit of paper, therefore producing paper more cheaply), it can shift all its resources into producing that good; if each country does the same, more of each good gets produced at a lower cost in terms of inputs consumed. There are more goods to go around (via trade), overall consumption increases, and therefore everyone benefits. Thus trade, as explained by economists, involves *specialization* and a *division of labour*. The great advantages, according to economists, occur through improved efficiency and the production of a greater volume of goods and services. (Some people today are questioning whether greater production is necessarily beneficial, however.)

Why do peoples from different countries engage in international trade? Consider what would happen in the absence of trade. A country's consumption would be restricted to those items that could be produced within its own borders. (This is a situation of *autarky*.) Take a simple mix of production, with only two goods: industrial and agricultural products. (Cloth and wine were what Ricardo used in the first explanation of comparative advantage, reflecting two products involved in an ongoing trade dispute.) The country could devote all its resources to the production of one good, to the production of the other, or to some mix of the two. Say country A just produced industrial goods; it could produce 300 units. If it just produced agriculture, it could produce 150 units. This establishes two important bits of information. First, if we were to draw a line representing the total production this country was capable of, these points would represent the endpoints of that imaginary line. In between would be all the other possible mixes of output (i.e., the country produced some of each type of good). We refer to this limit as the *production possibility factor* (PPF). Second, we would know the slope of that line, because we can calculate the rate at which production can be changed from one good to the other–for every unit of agriculture, it takes the same inputs as it would to produce two units of industrial output.

FIGURE 10: THE PRODUCTION POSSIBILITY FRONTIER

At some given rate, production can be shifted between these two products. This is referred to as the *rate of transformation*.[2] (Following Ricardo's early example, we represent the PPF as a straight line. In reality, most PPFs would be convex, since inputs are often hard to adapt to the production of one of the goods.) This same line also establishes the price for each good. It would take a reduction in output of agricultural goods of 30 units to get enough resources to produce an extra 15 units of industrial goods. In essence, it costs 2 units of agricultural goods to buy 1 unit of industrial goods in this country.

Now consider a second country. If it devoted all of its resources to producing industrial goods, it would produce 80 units; if it threw everything into the production of agriculture, it could produce 240 units. The relative price here is 3 units of agricultural goods per unit of industrial output. One country is very good at producing industrial goods, the other at producing agricultural goods. This can be seen in the price differences in the two countries—country A can sell industrial output at a higher price per unit in country B than at home (3 agricultural units rather than 2). From country B's perspective, it is possible to purchase industrial goods at a cheaper price in country A.

If each country then specializes, the result is the maximum of production possible out of any combination of production mixes. Country A specializes in industrial production (300 units) while country B specializes in agricultural production (240 units). Trade will take place because of the relative prices of the goods in the two countries. The notion of comparative advantage captures this sense of different prices in different countries; comparative advantage exists when one country can produce an item at a lower cost in terms of opportunities forgone than can the other country. (Absolute advantage, on the other hand, exists when a country can use fewer resources to produce a product than the other country. Absolute advantage does not replace comparative advantage, in that each country would still have different prices for the products domestically.)

It is important to recognize the assumptions that underlie the theory of comparative advantage. For instance, the results hold when one assumes each economy is at full employment and that trade is balanced. These assumptions are rarely met in the real world. Moreover, the availability and price of inputs can be altered via policy (hence the sections to be discussed below on *strategic trade policy* and infant industries).[3] And as we shall see below, several important observations about today's patterns of trade appear to be difficult to address using theories of trade based on comparative advantage. Despite these qualifications, theories of trade incorporating comparative advantage remain the most widely held. It provides the jumping off point for most other theories concerning the political economy of trade.

The Consequences of Specialization

The theory of trade based on comparative advantage recommends that countries focus their production on those goods they can produce more efficiently than others. It calls on states to produce one set of goods and trade some of them for goods whose production was forgone. Countries are supposed to count on other states to buy and sell with them.

According to the critics of neoclassical economics, the division of labour born from this trade structure may have serious political and economic repercussions. The Marxists, who developed the idea of the modern world-system, point to the example of the southern Baltic region in the 1600s. As trade first began to boom in early capitalism, the regions of what is today eastern Germany and Poland specialized in the production of grain. These areas exported grain to the Netherlands. The Netherlands was more urbanized and needed to import foodstuffs. In order to have wares to exchange for grain and other foods, the Netherlands specialized in manufacturing a variety of goods such as textiles. As time went on, the Netherlands became more industrialized and wealthier. Eastern Europe, on the other hand, continued to produce grain, failed to industrialize, and did not get any richer. Politically, the trade had enormous consequences as well. It increased the wealth of those who held the most land: the aristocrats. Trade enabled these landholders to continue to wield both economic and political power for centuries thereafter in these regions, while in the Netherlands the aristocrats declined in power and wealth as the merchant class ascended. According to the Marxists, some states enter into the international division of labour and get frozen in place; they are unable to escape the economic role in which they are initially cast. Since trade does not necessarily benefit states in the Marxist analysis, and certainly does not benefit states equally, there are important repercussions to being in one role or another. Being at the top of the international division of labour is certainly much better than being at the bottom.

Another criticism comes from the realists. According to the realists, states are pursuing power, not wealth. States want relative gains, not absolute gains. Realists argue that states are concerned with becoming richer than their neighbours, not just richer than they have been in the past. (Put another way, each state wants more money than its neighbour, not the most money it could possibly earn.) If the realists are correct, the prisoners' dilemma applies to trade as well as security. States will want their neighbours to pursue free trade while they themselves will apply protectionist policies. This would allow the state pursuing protectionist policies to control the distribution of gains from trade more directly than otherwise. As with the previous example of the security dilemma, in this game there is a dominant strategy. The end result depends on the decision each actor makes; each actor finds itself better off, regardless of the decision of the other actor, by selecting protectionism. The end result is joint protectionism, even though this joint outcome is not as satisfying as the result where both pursue free trade.

FIGURE 11: THE PRISONER'S DILEMMA APPLIED TO TRADE

A's hierarchy of preferences:

highest	=	to follow protectionism, but have B pursue free trade (4)
next highest	=	both to pursue free trade (3)
low	=	both to pursue protection (2)
lowest	=	to pursue free trade, while B follows protectionism (1)

B's hierarchy of preferences:

highest	=	to follow protectionism, but have A pursue free trade (4)
next highest	=	both to pursue free trade (3)
low	=	both to pursue protection (2)
lowest	=	to pursue free trade, while A follows protectionism (1)

B

	FREE TRADE	PROTECTIONISM
A FREE TRADE	3 , 3	1 , 4
PROTECTIONISM	4 , 1	2 , 2

As with the example of the security dilemma version of this game, the important point it illustrates is that two self-interested actors worried about relative gains will, through their interaction, make the outcome less than socially optimal. Both would be better off with free trade, but because both try to cheat, the outcome is rampant protectionism.[4]

The Domestic Impact of Trade

The idea of comparative advantage, first described mathematically by Ricardo, provided the basis for further developments in our understanding of trade. Two Swedish economists, Eli Heckscher and Bertil Ohlin, developed a more sophisticated model of trade to explain why a country should specialize in the production of one good or another. The *Heckscher-Ohlin* (H-O) *model* has since become the foundation for most modern economic analyses of trade. Heckscher and Ohlin argued that each country could be assessed in terms of its endowments of inputs, referred to as the *factors of production.* Starting with the simplest version, they described two countries with two factors of production (capital and labour). They argued that each country would export goods that intensively use the locally most abundant factor. Imports would then be composed of the goods whose production required intensive use of the locally scarce factor of production.

The great insight in this analysis is that the prices of factors of production vary from country to country, depending on their availability. Since the prices of goods and services reflect the costs of inputs, the comparative costs of inputs will allow us to compare the prices of final goods. In a country where labour is abundant compared to capital, labour will naturally be cheaper than capital. That country will be able to produce cheaply those goods that are labour-intensive. Goods that require intensive use of the locally scarce factor, capital, will be more expensive to produce. The cheaper, labour-intensive products will be easier to sell abroad; other countries, where capital is abundant and labour is scarce, will have cheaper capital-intensive goods to exchange for the labour-intensive exports. The sources of trade can thus be found in the different attributes of countries that allow them to produce different goods with greater or lesser costs.

IMPORTANT ASPECTS OF THE HECKSCHER–OHLIN MODEL

1. A country's endowments of the factors of production determine its exports and imports.
2. The results hold when the number of factors of production or the number of goods is increased.
3. The model is an elaboration on the theory of comparative advantage.

Using the Heckscher-Ohlin model, Wolfgang Stolper and Paul Samuelson developed a theorem in 1941 to examine the distribution of gains and losses within a country once trade took place. While expanded trade may lead to gains for the country as a whole, the H-O model does not tell us who within the country receives the gains. To test their ideas, Stolper and Samuelson applied their argument to a real case. They argued that the relatively scarce factor of production in the United States, labour, would lose real earnings when trade levels rose. Trade gives consumers the opportunity to import goods made intensively with labour in places where labour is relatively more abundant (and therefore cheaper to use as an input). Trade has the effect of substituting for flows of the actual factors of production. In a market where labour is relatively scarce compared to capital, labour-intensive imports will bid down the returns to labour. Since American labour is relatively scarce compared to capital, American workers enjoy relatively high wages, and because trade substitutes for flows of the factors themselves, the U.S. is likely to import labour-intensive goods that can be produced more cheaply abroad. Bringing in such goods has an effect similar to bringing in more labour. If labour is less scarce, it will earn a lower return. American labour therefore would try to prevent trade liberalization through political action. Conversely, because capital was relatively abundant in the U.S., returns to capital-intensive sectors within this market were lower than the returns these sectors could earn from exports. Capital-intensive sectors would profit from trade liberalization.

Since the Stolper-Samuelson argument assumes that labour and capital can easily and costlessly switch from employment in one sector to employment in the other, one single market would exist for each factor. This one market sets one rate of return for each factor regardless of the sector it is employed in. Stolper and Samuelson illustrated that while trade produces gains for the country overall (when compared with the situation absent trade), the distribution of the gains within the country is neither neutral nor unpredictable. By changing the relative prices of the two goods involved, trade engenders a redistribution of income. In the specific case Stolper and Samuelson analysed in 1941—labour in the U.S.—they demonstrated that increases in trade would drive the real wage down and the real return to capital up. Applying such a model, we should thus expect trade politics to be dominated by a division between the factors of production.

IMPORTANT ASPECTS OF THE STOLPER–SAMUELSON THEOREM

1. The holders of the scarce factor of production will oppose trade liberalization; the holders of the abundant factor of production will gain from trade expansion.
2. Trade increases gains for the country as a whole (or is neutral), but the specialization entailed redistributes income within the country.

Ronald Rogowski employed the Stolper–Samuelson theorem in a broad analysis of the formation of political coalitions.[5] Rogowski argued that changes in the level of trade sharpen the definition of economic interests, which in turn brings new political alliances into being. Some political coalitions form to influence trade policy, but these coalitions formulate other policies as well. Rogowski modifies the original Stolper-Samuelson model by considering three factors of production: capital, land, and labour. Following along the same lines of logic, the relatively abundant factors will form a coalition in favour of trade liberalization, while the relatively scarce factors will seek protection. Depending on which factors share relative abundance or scarcity, Rogowski expects two broad political patterns to emerge. In one, there is class conflict (because the interests of land and capital differ from that of labour), the other an urban-rural split (because labour and capital are divided from land).[6]

One shortcoming of the Stolper-Samuelson approach is that observable political activity concerning trade policy rarely falls completely along factoral lines (i.e., capital versus labour in the two-factor version), as would be expected. Instead, trade policy tends to be dominated by sectoral splits, where the different factors of production within a sector unite to oppose an alliance of factors drawn from another sector.[7] Such evidence suggests that it might be more useful for political analyses to assume that the factors of production are sector-specific, since these could better account for political alliances between capital and labour.

Once again it is important to recognize that these results depend on the assumptions theorists have made. The most important ones in the H-O model have to do with technology. For instance, if technology does not produce constant returns to scale (with constant returns to scale, when a certain percentage of all inputs is increased, output changes by the same percentage—when this is not present, the H-O model may not hold), or if some states possess much more advanced technology than others, it is not clear that the same results will occur.[8] Moreover, a host of other factors, such as preferences or marketing, can also affect trade. Most of these have been integrated into ever more sophisticated models, yet most still use the basic H-O model as their point of departure. For this text, we will focus on the simple version of the theory, but simply note that more refined and complex theories (which may also be more difficult to apply) may be available.

The H-O model also assumes that trade is the primary economic interaction taking place between different countries. Other options exist—if capital and labour are receiving very different rates of return for the same activities in different countries, trade in goods and services is one option, but movement in the factors of production themselves is also possible. Capital has traditionally been more mobile than labour, so international investment will receive more in-depth treatment in a later chapter. Increasingly, however, labour mobility has improved. The movement of people over international borders has increased in recent decades, and creates numerous political and economic issues. More research in this area will soon highlight the significance of such international flows in the factors of production.

Current Anomalies in Trade

When one is considering current trade relations, a number of different anomalies arise. According to the traditional theories of international trade, we should not expect to find that the greatest volume of trade exists between the most advanced countries, yet that is the case. After all, these countries have similar economies (all industrialized) with similar endowments of the factors of production, all characterized by similar cost structures (i.e., relatively expensive labour and relatively cheap capital). Moreover, the goods traded between these similar economies are mostly the same sort of products. Germany, Japan, France, Britain, Canada, and the U.S. all export automobiles—to each other. This intra-industry trade can be explained in a number of ways.

First, unlike the assumptions made in most trade models, perfectly competitive markets do not exist. Some markets may approach perfect competition, but these are rare, and rarer still at the international level. In fact, much international trade is dominated by *multinational corporations* (MNCs). Trade generated by MNCs often does not reflect a market transaction. Instead, it is the shipment of components from one branch of an MNC to another branch (e.g., a car engine from Detroit to Montreal); the price of the good isn't set by competition in markets; it is a decision made within a single corporation.

Second, these trade patterns may be driven by differences in taste. Economists have trouble incorporating variations in consumers' preferences into their models. If the hot car on the American market is made in Germany, German exports to the U.S. will likely rise. It may have nothing to do with any underlying economic forces (such as endowments of the factors of production) but might instead reflect a slick advertising campaign.

Third, in all the various theories of trade based on comparative advantage, trade results from differences in the cost of goods. Costs are shaped by a number of causes, not simply the relative distribution of the factors of production. Economists have turned to several other sources of cost differences to explain why trade patterns would be inconsistent with the H-O predictions. Examples of such sources of cost differences that may be familiar to students include economies of scale (that is, when the volume of output increases, it is possible to employ technology in ways that allow for more efficient use of inputs and thus reduce the price of the output) and learning curves in production, but there are many others.

Another major anomaly is known as the *Leontief paradox*. Wassily Leontief, a Harvard economist, was sceptical of the H-O results. He decided to conduct an empirical analysis to see if the H-O results held for the U.S. Taking data on American imports and exports (beginning in 1947), Leontief's analysis showed that the U.S. exported and imported a wide variety of goods—the mix did not clearly fit the expectations of the H-O model. Later replications of Leontief's work, using data from later years, produced similar results. The intra-industry trade mentioned above seems to play a vital role. Also, the number of factors of production in the analysis can be expanded, as we subdivide capital, labour, land, and other inputs into more discrete categories. Perhaps with a more sophisticated understanding of the range of factors of production, the Leontief paradox would disappear.

Despite these anomalies facing the H-O model, it remains the predominant theory economists use to understand the reasons trade takes place. While these anomalies have provided clues to the creation of possible alternative explanations of trade, the H-O model (and its derivatives) continues to provide the most comprehensive and convincing explanations for the content and patterns of trade. For political scientists interested in the politics of trade, the H-O model and Stolper-Samuelson theorem are an excellent foundation.

Strategic Trade Policy

In recent years, some economists have argued that comparative advantage is not fixed by the country's characteristics. Important assets a country can have include a skilled workforce (human capital) and other factors that can be manipulated by government policy. Moreover, if trade is driven by cost differences and all inputs are valued by domestic markets, and if government policy can intervene in these markets, then government policy can shape the prices of inputs in such a way that the country can export a different mix of goods. By choosing a strategic trade policy, states hope to change the benefits from trade, either by altering the position of particular firms or by changing the position of their economies in the international division of labour.[9]

A common, narrow definition of strategic trade policy places the concept within industrial policy; in Krugman's initial views on the subject, the international location of economic activity was driven by a host of factors such as historical accident, economies of scale, geographic location, etc., not simply comparative advantage as narrowly laid down in the H-O model.[10] This meant government policy was just as important for determining where things were produced as any other factor. In the words of Gilpin, "in a highly interdependent world economy composed of oligopolistic corporations and competitive states, it is possible, at least theoretically, for the latter to initiate policies that shift profits from foreign to national corporations."[11] In this view, strategic trade policy is primarily aimed at ensuring profitable firms in key sectors.

It is not such a far step to go from such thinking to the idea that a state could manipulate the position of its economy within the international division of labour.[12] Currently, many developing countries hope to emulate the economic development of the smaller states in Northeast Asia. South Korea, Taiwan, and Hong Kong appear to have used government policies to shift their comparative advantage away from labour-intensive production to industrial manufacturing. These countries have successfully changed the content of their exports and used their trade strategy to support their economic development. This *export-oriented industrialization* (EOI) has made these countries economic success stories. They have gone from exporting textiles and raw materials to exporting ships, automobiles, and computers.

The economics of such policies is of interest to us, primarily because of the political questions they provoke. How do states choose such a strategy? How can we explain such a dramatic change in trade policy? When do they decide to make such a move? We will try to answer these questions and more in the chapter covering South Korea's trade policy of the early 1960s.

It is important to remember that many factors shape the final results reaped from employing such policies. Just having decided to pursue EOI or a strategic trade policy is no guarantee that exports will be expanded or the economy will shift into those sectors designated as targets. These policies have worked in some cases and not in others. International competition has only intensified, making it harder for any exporter to achieve profits—the level of competition varies from sector to sector, so picking the right sector to target is extremely important; demand in the markets of the industrialized countries may unexpectedly sag or be blocked by trade barriers, leaving no other alternative consumers; the new regional trade deals often mean some countries will have an easier time implementing EOI, while others will find their goods displaced. In sum, deciding to pursue strategic trade policy is not enough to ensure success. Many other decisions must be made, and the policy well executed, for the state's goals to be attained.

Barriers to Trade: What Are the Possible Benefits of Protectionism?

More often, government policy is aimed at providing some form of protection against foreign competition. An economist would point out the costs to society of any sort of protectionism, yet such policies remain common. The answer lies in politics. The economist would say that protectionism results from a political failure—the state has adopted a policy that does not maximize the wealth of the society as a whole. The political scientist sees the same evidence very differently: protectionism reflects a political success by someone within the society. That person or group has been able to enrich itself at someone else's expense.

Different forms of protectionism have different economic and political consequences. *Tariffs* are merely a tax on goods as they cross a border. The tax raises the price of the good, discouraging consumers from purchasing the import. The additional cost to consumers is captured by the government, not the foreign producer of the goods. (Local producers can charge higher prices, of course, yet still undercut the price of the imports.) When tariffs were extremely common in the early nineteenth century, they provided governments with an important stream of revenue. Altering tariffs can still be difficult merely because of the fiscal strains such a step places on the government.

Quotas are another common type of barrier to trade. A quota limits the volume of goods coming into a country in a straightforward way—it establishes a specific quantity that may be imported. Compared to a tariff, a quota has rather different economic results. The quota leaves some of the local market unsatisfied by imports, and therefore local producers will be guaranteed some sales. Because the imports are made scarcer by the quota, the price of each unit tends to rise. This time, however, the high cost to consumers is translated into higher per unit profits to the foreign producer. (Therefore, foreign producers do not resist quotas as vigorously as they would tariffs.)[13]

The type of protectionism most common today is the *non-tariff barrier* (NTB). These barriers come in many forms and are difficult to identify because they are usually well hidden. Since tariffs are obvious, they are easy to eliminate with treaties. Governments regulate activities in many different areas, such as safety, environment, health, and many more. By skilfully crafting regulations in one of these areas, the government can effectively block foreign goods from entering the market. While such practices have been the target of international negotiations for a couple of decades now, they have proliferated.

What Has Been Predominant, Free Trade or Protection?

Given that economists have tried to explain how beneficial trade can be for both countries involved in an exchange, one might expect that free trade has been the norm. This intuition would be enhanced by the current situation, because today trade flows relatively freely among many countries. Historically, periods where free trade has reigned have been quite rare. The major economic powers pursued policies of free trade for several decades in the mid-eighteenth century, but then some began defecting from the free trade regime. World War I totally disrupted trade flows, but in the immediate years after the war a free trade regime was again established. This reconstructed trade regime was short-lived. Another free trade regime was erected after World War II, based on the General Agreement on Tariffs and Trade (GATT).[14] This regime has evolved in a new institutional arrangement (the World Trade Organization, or WTO) and appears to have a long future ahead.

What explains this coming and going of free trade? Why do some states adhere to a free trade regime while others default? These have been some of the major questions prompting analyses of past cases. The answers to these questions provide the insights that guide the design of regimes; with that information, regimes can be designed to last longer and to encourage more comprehensive adherence to the rules. To reach an understanding of some of these issues, examples of each of these problems have been included among the cases in Part III. We will investigate several examples of states deciding to liberalize their trade in some dramatic fashion (Britain in 1846; France in 1861; Canada in 1985), as well as two classic examples of states defecting from an existing free trade regime (Germany in 1896; the U.S. in 1930).

The rise and fall of free trade regimes suggests several points. First, despite the strength of liberal ideology, the world has been slow to learn what economists try to teach us. People seem to forget that free trade is mutually beneficial. Second, politics is always part of the story. As we have already seen, the realists would argue that politics is really the determining factor in the rise and fall of free trade. In their view, free trade occurs only when there is a single powerful state that wants free trade. Modern liberals (i.e., those who accept that market failures exist and that markets are not naturally self-correcting) see a role for powerful states to set up and enforce the rules necessary for a regime to operate smoothly.

The arguments used by both realists and liberals to explain the existence of free trade actually overlap in a curious way. The realists argue that free trade regimes (or, in fact, any regimes) are most stable and strongest when the system has a hegemonic distribution of power.[15] That single most powerful state can create a strong regime; it will choose to establish free trade because such a regime will feed into its own strength. The resulting theory has become known as *hegemonic stability theory*, because the presence of a hegemonic power is arguably necessary for the regime to be stable.[16] True to realism, the hegemonic state is pursuing a policy to maximize its strength relative to other states.

Liberals see the need for a hegemonic power, but in a different way. Modern liberals realize that markets often need some sort of management; markets are not always self-correcting and sometimes need to be stabilized. Only a powerful economic actor can actually stabilize an international market. Moreover, only a large actor would have the interests to stabilize a market—that actor would have to benefit enough from the market's stable operation that it would be willing to accept the costs of stabilization.[17] True to liberalism, what the hegemonic state is doing is maximizing its own wealth—the hegemonic state is unconcerned with the relative distribution of the gains from trade in this view.

Both these arguments were developed initially to explain periods when free trade seemed to be waning rather than on the rise. Liberals such as Charles Kindleberger created this sort of argument to explain the collapse of free trade in the early 1930s. Kindleberger argued that the U.S. would have been acting in its own interest if it had taken measures to stabilize international markets in the early stages of the Great Depression.[18] The logic was then applied to the policy issues contemporary to Kindleberger's writing: was the U.S. willing to make such sacrifices to keep international markets stable in the 1970s? At that time, realists were just beginning to argue that in fact the trade regime was breaking down because the U.S. was no longer enforcing the rules. Without enforcement, other states would try to maximize their power by defecting from the regime. Both theories then were extended backwards; if it takes a powerful state to keep the regime running, does it take a powerful state to establish the regime in the first place?

As will be seen in several of the cases, it isn't clear which of these two versions of hegemonic stability theory—liberal or realist—is more persuasive. In some of the historical applications, theorists often blend the two arguments together in a somewhat inconsistent manner.[19] Marxists will always mix together the economic and political arguments to form theories about the growth of the modern world-system; for Marxists the economic and political sides are always inseparable. Institutionalists and constructivists will offer totally different arguments for the development and evolution of trade regimes.

Summary: Questions to be Explored in the Cases

For our purposes, the two most important questions remain. For rival paradigms we ask, "what causes the trade regime to change?" The answers we find might help us understand the pressures working to support or undermine the current trade regime. For theories drawn from the different levels of analysis we ask, "why do states rapidly shift their trade policy in one direction or another?" The answers to this question could prove helpful for anticipating the behaviour of states that currently hold membership in the WTO, or even those states that have elected to stand outside the regime. Together, the answers to these two questions should provide insight into the future of trade relations in the coming decades.

Suggested Readings

Timothy J. McKeown, "Firms and Tariff Regime Change: Explaining the Demand for Protection," *World Politics* 36, 2 (January 1984), 215-33.

Helen Milner, *Resisting Protectionism*. Princeton, NJ: Princeton University Press, 1988.

Helen Milner, "Trading Place: Industries for Free Trade," *World Politics* 40, 3 (April 1988), 350-76.

Jonathan J. Pincus, "Pressure Groups and the Pattern of Tariffs," *Journal of Political Economy* 83, 4 (August 1975), 757-78.

Ronald Rogowski, *Commerce and Coalitions*. Princeton, NJ: Princeton University Press, 1989.

Notes

1   Adam Smith, *The Wealth of Nations* (Oxford: Clarendon Press, 1976; originally published in 1776); David Ricardo, *Principles of Political Economy and Taxation* (London: Dent, 1965; originally published in 1817).

2   This is merely the slope of the PPF curve.

3   Stephen D. Cohen, Joel R. Paul, and Robert A. Blecker, *Fundamentals of U.S. Foreign Trade Policy* (Boulder, Colo.: Westview Press, 1996), 59-60.

4   Robert Axelrod has developed an argument explaining how this type of outcome can be broken. See *The Evolution of Cooperation* (New York: Basic Books, 1984).

5   Ron Rogowski, *Commerce and Coalitions* (Princeton, NJ: Princeton University Press, 1989).

6   Ibid., 4-16.

7   See the research of Stephen Magee, "Three Simple Tests of the Stolper-Samuelson Theorem," in P. Oppenheimer, ed., *Issues in International Economics* (London: Oriel Press, 1978), 138-53; and Magee, "The Political Economy of Protectionism: Comment," in J.N. Bhagwati, ed., *Import Competition and Response* (Chicago: University of Chicago Press, 1982).

8   Cohen, Paul, and Blecker, *Fundamentals of U.S. Foreign Trade Policy*, 61.

9   For a brief discussion of such policies, see Richard G. Harris "The New Protectionism Revisited," *Canadian Journal of Economics* 22, 4 (November 1989), 751-78. For more in-depth information, see Paul R. Krugman, ed., *Strategic Trade Policy and the New International Economics* (Cambridge, Mass.: MIT Press, 1986). Also, for a review of the recent literature on the subject, see J. David Richardson, "The Political Economy of Strategic Trade Policy," *International Organization* 44, 1 (Winter 1990), 107-35.

10   Krugman, ed., *Strategic Trade Policy and the New International Economics*.

11   Robert Gilpin, *The Political Economy of International Relations* (Princeton, NJ: Princeton University Press, 1987).

12   As this statement makes clear, I see a close relationship between strategic trade policy and more general theories elaborating how states can develop policies to use trade for economic ends.

13   See Richard G. Harris, "Why Voluntary Export Restraints are 'Voluntary,'" *Canadian Journal of Economics* 18, 4 (November 1985), 799-809; Kent Jones, "The Political Economy of VER Agreements," *Kyklos* 37, 1 (1984), 82-101.

14 For an overview of the GATT's existence, see Jock A. Finlayson and Mark W. Zacher, "The GATT and the Regulation of Trade Barriers: Regime Dynamics and Functions," *International Organization* 35, 4 (Autumn 1981), 561-602.

15 Stephen D. Krasner, "State Power and the Structure of International Trade," *World Politics* 28, 3 (April 1976), 317-47; Robert Gilpin, *U.S. Power and the Multinational Corporation* (New York: Basic Books, 1975).

16 This phrase was actually coined by Robert Keohane in "The Theory of Hegemonic Stability and Changes in International Economic Regimes, 1967-1977," in Ole R. Holsti, R.M. Siverson, and Alexander L. George, eds., *Changes in the International System* (Boulder, Colo.: Westview Press, 1980), 131-62.

17 Charles P. Kindleberger, *The World in Depression, 1929-1939* (Berkeley: University of California Press, 1973).

18 These stabilizing functions are: (1) act as market for exports that otherwise will not find a market; (2) exchange rate management; (3) engage in counter-cyclical lending; (4) co-ordinate macroeconomic policies; and (5) assume the responsibility of international lender of last resort. See Charles Kindleberger, "The Functioning of Financial Centers: Britain in the Nineteenth Century, the United States since 1945," *Princeton Essays in International Finance* No. 157 (September 1985), 7-18.

19 Kindleberger's later writings illustrate some of the aspects of the overlap between the two paradigms and his attempts to separate such thinking. See Kindleberger, "International Public Goods without International Government," *American Economic Review* 76, 1 (March 1986), 1-13; Kindleberger, "Dominance and Leadership in the International Economy," *International Studies Quarterly* 25, 2 (June 1981), 242-54.

Eight

THE POLITICS OF
INTERNATIONAL
MONETARY RELATIONS

International monetary issues have traditionally been considered secondary to trade issues. Trade has long been treated as the most important form of economic intercourse, though this may have changed in recent years. Political scientists have shown greater attention to monetary issues in the last decade. Moreover, some of the best examples of how regimes constrain states and influence the ways in which states conduct economic intercourse come in the issue-area of monetary relations.

The Characteristics of Monetary Orders

Money performs three essential functions. It serves as a measure (or unit of value), as a medium of exchange (useful for intermediation), and as a store of value (or credit). Money is critical for the successful functioning of any complex market, for it facilitates transactions. Without money, trade could only take place via barter. This would require the complicated process of matching up buyers and sellers who each hold what the other wants—what economists refer to as establishing the "double coincidence of wants."[1]

If international markets are to work via market exchange, then some form of international money will also be needed. In this sense, the supply of money shares some of the features of a collective good. Exclusion may well be possible, but it would always be difficult. Non-rival consumption is clearly an essential characteristic of money; the more widely a money is used, the more effective it usually is.[2] Similar to so many other public goods, we typically find the government provides and manages the supply of money in the domestic economy.[3] Since the international political economy lacks an overarching political authority, the international political economy also lacks a true international currency.

In studying international monetary regimes, we use three main characteristics to describe and compare them: *exchange rates*, the nature of *reserves*, and the *convertibility* of capital (the nature of the links between capital markets).[4] The first characteristic refers to the rules governing how national currencies are traded. Exchange rates themselves are only the prices of one currency in terms of other currencies. The central question in terms of regime characteristics is whether exchange rates are fixed, freely floating, or somewhere in between. On one end of the spectrum, exchange rates can be fixed; that is, the rates at which currencies are exchanged are determined by political authorities. On a day-to-day basis, the rates are supposed to remain unchanged. In a regime with floating exchange rates, on the other hand, markets are left to determine the rates at which currencies are traded. Changes in the supply of and demand for the currency cause the rates to change. In such a situation, governments obviously can still use policy to shift supply and/or demand for currencies, so in a way political authorities may still be able to set exchange rates.

Reserves can vary widely in nature yet still serve their primary purpose. Historically, there have been two main types of monetary reserves. The first is a commodity. Most often in the past this commodity has been a precious metal such as gold or silver. These commodities can serve as a monetary reserve because they have some high intrinsic value recognized internationally. In short, these goods are extremely desirable in their own right. The second likely form of reserve asset is a national currency. A national currency can become internationally attractive because it is believed to have value and is widely accepted. This normally requires that foreign holders of this currency have access to the issuing country's domestic market (i.e., the issuing country should practise relatively free trade). A third possible form of reserves would be a money created by an international agency, though moneys issued by international organizations have historically played only minor reserve roles.

The third monetary regime characteristic, convertibility, involves the nature of controls on financial connections and/or capital flows. This characteristic refers to how open or closed the international financial system is. It also indicates how well national financial markets are integrated. This has significant ramifications not only for the amount of international investment that can take place (see next chapter), but also for the financing of trade and other economic activities.

According to W.M. Scammell, a successful international monetary system must have four integrated parts. These parallel the discussion above in that Scammell identifies the need for a medium of international exchange, adequate ties between nations' financial institutions (in order to use the medium of exchange), and some method (or methods) of managing balance-of-payments adjustments internationally (i.e., some agreed upon technique for paying for goods and services traded across borders). He added a fourth requirement to this list, which captures some of the issues involved with hegemonic stability theory: there must be management of the international monetary system.[5] Scammell was applying some of the modern liberal views on solutions to collective action problems—there is a clear role for a political authority to play.

Exchange Rates: Fixed versus Floating

Exchange rates are easy to understand if we think about them in terms of supply and demand. Exchange rates are simply the price of one currency in terms of the other. In decades past, the exchange rate between the Deutschmark (DM) and the U.S. dollar was 2 DM to $1. In other words, it took 2 DM to buy one U.S. dollar—or to put it another way, 50 cents would buy one DM. Today, however, the exchange rate between these two currencies is usually around 1.5 DM to $1. It now takes 65 cents to buy one DM. The change in the exchange rate affects how the prices of goods and services in each country appear. If a currency rises in value against another, the same amount of the first currency will buy more of the second than before; assuming domestic prices in each country are unchanged, people from the first country can take their money, purchase a greater volume of the second currency than before, and therefore purchase more goods in the second country than they could with the same amount of their own currency before the exchange rate moved.

To understand why the value of a currency changes over time, think of the price of a currency in its own terms. The price for money is established in interest rates, for interest is the price incurred when borrowing money. When you want to switch money from one currency to another, you must pay a price for the money you're buying. That price will be determined by the interaction of demand and supply of that other currency. If there is a lot of the currency available, then the price will fall; if the currency is scarce, then the price will rise. The same logic applies with domestic monetary policy and interest rates; the less money available, the higher the price (i.e., the interest rate goes up).

The supply and demand for a country's currency can be driven by numerous factors. The size and nature of a country's economy shape the supply of a currency. A country such as the U.S. has a large economy and therefore large amounts of currency in circulation, especially if compared to some smaller economy or one with a lower level of economic development. Also, the demand for a country's currency depends on the types of demands there are for making payments to that country, to purchase its goods and services. Transactions for goods and services or involving international investments therefore influence the exchange rate.

Exchange rates are also the target of government activities. Monetary policy refers to how government institutions manipulate the supply of a currency to make the interest rate rise or fall, thus making it easier or more difficult to borrow money. The government hopes to influence economic activity in this way. Different governments have different institutional arrangements that give them different policy instruments for adjusting the money supply. Along the same principles, the government can try to stimulate exports or imports by changing the relative price of its currency. Again, it does so by shifting supply. In addition, it can shift supply by selling more of its currency at cheap prices, thus driving the price down on exchange markets. Or it can force the rate up by purchasing much of its own currency using foreign currencies, thus bidding the price higher and reducing the supply. These are known as exchange rate interventions. Such a policy is often disguised as a floating exchange rate, and hence is referred to as a *dirty float*. As we shall see in some of the cases, the effectiveness of such policies have varied enormously in the past.[6]

The exchange rate affects exports and imports in a simple and direct fashion—the price of the currency is changed, the prices of the goods within the economy are being changed. This can make products or services appear cheaper, or more expensive, and thereby change the competitiveness of goods in trade. A higher value on the currency makes all the goods in the country look relatively more expensive—thus making it harder to export and more difficult to compete against imports. Conversely, a lower valuation of the currency has the effect of making all goods within the country look cheaper, thus making it easier to export and easier to compete against imports. Monetary policy can interact with or substitute for trade policy. One of the tricks to understanding foreign economic policies is understanding how trade balances, monetary policy, and exchange rate actions intertwine.[7]

The Balance of Payments

The *balance of payments* simply refers to a nation's accounting records. It is important to understand what goes into the different accounts in order to appreciate what these terms mean. Often there is confusion over the relationships between different terms. Like any balance sheet in accounting, there are credits (pluses) and debits (minuses), which give a balance (positive or negative). In this case, the effort is to establish how much wealth is coming into the country or going out.

The flows of goods, services, and funds are broken down into various subcategories. On the broadest level, the categories are divided between the *current account* and the *capital account*. Net changes in a country's claims on foreigners are handled in the current account, while the capital account largely records the borrowing, selling, or purchasing of assets. Within the current account, one category tracks merchandise exports and imports (the tangible goods shipped into and out of the country). A second category is made up of exports and imports of services (intangible economic exchanges, such as insurance, banking, consulting and so on). These two categories are added together to find a gain or loss, which is known as the balance of trade. While the balance of trade seems to measure all international intercourse (both in goods and services), it in fact does not include many other economic transactions. The balance of trade is therefore only a part of the balance of payments.

Other components of the balance of payments can be sizeable. Separate categories account for investment income and payments. This category tracks the money sent to other countries to pay off debts, or which the country has earned by lending abroad. Another category covers government exports and imports, plus any changes of funds caused by foreign aid flows. Joining these two accounts with the balance of trade produces the balance of the current account. Note that a country with a negative balance in trade could still have a positive balance on its current account if it is earning income from foreign investments or through the government's international transactions. And since we are usually more interested in overall payments— how much money is coming in or going out—we are not always interested in the balance of trade alone.

The balance on the current account still does not cover all international economic transactions. While this balance captures income generated by international investments, that income only represents the payments of interest on loans or dividends on stock—it is the earnings from international investments, but does not include the investment itself. Thus another account, the capital account, tracks the actual transfers of capital when an investment is placed in another country (or received from another country). This account often breaks investments down into other subcategories, such as long-term or short-term. (Beware the accounting principles used in the capital account. Exports of capital count as a debit and imports as a credit. This is confusing, since any investment placed in another country is actually an asset that will produce earnings, while any investment entering from abroad might have to be repaid. This category, however, is intended to keep track of capital flowing in or out of the country.) The balance on capital account is clearly important for understanding how states view the international investment regime.

The next category within the capital account is the measure of official reserves. This account has been more important in some eras than in others, as we will see in some of the historical cases. It is important to remember that changes in the official reserves represent attempts to pay for things purchased from abroad or deposits made with money earned from international dealings. When funds are transferred from one currency to another, the central bank has to accommodate these changes and thus alter its own holdings of currency. Today there isn't much concern with this measure, though it can be an important factor for countries that have fixed their currencies to others in some fashion. For such countries, reserves are necessary for intervening in international currency markets.

The last category on the balance of payments is an error term, representing statistical discrepancies. This ensures a real balance at the bottom of the sheet (since it is a common accounting practice to have all transactions sum to zero). Perhaps the most important point to remember is that the balance of trade is not the only measure of success in international economic transactions. As we shall see, some countries have been able to run balance-of-trade deficits for long periods of time, yet succeed economically because they are earning money on their international investments. The political ramifications of these actions are extremely interesting, as we shall see, especially in the area of international monetary relations.

FIGURE 12: THE BALANCE OF PAYMENTS

Current Account:	*Capital Account:*
net merchandise (or visible) trade	net direct investment
+ net services (or invisible trade)	+ net portfolio investments
= *balance of trade*	= *balance on long-term capital*

balance of trade	balance on long-term capital
+ net factor payments	+ net short-term capital
= *balance on current account*	= *balance on capital account*

balance on current account
+ balance on capital account
+ statistical discrepancy
+ changes in official reserves

= *total balance*

Balance-of-Payments Adjustment

People are usually interested in the balance of payments because they want to know how much their country is earning from or owes to its trading partners. It is important to remember that most economists now agree that the balance of payments is shaped by an array of economic forces, ranging from trade policy to domestic savings rates. International forces are only part of the picture. *Balance-of-payments adjustment* refers to the way in which states settle their bills. The methods for making such payments has varied from one monetary regime to the next. When a country has a balance-of-payments deficit, it is in effect taking in more in value than it is exporting. The extra value in imports has to be paid for in one way or another. One method is for the deficit country to make up the difference it owes by paying out monetary reserves. Another is to allow the deficit country time to increase its exports (or decrease its imports) in such a way that it can pay off its deficit. This can be helped by international rules or left to be done completely through domestic policy adjustments.

When a country pays out monetary reserves to adjust its balance of payments, there are numerous economic ramifications. First, no country has an infinite supply of reserves; in fact, most have very limited resources. Therefore, something else has to be done to restrain imports and enhance exports if reserves are not to be completely drained. But changes in reserves can actually catalyse the necessary economic policy changes. Under a set of rules where there is a fixed ratio between reserves and money in circulation, whenever reserves drop, the money supply should shrink. When the money supply contracts, prices drop (because there will be less money chasing the same amount of goods). This price drop makes the country's exports look cheaper, and therefore the country should sell more; imports will look relatively more expensive, and therefore the country will buy less of them. If the country has a balance-of-payments surplus rather than a deficit and adjustment occurs through reserve changes, then the same process is invoked, but in the opposite direction. Reserves expand, which increases the money supply. Inflation results, because now more money is chasing the same amount of goods. Inflation makes imports look cheaper and exports look more expensive. Whether in surplus or deficit, the change in monetary reserves will naturally stimulate the adjustment process.

Balance-of-payments adjustment that occurs through changes in monetary reserves has numerous economic effects. For example, adjustment through deflation usually means an economic downturn, including higher unemployment. To avoid such effects, other systems of adjustment have been tried. Under the Bretton Woods monetary regime, adjustment from a balance of payments deficit was supposed to be eased. Members of the regime deposited funds with an agency, the International Monetary Fund (IMF).

The IMF, in turn, would loan funds to countries that developed a deficit, so that these countries could make their payments in the short run while using other policies to alter the flow of imports and exports. Whether this regime has functioned well depends on one's perspective. Ultimately, trade flows have to be changed to achieve balance-of-payments adjustment. The ease with which such changes occur depends on a variety of actors and the other characteristics of the monetary regime.

The Distribution of Gains from Undertaking the Key Currency Role

A national currency that functions as international money is often referred to as a *key currency*.[8] Establishing an international money provides a valuable service to other members of the international economy, but it will also allow the leading state itself to garner specific advantages.[9] Because of the currency's dominance in finance, the state's control over the currency becomes a potential bargaining weapon vis-à-vis other states. Invisible earnings may be increased because others use the nation's services more than they would otherwise; financial actors with a base in the leading country have an edge in that they have greater access to the source of the international currency. Finally, practice has shown that the state whose currency is accepted as an international money has the option of allowing a deficit in its balance of payments, since working balances of its currency may accumulate abroad without any negative ramifications in the short run.[10]

Disadvantages to this specific form of leadership may emerge as well, making an overhang very possible.[11] An overhang occurs when foreign holdings of a currency on a fixed exchange rate expand beyond the value of reserves backing that currency (i.e., there are more claims on the reserves than there should be). If the national currency is the numeraire of the system (i.e., the standard of value for other national currencies), devaluation is not an option for resolving a balance-of-payments deficit. Other macroeconomic policies may then be slanted towards external targets rather than towards domestic goals. Finally, policies designed to maintain a country's money in the key currency role may support certain sectors and foster international investment but conflict with balance-of-payments policies and policies benefiting the competitiveness of other sectors.[12]

The Needs of the International Economy: Balancing Confidence and Liquidity

The reason Scammell argued that the international monetary system required some sort of management came from observations of domestic monetary systems. In the domestic economy, governments have established agencies (usually a central bank) to manage money supplies. The difficult task confronting such authorities is the balancing of the twin targets of *confidence* and *liquidity*. The three primary functions of money create conflicting pressures, for each suggests that a different amount of money be introduced into circulation. The less money in circulation, the better it can serve as a store of value. If too much money is introduced into the economy, inflation results; inflation erodes the value of the currency. When money is relatively scarce, people have confidence that the money will maintain its value. To serve as a medium of exchange, there has to be enough of the currency in circulation that it supports many transactions. The more money in circulation (or liquidity) the better it can serve as a medium of exchange.

In the domestic economy, central banks have developed a number of policy instruments to enable them to manage this balancing act. These instruments, however, are predicated on certain powers a government can exercise in the domestic realm. For instance, in most countries the domestic currency is legal tender. This means that merchants must accept the currency as payment—they cannot refuse it. Obviously, the same sort of mechanisms cannot be used in the international political economy, for there is no ultimate political authority. In the management of an international currency, domestic policies must be conducted in such a way that, in combination with international policies, foreigners can get enough of the money to undertake transactions but also have some assurance that their money will continue to retain its value over time.

For countries that decide to develop their currencies into the role of an international money, or for those that simply find their currencies fall into this role, monetary authorities inevitably confront more complicated choices. The political agencies managing the national currency would face two possibly competing sets of targets—a certain level of confidence and liquidity might be correct for the international economy but inappropriate for the national economy, and vice versa. How do national authorities handle such situations? How do national monetary policies affect other economic policies? Those questions will be addressed in two of our cases, where a national currency enjoyed the key currency role.

Hegemonic Stability Theory and Monetary Regimes

The idea that some countries might desire to manage the international economy returns us to the mixture of liberal and realist debates on hegemonic stability theory. Hegemonic stability theory argues that in the absence of an overarching international political authority, the collective goods that support liberal international economic relations will only exist when a state with the requisite capabilities decides to provide them. The establishment of an international money therefore is one of the classic issues hegemonic stability theory was intended to explain. If the hegemonic leader is trying to create and maintain an open economic subsystem, then it is necessary to establish a monetary regime where a stable international money is accepted throughout that subsystem. The more widely the international money is accepted, the more widely markets are integrated. In the absence of a single widely accepted currency, transaction costs rise and can become a formidable barrier to economic intercourse.[13]

Proponents of realism argue that monetary regimes require some sort of management by a hegemonic power, but also that the regime's characteristics and management will reflect the power and interests of the hegemonic country. Examples of ways in which the management of the regime is directed towards the hegemonic state's interest may be easier to identify. According to realists, if the hegemonic state wishes to see one set of exchange rate rules or one type of balance-of-payments adjustment, then the regime will have those very rules.

Liberals will examine the regime's characteristics from a different perspective, which underscores the links between liberals and institutionalists. Liberals are primarily concerned with how well the regime supports individuals' abilities to conduct economic transactions across international boundaries. It is the performance of the regime that most interests them—this emphasis on the regime's functions typifies an institutionalist analysis.

Marxists and dependency theorists look at these same issues from a different angle. They argue that monetary regimes are likely to be dominated by a single powerful state (or perhaps a small group of states), but that the monetary regime serves to reinforce the international division of labour. As such, the monetary regime enhances the concentration of capital in the hands of fewer and fewer people within the most economically advanced and politically powerful states. The monetary regime serves to integrate markets and is part of a comprehensive picture that includes international investment and trade patterns.

Comparing Monetary Regimes

If we consider the four characteristics of monetary regimes together, we get a quick and simple synopsis of any historical example we can use to make comparisons. For instance, the main traits of the classical gold standard are summarized in the box below.

FOUR CHARACTERISTICS OF THE
CLASSICAL GOLD STANDARD (1871–1914)

1. The exchange rate of each currency was fixed in terms of gold, hence all were fixed against each other.
2. Gold served as the only reserve.
3. Gold was allowed to flow freely from one participating member of the gold standard to another, both as the form of balance of payments adjustment, but also as capital flows.
4. Some have argued that Britain's Bank of England, as the monetary authority of the world's major trading power and international investor, was able to manage the gold standard.

The workings of the gold standard, the sterling overhang that developed, and the British policy response are explored in Chapter 13. After World War II, a new monetary regime was developed to mimic some aspects of the gold standard, but with modifications to enhance balance-of-payments adjustment and exchange rate management. The creation of this regime is discussed in Chapter 15; its downfall is then discussed in Chapter 17.

If we were to list the characteristics for the current monetary situation, the differences compared to the gold standard would be glaring. For the most part exchange rates are not fixed, though there are some attempts to fix exchange rates in some regional groupings. Dirty floating is the norm. Reserves are a mixture of foreign reserves and precious metals, though reserves have less meaning when exchange rates are not fixed. Capital controls in the major economic powers exist in only limited form these days, though capital controls are more extensive in other places. The U.S. dollar serves as the international money, though use of other currencies (especially the Japanese yen and the German Deutschemark) has risen in recent years. Whether the U.S. manages the international monetary order in any way is doubtful—certainly when compared to how the U.S. could manage affairs in the 1950s and 1960s when the Bretton Woods monetary regime was in place. Today's international monetary regime is based much more on co-ordination of policies among the major financial powers, as will be seen in Chapter 21.

Summary: Monetary Policies, Politics, and International Relations

The main questions concerning monetary regimes and international monetary policy reflect our efforts to untangle a variety of issues. On the one hand, national authorities must manage monetary policy in a way that meets domestic and international goals. If a country's currency is playing the role of an international money, balancing monetary goals becomes quite complicated. Policy decisions are also complicated because of the ways in which monetary policy can substitute for trade policy. Since monetary policy can manipulate the price of exports and imports, it can substitute for protectionist policies. At the same time, since monetary policy usually affects all tradeable goods and services, it is politically difficult to manipulate monetary policy without inviting opposition. Policy decisions may reflect national competition, the pursuit of power, the constraints of international regimes, the struggle between various domestic interests, or bureaucratic politics. Only an investigation of cases will persuade us of one point of view or another.

Suggested Readings

Richard Cooper, *The International Monetary System: Essays in World Economics.* Cambridge, Mass.: MIT Press, 1987.

Paul de Grauwe, *International Money: Postwar Trends and Theories.* Oxford: Clarendon Press, 1989.

Chris Milner, ed., *Political Economy and International Money, Selected Essays of John Williamson.* New York: New York University Press, 1987.

W.M. Scammell, *The Stability of the International Monetary System.* Totowa, NJ: Rowman & Littlefield, 1987.

Susan Strange, "The Politics of International Currencies," *World Politics* 23, 2 (January 1971), 215-31.

Notes

1 See, for instance, the discussion in Paul de Grauwe, *International Money: Postwar Trends and Theories* (Oxford: Clarendon Press, 1989), 1.

2 Non-rival consumption refers to the fact that one person's use of the money does not prevent another from using it. In this case, the more a money is used, the more effectively it serves as a medium of exchange. For a deeper discussion of the characteristics of money and their relevance for international exchange, see ibid., 1-4.

3 This was not the case in the past, and there remain many proponents of the "free banking" approach. If the free banking proponents are correct, then there should be few or no problems with a floating exchange rate system internationally.

4 Richard N. Cooper, "Prolegomena to the Choice of an International Monetary System," *International Organization* 29, 1 (1975), 63-97.

5 W.M. Scammell, *The Stability of the International Monetary System* (Totowa, NJ: Rowman & Littlefield, 1987), 9.

6 This, of course, shapes degrees of satisfaction with floating exchange rates. See Robert M. Dunn Jr., "The Many Disappointments of Flexible Exchange Rates," *Princeton Essays in International Finance* No. 154 (December 1983).

7 For a broader discussion, see Jeffry Frieden, "Invested Interests: The Politics of National Economic Policies in a World of Global Finance," *International Organization* 45, 4 (Autumn 1991), 425-51.

8 Susan Strange, "The Politics of International Currencies," *World Politics* 23, 2 (January 1971), 215-31.

9 For a similar discussion, see C. Fred Bergsten, *The Dilemmas of the Dollar* (New York: New York University Press, 1975), 101-12.

10 Scammell, *The Stability of the International Monetary System*, 55.

11 According to C. Fred Bergsten, such internationally used currencies typically develop overhangs. See Bergsten, *The Dilemmas of the Dollar*, pp. 129-130.

12 Scammell, *The Stability of the International Monetary System*, 55.

13 Of course, today, with extensive information and the ability to process it rapidly, such transaction costs can be greatly reduced. This was not true of most of the time periods considered in the cases.

Nine

....

THE POLITICS OF INTERNATIONAL INVESTMENT

International investments have become one of the fastest growing areas of concern in public debates about international political economic relations, especially in the United States. For many years, U.S. investors had purchased foreign businesses, established firms in foreign countries, or made loans abroad. American policy was primarily focused on creditors' rights and privileges; citizens of other countries were more interested in establishing debtors' rights. The U.S. has become a focal point for international investments in the last twenty years, causing Americans to reconsider the politics of international investments.

Some Reasons International Investment Takes Place

The obvious reason why international investment takes place is simply that someone wants to make a profit by taking capital from one country to another. As our discussion from the chapter on trade revealed, the factors of production are distributed unevenly. Because capital is relatively scarce in some areas and relatively abundant in others, capital earns different rates of return depending on which economy it is in. One response to these different rates of return is to engage in trade. Another response for the holders of capital where it is abundant (and therefore not earning as much as capital elsewhere) is to organize their capital and move it to someplace where capital is relatively scarce. Still another reason investment takes place between countries derives from the very fact that borders exist. Different countries exercise different laws, which translates into different economic practices and, ultimately, different profit rates from investments.

Less obviously, trade itself can drive firms' decisions regarding the location of investment. Several theories in economics consider the ways that firms compete and how they seek markets to be important factors driving investment abroad. Microeconomics tells us that firms do not always seek profits over other goals. In some situations, firms may well have to decide between maximizing today's profits or pursuing other goals that could enhance profits over the longer run. Thus firms may turn down immediate profits in favour of greater market share or attaining economies of scale in production. As part of their strategies aimed at achieving these other goals, firms often incorporate a plan to invest abroad. Individuals also invest internationally, but these investments depend on the international financial mechanisms available.

Politically, there are several contentious aspects to international investment. Are states willing to see money leave their own country and be spent on the economic development of another country? Realists will certainly have something to say about the wisdom of such a policy—though they must also be able to explain why so much international investment takes place. Liberals will have no trouble answering this last question by relying on the arguments of economists. Yet in providing explanations for fluctuations in the forms and volume of international investment over time, liberals will have some of the same problems that appeared in their theories about the evolution of trade. The challenge for liberals is to provide consistent arguments over time.

Of course, the countries hosting the international investment may also question the value of international investments. The host country receives money to help it develop, but at what cost? Is it beneficial to receive funds if the price is handing over critical decisions determining the country's economy to foreigners? Liberals, realists, Marxists, and others will naturally disagree about the answers to such questions. We can only discuss how political scientists analyse decisions made about international investment by first recognizing some of the different forms in which international investment takes place. Each form has different consequences for the home country, the host country, investors themselves, and the borrowers. Different forms have also been popular at different points in time.

The Different Forms of Investment

Different forms of investment reflect a combination of contemporary business practices (which are constantly changing), but they also reflect reactions to the problems of particular historical periods. In international business, some problems have been constant: how can risks be reduced? how can geographically dispersed operations be co-ordinated? how can profits be amassed and redeployed? These questions have been more perplexing in some periods than others, but in each case the answers are profoundly shaped by political factors.

The initial form of international investment in the modern period was to keep the business in the family. To overcome the risks involved with international operations in a period when communications were underdeveloped and legal controls were likewise primitive, operations were kept within the family. In the seventeenth century, for instance, if a Dutch businessman wanted to purchase grain in the Baltic region, ship it to the Netherlands, convert that grain into gin or some other type of liquor, and then sell that liquor in Britain, how was he to establish a business in these other countries? If he simply handed over capital to someone in these other countries or hired someone in the other countries to handle the local operations, he bore the risks concerning the foreigner's honesty. Given that it would take some time to get information about any problems, if the foreigner simply took the capital, the investor would be in trouble. The host government would be unlikely to care about the foreign investor's dilemma.

The common solution to such problems was to dispatch sons. In the example above, one son would live in a Baltic coast town and run that end of the business. Another son (or son-in-law) set up a business in London to handle business affairs there. In this situation, risk was lowered because family ties kept the managers of the disparate units loyal to the overall firm. While that reduced some of the economic risks associated with international investment, the political risks remained. Monarchs claiming absolute political power could always try to seize their citizens' property—foreigners' investments were an even easier target for such rulers.

Other major obstacles remained during this period. Communications were undeveloped, so co-ordination of operations was still difficult. More importantly, many countries practised mercantilism. *Mercantilism* prevented individuals from taking capital out of their home country. However, the citizens of those countries that did allow capital exports (such as the Dutch Republic) confronted a second problem. Once capital was placed in another country (one practising mercantilism), removing any profits would probably be prevented. Those countries pursuing mercantilist policies pushed investments into large trading companies, which invested in the home country's colonies rather than in the economies of other major powers. These trading companies, such as the Hudson's Bay Company and the East India Company, often exercised a monopoly over the trade from a particular colony or region, or perhaps over the trade in a specific item, and thus they made huge profits. Under mercantilism, investment patterns and trade flows were closely linked.

Some of these trading companies were the first to issue shares, which allowed them to operate as limited liability companies. Previously, firms either were individually owned or were partnerships. Partnerships could only raise money to the extent that they could bring people together; moreover, partnerships (or firms owned by a single individual) did not have a separate identity. If such a firm had debts, the owner or owners were personally responsible. In a limited liability operation, control was exercised through stock ownership; the firm was an entity unto itself. If the firm went bankrupt, the stockholders lost money in the value of their stock, but they were not personally liable for the firm's debts. This innovation obviously encouraged investment by people with small amounts of capital and allowed for many small amounts of capital to be pooled together into larger amounts.

Another important distinction has to do with the management of limited liability firms. In most instances of partnerships, the partners ran the day-to-day operations themselves. In limited liability firms, the ownership was divided among numerous stockholders, each with only a small stake in the firm; none would likely be in a position to claim the right to run the firm. Instead, professional management would be brought in to handle the company's operations. This division between ownership and management is important for understanding how portfolio investments work, as well as for appreciating the differences in the political consequences of portfolio investment compared to other forms of international investment.

Portfolio Investments

A *portfolio investment* is an indirect investment—one where ownership or investment does not entail direct management of the economic activity resulting from the investment. The most common portfolio investments are stocks, bonds, or simple bank loans. The term "portfolio" refers to the nature in which investors handle these investments.

Portfolio investments have occurred since the development of the modern international political economy. For instance, in the seventeenth century several governments (the Dutch especially) became adept at floating bonds that their public would purchase. Dutch citizens became accustomed to earning steady returns on such items. Such portfolio investments became international and occurred on a large scale once Britain's Parliament assumed political dominance in the Glorious Revolution of 1688. William III, who as Prince of Orange was already the most important political figure in the Netherlands, was invited to become King of England; England and the Netherlands became steadfast allies. To the Dutch public, investing in English parliamentary bonds was sensible because they trusted Parliament to repay its debts, English and Dutch political interests were interwoven (and with William III involved in both governments, policies were loosely co-ordinated), and the investment could even be seen as patriotic. Since the Dutch were not practising mercantilism, Dutch investors became the first to invest heavily in the form of international portfolio investments.

When we consider the political questions circling international investment, the particular characteristics of portfolio investments are critical to keep in mind. Portfolio investments link together capitalists from different countries. No matter what the specific type of investment (bank loan, bond, or whatever), capitalists in one country are lending money in one form or another to capitalists (economic agents, public or private) of another country. The capitalists therefore share an interest in seeing that the investments earn a return. Portfolio investments are an economic bond between capitalists. If the deal is entered into voluntarily, why should such lending ever lead to economic friction between the home and host?

Look at the basic economic cause of the investment in the first place. Capitalists in a country with relatively abundant capital will wish to earn higher returns on their investments by placing that capital in a country where this resource is relatively scarcer. In the end, however, portfolio investments always mean that more capital is supposed to leave the host country than went in—more capital will flow back to where capital was already relatively abundant. Why? Because with portfolio investments, such as a simple loan, the debtor always has to pay back the principal (the amount borrowed) plus interest. The trick is for the borrower to spend the money wisely, making enough to pay back the principal and interest, and still have some left over.

In the nineteenth century, the country with the most capital to invest at home or abroad was Britain. For a variety of reasons, Britain's investments primarily took the form of portfolio investments. At first, these investments enhanced British trade. Portfolio loans in the form of stocks or bonds were floated on the London markets, often by foreign national or municipal governments. The foreign governments used the money to invest in their own public infrastructure. They spent the funds they had borrowed on new canals, bridges, port improvements, and above all, railroads. Construction of train lines, such as the Grand Trunk Railway in Canada, meant these same actors would have to purchase iron rails, steam engines, and railroad cars. Britain, as the first country to experience the Industrial Revolution, held a huge technological lead in producing these items efficiently. By loaning money to foreigners, British investors stimulated the demand for British industrial exports.

That, at least, was true for the first half of the nineteenth century. As other countries began to industrialize, their exports began to compete with Britain's. British loans could be spent purchasing goods produced elsewhere. The situation changed even more dramatically by the end of the 1800s. British investments were increasingly fuelling the creation of economic rivals, for capital flowing from Britain was being used to establish industries themselves. Capital was being taken abroad and used by foreign borrowers to create their own steel mills and factories. These producers then competed directly against British exporters.

Such patterns had an impact on Britain's policy stance on trade. The investments hurt Britain's trade in goods (though interestingly, Britain had already been running a deficit in the trade of visible goods). Britain remained committed to a policy of free trade despite its changing fortunes in the trade in merchandise because of the income generated through international investments. The free trade regime remained important to Britain because foreign borrowers had to be able to sell their goods in order to repay their debts.[1] As the prime source of capital for the financing of trade, insurance, transportation, etc., Britain also did very well in the free trade regime.

The Multinational Corporation

After World War I, international financial leadership was increasingly shared between London and New York. Americans had amassed vast amounts of capital to invest prior to 1914. World War I accelerated these economic trends. The British had been forced to sell off some of their international investments to finance the war effort. As part of these wartime measures, Britain had even been forced into debt by borrowing from private banks in New York. These war loans were typical of the initial American investments abroad. At first, such American activity abroad was primarily composed of portfolio investments.

This pattern of change was accelerated further by World War II. Britain once more had to sell off international holdings to purchase war material from abroad. The British government and other allies mostly borrowed from the U.S. government rather than from private banks. As we saw in the previous chapter, monetary policy practices had changed just prior to World War II, so governments everywhere were much more willing to run very large budget deficits.

But most of the American private investments after World War II took a different form. Instead of exercising indirect control— loaning money out but not managing how it was invested—American capitalists tended to practise direct investment. This reflected the form of capitalism dominant in the U.S. in the twentieth century: the corporation. Most often in the post-1945 era, American corporations invested abroad by purchasing an existing business within a foreign country. The foreign firm would then be integrated into the American company's corporate structure. Sometimes the American corporation moved into the foreign market by establishing an entirely new enterprise, but either way, the U.S. firm ended up with a subsidiary it would operate directly.

The political consequences associated with *foreign direct investment* (or FDI) are not at all like those associated with portfolio investment. With FDI, foreign capitalists are entering into direct competition against local entrepreneurs.

Whereas portfolio investment builds links between capitalists from the investing country and the host country (so that they share an interest in seeing the investment make a profit), FDI turns the investing capitalists into competitors vying within the host country.

The Reasons Firms Choose To Go Multinational

There are several reasons firms might choose to establish multinational operations. First, the firm might be seeking either vertical or horizontal integration to exercise market power. Second, oligopolistic practices and pressures may push a firm to pursue market shares. Third, firms may try to protect and exploit their intangible assets. All of these factors seem to be in play in the decision of so many large American firms investing abroad in the post-World War II era.

Vertical integration refers to the uniting of the various stages of production. A firm producing aluminum cans has to worry about securing sources of its key input, aluminum. Aluminum is produced from bauxite ore. Processing the ore requires a large amount of energy. To secure a steady supply of cheap aluminum, a firm producing cans would try to control some source of bauxite plus cheap sources of energy. Bauxite isn't found in that many places so the firm might well have to move into foreign operations to control this input.

Vertical integration was often a response to the threat that someone else might take control of the world's supply of a particular input. To follow with the previous example, a firm might wish to establish a monopoly over the world's supply of bauxite and therefore be in a position to charge a monopoly price for that input. That would be an example of *horizontal integration*—expanding a firm so as to establish a monopoly over a single step in the production process. Horizontal integration can therefore also be a reason for firms to go multinational. If foreign competitors exist, then one way to eliminate or control that competition is to take over the foreign suppliers. Strategies of market control, and counter-strategies, were often reasons for the very first multinational investments.

The Product Cycle

One of the most popular explanations for international investment, developed by Raymond Vernon, is known as the *product cycle*.[2] He focused on a particular set of firms producing specific sorts of products. (Consumer electronics is a perfect example.) These products go through a characteristic life cycle, and this life cycle determines whether production will be internationalized. The first stage in the product cycle is product innovation. Here a firm in an economically advanced country develops a new product that is expensive to make, for the home market is composed of wealthy consumers. The firm may initially have a monopolistic edge over competitors because of its innovation.

The second phase comes as the home market is saturated with the good and the product is exported to other markets. Because of economies of scale or learning curves in production, production costs tend to fall over time. As the price falls, the product can be sold in other markets where the population has less disposable income. The firm responds to this opportunity by exporting the good to these other countries. The next phase is the product maturation phase. This is when FDI first occurs. Exports of the product serve to disseminate the technology necessary to produce the good. If the product goes to consumers, a number of firms will arise to service these goods. If one understands how the technology works, however, one also understands how to produce similar goods. Since there is the risk that foreign firms may try to produce similar goods, the home producer establishes foreign branches to pre-empt any rivals from arising.

Once foreign competition does emerge, the innovating firm's margin of profitability is cut. The original firm must lower its prices, thus making it sensitive to any factors that might increase the cost of the good, such as transportation, marketing, and labour. Differences in these costs between what the innovating firm is paying versus what its foreign rival pays could make all the difference in whether the firm turns a profit. The firm can respond by locating production as closely as possible to the new markets, thereby reducing transportation costs—yet another reason to pursue FDI. The final phase is product standardization, which occurs when production has become so mechanical and so routine that production goes to the country wherever labour costs are lowest. Firms shift all their production to the labour-abundant, less economically developed countries in an effort to control production costs. Ironically, the firm can only supply the original home market by exporting these goods from its foreign operations.

This is exactly the pattern of trade and investment we have seen in several products, but perhaps the most striking examples have occurred in consumer electronics. Colour television was originally developed in the United States. At one point colour TVs were only produced in the U.S. Eventually, the production spread to the other economically advanced countries, and then to the less economically advanced countries, until finally all production shifted to the less developed countries. For some time, colour TVs were no longer produced in the U.S. at all.

Other Economic Explanations for FDI

One of the most powerful new explanations for the rise and spread of MNCs looks at the incentives firms face, just as Vernon's product-cycle explanation does. Instead of focusing on technology as the driving force or treating integration of production as the key factor influencing the decision to invest abroad, this explanation looks at the control of transaction costs. In several sorts of transactions, it is difficult for firms to know what price to charge. This holds true for tangible goods such as technology but is even more true for intangible assets, such as brand names or marketing information.

By tapping into the importance of marketing, this explanation highlights a critical factor in the success or failure of many firms. Brand names are very valuable to corporations. Businesses spend millions to develop and protect the images of their products. Successfully developing an image in one country often has a natural spillover in other nearby markets. To license a foreign firm to produce and market the same type of good involves a calculated risk. The original firm may earn high payments in the short run, but if the foreign firm operating under licence produces goods of poor quality, the product's image can be severely damaged in other markets. Given the high risks involved in the licensing of production and use of brand names, firms may be uncertain of the proper fees to charge in such deals. It is difficult to develop a licensing scheme that would adequately cover the original producer's risks and still leave the new foreign producer a reasonable profit.

As Richard Caves explains, firms that do not know what price to charge for such intangibles may simply internalize the transaction by refusing to sell the asset at stake (technology, information, trademark, or whatever).[3] Instead of selling rights to the asset to a foreign firm, the corporation may create a foreign subsidiary. In this way, the corporation can retain the profits derived from the corporation's asset. Such arguments fit nicely into other theories of oligopolistic competition (i.e., situations where a few large firms dominate the market), because whenever FDI has been spurred by uncertainty over transaction costs, it generates other consequences that may benefit an oligopolistic firm. By moving abroad, the firm can limit the development of foreign rivals. Rather than allow a foreign firm to develop competitive goods in a foreign country, the firm may seize that opening and squeeze potential competitors out of the market. Since the oligopolistic firm can use technology (or trademarks, or any other intangible asset or combination of assets) already developed, this strategy builds on sunk costs and entails few new risks.

Another reason for firms to go international is to capture economies of scale. Firms may simply produce for foreign markets and achieve the economies of scale necessary by relying on exports. But they may also be drawn into foreign countries to pursue the linkages in production needed to support economies of scale. This is another argument based on the obvious fact that most firms involved in multinational production are oligopolies. Caves, having noted that there are several types of oligopolies, has used these firms' characteristics to provide several possible explanations for MNCS' investment activities.

Caves identifies three sorts of MNCS: horizontally integrated, vertically integrated, and diversified firms. Horizontal and vertical integration have already been discussed. Diversified firms are involved in the production of similar sorts of goods as well as totally dissimilar ones. This can only be explained as either a combination of the above patterns or risk avoidance. Firms may expand in other areas alien to them (i.e., not only foreign but also technologically different) in order to learn more about another country or another area of production. For instance, a Japanese firm might buy an American firm in a completely unrelated field, not because it wants to merge the two firms but because the Japanese company wants to learn more about the American market. This information will help the Japanese firm decide if it should expand its operations in the U.S. In just such a transaction, General Motors bought another multinational, Hughes Aircraft, in the hopes that GM could learn more about high-tech production techniques. While there was the possibility that GM could generate some aerospace spin-offs to use in their automobiles, its real reason for wanting Hughes Aircraft was to see how Hughes managed its automated production.

The Returns to Foreign Direct Investment

Unlike portfolio investments, foreign direct investment does not automatically mean that capital should ever flow out of the host country at a higher rate than it is coming in. A foreign firm that invests in a country may decide to leave its investments there or plough its profits back into the firm—or it may not. This creates a strong contrast with portfolio investments. As mentioned above, when the transactions made in the form of portfolio investments work according to plan, more capital leaves the host country than entered; the borrower must pay back the principal plus interest.

With foreign direct investment, this, too, may be the case. The MNC may decide to end its investment by selling off the operation. It would clearly prefer to make a profit, thus taking more money out than it initially invested. But if an MNC opens up a factory in a foreign country that services the local market and the factory is successful, the MNC would presumably continue the operation. Profits might be taken out, but the original investment would remain (as an asset held by foreigners, of course).

Interestingly, the political reaction to each form of investment is often quite different. In either case, more money is being pumped into the host economy. That translates into more jobs (higher wages, as workers' pay is bid up), greater demand for other local inputs, and a stimulation of the economy. (None of this stimulation necessarily penetrates very deeply into the economy, however. Often this type of stimulation creates economic distortions with unwanted side-effects.) Yet portfolio investments usually do not generate political opposition, whereas foreign direct investment does. This obviously comes from two points: first, with portfolio investments, key decisions on day-to-day matters remain in the hands of locals. Second, in portfolio investments, local capitalists have a role to play, whereas FDI means competition with local capitalists. Capitalists from the host country therefore prefer portfolio investment over FDI, and thus the politics associated with FDI has been much more nationalistic compared to the politics associated with portfolio investments.

The State versus the MNC? The Issue of Regulation

Discussions about the politics of foreign investment span a wide spectrum. At one point, some people believed that firms, organized around economic ends, were not only becoming more powerful than nation-states but would soon replace political units in degree of importance. As one proponent of this viewpoint argued, "the nation-state is just about through as an economic unit."[4] While this comment was made in the 1960s and was echoed by many others at the time, it perhaps reflects an extreme view. None the less, MNCs can be seen as having a commanding role in the international economy. Statistics for the late 1980s show that U.S.-based MNCs accounted for nearly two-thirds of American merchandise exports, so clearly MNCs play a major role in international trade.[5]

Of course, on the other extreme, we have the realist viewpoint, which has always assumed that states are the most important actors in international affairs. The classic realist response to the extreme liberal viewpoint of someone like Kindleberger (or George Ball) came from Sam Huntington, who stated in 1973:

> Predictions of the death of the nation-state are premature. They overlook the ability of human beings and human institutions to respond to challenges and to adapt themselves to changed environments. They seem to be based on a zero-sum assumption about power and sovereignty: that a growth in the power of transnational organizations must be accompanied by a decrease in the power of nation-states. This, however, need not be the case.[6]

Another realist counterpoint came from Waltz, and was perhaps less prophetic. In commenting on Kindleberger's views, he posed the question: "Who is likely to be around 100 years from now—the United States, the Soviet Union, France, Egypt, Thailand, and Uganda? Or Ford, IBM, Shell, Unilever, and Massey-Ferguson? I would bet on the states, perhaps even Uganda."[7]

Of course, there are several good reasons why governments would be wary of FDI. Multinational corporations do indeed pose a challenge to governments, for they can use their mobility to evade and even overturn governments' policies. In some ways that is one of the reasons firms undertake multinational operations: to link markets or production centres that are kept politically separate.

The challenge MNCs pose to governments must be noted for other significant reasons. MNCs do have home bases, where they often have political links. They can protect their interests by calling on one government to oppose the actions of another government.[8] This often pits an economically advanced country of the North against an economically developing country of the South, but it also may pit northern countries against each other (as when the U.S. and Canada argue over the treatment of American corporations in Canada) and now also may foster South-South tensions, as more MNCs of southern origin arise (as when a Korean MNC begins operations in the Philippines).

Part of the North's response to the inability to control MNCs or regulate their activity has led to an increase in attempts to exert *extraterritoriality*, i.e., the extension of national jurisdiction beyond a nation's own borders. Thus a country such as the U.S. tries to implement its own anti-trust laws to keep an American-based corporation from buying up its competitors even outside the U.S. The U.S. government also tries to keep MNCs from engaging in international sales of equipment or technology deemed strategically significant. For example, in the 1980s the U.S. enacted sanctions against Toshiba's operations in the U.S. to show its displeasure with Toshiba-Japan selling high-tech engineering equipment to the Soviets. Although this deal violated an agreement between the U.S. and Japan, it is not clear why the dispute was not resolved between the Japanese government and Toshiba or why the subsidiary in the U.S. should have been punished.

In a similar vein, taxation schemes based on the notion of extraterritoriality are becoming more and more common. Rather than taxing an MNC on its operations within a particular government's jurisdiction, some governments are now assessing each MNC on the basis of its global operations. The state of California, for instance, wishes to tax corporations on their total global returns, not just their operations within California or even within the U.S. The state's right to do this is not clearly established in international law or by any precedents; the real question probably remains with enforcement, in any case. If an MNC doesn't comply with the state's regulations, the state can deny the corporation licences necessary for conducting business there. If the state in question is California, enforcement means cutting the MNC off from a lucrative market, and therefore such regulations must be taken seriously. (This particular example involving California's tax code was not upheld by the U.S. Supreme Court, though the issue is certain to resurface.)

Because many less economically advanced states do not have large markets or other benefits they can deny MNCs, they have a harder time exerting controls within their own jurisdictions, let alone enforcing extraterritoriality. At the same time, at the basic theoretical level the issue facing both the economically advanced countries and the economically less developed states is the same: how should the state go about regulating the MNC's activities? There is considerable overlap in all states' goals in implementing regulation, since all states would like a greater success rate in meeting their policy objectives and in raising taxes. This shared interest in regulation should prove a fertile ground for some sort of international agreement to regulate the practices of MNCs—yet little progress has ever been made in this area.

The problem over regulation is a classic example of failed collective action. If it is possible for all states to agree on an issue that would make them all better off, such as raise taxes on MNCs, why don't they all do it? The problem is getting all to act together (another example of the prisoners' dilemma). If all raise their taxes to the same level at the same time, MNCs could not easily evade the tax hike. But if one state fails to raise its taxes, that would leave an opening for the MNCs to exploit (e.g., Panama in regard to shipping regulations). Since the governments are interested in total taxes collected rather than rates per se, the greater volume generated by being a tax haven could easily mean more tax revenues. So there is going to be a defection problem with any collective action on regulation of MNCs. This same sort of collective action problem hampered the regulation of corporations in the U.S. at the turn of the century, when regulation of business activity was in the hands of the individual states—firms could play one state off another. Eventually the federal government had to take over business regulation. At the international level, there is no higher body to turn to; states must come together and agree on minimum regulations. Resolution of the collective action problem is an inherently political activity.

The Resurgence of Portfolio Investments

While MNC operations were the norm in the 1950s and 1960s, portfolio investments never disappeared. In fact, they made a resurgence in the 1960s and 1970s, and this growth has continued to mushroom. As a potential threat to sovereignty, governments in many developing countries increasingly opposed FDI. The creation of large pools of cheap and available capital meant that these countries could turn away from MNC investments and replace them with borrowing from foreign sources. The most prominent source of portfolio investments was European banks, which had U.S. dollars to lend.

This *Eurodollar market*,[9] as it was called, had been created as a way of avoiding certain government regulations concerning financial markets. U.S. dollars were the most attractive currency to hold in the post-World War II years. It was the currency used in most international transactions and the currency used to price goods sold on international markets. When the Soviet Union exported diamonds or natural gas, the prices were set in dollars. Payment was normally made in dollars as well. Yet for a wide variety of goods, the U.S. dollar was only accepted as payment in the U.S. itself. Banks had only been interested in handling local money, so if people earned a foreign currency they would traditionally exchange that for their own currency or take that currency back to its country of origin to deposit it there. When the Soviet Union earned dollars from the sale of resources, it didn't want to exchange them into Russian money (what was the point?) and, in fact, would desire to spend those dollars on international markets. The money was very useful—but where should the Soviets put it? They were supposed to take those dollars and deposit them in a bank in the U.S.

The Soviet government was worried about this option, however. If it held large deposits in American banks, it left itself open to some sort of retaliation or pressure by the U.S. government. The U.S. government could order the freezing of these assets. To avoid such problems, the Soviet government convinced a British bank to hold the Soviet's dollar deposits. With that, the Eurodollar market was born—U.S. dollars held by banks outside the U.S. government's jurisdiction. This opened up a whole new range of economic activity.

Banks make a profit by lending out depositors' funds. As other countries and firms began to make deposits in U.S. dollars, the banks found they had a large amount of U.S. funds to lend. Moreover, these accounts were largely unregulated—that is, national laws were unclear as to how such accounts were to be managed. In most countries, commercial banks receive deposit insurance from the central bank in exchange for accepting the central bank's regulation. The central bank oversees that each bank does not engage in overlending; this is the way the banks avoid their own collective action problem of overcompetition. The central bank usually asserts control by issuing regulations that a certain percentage of deposits must be on hand at all times, so as to meet depositors' potential demands. Banks may decide to hold even more. In return, the central bank promises that if the commercial banks make sensible transactions but find that for an unexpected reason they lack enough funds to meet demands from depositors, the central bank will loan the commercial bank the necessary funds. When the Eurodollar market developed, such rules and promises only applied to deposits in national currency. Without any rules forcing the commercial banks to maintain a certain percentage in reserve, the banks became less and less prudent. They began to keep ever smaller amounts of money on hand and loaned out more and more; they also charged less and less interest over time. Competition forced them to play an ever riskier game.

These tendencies were exacerbated by new U.S. dollar funds accumulating in these offshore accounts. Other depositors wanted their dollar holdings kept outside the legal boundaries of the U.S. When the Arab states organized the OPEC oil embargo in the early 1970s, they forced the price of oil much higher. This translated into increased earnings of U.S. dollars, but there was a fear that the U.S. government would retaliate by freezing the OPEC countries' assets. The massive amounts of money earned could not be spent right away, so the OPEC countries deposited these petrodollars (as they were known) in the Eurodollar market. Competition between the banks to place loans simply intensified.

On the positive side, the international system could handle the huge jump in the price of oil thanks to petrodollar recycling. The profits made by OPEC were deposited in European banks, which loaned the money out to developing countries, which often spent those dollars on purchases of oil. The dollars could be recycled because the market mechanisms were in place. With so much money available to be lent out, countries could refuse to accept FDI or could place stringent terms on new FDI by replacing the lost investment capital with money borrowed on the Eurodollar market. International bank lending in 1975 accounted for perhaps $40 billion; by 1990 that figure had risen to $300 billion. Bond lending, too, had increased from less than $20 billion in the mid-1970s to more than $170 billion in 1990.[10] The side-effect was that countries amassed large debts to the private commercial banks, which would eventually have to be paid back with interest.

The Changes in the Investment Regime over the Centuries

These descriptions of recent patterns of investment underscore the fact that the international investment regime continually changes. One of the most critical questions about the international investment regime concerns the rise and fall of international investment levels over time. Realists provide possible answers to some of our key questions about the evolution of this regime. Low levels of international investment occurred prior to the nineteenth century, but when Britain began to pursue portfolio investments the level rose steadily. Investments increased in the twentieth century, but with some periods of reduction—especially in the 1930s.

Liberals follow the economists' arguments and therefore would expect to see fairly consistent patterns of international investment. How well can they explain these fluctuations? Realists, on the other hand, offer hegemonic stability theory. Investments rise and fall, according to the realists, because investors must make political calculations as well as economic calculations. The economic incentives to invest are constant; but investors do not always have the guarantees that their property rights will be protected or that capital will be allowed to flow freely over borders (allowing them to move their profits wherever they wish). Realists argue that states still remain the most important actors—if governments don't want investments, they can exercise sovereignty and block them, or even block investors from taking their capital out of the home country. How realistic is such a view today? With governments everywhere in debt, international lenders can often exert immense pressure on them.

Marxists make similar analyses to the realists, since they argue that the powerful states are able to impose their investments on weaker states. Moreover, Marxist analyses cause us to consider several related questions. Marxists usually believe that international investments are one more mode of integrating nation-states into the international division of labour. Investments therefore serve the interests of the home country (and their capitalists) and are not mutually beneficial. As such, international investments make the host countries dependent on the home countries.

There are other important questions about the international investment regime. Why does one form of investment dominate at one point in time? Is it merely a reflection of capitalist practices, or does the form of international investment reflect the practices of the hegemonic country? How are investors' rights protected? Are they protected at the expense of states' ability to exercise sovereignty?

Today, international investments are powerfully influenced by technology. Capital markets are large, fast, and interconnected. Capital can flow across borders with electronic transfers; billions of dollars are traded across borders each day. MNCs have extensive holdings—a single MNC may operate in dozens of countries. The largest MNCs, such as General Motors and IBM, operate with budgets larger than the GNP of many countries. The value of international investments and capital flows has come to overwhelm the value of trade itself.[11] Our ability to answer these questions about the international investment regime are more important than ever.

The Opportunities and Problems of International Investment

The activities of MNCs are characterized by their ability to operate internationally, across several political jurisdictions. This mobility means they can upset or offset government policies. Clearly, MNC operations can counteract government attempts to rectify balance-of-payments problems. MNCs are large holders of currencies, with wide-ranging knowledge, and great flexibility to respond to market incentives. When governments try to shift their exchange rates, MNCs can respond quickly and massively to garner profits. This often makes the government's job of stabilizing or hitting an exchange target that much more difficult. Remittance of profits, internal pricing, and other MNC activities profoundly affect the exchange rate, too, by determining which currencies are actually exchanged. As major actors in international trade, MNCs' corporate strategies can also affect trade policy.

In the area of government revenues, MNCs often locate as much of their activities as possible in the areas where taxation is the lowest. Competition between countries for MNC operations follows, with the country asking for the least in taxes often winning, which means that all countries are forced to ask for less in taxes. This same mobility in terms of locating production allows MNCs to play a major role in broader macroeconomic policies, such as employment levels and overall performance of the economy.

Multinational corporations are also a possible resource. They are not only the purveyors of jobs or the source of taxes. These are things they obviously provide, because these are the very things that may cause them to move elsewhere. MNCs also possess technology. They control the technology both physically and legally. Because they hold patents on technology, they have the ability to monopolize its use. MNCs also control information and communication networks and often employ the latest in technology, and therefore their networks are quite advanced. Several MNCs have the capability to garner and assess economic information on a global basis.

MNCs also are often the masters of expertise. Large corporations are knowledgeable about their own activities and products, and often have impressive amounts of knowledge about other markets and political economic factors. In order to develop marketing strategies, corporations form profiles of consumer types and their locations. This information is quite detailed and often much better than government census material. Corporations know how to do certain things better than many governments because often they are more experienced than those governments. When a Third World country decides to build its first chemical plant, for instance, it has no first-hand expertise on this subject, whereas several large European or North American construction firms have built dozens of such plants. This expertise is important for doing jobs correctly and most cost-efficiently.

In this sense, MNCs not only pose problems for governments, but they also represent opportunities. Whether the MNCs are viewed as an opportunity or a threat depends on the balance of power between the government and the MNC. These relationships between MNCs and governments are true for both economically advanced countries and those countries just beginning to industrialize and develop their economic potential. The less economically advanced states, however, are more vulnerable to the actions of the MNCs. It isn't so much that the MNCs' power varies; rather, the governments of the North are better able to regulate the MNCs' activities than the countries of the South.

One of the obvious differences here, though, is that the economically less developed countries have different goals from those of the economically advanced countries. While both are concerned about taxes and employment levels, the less economically developed countries are also concerned with economic issues such as development and political issues surrounding the issue of nation-building (though Canadians often appear to have this problem, too), and they are more sensitive to foreign ownership.

Summary: Questions To Be Explored in the Cases

The questions we might pose about the international investment regime parallel those we asked about the evolution of the trade and monetary regimes. Why does the regime change when it does? Moreover, we will examine how the investment regime influences decisions in monetary affairs, especially when a country responds to a currency overhang (as explored in Chapters 13 and 17). We will also look at the debtors' views. Why would a state allow itself to become so indebted? How does a state respond to situations where it is deeply in debt? These are explored in Chapter 18, where Brazil's actions in the debt crisis are explored. Part III begins, however, with cases concerning the creation of a free trade regime in the nineteenth century.

Suggested Readings

Richard Caves, Harold Crookell, and J. P. Killing, "The Imperfect Market for Technology Licenses," *The Oxford Bulletin of Economics and Statistics* (August 1983), 249-67.

Benjamin J. Cohen, *In Whose Interest?* New Haven: Yale University Press, 1986.

John H. Dunning, *Explaining International Production*. London: Unwin Hyman, 1988.

Jeffry Frieden, "Capital Politics: Creditors and the International Political Economy," *Journal of Public Policy* 8, 3/4 (July-December 1988), 265-86.

Robert Gilpin, *U.S. Power and the Multinational Corporation*. New York: Basic Books, 1975.

Eric Helleiner, *States and the Reemergence of Global Finance*. Ithaca, NY: Cornell University Press, 1994.

Ethan Kapstein, *Governing the Global Economy*. Cambridge, Mass.: Harvard University Press, 1995.

Stephen D. Krasner, *Defending the National Interest*. Princeton, NJ: Princeton University Press, 1978.

Charles Lipson, *Standing Guard: Protecting Foreign Capital in the Nineteenth and Twentieth Centuries*. Berkeley: University of California Press, 1985.

Raymond Vernon, *Sovereignty at Bay*. New York: Basic Books, 1971.

Notes

1 Jeffry Frieden, "Capital Politics: Creditors and the International Political Economy," *Journal of Public Policy* 8, 3/4 (July-December 1988), 265-86.

2 Raymond Vernon, "International Investment and International Trade in the Product Cycle," *Quarterly Journal of Economics* 80, 2 (1966), 190-207.

3 Richard Caves, *Multinational Enterprise and Economic Growth* (New York: Cambridge University Press, 1982).

4 Charles P. Kindleberger, as quoted in Andrew Walter, *World Power and World Money* (Hertfordshire: Harvester Wheatsheaf, 1991), 12.

5 Ethan Kapstein, *Governing the Global Economy* (Cambridge, Mass.: Harvard University Press, 1994), 3-4.

6 Sam Huntington, "Transnational Organizations in World Politics," *World Politics* 25 (April 1973), 363, as quoted in Kapstein, *Governing the Global Economy*, 11-12.

7 Kenneth Waltz, *Theory of International Politics* (Menlo Park, NY: Addison-Wesley, 1979), 95.

8 See Jeffry Frieden, "The Economics of Intervention: American Overseas Investments and Relations with Underdeveloped Areas, 1890-1950," *Comparative Studies in Society and History* 31, 1 (1989), 55-80.

9 A Euromarket has been defined by Benjamin Cohen as "an organized market for foreign currency deposits." See B.J. Cohen, *In Whose Interest?* (New Haven: Yale University Press, 1986), 19. See the general discussion in Kapstein, *Governing the Global Economy*, 32.

10 Kapstein, *Governing the Global Economy*, 4.

11 Jeffry Frieden, "Invested Interests: The Politics of National Economic Policies in a World of Global Finance," *International Organization* 45, 4 (Autumn 1991), 425-51.

Part Three

TURNING POINTS IN
FOREIGN ECONOMIC
POLICY BEHAVIOUR

Ten

BRITAIN'S REPEAL
OF THE CORN LAWS

Britain's Mercantilist Past
and the Industrial Revolution

Mercantilism had been the dominant form of foreign economic policy followed throughout Europe since the advent of capitalism. Mercantilism was based on the assumption that wealth and power were synonymous.[1] Wealth could easily be turned into power (since armies were largely composed of mercenaries), and power could easily be translated into wealth (via conquest, especially of rich native peoples in North America, Africa, or Asia). Wealth was defined only in terms of precious metals such as gold and silver. Since there is a finite amount of these precious metals, people treated the pursuit of wealth as a zero-sum game—if one country got more gold, that left less for all the others. Since wealth and power were one and the same, foreign economic policies were geared to maintaining a positive balance of payments (i.e., an inflow of gold). Mercantilism entailed a set of policies designed to maintain an inward flow of money, but these policies were barriers to trade and international investment. In trying to prevent their neighbours from earning any money internationally, mercantilist countries were merely hurting themselves.

Britain had moved away from mercantilism in the 1780s, only to return to such policies during the wars with Napoleonic France. By the 1830s, however, the old pressures for trade liberalization re-emerged. These pressures resurfaced in a more sophisticated form, as the gains from trade were now better understood in economic models. Specifically, the works of David Ricardo illustrated in good liberal fashion how international trade and specialization in national comparative advantages could lead to a more efficient use of international resources. With greater overall production, someone had to be made better off through trade, since there was more to consume.

Britain's comparative advantage in the 1830s and 1840s lay in the production of manufactured goods. The development of domestic markets, the transition to full-blown capitalism, and the impetus of war production had caused Britain to enter the Industrial Revolution. Britain was the first to experience this shift, so in 1840 it was far ahead of other countries in using non-renewable resources (e.g., coal and iron) and capital embodied in machinery. Technologically, Britain stood on top. Following the then recent liberal ideas, Britain should trade manufactured goods for the import of raw materials. This was the lesson from Ricardo's theories on international trade, and it was a popular idea for the British capitalist class. The domestic market was being developed, but profits could also be made in foreign trade because British manufacturers' technical edge meant they could outcompete other producers. Profits could be increased if other countries would accept British exports.

Several significant domestic barriers remained, though. Britain's own mercantilist policies had limited all kinds of imports. In Britain as elsewhere, mercantilism protected inefficient sectors. One very important and well-protected area was agriculture. During the Napoleonic Wars, mercantilist legislation had been reasserted to stimulate home production of grain. During the wars, France had attempted to block European exports to Britain. Britain, in turn, took measures to make its economy self-sufficient, especially in food production. A set of regulations, known as the Corn Laws, established a floor price for grain (i.e., the laws made sure that the price of grain did not fall below a certain level). Anytime grain imports threatened to push prices down, tariffs were automatically applied to keep the price of grain high enough that farmers weren't hurt. This guaranteed British grain farmers a profit and kept them producing grain.

After the Napoleonic Wars had ended, debates over Britain's proper foreign economic policies resumed. While some elements of the mercantilist barriers were dismantled, new barriers were actually erected.[2] Meanwhile the Industrial Revolution, stimulated by the war effort, continued to alter the British economy and society. Britain's political institutions had not been changed in some time; pressure had been growing for political adaptations to bring Parliament in line with the economic changes. Where there had been only fields a century before, industrial cities had sprung up. Tens of thousands had left the countryside for the towns and cities. Yet parliamentary districts failed to reflect these changes. The reformers (a coalition of groups allied with one party, the Whigs) were finally able to push through the Reform Act of 1832. This Act redrew district boundaries, redistributing political power away from the conservative agricultural areas (dominated by the Tories) to the new industrial classes. (It is important to recognize that only a small portion of males could vote for Parliament at this time. The working class would not participate fully until universal male suffrage was adopted in 1918. The redistribution of political power, therefore, was merely between the capitalists in the agricultural sectors—largely aristocrats—and the new industrial capitalists.)

The leader of the conservatives, or Tories as they were called, was Sir Robert Peel. The conservatives received most of their political support from aristocrats and rural areas. Despite the Reform Act, they remained the single most powerful party in Parliament. Peel and others were concerned, however, that further pressures might build for greater democratic reforms. These same conservatives also stood to lose economically if the protectionist barriers were lowered and foreign grain competed against their own production. Yet as prime minister, Peel would be the one to enact the repeal of the Corn Laws—dividing his party and being forced out of office in the process.

The repeal of the Corn Laws was completed on 26 June 1846, and is seen as the final, conscious step in Britain's abandonment of mercantilism. Within a few years, the last remaining pieces of protectionist legislation were also removed.[3] Britain embraced foreign competition, trusting its economic future to the international market. British agriculture would survive, somewhat battered, by shifting into more specialized production. It represents the first time a major economic power would adopt free trade.

Systemic Theory: The Rise of a New Hegemonic Power?

From a realist perspective, Britain's adoption of freer trade merely reflected the new distribution of political and economic power in the international system. Britain had emerged victorious from the Napoleonic Wars and held the necessary ingredients for dominating the international political economy. Militarily, the country commanded the world's most powerful navy and also controlled a system of bases strung around the globe that enabled the Royal Navy to maintain fleets wherever necessary. While the British Army was not so large, it had played a pivotal role in the defeat of France. Economically, Britain alone was industrialized.[4]

According to this perspective, Britain was pursuing power by liberalizing international trade.[5] As Krasner put it, "a hegemonic distribution of potential economic power is likely to result in an open trading structure."[6] Moreover, the argument is that the hegemonic power will create and maintain an open international economic order. Krasner was careful to elaborate his view of hegemony in largely economic terms. As indicators of the distribution of economic power, he used per capita income, aggregate size of the economy, share of world trade, and share of world investment. In each of these categories (except for size of the economy), Britain led the world in the nineteenth century. According to the realists, this structural position provides both the interest and the capability to shape the international political economy. Britain should be seen to follow foreign economic policies that would ensure it stayed ahead of other countries in terms of economic and political power. Since Britain stood to gain from free trade because it was in a unique position in the world economy, its own trade liberalization was an effort to maintain its dominance.[7]

Several questions arise with this interpretation of events, however. First, the timing seems questionable. After all, Britain stood militarily victorious in 1815, yet the economic policy associated with Britain's new structural position wasn't enacted until the 1840s.[8] Second, Britain's military power was waning over this time; that is, Britain's naval dominance fell between 1815 and 1846, only to be reasserted later. Third, the trade liberalization was unilateral. Britain was not sending out ambassadors to negotiate new trade treaties, at least not at first. (To be fair, Britain was using force to open up trade with weaker powers outside of Europe.)

Was Britain acting hegemonically when it unilaterally lowered its tariffs? What sort of leadership was this, if no international negotiations were undertaken?[9] Peel's own writings, however, do not mention any concern with foreign responses to Britain's actions.[10] Since these sorts of details are missing in the support of the systemic arguments, numerous counter-arguments from the other levels of analysis have been constructed.

Domestic Politics: Economic Interests, Parliamentary Reforms, and the League

The alternative interpretation most often proposed can be found at the level of domestic politics. Timothy McKeown, for instance, argues that the most parsimonious explanation for the repeal of the Corn Laws can be found without examining the structure of the international system.[11] Instead, McKeown and others have argued that the repeal of the Corn Laws can be understood purely in domestic political terms—though one must first consider the economic consequences of trade liberalization to understand the motivations for the different political groups within Britain.

Labour wanted to repeal the Corn Laws because after trade liberalization, cheaper grain could enter the country. Workers would be able to spend less on food and more on other goods. The industrial capitalists wanted to eliminate the Corn Laws for two reasons. First, domestically, the end of the Corn Laws would mean cheaper grain. The industrialists wanted cheaper food prices, because cheaper food prices meant they could reduce the wages they paid to labour. Moreover, since food was a major expense for most workers, falling food prices might placate labour for some time.

The second reason the industrial capitalists wanted an end to the Corn Laws reflects the industrialists' international interests. Foodstuffs that could be more efficiently grown in the Middle West of the U.S. or in Canada, or on the plains of Eastern Europe, could be imported; these imports would be paid for by the greater export of manufactured goods. Meanwhile, the aristocrats who owned much of the land remained in favour of maintaining the Corn Laws. The Corn Laws were supporting the price of their output and thus maintained their incomes. This illustrates how specialization in trade would reflect the endowments of the factors of production (as in the H-O model), but we can also see operative here a redistribution of domestic wealth through international trade (Stolper-Samuelson theorem).

Britain was endowed with several factors of production giving it an edge in the area of industrial manufacturing. The country held the premier position in terms of capital per worker, which manifested itself in low interest rates, extensive use of machinery, and higher technology. Britain's capital-intensive service sectors also did a booming business, especially banking, insurance, and the financing of trade. These economic sectors did well in international competition by using the cheap capital available to them, just as the H-O model would have predicted. Moreover, freer trade increased the profits going to these sectors and reduced those flowing to agriculture—just as the Stolper-Samuelson theorem would have predicted.[12]

Understanding the interests of the various groups is not enough to explain political outcomes, however. At least two other steps have to be undertaken. First, how easily can each group organize its members for political action? Second, once organized, how do these groups interact with political institutions to affect policy? In this case, the aristocrats held the upper hand. Only aristocratic landholders sat in the House of Lords, and at that time the House of Lords still played an important role in the passage of legislation. Also, aristocrats used their local influence and patronage to control voting for the House of Commons.

One argument holds that the repeal of the Corn Laws was only possible because the political power of the old landed aristocracy was lessened through a revision of political institutions. Specifically, the aristocrats' power in Parliament declined after the Reform Act of 1832. Since the Reform Act altered the pattern of representation in the House of Commons and redistributed political power to the new industrial capitalists, some have suggested that this enabled the industrial sector to drive policy to its advantage. The Reform Act redrew district boundaries to take account of demographic changes driven by the ongoing economic revolution, reflecting the rise of the new industrial towns. It was only after this political shift that we see the effective pressure for an alteration in Britain's foreign economic policy.

There are several problems with this account, however. A Tory administration carried out the repeal, so the Tories would be on the wrong side in the dispute. Why would Tories have voted for the changes? Two competing alternative explanations, which attempt to provide a deeper understanding of the situation, have recently been put forth. The first, developed by Cheryl Schonhardt-Bailey, argues that the economic divisions so easily identified in theory were blurred in reality.[13] Schonhardt-Bailey executed extensive field research to develop economic profiles of particular voting districts. Her insight was that aristocrats played a double role—they earned an income from their land, but at the time they were also the major holders of investment capital in Britain. They were the investors backing many of the new industrial enterprises. They would therefore have mixed motives in any questions concerning trade liberalization.

In the other new rendering of these political events, Michael Lusztig places the repeal of the Corn Laws within the broader context of domestic politics.[14] The prime mover in the policy game was the prime minister, Robert Peel. Trade was merely one issue among several, including pressures for political reform and crop failure in Ireland. For Lusztig, Peel was primarily motivated by a wish to defend Britain's existing political institutional structure from new pressures for reform. Some reform had already taken place. The Reform Act of 1832 had changed some of the rules respecting parliamentary elections, but by and large the revisions had not altered the power of relative groups represented within Parliament.

The Anti-Corn Law League was formed to attack the series of laws protecting agriculture from foreign competition. By itself, the League was not powerful enough to overturn the institutional structure—yet Peel worried that it might have the ability to increase its power by mobilizing other groups interested in reform. A number of such disgruntled groups existed: the urban working class was not yet allowed to vote, many of the workers in the cities had been forced off rural land (and thus were unhappy about the impact of industrialization on their lives), and several groups were displeased with the political power exercised by the House of Lords.

Much of Lusztig's interpretation relies on a close analysis of Peel's bargaining and political tactics. In discussions over how to respond to the crop failure in Ireland, Peel suggested it was time to repeal the Corn Laws. Peel's Tory Party was split. Whig leader Lord John Russell placed his party squarely behind the notion of repeal. Yet without the Tories in both the House of Commons and the House of Lords in full support, no one believed Peel could get the repeal passed. Peel then pulled off a risky political ploy. He resigned—throwing the ball into Lord Russell's court. Yet Peel knew full well that Russell did not have the support in the House of Lords to get repeal accepted. After Russell was unable to gather enough support to be an effective prime minister, Peel resumed the prime ministership (having illustrated that he was the only person likely to cobble together the coalition to achieve repeal).

For Peel to get the repeal through the House of Lords, he had to use his close connections with the key conservative leader in the upper house, the Duke of Wellington. Peel did so by underlining the likelihood of some sort of retribution against the House of Lords if it stood in the way of such a publicly popular bill. Thus, in the Commons Peel used the Whigs' support, however many of the Tories he could bring along, and the members of the Anti-Corn Law League, plus the conservatives in the House of Lords led by the Duke of Wellington, to repeal the Corn Laws. But such tactics had a price—within days Peel's government fell to attacks from Tory back-benchers. The Tories were split over the wisdom of his manoeuvres, and many viewed the repeal of the Corn Laws as too great a sacrifice, regardless of the alternatives.

Lusztig's account differs from Schonhardt-Bailey's because he emphasizes the role of political parties and the "nesting" of the tariff issue within a broader political game. Lusztig also suggests some of the explanation rests with Peel himself and his attitudes towards change.

Bureaucratic Politics: Tariffs as Revenue

Another factor is the role of tariffs in generating revenues for the government. Britain had been at war against France for some twenty years by 1815. To conduct their war effort, the British government incurred extensive debts. In the years between 1815 and 1846, this debt was reconsolidated but it remained large. The government's primary source of revenue was the tariff. Any reduction in the tariff would have tremendous consequences for the government's ability to pay down this debt. In fact, most European governments raised the bulk of their funds through the tariff. High tariffs on a small range of goods (such as tea, coffee, sugar, and tobacco) were the source of most revenue, so dumping tariffs on those few goods was especially risky, since that might destroy the government's major source of funds.

Reducing tariffs therefore involved not only those interested in trade policy, but also the Treasury. In Britain, the government was only willing to drop tariffs because it could reinstitute the income tax. This was somewhat unpopular, however, because the income tax had never been used in peacetime in Britain before then. People associated the income tax with emergencies.[15] Without this ability to substitute a new revenue stream, Britain would have had a hard time altering the tariff.

The budget of 1842 included several new measures, including the standardization, simplification, and a minor reduction of tariffs. These changes caused the Treasury to anticipate a fall in the government's annual revenues of £3,780,000. The reintroduction of the income tax was supposed to counter the shortfall. The actual revenues lost that year turned out to be around £3,979,000, due to an error in the timing of the collection of taxes. Once this error was corrected, the next year's budget moved into surplus to the tune of £4,165,000.[16] This set the stage for tariff reform. To a certain extent, the fiscal changes prevented an impending bureaucratic struggle, for the Treasury would otherwise have blocked tariff reform. The bureaucratic politics aspect of the tariff reform is largely missing as a result.

Individual Level: Peel the Conservative Reformer?

Lusztig comments that Peel was concerned with the likelihood of grievances among the lower classes leading to some sort of radical (if not even revolutionary) change in Britain. The aristocratic class still enjoyed incredible privileges. The experiences on the Continent—especially in France, where revolution had occurred in 1789 and then a second serious uprising erupted in 1830—sent a message that Peel thought should have been clear to Britain's élite: they had a duty to respond to the problems of society's aggrieved. If they did not, they risked the consequences.

Lusztig argues that Peel feared further democratic changes in Britain. The Reform Act of 1832 was potentially the beginning of a series of such reforms. To head off such changes, Peel thought it was important for the élite to make some sort of economic sacrifices that might improve the average person's lot in life. By dropping protection of aristocratic estates' agricultural production, food prices could be lowered. Such logic can be found expressed in Peel's speeches to Parliament. These views were not unanimously held, however. Peel's vision was hardly popular among the Tories, which is why the repeal of the Corn Laws cost him his office. Lusztig is suggesting that if someone else had been leader of the Tories, the calculations might have been quite different. Certainly the political manoeuvring Lusztig details would have been undertaken in a somewhat different fashion.

The Consequences of the Repeal of the Corn Laws

The repeal of the Corn Laws was just about the last step in making Britain's trade "free"—in 1849 the last of the Navigation Acts was repealed. In 1840 the number of items that had duties placed on them had been 1,146; by 1860 that number was down to 48—and of these only 36 were to protect British producers from foreign competition, with the other 12 being luxury goods the government levied customs on to raise money.[17]

Peel's domestic political strategy seems to have worked. When liberal revolutionary challenges swept the governments of Europe in 1848, similar disruptions failed to materialize in Britain. Peel, according to Richard Cobden, noted that Britain's government had already responded to popular pressures—even if those pressures hadn't been expressed through direct political or electoral channels.

One of the first reactions to Britain's unilateral moves was an implicit deal between the United States and Britain concerning the repeal of the Corn Laws. The U.S. watched to see what the British were doing in 1846, and when Britain actually repealed the Corn Laws, the U.S. moved to lower tariffs on manufactures. The Americans were willing to do this because they now believed they could successfully export grain to Britain. This new lower American tariff was the Walker Tariff. Russian grain exports to Britain surged after 1846 as well.

Britain's unilateral actions, then, could be seen as one possible way of encouraging others to lower their tariffs unilaterally: Britain offered its domestic market to other countries (unilaterally) and hoped these other countries would realize their comparative advantage through free trade. The only countries that readily moved in this direction, though, were those that already specialized in agricultural production, such as the U.S. (where the South produced cotton for the British textile mills and the West produced grain to feed British cities) and Denmark (which produced ham, cheese, and butter for export to Britain). It would take more direct negotiations to spark a widespread opening of the European markets. Such negotiations would begin with Britain and France, and lead to the Cobden-Chevalier Treaty in 1860, as discussed in the next chapter.

Suggested Readings

Gary Anderson and Robert Tollison, "Ideology, Interest Groups and the Repeal of the Corn Laws," in Charles Rowley, Robert Tollison, and Gordon Tullock, eds. *The Political Economy of Rent-Seeking.* Boston: Kluwer Academic, 1988, 199-216.

David Eastwood, "Peel and the Tory Party Reconsidered," *History Today* 42 (March 1992), 27-33.

A.C. Howe, "Free Trade and the City of London, c. 1820-1870," *History* 77, 251 (October 1992), 391-410.

Douglas Irwin, "The Welfare Effects of British Free Trade: Debate and Evidence from the 1840s," *Journal of Political Economy* 96, 6 (December 1988), 1142-64.

Michael Lusztig, "Solving Peel's Puzzle: Repeal of the Corn Laws and Institutional Preservation," *Comparative Politics* 27, 4 (July 1995), 393-408.

Timothy McKeown, "Hegemonic Stability Theory and Nineteenth Century Tariff Levels in Europe," *International Organization* 37, 1 (Winter 1983), 73-92.

206 » TURNING POINTS

Timothy McKeown, "The Politics of Corn Law Repeal and Theories of Commercial Policy," *British Journal of Political Science* 19 (July 1989), 353-80.

John Vincent Nye, "The Myth of Free-Trade Britain and Fortress France: Tariffs and Trade in the Nineteenth Century," *Journal of Economic History* 51, 1 (March 1991), 23-46.

Cheryl Schonhardt-Bailey, "Specific Factors, Capital Markets, Portfolio Diversification and Free Trade: Domestic Determinants of the Repeal of the Corn Laws," *World Politics* 43 (1991), 345-69.

Scott James and David Lake, "The Second Face of Hegemony: Britain's Repeal of the Corn Laws and the American Walker Tariff of 1846," *International Organization* 43, 1 (Winter 1989), 1-29.

Richard Francis Spall Jr., "Free Trade, Foreign Relations, and the Anti-Corn Law League," *International History Review* 10, 3 (August 1988), 405-32.

Jeffrey Williamson, "The Impact of the Corn Laws Just Prior to Repeal," *Explorations in Economic Literature* 27 (1990), 123-56.

Notes

1   For the best discussions of the characteristics of mercantilism, see Jacob Viner, "Power versus Plenty as Objectives of Foreign Policy in the Seventeenth and Eighteenth Centuries," *World Politics* 1, 1 (October 1948), 1-29; Eli Heckscher, *Mercantilism*, 2 vols. (London: George Allen & Unwin, 1934).

2   For example, the Reciprocity of Duties Act was enacted in 1823.

3   Most notably, the last of the Navigation Acts controlling the use of shipping was taken down in 1849.

4   Robert Gilpin, *U.S. Power and the Multinational Corporation* (New York: Basic Books, 1975), 81-82. Also see Stephen Krasner, "State Power and the Structure of International Trade," *World Politics* 28 (April 1976), 317-47.

5   We should note how the modern world-system perspective largely parallels the arguments of the realists, with only a few differences. The major differences involve the motivations for Britain's actions. From the modern world-system perspective, Britain was acting at the behest of its most important capitalists—the new industrialists. Britain chose free trade as the best policy to implement in order to restructure trading relations so that Britain's capitalists would benefit. Otherwise, this perspective also emphasizes Britain's military and strategic power.

6   Krasner, "State Power and the Structure of International Trade."

7   It is worth noting that one contemporary observer, Friedrich List, agreed with this assessment. List proposed that German states continue with mercantilism to counter Britain's attempt to dominate the international political economy. See List, *The National System of Political Economy* (New York: Augustus M. Kelley, 1966; originally written 1841-44).

8   This and other questions are raised by Timothy McKeown. See McKeown, "Hegemonic Stability Theory and Nineteenth Century Tariff Levels in Europe," *International Organization* 37, 1 (Winter 1983), 73-92.

9   This is simply restating the question driving the article by Scott James and David Lake, "The Second Face of Hegemony: Britain's Repeal of the Corn Laws and the American Walker Tariff of 1846," *International Organization* 43, 1 (Winter 1989), 3.

10 See Michael Lusztig, "Solving Peel's Puzzle: Repeal of the Corn Laws and Institutional Preservation," *Comparative Politics* 27, 4 (July 1995), 393-408.

11 McKeown, "Hegemonic Stability Theory and Nineteenth Century Tariff Levels in Europe."

12 For more details, see Mark R. Brawley, *Liberal Leadership: Great Powers and Their Challengers in Peace and War* (Ithaca, NY: Cornell University Press, 1993).

13 Cheryl Schonhardt-Bailey, "Specific Factors, Capital Markets, Portfolio Diversification and Free Trade: Domestic Determinants of the Repeal of the Corn Laws," *World Politics* 43 (1991), 345-69.

14 Lusztig, "Solving Peel's Puzzle."

15 Arthur A. Stein, "The Hegemon's Dilemma: Great Britain, the United States, and Economic Order," *International Organization* 38, 2 (Spring 1984), 355-86.

16 J.F. Rees, *A Short Fiscal and Financial History of England* (London: Methuen, 1921), 90-92.

17 See Trevor May, *An Economic and Social History of Britain, 1760-1970* (New York: Longman, 1987), 184-85. This view is contested by several recent accounts, which argue that protectionist measures remained effective. See John Vincent Nye, "The Myth of Free-Trade Britain and Fortress France: Tariffs and Trade in the Nineteenth Century," *Journal of Economic History* 51, 1 (March 1991), 23-46; Patrick K. O'Brien and Geoffrey Pigman, "Free Trade, British Hegemony, and the International Economic Order in the Nineteenth Century," *Review of International Studies* 18 (April 1992), 89-113.

Eleven

THE COBDEN–CHEVALIER TREATY

In the previous chapter, we saw how Britain changed its own foreign economic policy in favour of free trade. Also, there was brief mention of some of the responses from other states. Yet overall, the impact of the repeal of the Corn Laws was limited to changes in the content and pattern of trade flows. Other states adjusted their exports and imports as Britain specialized in industrial production, but most states were reluctant to abandon mercantilism. It would be impossible to characterize the international trade regime as free. Other countries needed more encouragement and prodding to open up their trade and lower their tariffs.

One of the first specific missions sent by Britain to negotiate lower tariffs after the repeal of the Corn Laws was when Richard Cobden was sent to France in 1860. Behind the scenes contacts had been made many years before, so that the setting was ripe for a trade deal between the two countries. Napoleon III had recently been proclaimed the Emperor of France, though his actions were still constrained by Parliament. Napoleon III was interested in establishing closer commercial ties with Britain, though his motivations remain the subject of much debate. The French government agreed to lower tariffs on British goods, even though this was not popular in France. Napoleon III had in fact been unable to pass the tariff through his own Parliament until he had signed the deal with Britain. Moreover, the agreement had some specific strategic ramifications. These aspects of the treaty's negotiations provide the seeds for several different theoretical interpretations of the event.

Systemic Theory:
The Lure of British Power

The realists naturally focus on the role of Britain in these negotiations.[1] Realists would expect to see Britain taking the initiative, attempting to construct a free trade regime. Repeal of the Corn Laws had been a unilateral act, but now, with Cobden's mission to France, Britain was taking direct action. Moreover, realists point to the role of British power in achieving the results desired. Rather than seeing Britain's power purely in coercive terms, the realists suggest that this power may have made Britain an attractive ally. France, in short, wanted Britain as a political ally and was willing to make trade concessions in order to develop a closer relationship.

In return for France's lower tariffs on British manufactures, Napoleon III negotiated Britain's acquiescence to French imperial ambitions. Napoleon III was letting Britain get the economic deal it desired as long as Britain promised to accept Napoleon III's military adventures.[2] Napoleon III had ordered his army to invade northern Italy to attack the Austro-Hungarian Empire's Italian provinces. Britain remained neutral. (It is worth noting that Napoleon III tried to achieve glory in Italy, but in the end military affairs were his undoing. France's defeat in the Franco-Prussian War in 1870 ended his rule.)

Napoleon III had important reasons to seek Britain's favour. Austria had been defeated at the battle of Solferino in the previous months and peace negotiations were under way in Zurich when the possibility of a commercial treaty was raised. Britain wanted Italy to become a unified state, and therefore viewed Napoleon III's moves in the annexation of Savoy with great suspicion and disapproval.[3] When one Englishman asked Michel Chevalier, an academic and adviser to the French government, if the 1860 commercial treaty had been signed simply to reconcile Britain to Napoleon's moves in Italy, Chevalier responded "Utterly false." Chevalier's position was that the treaty could not have been a ploy on the part of Napoleon III because Chevalier himself had initiated the talks via communications with Cobden in Britain and with members of Napoleon's cabinet. Chevalier realized, however, that Napoleon III may well have thrown his support behind the treaty in order to improve relations with Britain.[4]

This was one example of how Britain could use military power in a positive sense to support those who were willing to make economic deals. This was done explicitly in the case of the Cobden-Chevalier Treaty, but was done implicitly as well. Spain had been overrun by France during the Napoleonic Wars, and during that time and right afterwards, some of Spain's American colonies rebelled and became independent countries. The U.S. enunciated the Monroe Doctrine, claiming the Western hemisphere should be kept separate politically from the conflicts and problems back in Europe, but there really wasn't much the U.S. could do to back that up. Instead, Britain prevented outside interference with the new South American states, which Britain was able to back up with force thanks to the strength of the Royal Navy. The British were quite willing to do this because these South American countries were basically exporters of raw materials and importers of manufactures. It was in Britain's economic interest to keep these countries independent and outside of any other country's closed mercantilist system.

Britain, of course, could and did use military power in the more obvious coercive sense—forcing countries to adopt free trade. Those same South American countries could be bullied by the Royal Navy to loosen up their trade barriers. Among the more egregious examples was the Opium War against China. Opium was produced in the British colony of India and sent to China, where it was being consumed in ever larger proportions. This was a great money-earner, but one that clearly was costly to the Chinese economy and society. The Chinese government decided this was unacceptable and therefore barred the importation of opium. British ships and troops attacked China. Britain forced Chinese ports to accept opium shipments. The Opium War was perhaps one of the crudest exercises of power, but there are other examples of British policy that weren't quite so brutal or when trade was much less morally troublesome and more even.

Therefore, realists tend not to worry about the domestic changes in Britain—they instead focus on the importance of the Napoleonic Wars (ending in 1815) when Britain emerges as the dominant power in the system. Britain's empire circled the globe. (It was said in those days that "the sun never sets on the British Empire.") The Royal Navy was the strongest in the world and could project British power virtually anywhere. The realists see this political position develop and argue that it enabled Britain to make the rules of the international economy and get everyone else to agree to those rules.

The realists go on to argue that Britain's unique position meant that it would establish a particular set of international rules. Realists, of course, claim that states maximize their power; Britain should therefore set up a system with rules to its own benefit. The British had a technological lead, and with this headstart they were quick to desire free and open international economic competition, knowing that they would dominate.

The Domestic Level: The Interplay of Sectoral Interests and Political Institutions

Since it considers both the domestic and system levels, the modern world-system interpretation for this case actually spans the most important aspects of the realist view and a more sophisticated liberal interpretation. The modern world-system theorists look first at the domestic politics within Britain, see the rise of the capitalist class economically and politically, and then centre their attention on how the British bourgeoisie could control Britain's foreign economic policies to further their material aims. This approach should also sound similar to the realists' arguments, since in its explanation of systemic changes it, too, emphasizes Britain's international role. Of course, not all the bourgeoisie in Britain gained from free trade, and given Schonhardt-Bailey's arguments noted in the previous chapter that the aristocracy and the bourgeoisie were intermixed, it is difficult to see a class acting here. Instead, part of the British bourgeoisie was getting its way despite the wishes of other sections of the bourgeoisie. The liberal view therefore has some advantages over a class-based analysis.

The typical domestic politics explanation of trade liberalization would begin with the Stolper-Samuelson theorem. Having identified which groups should benefit from free trade and which should lose, we would then consider how each group organized and then interacted with domestic political institutions to set policy. This argument does not work well for explaining French policy in this case. While some sectoral interests stood to gain from free trade, these were on the whole much less well organized and much weaker than those interests that feared the impact of liberalization.

There was in France a long prior tradition of public support for protectionist policies.[5] Agricultural groups were the most important. French agriculture was dominated by small landholders, since the Revolution had eliminated many of the large landholders. As one contemporary, Auguste Arnauné, put it in 1848: "Our land is in the hands of a peasant democracy. The duties on the products of agriculture and on livestock seem to be imposed, not in the interest of a few great landowners, but for the benefit of a whole nation of farmers, both large and small."[6]

The big negotiating point for France, therefore, was the British wine tariff. While Britain had unilaterally reduced or eliminated most tariffs, some had been retained for revenue purposes. Wine and alcoholic spirits were among the important goods on which Britain still imposed a tariff. These were obviously important export items for France. Convincing Britain to reduce those tariffs became an important issue in the negotiations.[7] In the end, Britain kept some small tariffs on wine and spirits, but it was willing to exchange lower tariffs on these items for France's reductions on many of its tariffs.[8] On the other hand, French officials were also interested in placating consumer demands. To bring the emergent industrial sector on board, it was important to get cheap access to British coal. Thus the French asked for Britain to agree to prohibit any limits on the export of coal in the future and to prohibit any export duties on coal.[9]

The French negotiators were very interested in garnering benefits they could use to construct a pro-free trade coalition. They knew they would have problems in this, since the government had already failed in prior efforts to lower French tariffs unilaterally. The opposition from the agricultural sectors (which needed some sort of benefits in terms of new markets), artisans (the hand-manufacturing sectors), and the newly emerging industrial sectors (which were afraid of British competition) had previously blocked the government's attempts to reduce tariffs.

As a result, Napoleon III's government carried out its negotiations with Britain in secret. Precautions were taken to prevent public discussion of the treaty within France until after it had been completed. If the public had been aware of the talks, protests would have erupted, the Chamber of Deputies would have become a battlefield for the protectionists to air their views, and in all likelihood the treaty would have never come to pass.[10] The negotiations only took about three months, but then the deal had to be sold to both governments and the publics. The domestic ratification process in the two countries would take nearly a year.[11]

Once the deal had been put together it was made public. In France, the opponents demanded and received a public inquiry. The inquiry in the Chamber of Deputies was stretched out and in the end the protectionists had their say, but the process seemed to take the wind out of the protectionists' sails. They were forced into publicly declaring their inability to compete, a step that few were willing to take in the end. Moreover, the treaty did include aspects meant to weaken some of the opposition, and these measures may have had some impact. Ultimately, as well, the opposition would have had a tough time overturning the treaty in any event.

The institutional structure of the French political system had introduced an avenue for Napoleon's government to circumvent most parliamentary powers. Arnauné, in the quote above, was bemoaning the fact that the peasants dominated the democratic political institutions in 1848. Institutional arrangements had changed within a short time. In December 1852 the Second Empire was proclaimed. Napoleon III was given the title of Prince-President, which brought with it special powers (all through popular measures). Parliament was willing to hand over discretionary powers in several areas, which included important responsibilities in foreign affairs. Already, with the Constitution adopted on 14 January 1852, the then Prince-President had been given the power to sign treaties. The role of the Chamber of Deputies and Senate had not been clear, however—would they retain the right to ratify deals the Prince-President had signed? Once Napoleon III was made Emperor, the Senate approved (64-7), giving the Emperor power to sign commercial treaties without the assent of the Parliament.[12]

This introduces the possibility that the Cobden-Chevalier Treaty resulted from a domestic strategy employed by Napoleon III's government. If the government was convinced that free trade was the best policy for France, yet the public opposition was too fierce to get the policy approved in Parliament, unilateral free trade was not a possibility. But the government could turn to the area where it had autonomy from Parliament—foreign affairs. Free trade was therefore enacted by treaty rather than through domestic legislation. This interpretation raises some interesting questions, however. How do we explain the government's preference for free trade, if it wasn't a reflection of domestic interests? To explain that, we need to consider bureaucratic politics, individual personalities within the French government, and the force of ideas.

The Budget and the Evidence of Bureaucratic Politics

In Britain, the biggest potential bureaucratic fight with the repeal of the Corn Laws had revolved around the budget. Most of the tariffs had been removed, and the income tax put in place. When the Cobden-Chevalier Treaty eliminated some of the last tariffs, those that had specifically been left to generate revenues, the income tax had to be increased. Enough people in Britain stood to gain from the increased trade that this was acceptable. Napoleon III's problem was different, for he had to sell the tariff deal to the public.

Once again, the budgetary situation had to be favourable for the government to be willing to reduce its own revenues. The bureaucratic politics battle was essentially missing here, as well. As long as the budget allocations to the different departments were not upset, few internal battles arose. The fights within the cabinet reflected personal beliefs, not bureaucratic interests. Yet the French government had to go even further in its budgetary changes than the British had had to in 1846. The treaty was sold to the French public by packaging it with various measures aimed to assist in the adjustments associated with specialization for trade. The package included money for reforestation in agricultural areas, assistance in improvement of drainage for better agricultural production, funds for the construction of canals and railroads, and government loans to industry.[13]

Interestingly, the shortness of the war with Austria had opened up the possibilities of such assistance to Napoleon III's administration. The government had borrowed for the war in 1859. The government's loan had been oversubscribed (that is, people were willing to lend more money than the government required), so the government had borrowed extra funds. The war in Italy went well, and the government did not need to spend all it had borrowed for this purpose. With abundant resources on hand, the government could compensate those who might be hurt by the trade liberalization. Most importantly, it could make cheap loans to industry, the one sector most likely to feel the pressure of competition from Britain.[14] While this evidence helps clarify how the government enacted its policy, it still does not provide insight into why the government preferred free trade in the first place.

Individual Level: The Ideology of Cobden and Chevalier

Once we turn to the individual level of analysis, explanations emphasize the role of knowledge, in particular, the spread of the perception that free trade was mutually beneficial. As people came to understand this, after Adam Smith and David Ricardo had written and explained how free trade works, free trade became the dominant policy. Naturally, the analysis turns to the particular individuals involved in arranging the negotiations. Richard Cobden, the chief British negotiator, had clearly been a powerful proponent of liberal ideology for several decades.[15] Cobden had played a critical role in the repeal of the Corn Laws.

On the French side, an important role was played by Michel Chevalier. Chevalier was a professor at the Collège de France. From his academic post he spoke out constantly about the benefits of free trade. He had already enjoyed a brief career as a politician, though the unpopularity of free trade had prevented this from being much of a success. In 1845, Chevalier had been elected to the Chamber of Deputies (for the Department of Aveyron). He spoke passionately in favour of free trade. In the next election, a competing candidate ran on a protectionist platform and easily defeated him.[16]

What gives particular power to the individual level of analysis in this case are the close connections between the two negotiators. Cobden and Chevalier had met in 1846, when Cobden was conducting an international tour in the wake of the repeal of the Corn Laws. Cobden was basking in the glory of his political success and other liberals listened intently to his advice. From that point on, Chevalier and Cobden exchanged letters. In short, they knew each other quite well, not simply from reputation. From their letters we can surmise that Chevalier was the true initiator of the discussions leading up to the treaty. In his letters from 1856, we see him transmitting his specific ideas on a treaty between the two countries.[17]

Chevalier did not hold an official post and therefore had little role in the negotiations once they began. His role was behind the scenes.[18] On the French side, the most important individual would undoubtedly have to be Napoleon III himself. Without his support the treaty could never have been signed. Yet it is unclear as to whether Napoleon III believed in the mutual benefits of free trade or merely saw the treaty as part of a broader international strategy involving his imperial ambitions.

Another important sign of the roles individuals can play can be found in the intrigues within the French cabinet. Walewski, the Foreign Minister, opposed Napoleon III's goals in Italy. Walewski was also leary of any deals with the British and apparently was a believer in protectionism. He had to be excluded from the negotiations completely. Baroche, the Minister of Commerce, was in favour of some liberalization. He supported both Napoleon III's policy towards Italy and the commercial treaty with Britain. Within two weeks of Walewski's discovery of the secret negotiations with Britain, Baroche was brought in to replace Walewski as Minister of Foreign Affairs.[19] Walewski's removal was to assure that the right individuals were in control of the key positions within the cabinet. In this case, idiosyncratic personalities mattered more than official roles.

An Early Constructivist Interpretation? The Power of Liberalism as an Ideology

One of the most well-known interpretations of the Cobden-Chevalier Treaty and its consequences comes from Charles Kindleberger.[20] Kindleberger examines the roles of sectoral pressures, British power, and individuals in the French decision to engage in these negotiations. He finds evidence that all could have played a part. Yet he is also interested in explaining why other states chose to pursue free trade in the same period.

To explain the French decision, but also the British decision to repeal the Corn Laws and the decisions of the German states and the Netherlands to pursue free trade a short time later, Kindleberger reaches for a broader causal factor. The politics within each country differed, both in terms of the arrangement of proponents and opponents of trade liberalization and in terms of political institutional arrangements. For Kindleberger, the fact that all turned to the same policy at roughly the same time could best be explained by a single force sweeping through Europe: the power of liberalism as an ideology. Liberal practices were new and appealing since they seemed to be working so well for Britain.

The only problems with this explanation, unfortunately, are difficult to resolve. On the one hand, this explanation is difficult to falsify. People must have believed in the efficacy of liberal policies if they chose to pursue them;

thus their beliefs in these ideas had to matter somewhat. Did they follow these beliefs against their own economic interests? That would be hard to show, since liberalism argues that all benefit from free trade in the long run. Second, this explanation only works with the change occurring in one direction—the rise of free trade. If free trade spread because of the power of liberal ideas, why didn't states stick with liberalism? What explains the defection of states from the free trade regime? After all, the first serious protectionist barriers were re-erected at the end of the 1870s—less than a quarter of a century after free trade had swept across Europe.

The Consequences of the Cobden-Chevalier Treaty

The one particular event that signals the shift of the international system towards freer trade was the Cobden-Chevalier Treaty. It is worth explaining how this treaty sparked the wider changes within Europe. When Britain and France signed the treaty, they negotiated and agreed to lower tariffs on a whole number of items. Moreover, the treaty was written in such a way that it could easily be extended to third parties.[21] In so doing, the changes were transmitted into other international relationships through the most-favoured-nation clauses in existing trade treaties.

"Most-favoured-nation" is a designation in trade treaties meaning the country holding this status gets the same treatment as the third party with the best existing trade deal. MFN status traditionally comes in two forms—conditional and unconditional. Conditional MFN status says that concessions given to one country are only extended to others if they take steps to earn the concessions. For example, assume that France and Belgium have a trade treaty that grants Belgium conditional MFN status on French tariffs on coal. Britain and France later negotiate the Cobden-Chevalier Treaty, and as part of that, Britain wants to export more coal to France. Britain negotiates a lower French tariff on coal in return for lower British tariffs on French wines. Belgium would have the right, then, to use the lower French tariff on coal, as long as Belgium also took the lower tariff on wine imports. That would be an example of how conditional MFN clauses can spread the results of bilateral negotiations to third parties.

Unconditional MFN works much more simply. Assume Belgium had unconditional MFN status with France. As soon as Britain and France agree to lower the French tariff on coal, Belgium can use the new low tariff. With unconditional MFN, Belgium can use the tariffs at the same rate as the most favoured nation's tariff without ever having to make any concessions.

In 1860, many European countries were linked in trade treaties with MFN clauses, but since tariffs were only going up the MFN clauses had no positive impact. When the Cobden-Chevalier Treaty was signed, the MFN clauses served to spread the impact of liberalization. Because Britain and France signed a treaty lowering tariffs on an extensive range of important goods, and they were already linked to third parties through these MFN clauses, changes occurred throughout these relationships. Tariffs governing trade among many European countries were reduced as a result of a chain reaction. Within a short time, most of the major European governments were practising free trade—the international trade regime had been transformed. Yet, as noted in the previous section, this free trade regime did not last long. The reasons for some of these defections are addressed in the next chapter.

Suggested Readings

Peter Cain, "Capitalism, War and Internationalism in the Thought of Richard Cobden," *British Journal of International Studies* 5, 3 (October 1979), 229-47.

Charles P. Kindleberger, "The Rise of Free Trade in Western Europe," *Journal of Economic History* 35, 1 (March 1975), 20-55.

Barrie M. Ratcliffe, "Napoleon and the Anglo-French Commercial Treaty of 1860: A Reconsideration," *Journal of European Economic History* 2, 3 (Winter 1973), 582-613.

Louis Reybaud, *Economistes modernes*. Paris: M. Levy Frères, 1862.

Jean Waleh, *Michel Chevalier économiste Saint-Simonien 1806-1879*. Paris: J. Vrin, 1975.

Notes

1   See Charles P. Kindleberger, "The Rise of Free Trade in Western Europe," *Journal of Economic History* 35, 1 (March 1975), 20-55.

2   The logic may have worked in the opposite direction as well. Despite the strength of the Royal Navy, Britain had reason to fear France. Several war scares racked Britain in 1858-59. The presence of another Napoleonic Empire across the English Channel was enough ammunition for the popular press to conjure up images of a possible invasion. Such ideas not only gripped the public imagination, they also influenced the politicians. Britain suddenly began to invest in military defences on the British Isles. The budget allocated money not only for the Royal Navy but also for fortifications. To avoid any conflict, or simply to avoid the greater expenditures associated with these defences, Britain's political leadership was interested in improving political relations with France. See Arthur Lewis Dunham, *The Anglo-French Treaty of Commerce of 1860* (Ann Arbor: University of Michigan Press, 1930), 50-52.

3   Ibid., 61-62.

4   Ibid., 61, 77 n 23. Dunham, one of the historians who has looked closely at the Commercial Treaty of 1860, argues that the treaty's primary impact was economic. There may well have been other goals for Napoleon III and the French, but these diplomatic aims were short-lived. Britain and France did not enter into close enough relations to form a true alliance.

5   Ibid., ch.1.

6   As quoted ibid., 17.

7   Ibid., 88-92, 99-100. Interestingly, Patrick O'Brien and Geoffrey Pigman have recently argued that these tariffs were left on in Britain as a protectionist measure for agriculture, not for revenue purposes. See O'Brien and Pigman, "Free Trade, British Hegemony, and the International Economic Order in the Nineteenth Century," *Review of International Studies* 18 (April 1992), 89-113.

8   In order to keep the budget in order, the income tax had to be raised again. The number of articles covered by a tariff fell from 419 to 48, and the revenues thereby lost totalled £2,000,000. See Dunham, *The Anglo-French Treaty of Commerce of 1860*, 110.

9   Ibid., 99-100.

10 Ibid., ch. 4.

11 Ibid., 102.

12 Ibid., 38.

13 Ibid., 124.

14 Ibid., ch. 8.

15 Peter Cain, "Capitalism, War and Internationalism in the Thought of Richard Cobden," *British Journal of International Studies* 5, 3 (October 1979), 229-47.

16 Dunham, *The Anglo-French Treaty of Commerce of 1860*, 34.

17 Ibid., 44.

18 Ibid., 59.

19 Ibid., 62.

20 Kindleberger, "The Rise of Free Trade in Western Europe."

21 Dunham, *The Anglo-French Treaty of Commerce of 1860*, 102.

Twelve

THE FAILURE OF CAPRIVI'S NEW COURSE AND IMPERIAL GERMANY'S DEFECTION FROM THE FREE TRADE REGIME

Germany was one of the first states to defect from the free trade regime. The country had been unified under the leadership of Prussia, as the numerous German states that fought alongside each other in the Franco-Prussian War came together. Prussia's Otto von Bismarck led this diplomatic manoeuvring and then took up the most important executive post (after the monarch) in the new German government. The political structure of the new German Empire was dominated by Prussia—and Prussian interests. The new state would first adopt free trade because it was in the interest of Prussia's aristocrats, the Junkers. The Junkers owned large tracts of land and grew grain. Since Germany was endowed with much land and was not yet industrialized, the country exported those goods that used its factors of production most intensively. The international economy was rapidly changing, however. In the 1870s, improved technology expanded the number of countries and the volume of commodities involved in international trade. These changes altered the competitiveness of various sectors in the German economy, as will be explained below.[1]

Bismarck now had a different domestic political task on his hands. He wanted to protect the economic, political, and social status of the Junkers. He had to protect their income from grain production by establishing a protectionist tariff and gathered together a coalition uniting the conservative agriculturalists and the new industrial capitalists—a coalition referred to as the "Coalition of Iron and Rye." The tariff was Bismarck's single most important tool—the Junkers did not want to face the agricultural competition from the developing countries, while the industrialists did not want to face exports from Britain.[2] Most analyses of Germany's trade policies between 1870 and 1914 focus on Bismarck's machinations and leave us with the impression that the Coalition of Iron and Rye held sway right up until World War 1.

What we examine in this chapter, however, is something a little different. Germany's policies did not run in a smooth, consistent pattern from 1879 until 1914. The protectionist coalition of Bismarck actually came unglued, and a free trade coalition held power for a brief period. Given what economists tell us about the pay-offs from free trade, the free-traders should have been in a position to compensate the protectionists (or at least part of them) and thereby solidify their hold on power. Why didn't this occur? Peter Gourevitch notes that the free trade coalition should have been able to hold onto power since it was "perhaps even a majority of the electorate."[3] The free trade coalition was given the opportunity to consolidate its preferences after the election of 1890, when Leo von Caprivi took over the chancellorship. As Gourevitch asks, "Why did this coalition lose over the long run?"[4] Is it simply a domestic-level story—as suggested by our discussion so far—or were there other factors at work as well?

Background: Bismarck's "Coalition of Iron and Rye"

Prior to Germany's unification in 1872, the Junkers had been dominant politically in Prussia. This political dominance was maintained within the federal government of the new united Germany through institutional arrangements. Prussia dominated the new Germany, and the Junkers dominated Prussia. As large-scale producers of grain, the Junkers had long been successful exporters. They had naturally supported free trade.[5] This makes perfect sense when we use the H-O model (and the Stolper-Samuelson theorem) to assess Germany's position vis-à-vis the country's main European trading partners; Germany's abundant factor of production was land. Manufacturing interests, primarily in the west regions of Germany, were more interested in protection from British goods, reflecting Germany's lower ratio of capital to labour compared to Britain. During the formulation of Germany's original tariff policies just after the country unified, industry argued for protection while agriculture pressured for free trade.[6] The Junkers' dominant political position meant Germany adopted low tariffs.

By the end of the decade, however, the European economy soured. Prices dropped as new trade competitors emerged. Cheap grain flowed into Europe from the plains of the U.S., Canada, Russia, and Argentina. These agricultural regions were suddenly able to export bulk commodities such as grain due to the extension of the railroads. Railroad penetration into the interior of continents lowered transport costs substantially.[7] Since one assesses a country's factor endowments relative to its trading partners, and Germany's trading partners were essentially different now, Germany could no longer be considered relatively abundant in land. The Junkers could no longer produce grain at competitive prices. Naturally, they reversed their stance on trade.[8] Since industry still desired protection from British competition (and this was intensified due to an economic downturn that meant lower demand), Bismarck could now offer a protective tariff to industry. The tariff would unite heavy industry and the Junkers. Bismarck reorganized the conservatives into a new political party, developing the party's program around economic policies designed to appeal to agrarian interests.[9]

The pattern of change, however, is not straightforward. Between the Coalition of Iron and Rye in 1879 and the outbreak of World War 1, Germany's tariffs briefly moved back towards freer trade, only to reverse direction again. In the early 1890s, the government of von Caprivi tried to lower Germany's tariffs. These efforts were short-lived, and when Caprivi's government fell, trade policy swung back to protectionism.

The System Level: Retaliations—Or the Lack Thereof?

If the German tariff of 1879 signalled Germany's defection from the free trade regime, how did other countries react? One of the obvious things to remember, when we consider the systemic factors at work in the late nineteenth century, is that the free trade regime in place was completely informal. There may have been international norms created by Britain's repeal of the Corn Laws, and then the Cobden-Chevalier Treaty, but there were no explicit obligations to the regime. The regime had taken some time to establish itself and had been created in an ad hoc fashion. Now it would fall apart slowly, and in an ad hoc fashion. The erosion of the regime is often blamed on Germany, along with some other states.

The only kind of restraints placed on Germany's policies by the regime, therefore, were the implicit threats of retaliation from those wishing to continue to pursue free trade. These retaliations had not been very strong in 1879; demand had fallen already, so what were these other states denying Germany? Since their purchases of German exports were already low, retaliation would not have achieved much. Perhaps this explains the reaction of Britain: as stated earlier, Britain earned substantial sums from the services associated with international trade and could afford to have a balance-of-trade deficit, because it made so much more off of international investments and services that it still came out ahead in the overall balance of payments. If Britain had retaliated against the protectionist policies of Germany or other countries, it would have been hurting itself. In response to the erosion of the free trade regime in the 1870s and 1880s, Britain did nothing.

What were the rewards, then, for Caprivi's government to liberalize Germany's tariffs in the early 1890s? For one thing, Germany had begun to export an assortment of goods. The German economy's characteristics were changing. The economy was much more industrialized, and the country itself had become more urbanized. Germany's leading economic sectors (e.g., chemicals, electrical goods, steel, etc.) were at the forefront of technological development. The country was ready to compete internationally in industrial production. These groups, while competitive, nonetheless benefited from protection since the tariffs allowed them to charge higher prices within Germany. To continue to grow, however, these businesses needed export markets. The Coalition of Iron and Rye was headed to a divorce, since the agriculturalists were declining in competitiveness and required protectionism more than ever, while the industrial sectors could afford to abandon protectionism.

Specifically, the exporters were concerned about the series of trade negotiations nearing in the 1890s. The most important market at stake was the United States. Unlike Britain, the U.S. had no large earnings from international services yet. In fact, the U.S. had had its own form of protectionism in place for some time. German industrialists wanted to gain entry into the American market, but Germany's high grain tariffs were clearly an obstacle for reaching any positive agreement. The Americans exported vast amounts of grain, and American farmers wanted access to the German market. Since the Americans were not going to let German industrial goods in without first being able to export its own agricultural goods, and the American market was critical for heavy industry's exports, Germany's industrial sectors began to speak out against high agricultural tariffs. The chemical industry led the change in direction when it formed a new lobbying organization (the Centralverband der Industriellen, or CdI) early in 1891.[10] The CdI would be a powerful voice for trade liberalization, but it would need allies.

There was additional systemic pressure to reverse some of the protectionist tariffs. Germany's military and political strategies had to be supported by foreign economic policies. While many scholars have stressed how agricultural self-sufficiency was a goal pursued for military purposes, the truth is a bit more mixed. By 1890, German politicians were concerned about encirclement and about being isolated by an opposing coalition. The alliance between France and Russia put tremendous pressure on the German decision-makers. Securing stable allies became a top priority. One way of attracting and solidifying alliances was to offer economic concessions. Some concessions on agricultural tariffs were made to the Scandinavian countries, making it easier to import pork products into Germany. Tariff negotiations with Austria-Hungary were ongoing at that time as well, and that country would almost certainly be seeking to export agricultural goods to Germany.[11] Germany needed Austria-Hungary as an ally and therefore some sort of trade concession would have been extremely useful.

By the summer of 1891, agricultural prices seemed to be headed in an upward spiral, thrust to higher levels by the tariff. Germany's agricultural production was not increasing in response to the higher prices; exporters felt that their interests were certainly threatened. The opposition to protectionism, which had only been voiced previously by the heavy industrial sectors, now started to gel. Because grain prices continued to rise in 1891, Caprivi was forced to take action.[12]

When he took office in 1890, Caprivi had two choices. If protectionism continued or even increased, there would be trade wars on several fronts. If, on the other hand, he led a change in Germany's policies, it would be possible for Germany to negotiate the opening of several important markets. With this second path in mind, Caprivi undertook talks with the Austro-Hungarian Empire, Italy, Switzerland, and several other countries. Germany would pursue trade policy in a new direction until Caprivi's administration fell in October 1894.[13] So while the systemic factors have largely been downplayed in most accounts of Germany's tariff decisions in the 1890s, they in fact play a role.

The Domestic Level: Economic Changes and Interests

According to the Stolper-Samuelson theorem, as the German economy changed, the distribution of benefits from trade should have been redistributed. After 1870 the German economy was characterized by rapid capital accumulation. This capital accumulation manifested itself in a spurt of industrialization, the application of more machinery in production, and higher rates of savings and investments. These changes in the endowments of the factors of production should have led to a realignment of the political supporters of free trade and protection. Those interested in free trade should have gained strength over time, as key components of the protectionist Coalition of Iron and Rye lost interest in maintaining barriers against imports.

In the 1870s, two-thirds of Germany's population lived on the land; by 1914, two-thirds of the population lived in the cities. Industrialization was clearly the motor behind such changes.[14] Among the fastest growing elements of this industrializing economy were iron and steel production, along with those businesses that transformed iron or steel into other products. Production of machinery and instruments grew rapidly. Trade and banking grew apace.[15] The railroad network in Germany increased in scope and scale. In 1878, there were 5,000 kilometres of tracks established; by 1890 the length of track laid had risen to 25,000 kilometres. But that wasn't the end

of the construction boom—by 1910 the amount had risen to 37,000 kilometres.[16]

As noted earlier, Bismarck had cemented the Coalition of Iron and Rye
by raising the tariff but also by forming a new conservative party. This party
was centred on the interests of the Junkers. It had pulled in heavy industry
at first. Yet in the 1890s, elements of heavy industry were ready to re-enter
an alliance with small businesses. The small businesses had long backed the
various liberal parties. There were other important political parties, though,
reflecting other interests. Labour was represented by the Social Democratic
Party. Catholics were represented by the Centre Party. As the economic
characteristics of the country changed, the capital-intensive sectors became
more interested in expanding exports and less fearful of foreign competition;
the land-intensive sectors (i.e., agriculture), on the other hand, were increasingly less competitive compared to international rivals and therefore became
more interested in protection. Labour was divided—it wanted freer trade as
a way to reduce the price of food, but it, too, feared that foreign competition would lead to lower wages.[17]

Of course, to follow through on the domestic politics model, we next
need to see how the different economic interests organized themselves for
political action and then interacted with the various political institutions. In
the 1890s, organized interest group activities began to matter much more
than they had in the past, primarily because the cost of elections rose.
Political parties had to raise more money to compete. Trade policy
remained where Bismarck had placed it—at the top of the political agenda;
it proved to be one of the strongest forces provoking groups to organize and
to donate funds to political parties.[18]

One of the groups most interested in challenging the existing policies of
protectionism was the working class. In many sectors, workers were already
organized in unions. The labour movement was divided, however, between
the socialists and the Catholics, with each set of unions having a relationship
with a specific party. The rising price of bread ate into the real earnings of
workers, and as a result working-class agitation rose. The number of strikes
in 1889 represented a sharp increase from preceding years. The workers'
greatest weakness, however, was their inability to win power in state elections. The single most powerful state in the German federation was Prussia,
and in Prussian state elections the workers were completely underrepre-
sented. (Voting rights were linked to taxes and wealth; the poor could be
effectively excluded.) Prussia's policies were determined by the Junkers.

The various state governments sent their representatives to Germany's
upper legislature, the Bundesrat. Prussia held enough power here to veto
most policies and since the Junkers controlled Prussia they could indirectly
dominate the German government. If the workers were ever to play a significant role their unions and political parties would have to join forces with

others. There were potential allies, since a second group—exporters—was interested in overturning the protectionist policies. In the closing years of the 1880s, German exports had been relatively stagnant. Exporters were beginning to blame Germany's protectionism for the closure of other markets to German goods. Exporters believed their interests were not being taken into account. The exporters would form several organizations to raise money and promote the liberalization of trade; the two most important were the Bund der Industriellen and the Hansa-Bund.

Caprivi used trade liberalization to get support from the Liberals, and even from the Social Democrats and the Centre Party. A coalition between the industries that produced for export and the workers was simply not very stable. While Caprivi would try to forge some of these links once he came to power in 1890, the disagreements between the workers and employers were simply too deep to overcome. Certainly, trade policy alone could not bridge their differences; other policies, such as tax reform, voting reform, and expanded social benefits, would have to be enacted to keep such a coalition together. Caprivi was never able to satisfy so many different groups with different demands at once.

Caprivi latched onto some aspects of the idea of trade liberalization and attempted to use liberalization to sever the relationship central to the conservative protectionist coalition: the tariff binding heavy industry and agriculture. Heavy industry was in fact interested in liberalization, and at first seemed to throw its support behind Caprivi's "New Course." This sector was easy to organize—there were few actors, since these areas were dominated by monopolies and cartels. Heavy industry had formed the Centralverband der Industriellen (CdI) during the 1870s to promote protectionism, and this group still played an important role. It was the primary channel of support for the National Liberal Party, a critical ally for the Conservatives outside of Prussia. The fact that these industries were largely monopolized or cartelized might also explain their tendency to support protection—the monopolies were able to charge higher than market prices and therefore needed tariffs to keep foreign competitors out. Caprivi could bring some firms over to his side, but on the whole the CdI stuck with protection.

Caprivi tried hard to connect trade issues to an issue dearer to the hearts of the agrarians—emigration—by arguing that Germany would have to export either goods or people. Without an expanding economy based on exports of manufactured goods (which were necessary to pay for imports of raw materials, including foodstuffs), Germany could not maintain employment at levels conducive to social order.[19] Thus, Caprivi was playing on the Junkers' two greatest fears: political unrest at home, and the loss of the rural workforce. The Junkers were unswayed.

Instead, the Junkers responded by copying the tactics of the promoters of free trade. The proponents of lower tariffs had formed mass organizations to build support and raise money; the Junkers would do the same thing, via the Bund der Landwirte (BdL). The financial clout of the BdL came from the Junkers, but the organization created links between the Junkers in the east and small farmers in the west and south of Germany. It soon became extremely powerful.[20] The BdL blamed falling grain prices and the general hardship in the agricultural sector on Caprivi's policies. The CdI and the BdL working together soon engineered the downfall of Caprivi's administration. The succeeding regimes would have to wait until Caprivi's trade treaties expired, but once they did, Germany's tariffs would be brought back up to high levels.

Consensus among the Experts, and the Minor Role of Ideas

If we try to locate the role of ideas among the shifts from protectionism to free trade, we run into some difficulties. Trade policy was rarely seen in a vacuum. The economic experts might have agreed on one policy, but the Junkers saw the tariff largely in terms of the support it gave to their own incomes, which in turn was the foundation for the continuation of their own social standing. End the tariff, the Junkers would argue, and you change not just the economy but the entire society. Others viewed the tariff in strategic terms, arguing that Germany needed to stay focused on agricultural production if it was to have the basic materials and manpower needed for a large army. (This was obviously foolish, since industry provided the real sources of military strength.)

Perhaps unsurprisingly, the economists of the day were largely opposed to protectionism—though this statement must be qualified. The opponents of protectionism could call on a number of the most famous economists in Germany (Gustav Schmoller, Lujo Brentano, etc.) for support. Yet these economists were not die-hard liberals. Orthodox liberalism had been decisively discredited when the European economy had collapsed in the 1870s, and it had not been able to right itself. No one therefore proposed that markets could stabilize themselves. Government intervention in the economy was not opposed on principle; it was the manner of the intervention that was debated, and therefore the economists had to use their skills to illustrate and underscore political points. Instead of engaging in theoretical debates on principles, the economists had to argue about the degree to which one group or another benefited from the policies at issue.

The economists who favoured freer trade were naturally located at universities in regions where the local interests were in favour of free trade. Schmoller, for instance, was at the University of Leipzig, in Saxony. The most important firms in Saxony were textile manufacturers and other producers of finished goods. Heavy industry was located far to the west and the Junkers to the east. Saxony elected representatives from liberal parties who naturally argued for lower tariffs. It is a good example of the links that develop between the political forces and those agents needed to promote particular ideas.

In this particular case, it is difficult to distinguish an independent role for ideas. There was no clear division in terms of ideas, and no clear principles strongly divided the experts. Nor was there any clear consensus on one specific policy. Since the experts agreed that some sort of government intervention was probably necessary but couldn't agree on what that intervention should entail, it is not clear that ideas had a powerful role to play in these debates.

The Reactions to Caprivi's Policies

Caprivi's term ended much the same as it had begun, full of sharp disagreements over trade policy. The BdL actively opposed any further treaties that might reduce protectionism, and the agrarians were especially against any deal with Russia. As a result of the BdL's ability to block a treaty, a tariff war between the two countries erupted in August 1893. Industrial exporters perceived significant losses as a result, since they had trouble entering the Russian market. The McKinley tariff in the U.S. was already hurting industrial exporters.[21]

Caprivi's successor, Fürst zu Hohenlohe, was in office from 29 October 1894 until October 1900. In trade policy, Hohenlohe tried to work around the margins, that is, he did not attempt to undo the treaties Caprivi had negotiated, though he did move in minor ways to provide some additional protection for the agricultural sectors. He raised export duties on some products not previously taxed and placed customs on products outside the agreements signed by Caprivi's government.[22] This, however, left the protectionist forces unsatisfied.

The next government was led by Fürst Bülow and was in power from October 1900 until 1909. This administration worked much more actively to return Germany's trade policy to protectionism. Bülow, too, had a choice to make, similar to that which Caprivi had faced. Caprivi had chosen to pursue freer trade in the hopes of making Germany a "trading state" and of building a stable dominant coalition to support his government. He had failed. Bülow would now try the opposite strategy: support agricultural interests against the interests of industry, even if it sparked retaliations abroad.[23]

The tariff passed in 1902 (which only came into force in March 1906) was intended to strengthen the agricultural sectors. The tariff rates on grain were raised, as were the rates on other agricultural products. Higher tariffs were charged on horses, cows, and various animal products.[24] As expected, other countries retaliated by charging higher tariffs on Germany's industrial exports. Also as expected, the higher grain tariffs helped the agrarians, not least by putting upward pressure on their income and land prices again. The big owners—the real supporters of the BdL—came out ahead.[25]

Industry was wary about the return to protectionism. There were three reasons for this anxiety: first, by 1900, fewer elements of big business needed protection from foreign competition because they now held technological advantages; second, some industrial sectors had important concerns about exports, and their experiences in the previous decades showed that a higher agricultural tariff resulted in losses in these markets due to retaliation; third, many of these same firms had seen strong growth in the 1890s as a result of Caprivi's policies and therefore were deeply suspicious of the policies Bülow was pursuing.[26] The conservative leaders thus exerted immense effort to solidify the capitalists in one coalition, and they did so by painting the socialists as the enemy. This Sammlungspolitik, as it was called, was intended to bind together the capitalists and unite them in struggle against the Social Democratic Party.

The Consequences of Protectionism: Economic Competition, Rivalry, and World War I

The failure of Caprivi's "New Course" had a number of significant consequences. Germany's return to protectionism has been linked on the international level to increased friction between Germany and other major powers, especially Britain and Russia. The differences over economic policies certainly did nothing to build goodwill between the countries, and in that sense may have played a role in the rising international tensions prior to 1914.

The economic conflicts within Germany itself also had repercussions. The instability of the German regime is often cited as a reason for Germany's role in the initiation of World War 1. The regime was built on a coalition of politically conservative groups—the Junkers and heavy industry—yet the distributional impact of trade continually threatened to push these two groups apart. To keep them together, and to keep the working class and liberals apart, policies were packaged in ways that created problematic side-effects. Some argue that Germany's foreign policy was manipulated.[27] The conservatives could agree on nationalistic programs, so these became the centrepieces of foreign policy, which then enveloped foreign economic policy. This had the advantage of downplaying class divisions within society.

The other view, put forth recently by Jack Snyder, is that protectionism was one facet in the logroll that kept Germany's conservative coalition together.[28] Logrolling is a legislative tactic, where a coalition is kept together by essentially promising every group whatever it is they want. In this case, protectionism and imperialism were used as blanket policies the government could use to promise benefits to its varied bases of support. When the government tried to deliver on these promises, it merely got Germany involved in international crises, entangling alliances, and arms races. These problems, in turn, played a critical role in the outbreak of World War I.

World War I reshaped the map of Europe and altered the distribution of economic and financial power around the world. The war sparked economic development in the U.S. and Japan, boosting them to the fore as economic powers. Germany would be initially weakened by defeat; Russia would drop out of the conflict before it was over, thanks to the Russian Revolution. The war would make New York a powerful financial centre. Yet it took some time—and many economic conflicts—for contemporaries to recognize these changes. Among the most important yet largely unappreciated effects of the war would be the relative decline of Britain. Britain emerged victorious in 1918, but with a very different economic, financial, and military position. There would be great difficulty in adjusting Britain's policies to fit its new stature, which takes us to the next chapter.

Suggested Readings

Mark R. Brawley, "Factoral or Sectoral Conflict? Partially Mobile Factors and the Politics of Trade in Imperial Germany," *International Studies Quarterly* 41, 4 (December 1997), 633–53.

Peter Gourevitch, "International Trade, Domestic Coalitions, and Liberty: Comparative Responses to the Crisis of 1873–1896," *Journal of Interdisciplinary History* 7 (1977), 281–313.

Eckart Kehr, *Economic Interest, Militarism and Foreign Policy*, ed. Gordon Craig. Los Angeles: University of California Press, 1977.

Ron Rogowski, *Commerce and Coalitions*. Princeton, NJ: Princeton University Press, 1989.

Jack Snyder, *Myths of Empire*. Ithaca, NY: Cornell University Press, 1991.

Notes

1 For a broader application of this type of argument, see Ronald Rogowski, *Commerce and Coalitions* (Princeton, NJ: Princeton University Press, 1989).

2 Peter Gourevitch, "International Trade, Domestic Coalitions, and Liberty: Comparative Responses to the Crisis of 1873-1896," *Journal of Interdisciplinary History* 7 (1977), 281-313.

3 Ibid., 288.

4 Ibid., 289.

5 Hans-Ulrich Wehler, *The German Empire 1871-1918*, trans. Kim Traynor (Dover, NH: Berg, 1985), 11-12.

6 Ivo Lambi, *Free Trade and Protection in Germany 1868-1879* (Weisbaden: Frantz Steiner Verlag, 1963), 59.

7 Ibid., 132; Gourevitch, "International Trade, Domestic Coalitions, and Liberty."

8 Wehler, *The German Empire 1871-1918*, 36.

9 Hajo Holborn, *A History of Modern Germany 1840-1945* (Princeton, NJ: Princeton University Press, 1982), 266.

10 Rolf Weitowitz, *Deutsche Politik und Handelspolitik unter Reichskanzler Leo von Caprivi 1890-1894* (Düsseldorf: Droste Verlag, 1978), 22-23.

11 Ibid., 19.

12 Ibid., 25, 34.

13 Jürgen Schneider, "Die Auswirkungen von Zöllen und Handelsvertrgen sowie Handelshemmnissen auf Staat, Wirtschaft und Gesellschaft zwischen 1890 und 1914," in Hans Pohl, ed., *Die Auswirkungen von Zöllen und anderen Handelshemmnissen auf Wirtschaft und Gesellschaft von Mittelalter bis zur Gegenwart* (Stuttgart: Franz Steiner Verlag, 1987), 294.

14 John C.G. Röhl, "Beamtenpolitik im Wilhelminischen Deutschland," in Michael Stürmer, ed., *Das kaiserliche Deutschland, Politik und Gesellschaft 1870-1918* (Düsseldorf: Droste Verlag, 1970), 288-89; Hans-Jürgen Puhle, "Parlament, Parteien und Interessenverbaende 1890-1914," in Stürmer, ed., *Das kaiserliche Deutschland,* 342.

15 Siegfried Mielke, *Der Hansa-Bund für Gewerbe, Handel und Industrie 1909-1914, Der gescheiterterte Versuch einer antifeudalen Sammlungspolitik,* Kritische Studien zur Geschichtswissenschaft (Band 17) (Göttingen: Vandenhoek & Ruprecht, 1976), 14-15.

16 Röhl, "Beamtenpolitik im Wilhelminischen Deutschland," 288-89.

17 This argument is laid out in more detail in Mark R. Brawley, "Factoral or Sectoral Conflict? Partially Mobile Factors and the Politics of Trade in Imperial Germany," *International Studies Quarterly* 41, 4 (December 1997), 633-53.

18 Thomas Nipperdey, "Interessenverbände und Parteien in Deutschland vor dem Ersten Weltkrieg," in H.-U. Wehler, ed., *Moderne deutsche Sozialgeschichte* (Berlin: Kiepenheuer & Witsch, 1966), 378; Thomas Nipperdey, *Deutsche Geschichte 1866-1918, Zweiter Band, Machtstaat vor der Demokratie* (München: Verlag C.H. Beck, 1992), 577; Hans Jaeger, *Unternehmer in der deutschen Politik (1890-1918)* (Bonn: Ludwig Röhrscheid Verlag, 1967), 149.

19 Weitowitz, Deutsche Politik und Handelspolitik, 6-7, 14. Also see Friedrich-Wilhelm Henning, "Vom Agrarliberalismus zum Agrarprotektionismus," in Pohl, ed., *Die Auswirkungen von Zöllen*, 254. Caprivi is quoted as saying: "Wir müssen exportieren: entweder wir exportieren Waren, oder wir exportieren Menschen." See Hans-Peter Ullmann, *Der Bund der Industriellen*, Kritische Studien zur Geschichtswissenschaft (Band 21) (Göttingen: Vandenhoek & Ruprecht, 1976), 22.

20 Schneider, "Die Auswirkungen von Zöllen und Handelsvertragen," 310; Ullmann, *Der Bund der Industriellen*, 23-25.

21 Ullmann, *Der Bund der Industriellen*, 23-25.

22 Schneider, "Die Auswirkungen von Zöllen und Handelsvertragen," 295-96.

23 Ibid., 296.

24 Ibid., 296-97.

25 Ibid., 311.

26 Ibid., 304.

27 Eckhart Kehr, *Economic Interest, Militarism and Foreign Policy*, ed. Gordon Craig (Los Angeles: University of California Press, 1977).

28 Jack Snyder, *Myths of Empire* (Ithaca, NY: Cornell University Press, 1991).

Thirteen

BRITAIN'S RETURN TO
THE GOLD STANDARD
AFTER WORLD WAR I

Introduction: How the Gold
Standard Supposedly Worked

With the spread of free trade in the middle of the nineteenth century, and the increasing levels of international trade after that, ever larger international payments had to be made. The shift away from mercantilist policies in trade created pressures to change international monetary relations to facilitate trade. Paying off international debts requires some kind of international currency, some means of payment accepted almost universally. The nineteenth-century solution to this problem stressed the ideological links to free trade. The gold standard was in effect a market solution to the international payments problem, one that integrated some national markets together quite well.

The gold standard solves the international payments problem because all currencies participating in the gold standard are convertible into gold. Every currency can be cashed in at its central bank for a specified amount of gold. If you turn in gold at the central bank you can get currency at the same fixed rate of exchange. Ultimately, gold is the medium of international exchange. If a German wanted to do business in France, he or she would exchange German marks for gold at the German central bank, take this gold to France, and buy French francs at the central bank there.

With mercantilism, official policy is completely reversed. Under mercantilism, all international flows of gold were supposed to be strictly managed or blocked; gold was hoarded within the countries and national policies were designed to achieve that end. In the period of Pax Britannica and free trade, gold was supposed to flow freely between countries and national policies were redirected towards this.[1] It was believed free trade, over time and under ideal conditions, would lead each country to balance its exports and imports automatically. Liberals argued that in the long run the market would automatically drive countries towards a perfect balance in the value of imports and exports—an equilibrium. If this was the case, there would be no problem with international payments; the liberals liked this situation because it was a pure market solution and therefore did not involve the exercise of power. If a country participated in the international market, it would eventually find its correct equilibrium point. This fit with the liberals' notions that the international market was a natural, neutral forum for solving international payments problems.

The gold standard system was intended to be part of this natural and neutral system. Gold was seen as one "special" good that would make up any marginal differences in the balance of trade. Imports and exports of gold would be linked to the volume of domestic currency, and therefore the flows of gold would influence domestic prices. This connection between flows of gold and prices caused many to describe the gold standard as a "corrective mechanism," since the changes in prices would affect competitiveness.

How was this supposed to work? Let us begin with the example of a country in a balance-of-payments deficit. The country is importing more goods than it is exporting. To pay for the greater value of imports coming in, gold has to flow out. Being on the gold standard meant that the amount of currency in circulation was tied directly to the amount of gold the country held. In other words, the domestic money supply was determined by the amount of gold people brought to the bank and exchanged for currency. If they had to make payments overseas, people brought currencies in and took gold out of the bank to give to foreigners (or foreigners paid in the national currency converted it to gold before transporting it home, where they would exchange it for their own currency). If gold left the country, then the amount of currency in circulation was also affected—an outflow of gold automatically constricted the money supply. A reduction in the money supply, in turn, affects domestic prices. When the money supply drops, there is less currency chasing the same amount of goods (i.e., deflation), which means prices fall.

This pushes the country towards an international payments balance because when the prices of domestic goods are falling, domestic goods look cheaper to domestic consumers than international goods. So within the country a change brought about by this deflation makes imports less competitive. Internationally, the same thing happens: cheaper prices for things domestically mean that goods can be exported at cheaper prices, so that exports are more competitive on international markets than previously. Thus, this same set of links worked as a corrective for a balance-of-payments surplus. If a country successfully exported more than it imported, other countries paid off debts in the form of gold, so the first country's domestic gold supply increases, its money supply increases, inflation occurs, and domestic prices rise. This rise in domestic prices would affect the country's appetite for imports—the price of domestic goods has risen, so imports by comparison become cheaper. At the same time exports begin to look expensive to everyone else. The country would be driven out of this balance-of-payments surplus back towards an equilibrium. Because the system drove countries back towards equilibrium whenever they deviated from it, the system is described as corrective or self-correcting. With a balance-of-payments deficit, the gold standard drove a country back towards surplus; if it started with a surplus, the gold standard drove it back towards deficit.

The Benefits of the Gold Standard

Liberal theorists still see real beauty in this system in that it worked through the market and contained no role for power (or government intervention). The system was self-regulating and self-equilibrating. Theoretically, the government could join the gold standard, establish the links between the domestic currency and gold, and forget about balancing trade—the market would do that. While it wasn't that simple, it may have seemed so to contemporaries. After the major powers joined the gold standard in the late nineteenth century, international monetary affairs took on a whole new set of characteristics. First, the system of exchange rates had to be stable if all this was to work. Given that gold is the same everywhere, if a currency is fixed to a set amount of gold and all the other countries are also fixing their currencies at a set rate versus an amount of gold, then countries can figure out how much of their currency will buy of any other currency also on the gold standard. Since these currencies were fixed in terms of gold (and weren't supposed to be changeable) and indeed remained fixed for long periods of time, merchants and investors knew what exchange rates were going to be for the foreseeable future.

That stability of exchange rates allowed for economic predictability. Economic actors could figure out future returns on international deals without having to risk fluctuations in currency exchange rates. As long as another country is on the gold standard, its currency can be accepted and exchanged for gold, which can then be exchanged into one's own currency. Holding this foreign currency for a while would not be very risky (in terms of the value changing) vis-à-vis one's own currency. This predictability also affected how involved actors would get in another country's economy. They could more easily make long-range plans, even though communication systems were underdeveloped.

The extensive use of the gold standard radically altered the policies prohibiting or limiting international investment. First, gold can be moved internationally. If someone decided to invest in another country, he or she could take gold there. Most importantly, contra mercantilism, states would not prohibit individuals from removing gold from their own country. Moreover, if they wanted to invest in another country, they may be able to use their own currency to pay for things in other places because their currency is convertible into gold and in turn into other currencies—their currency should be as good as gold! Since foreigners can take their currency into their central bank and get gold in return just as easily as locals, they may merely accept foreign currency as something equivalent to gold. That was another advantage to this system of payments that stimulated international investment and trade.

We can now turn to how the gold standard solved the international confidence and liquidity problem. Confidence in gold was high, and when a country fixed its currency in terms of gold the currency took on that same confidence. Gold was accepted in international deals, but so were currencies backed by gold; so national currencies on the gold standard enjoyed international confidence. People had confidence in their value. The system was specifically designed to solve that problem—the confidence issue was largely eliminated. Confidence meant people were willing to accept something because they valued it. High confidence is then associated with high value—if people tend to hold onto or hoard things they value, there may not be enough to go around. In this case, if gold is accepted everywhere and everyone wants to use it internationally, will there be enough to go around? Or will a liquidity problem arise internationally? Moreover, there was a close connection among free trade, the rising levels of trade, and the gold standard. More trade was taking place, which required more gold or currencies to be used to facilitate trade. High confidence and increased demand in general would lead us to expect a liquidity problem.

Where did liquidity come from under the gold standard? Well, as the model of the payments disequilibrium showed, all domestic money supplies were supposed to be determined by the supply of gold in each country. Domestic liquidity and international liquidity depended on the global supply of gold. Control over the domestic supply was removed from government policy-making, which in effect should have also removed international liquidity from the realm of government policy manipulation.

The supply of gold depended on the discovery of new sources of gold. It just so happened, purely by accident, that new sources of gold were discovered. The gold rush in California in 1849 and the subsequent development of gold mines there provided an initial spurt to the supply of gold. In the later nineteenth century, there were periods when the liquidity problem reemerged. But in the long run, there were other gold strikes and new mines developed–there were gold rushes in Alaska, the Yukon, and, of course, in South Africa. Each helped relieve the liquidity squeeze on the international system as the volume of payments and investments grew. At an international level the liquidity problem didn't appear to matter because of these fortuitous discoveries. At the national level, though, there were problems with liquidity, because some countries were growing at a faster rate than their money supply. Being on the gold standard, these governments effectively tied their hands when it came to domestic monetary policies. Some countries got stuck in deflationary trends they had trouble escaping.

A second source of liquidity also existed: British pounds. Since Britain had honoured the gold standard rules for so many years, foreigners had confidence in the future value of sterling. London was the source of so much finance and investment, and so many other goods could be found in London, that it was easier for foreigners simply to hold on to their pounds. They held on to their pounds outside of London. Balances soon built up, and these plus credits from London provided additional international liquidity.

All of this has been about how the system was supposed to work. The design of the gold standard fits very closely to the way liberals wanted things to work—in particular, note how the system was supposed to be neutral and natural. The markets were self-equilibrating, and there was no reason for governments to intervene in international exchange markets.

The Sterling Overhang and the Impact of World War I

The gold standard worked well for the decades prior to 1914 in terms of how well international payments and investments were eased by the monetary regime. Flaws were building up, however. One of the most obvious was that the amount of British pounds in circulation was well beyond the amount backed by gold in the vaults of the Bank of England. An overhang occurs when, in a system of fixed exchange rates, there is so much of a currency in circulation that the supply overwhelms the reserves set aside to back the currency. Despite the supposedly rigid rules of the gold standard, several countries were holding extensive amounts of currencies as reserves alongside gold and/or silver. Sterling remained the most important single foreign currency in other countries' reserves. By 1913, sterling holdings clearly outstripped the combined gold reserves of the Bank of England and all other private banks in Britain (by a ratio of at least 2 ½ to 1).[2] This weakness was not a problem so long as there were no other attractive alternative currencies. When World War 1 broke out, countries no longer wanted to adhere to the gold standard rules.

The gold standard was suspended by war, but just as in trade, there were attempts to reconstruct these international regimes. The attempts failed. To a great extent the developments in monetary relations parallel those in trade, so one story is linked to the other. As part of the war effort, countries blocked any exports of essential materials, including gold—which meant they had to abandon the gold standard. Moreover, going off the gold standard allowed the governments to manipulate their domestic money supplies to conduct policies supporting their war efforts. By going off gold they could follow deficit spending programs by simply pumping more cash into the domestic economy. This naturally created inflationary pressures, but these inflation rates varied across countries.

Having independent, unconnected inflation rates undermined the old system of fixed exchange rates. In Germany, there had been very high inflation during the war; in Britain and France there had been moderate inflation; and in the United States there was much less, as the U.S. adhered to most of the gold standard rules. The exchange rates should have been adjusted to take into account the different rates of inflation (i.e., the new real values of the currencies). In the early 1920s, the currencies were allowed to float, in order to find their true values vis-à-vis each other.

The real problem emerged when countries tried to fix their exchange rates again and once again honour the rules of the gold standard. (Germany returned to the gold standard in 1924, Britain in 1925, France in 1927.) The pound had fallen in its real value versus the dollar, and the attempt to bring it back onto the gold standard at its pre-war value proved disastrous for Britain's industry. The overvalued exchange rate made British prices relatively uncompetitive internationally. Britain's policy hurt trade competitiveness, but of course the opposite could be done. France, for instance, maintained an undervalued rate for the French franc at this same time. This made French prices very competitive internationally, making French exports rise. The French were able to improve their balance of payments without resorting to high tariffs because this undervaluation of the currency helped all sectors. The earnings of foreign currency allowed the French central bank to collect gold from the other central banks, so France went from being a minor holder of gold in the early 1920s to the second largest in the early 1930s.

British Monetary Policy
Immediately after World War I

While there had been some pretences of returning to the gold standard right away, the British government decided to break the links between the pound and gold in 1919. The decision was reached by the cabinet, not the Bank of England, the traditional authority in charge of exchange rate policies. The government did not want to defend Britain's gold reserves under the gold standard rules, since that would drive up unemployment. The government also wished to stimulate trade, particularly in goods transiting the country. The two bureaucracies responsible for monetary policy, the Treasury and the Bank of England, had other concerns. The Treasury feared that the government's debts were already so high that taxes would have to be kept extremely high for the foreseeable future. If the government failed to repay its debts, business would lack the capital necessary for new investments. Additional government debt was out of the question, since that would push interest rates higher, thus making the existing debt even more expensive to carry.[3]

The Bank of England, on the other hand, considered the restoration of the pre-war financial system, with London as the key financial centre, as its primary goal. The Bank wanted government debt to be paid down quickly, a new funding of other short-term debt as soon as possible, and a policy to restore confidence in the pound.[4] Despite concerns about official debts, the Treasury would accept an upward valuation of sterling—as one Treasury official put it in 1920, "the community as a whole stands to gain enormously from the improved standing of British credit."[5] Interest payments on government debt had been only a minor concern before, but after the war they accounted for about 30 per cent of government expenditures. The initial split between the Bank of England and the Treasury after the war was not over the ultimate goal of monetary policy, since both agreed the value of sterling needed to be raised, but rather over the means to pursue that end. The Bank wanted to reassert its control over financial markets, pushing interests rates up. The Treasury was concerned that this would make it difficult to sell new Treasury bills (and other forms of short-term government debt). Yet since both feared inflation, their agreement that the top priority should be sterling's confidence formed the basis of the Cunliffe Committee (officially known as the Committee on Currency and Foreign Exchange) findings, which guided official decision-making.[6] The committee's report had simply assumed that the goal of British monetary authorities was to return to the gold standard as soon as possible. The Committee on Financial Facilities, which was made up of representatives from industry and commerce, reported at this same time and also assumed the same goals for monetary policy. The recommendations from both committees agreed that the government should stop borrowing money as soon as possible; that "Bank rate" (the interest rate the Bank of England charged others) should be used to stop any drain of gold reserves, as well as deflect inflationary pressures at home; and that national gold reserves should be concentrated in the hands of the Bank of England.[7]

Yet the monetary authorities were slow to realize how the setting for action had changed. The success of the government's own war financing effort had changed the mix of assets in the London market. This naturally affected the relative utility of different policy tools. Treasury bills were much

more important than before, since they now made up around half of the
market for monetary devices. Before the war, monetary policy had relied on
the use of Bank rate to maintain exchange markets. Bank rate would not be
as effective as it once had been, since it would have to drive up the rates
offered on Treasury bills to draw in money from outside Britain. Investors
did not necessarily find Treasury bills attractive enough to transfer money
from other countries to London.[8] If the Bank of England were to rely on
Bank rate alone to draw in foreign funds or block the expansion of trade
credit, it would now have to change the rate more dramatically. This was
especially true now that New York was a rival source of credit and an alternative destination for deposits. These new factors were not considered in the
Cunliffe Committee's analysis.

The overhang created the desire to tighten credit, while a return to a
peacetime economy created the desire for economic growth. The British
economy boomed briefly when the government, fearful of unemployment,
had initially loosened wartime controls. This was followed by a slump in
1920-22, but the economy had largely recovered by 1924. Problems
remained with the export-oriented sectors, however; exports in 1924 were
still only about three-fourths those of 1913.[9] The government was interested
in policies promising to assist in the recovery of these sectors.

Recovery could not be allowed to stimulate inflation, however. If inflation sparked a devaluation of sterling, this would undermine the real value
of Britain's income from overseas investments denominated in sterling and
set at fixed amounts. Without examination, it was assumed that inflation
hurt the internationally oriented service sectors, too. In fact, inflation might
not have hurt the service sectors as feared, since services tended to charge
commissions. Commissions are often percentages of transactions, and therefore would have risen with inflation.[10] As long as the Bank and the Treasury
feared inflation the most, policy would emphasize the bolstering of sterling's
international value.[11] A fall in confidence in the currency would cause foreigners to unload their holdings of pounds and shift into stronger currencies.

Monetary policy decisions could have been influenced from a variety of
forces. On the one hand, there were systemic factors, especially the rise of
an attractive rival currency (the U.S. dollar). There were the ingredients
necessary for a decision to be shaped by bureaucratic politics, since the
Treasury and the Bank of England had overlapping responsibilities and over
time their goals diverged. Sectoral interests also may have played a role,
since the impact of monetary policy was felt differently in different sectors.
Each of these theories offer insight into the decision actually taken: to place
the pound back on the gold standard in 1925, at the pre-war exchange rate.

Systemic Theory:
Britain's Hegemonic Afterglow

The typical systemic argument for Britain's difficult policy choices in this period draw on the changing distribution of capabilities in the international system. World War 1 heralded the relative decline of British economic and financial power and the rise of the United States. Britain was no longer the single most important source of credit or trade—it had to share that role with the U.S. The U.S. had its own uncertainties about the role it was to play in the international political economy. Whereas Britain would struggle to retain the premier position, the U.S. would avoid much of the responsibilities it perhaps should have undertaken.[12] In short, there was no clear hegemonic power during this period of transition.[13]

If Britain was no longer clearly dominant, why then did it persist in the pursuit of hegemonic policies? This example of hegemonic "afterglow" can really only be described by adding in other causal variables from other levels of analysis. For instance, when Stephen Krasner sought to explain why Britain retained hegemonic policies into the 1920s, he argued that it was because these policies were supported by domestic arrangements constructed during hegemonic ascendance. In Krasner's words, "the British state was unable to free itself from the domestic structures that its earlier policy decisions had created."[14] Susan Strange made essentially the same point to explain British international monetary policy at a later time: "it has been the misfortune of British policy since the Second World War to have inherited from this distant imperial hey-day, associated ideas which no longer apply to Britain's changed situation, but have nevertheless proved remarkably hard to shed or modify."[15]

These scholars were noting that Britain's international monetary policy after World War 1 (and even much later) was not rational from the perspective of the nation as a whole. Industry's competitiveness in particular was hurt by the monetary policies of the 1920s. Most researchers also link these policy outcomes to an institution created much earlier—the Bank of England. As an essentially systemic-level argument, hegemonic stability theory has been ill-equipped to deal with such questions. Krasner's immediate intention in suggesting a role for domestic institutions was to explain the time lags he observed between the onset of hegemonic decline (in structural terms) and the end of leadership (in terms of policy). By introducing domestic factors, his explanation for the afterglow was an addendum to an otherwise structural theory. It suggests that hegemonic stability theory could not explain everything on its own. A similar problem arises, as will be seen in the next chapter, when we consider what the U.S. was doing at this time.

The Domestic Level:
Industry versus the City of London

The basic alternative arguments, drawn from the level of domestic politics, support this assessment. The proponents of these arguments would question why systemic factors would be considered at all. Instead, they would suggest that the policy decisions can be best understood by looking at the winners and losers involved. On one side stood the set of financial actors (banks, insurance firms, etc.) loosely termed "the City" and on the other side was British industry. At first glance, one might think the two sets of actors would have many links, but in fact the City had always been involved more heavily in investing abroad and in financing international trade rather than investing in home industry.[16]

The City was concerned with dealing with the overhang in such a way that international confidence in sterling remained high. As Peter Katzenstein put it, "the British definition of policy objectives reflects a 'banker's' rather than a 'business' view of the world. The former view has found its most ardent proponents in London's City, whose economic survival, it was thought until the mid 1960s, depended on defending the position of sterling as a reserve currency."[17] In short, they wanted interest rates to continue to be high, in order to draw in pounds from abroad as well as encourage people to hold their sterling in savings rather than spend it. The City feared that if foreigners lost confidence in the pound, they would switch their transactions to U.S. dollars; as a result transactions would go through New York rather than London and the City's income would fall. The financial actors considered their own competitiveness to be aided by a strong pound.

A strong pound would make industry's products look relatively expensive on international markets, however. Industry's international competitiveness had already been on the wane for some time. British industry had been at the forefront of manufacturing technology in the first half of the nineteenth century, but as new technologies were created that position slipped. Others found it easier to adopt the new technologies. British industry was uncompetitive and needed lower interest rates so it could finance retooling. Yet that went directly against the interests of the City. And as noted earlier, Britain earned more from international services and international investments than it did from trade in goods. The City was in a better position to argue its point of view.

Yet at first, this domestic split was not all that apparent. Representatives of the Federation of British Industry, the central organization for industry, went before one government advisory committee in 1924 to argue for a return to the gold standard "in the interests both of the financial position of this country and also for its advantages and benefits to the industry and business of this country." The same representatives also noted, however, that "a British initiative in restoring the gold standard at an early date ... would be premature and inadvisable" because it would lessen their ability to sell exports and therefore likely increase unemployment.[18] The committee listened to this information, yet recommended a return to gold at the pre-war level. In 1925 the exchange rate against the dollar was set at its pre-war level ($4.86 = £1), and industry soon faced serious difficulties.

This exchange rate certainly placed too high a value on sterling, but debate remains as to how much this accounted for British industry's difficulties. The overvaluation of sterling cannot be separated from broader economic problems. The high pound did not cause all of the broader adjustment problems that industry faced, but it surely eliminated some policy options. The underlying difficulties were therefore that much more difficult to deal with.[19] After 1928, there was wider recognition that industry's most pressing problem seemed to be the combination of deflation at home and the overvaluation of sterling.[20] The higher value of sterling caused domestic demand to fall off, made it more difficult to invest in new machinery, hurt overseas sales, and forced industry to begin laying off workers. The workers responded with a nationwide strike in 1928. Because of the way in which the gold standard had supposedly worked in the past, domestic goals (such as employment levels) were being sacrificed for international targets.

This was a more dangerous game to play in the 1920s, however.[21] As part of the government's attempts to stimulate the war effort, Britain had finally extended the vote to the working class in 1918. For the first time, the workers in Britain had their own powerful voice in Parliament: the Labour Party. The politics associated with monetary policy would be played out differently, since the workers would be more interested in domestic priorities.

Bureaucratic Politics: The Treasury and the Bank of England

A rival explanation for Britain's monetary policy decision in 1925 can be found in bureaucratic politics, though it is difficult to untangle this argument from the domestic politics discussed above. The different parts of the economy had close ties with particular parts of government. The City naturally had many links with the Bank of England. The Bank of England would have interacted with the financial actors quite regularly. Moreover, the Bank's responsibilities had always been presented in terms of defending the pound's international value. The Treasury, on the other hand, had the government's budget as its primary responsibility. Moreover, the Treasury had obligations to cabinet and, therefore, to the electorate.

In the early 1920s the Treasury and the Bank of England largely agreed
on policy, perhaps because the government's annual budgets were still in
surplus. Both institutions agreed on a return to the gold standard as the best
way to improve trade and increase employment. At the same time, leaders
of both institutions failed to consider all the consequences associated with
moving Britain from its existing position to the one they wanted. Rather
than understanding the gold standard and the exchange rate as means to an
end, the return to the gold standard became an end in itself. In the early
1920s, policy-makers from each institution shared a common goal—the
wish to retain London's role as the premier international financial centre,
which they understood also meant keeping sterling in its international role.[22]
Sectoral influences do not seem to have had an impact on the institutions'
policy positions up to this time, except to the extent that both were influenced by the financial sector. The only serious disagreement between the
two bureaucracies would come over the policies to be used.[23] The Bank
wished to employ higher interest rates to strengthen the pound, while the
Treasury felt this would lead to higher interest charges; debt service had
accounted for a mere 11 per cent of government expenditures in 1913 but
had risen to 24 per cent in 1920. This would climb to more than 40 per cent
by 1930, and would drive the two institutions apart.

If anything, the bureaucratic politics argument suggests that a common
set of sectoral interests emanating from the City may have dominated both
institutions, but bureaucratic politics led to a division. The public airing of
this division in institutional views opened the way for others to enter the
debate over monetary policy, and this in turn created the opportunity for
the institutions to mobilize groups for political action in ways that were
never possible in the pre-World War 1 era.[24] In short, this view argues that
the bureaucratic politics explanation is reinforced by domestic political
struggles.[25]

The Bank considered its primary obligation to be the maintenance of the
international exchange value of sterling.[26] Though the Bank and the
Treasury were not acting completely independent of each other, co-ordination between the two could have been much better. The Bank did not
notify the Treasury of its complete resources or of its actions. The Treasury
eventually took action via Parliament. The Currency and Bank Notes Act
of 1928 gave the Treasury access to more information on the Bank's foreign
exchange reserves held by the Issue Department (but the Treasury could not
find out about all of the Bank's foreign currency holdings, which the Bank
was starting to use to intervene in exchange markets).[27]

The Bank was searching for alternative policies that would allow it to
avoid relying on the government. When the question of going back on the
gold standard arose in the early 1920s, Bank Governor Montagu Norman
worked in close co-ordination with the New York Federal Reserve Bank,

often with little guidance from the government. Norman successfully co-ordinated some aspects of British and American monetary policies. While the Fed relaxed interest rates in New York, the Bank of England raised interest rates in London, thereby adjusting the exchange relations between the two markets. International borrowing focused on New York, making it easier for Britain to keep sterling's value high and hence resume participation on the gold standard.[28]

The Treasury's vulnerability to broader societal pressures played a role in the battles between the two institutions after 1925, though these concerns were hardly linked to the lobbying activities of any specific sectors. By 1928, the Treasury would deter greater deflation. The Treasury feared that rising unemployment would be politically and fiscally unacceptable. One of the major expenditures that worried the Treasury most was the unemployment insurance fund. The Treasury prevented a higher Bank rate, taking away the Bank's most important short-term policy instrument. The Bank was forced to turn to international co-operation more often.[29]

Once Britain returned to the gold standard at a high valuation of sterling, it was all too clear that some sectors were hurt by the Bank's use of interest rates. As the *Westminister Bank Review* stated in 1929, finance and industry no longer had similar interests.[30] It remains somewhat debatable whether the Bank was ready to allow industry to be continually run down in order to stay on the gold standard at the high valuation. In negotiations with the Bank of France in May 1927, Norman threatened to take Britain off the gold standard lest there be further damage to the competitiveness of British industry. When defending the high exchange rate in the later months of 1928, the Bank chose not to use Bank rate to avoid further harm to British industry. Instead, Norman relied more on direct intervention in the exchange markets.[31]

Publicly, Norman continued to argue that industry and finance had the same interests. When testifying before the Macmillan Committee in March 1930, he was asked whether "the advantages of maintaining the international position outweigh in the public interest the internal disadvantages which may accrue from the use of means at your disposal." Norman replied:

> the disadvantages of the internal position are relatively small compared with the advantages to the external position ... we are still to a large extent international bankers. We have great international trade and commerce out of which I believe considerable profit accrues to the country; we do maintain huge international markets ... and the confidence and credit which go with them, are in the long run greatly to the interest of finance and commerce.[32]

The Macmillan Committee's report mirrored the Bank's position. The committee's conclusions rebuffed calls for a devaluation on the grounds that such an act would undermine faith in sterling. Even though this committee assessed a wider spectrum of views than most of the earlier inquiries precisely because they were responding to industry's frustrations, the committee's report stated that Britain's "international trade, commerce and finance are based on confidence."[33] Despite the committee's recommendations, Britain would in fact have to devalue sterling in a few years.

Ideas: The Faith in Liberal Ideology

Perhaps a more powerful explanation can be found in the realm of ideas. Liberal ideology was so strong that it drove many of the policy decisions in the years immediately after 1918. Britain had been so successful economically in the years before the war that policy-makers and the public may have failed to consider why this had been and how the world had changed. The greatest evidence in favour of this type of explanation comes in the form of the questions that were not asked.

For example, in the debates concerning the return to the gold standard in 1924, policy-makers focused intently on the rate at which the currency would be fixed. Little thought was given to the timing of the revaluation itself.[34] Moreover, few policy-makers challenged the assumption that the gold standard was the best international monetary regime for Britain. Winston Churchill, who had been made head of the Treasury, never really questioned the wisdom of returning to the gold standard at the old parity. He only wanted a monetary policy that would complement free trade.[35]

The goal of returning to the gold standard at the old rate was persuasive because nearly a century of experience had shown that the standard and Britain's adjustment mechanisms had worked smoothly and swiftly. Sterling's value had effectively been fixed since 1821, and the other major currencies had not changed in value much in the thirty years prior to 1914. These experiences and beliefs meant other possible options were not adequately explored, even when officials accepted that the transition to such a high exchange rate would be difficult.[36] These beliefs could very well have muted any sectoral opposition to a return to gold as the solution to the overhang.

Consequences: The Short-Lived Reconstructed Gold Standard

The difficulty in this case comes in measuring the impact of ideology separate from institutional factors.[37] Systemic theories also contribute something, if only to provide insight into how the problem of the overhang came about. Since all the arguments point to similar outcomes, the only way to test them is to compare more details in the evidence. It is also possible to specify our questions in different ways. For instance, we could compare how each type of theory explains the specific timing of the return to the gold standard, or in what order the different types of actors organize and act. The bureaucratic politics argument may give us more insight here, simply because of the nature of the issue. It is hard for domestic groups to ask for monetary policy changes without some sort of disagreement among the monetary institutions.

After Britain had struggled to get back on the gold standard, and even sacrificed industry's interests, defending the overvalued exchange rate was still difficult. The problems eventually came to a head in 1931 when financial crises in other countries caused many banks to hoard gold. Pounds were brought back to Britain and cashed in for gold—on Wednesday, 16 September, 5 million pounds were exchanged for gold. The following day the figure rose to 10 million, and then on Friday to 18 million. The Bank of England only had another 130 million pounds worth of gold left, so over the weekend it was decided to suspend convertibility into gold, lest the reserves be drained completely. (France had been part of the problem, since the French central bank had been converting pounds into gold all summer. After Britain suspended convertibility, the French central bank was stuck holding £62 million.)

Britain's move was followed by others. The U.S. went off in 1933; France held out until 1936, which was much too late. By staying on gold for so long, the French policy-makers constrained their own choices, which prevented economic recovery before World War II. By going off gold, the other countries were able to replicate some of the policies they had pursued to their advantage during the war. They were free to manipulate the money supply. They all first tried to devalue quite quickly—what is also known as a *competitive* or *predatory devaluation*, since devaluing has the effect of lowering your prices relative to everyone else. The aim was to expand exports, which should stimulate production and pull the economy out of the downward spiral. There is a great incentive to be the first to devalue, since whoever goes first gets the most gain. Of course, within a relatively short time many of the major economies had done exactly the same thing, so none gained any special advantage.[38]

Countries began to exert greater control over international transactions and international exchange, with repercussions in other issue-areas. The Germans, to prevent money from leaving the country, had already set up barriers preventing capital exports in August and September 1931. Other countries soon adopted similar policies. As a result, new international investments fell off, and it became harder to pay debts from existing international investments. Meanwhile, countries had already been doing some of the very same things in the area of trade. Britain set up a monetary bloc within the colonies and Commonwealth based on use of the pound. The Japanese set up a yen bloc in Asia. The U.S. had a de facto dollar bloc in Latin America. These blocs made trade flow along preferential lines, since payments were easier within the blocs. Trade had already started to be closed down soon after the economic downturn following the stock market crash of 1929. The American response had been to implement the trade policy equivalent of predatory devaluations. The reasons for that, and the consequences, are examined in the next chapter.

Suggested Readings

Stephen Blank, "Britain," in Peter Katzen-stein, ed., *Between Power and Plenty.* Madison: University of Wisconsin Press, 1978, 89–137.

Michael K. Bordo and Anna J. Schwartz, eds., *A Retrospective on the Classical Gold Standard, 1821-1931.* Chicago: University of Chicago Press, 1984.

Barry Eichengreen, *Golden Fetters: The Gold Standard and the Great Depression.* Oxford: Oxford University Press, 1992.

Jeffry Frieden, *Banking on the World.* New York: Harper & Row, 1987.

John Maynard Keynes, *The Economic Consequences of Mr. Churchill.* London: Hogarth Press, 1925.

Diane Kunz, *The Battle for Britain's Gold Standard in 1931.* London: Croom Helm, 1987.

Notes

1   There were significant departures from this ideal operation of the standard in practice. In fact, large countries had so little of their economies involved in trade that the flows of gold were too small to force through the adjustments described here; Britain developed practices that manipulated the flows of capital in and out of London so that it could avoid adjustments if desired; not all countries could maintain the gold standard rules because they lacked the domestic institutions necessary. The system could hardly be considered natural and neutral. See Marcello de Cecco, *Money and Empire* (Totowa, NJ: Rowman & Littlefield, 1975); Donald N. McCloskey and Richard J. Zecher, "How the Gold Standard Worked, 1880-1913," in Jacob A. Frenkel and Harry G. Johnson, eds., *The Monetary Approach to the Balance of Payments* (London: Allen & Unwin, 1976).

2   See Peter Lindert, "Key Currencies and Gold, 1900-1913," *Princeton Studies in International Finance* No. 24 (August 1969).

3   Susan Howson, *Domestic Monetary Management in Britain 1919-1938* (New York: Cambridge University Press, 1975), 11-13.

4   Ibid., 4.

5   Ibid., 25.

6   Ibid., 28.

7   John Guiseppi, *The Bank of England* (Chicago: Henry Regnery, 1966), 147.

8   D.E. Moggridge, *The Return to Gold, 1925: The Formulation of Economic Policy and its Critics* (London: Cambridge University Press, 1969), 23; Alec Cairncross and Barry Eichengreen, *Sterling in Decline* (Oxford: Basil Blackwell, 1983), 50-51.

9   D.E. Moggridge, *British Monetary Policy 1924-1931* (New York: Cambridge University Press, 1972), 28-29; Howson, *Domestic Monetary Management in Britain*, 24.

10 Moggridge, *The Return to Gold*, 21.

11 Howson, *Domestic Monetary Management in Britain*, 1.

12 M.E. Falkus, "U.S. Economic Policy and the 'Dollar Gap' of the 1920s," *Economic History Review* (2nd ser.) 24, 4 (November 1971), 599-623.

13 This is well laid out in David Lake, "International Economic Structures and American Foreign Economic Policy, 1887-1934," *World Politics* 35, 4 (July 1983), 517-43.

14 Stephen Krasner, "State Power and the Structure of International Trade," *World Politics* 28, 3 (April 1976), 342. This argument is also consistent with that put forward by Judith Goldstein in *Ideas, Interests, and American Trade Policy* (Ithaca, NY: Cornell University Press, 1993). As she puts it (p. xii), "the creation of rules and procedures to enforce a particular economic strategy at one point acts as a constraint not only on current behaviour but also on the range of options available to future entrepreneurs." This also fits in with broader theories about institutions and path-dependency. As Geoffrey Garrett and Peter Lange point out in their assessment of historical structural arguments on the role of institutions in "Internationalization, Institutions and Political Change," *International Organization* 49, 4 (Autumn 1995), 628, "institutions invariably outlive the constellations of interests that created them, and hence provide barriers to market-driven policy change."

15 Susan Strange, *Sterling and British Policy: A Political Study of an International Currency in Decline* (New York: Oxford University Press, 1971), 47.

16 Michael Edelstein, "Rigidity and Bias in the British Capital Market, 1870-1913," in Donald N. McCloskey, ed., *Essays on a Mature Economy: Britain after 1840* (Princeton, NJ: Princeton University Press, 1971), 83-105.

17 Peter Katzenstein, "Conclusion: Domestic Structures and Strategies of Foreign Economic Policy," in Katzenstein, ed., *Between Power and Plenty* (Madison: University of Wisconsin Press, 1978), 309.

18 Moggridge, *British Monetary Policy 1924-1931*, 46.

19 Bernard Elbaum and William Lazonick, "The Decline of the British Economy: An Institutional Perspective," *Journal of Economic History* 44, 2 (June 1984), 581.

20 Moggridge, *British Monetary Policy 1924-1931*, 236-37.

21 For a more in-depth discussion, see Beth Simmons, *Who Adjusts?* (Princeton, NJ: Princeton University Press, 1994).

22 Moggridge, *British Monetary Policy 1924-1931*, pp. 99-100.

23 Howson, *Domestic Monetary Management in Britain*, 36, 141.

24 Cairncross and Eichengreen, *Sterling in Decline*, 41.

25 Mark R. Brawley, *Afterglow or Adjustment?* (forthcoming).

26 Moggridge, *British Monetary Policy 1924-1931*, 145.

27 Ibid., 160-61.

28 Strange, *Sterling and British Policy*, 50; Howson, *Domestic Monetary Management in Britain*, 56.

29 Moggridge, *British Monetary Policy 1924-1931*, 237; Howson, *Domestic Monetary Management in Britain*, 9.

30 As cited in Cairncross and Eichengreen, *Sterling in Decline*, 38.

31 Ibid, 46-47.

32 As quoted ibid., 54.

33 Ibid., 60-61; M. June Flanders, *International Monetary Economics, Between the Classical and the New Classical* (New York: Cambridge University Press, 1989), 87-88, 100.

34 Moggridge, *British Monetary Policy 1924-1931*, 86-87.

35 Ibid., 57-58.

36 Ibid., 3-4; Moggridge, *The Return to Gold*, 65; also see Cairncross and Eichengreen, *Sterling in Decline*, 29.

37 It is easier to treat these as two separate but reinforcing forces; see Goldstein, *Ideas, Interests, and American Trade Policy*.

38 The depreciations may have helped stimulate some recovery none the less: see Barry Eichengreen and Jeffrey Sachs, "Exchange Rates and Economic Recovery in the 1930s," *Journal of Economic History* 45, 4 (December 1985), 925-26.

Fourteen

THE PASSAGE OF THE SMOOT–HAWLEY TARIFF

Introduction:
The Trade Regime after World War I

Just as monetary relations were upset by the war, so, too, were trade patterns. During the war, each country tried to manipulate its international economic relations to aid its own war effort. The European governments acted to direct trade and international payments towards political goals. Even Britain finally moved away from free trade. Two significant measures were taken by Britain to protect domestic industry and reduce imports (Britain wanted to spend precious foreign currency on war material only and not on foreign goods that could be produced at home). The first step away from free trade occurred with the enactment of the McKenna Duties, which were put in place during World War 1 (in 1916). After the war, in 1921, they were reinforced and rationalized by the postwar Safeguarding of Industries Act. These represent the first times since 1846 that Britain raised tariffs.

Other countries raised tariffs during the war. The United States moved towards free trade before the war broke out with the passage of the Underwood Tariff in 1913. The Underwood Tariff was the lowest tariff the U.S. had adopted up to that time. But since the war was seen as disrupting existing trade patterns, the U.S. decided to insulate its own economy from these disruptions. This gave it incentives to pass new, higher tariffs. These incentives were especially strong since all the major combatants had raised tariffs on industrial goods during the war, but most had been eager to import food. The U.S. had managed to increase its agricultural exports during the war; however, once the war ended, the European countries tended to keep their industrial tariffs in place and likewise began to protect agriculture in order to shift back to more normal production mixes. In some regions, the war had altered political settlements, such as Eastern and Central Europe where several old empires were dissolved. The new countries in Central and Eastern Europe established after World War 1 had political economic goals that made it more likely they would employ tariffs. Each wanted to develop its own industrial base, which meant they all adopted high tariffs to discriminate against exports of finished goods.

The U.S. became concerned with the role of tariffs in the postwar adjustment process as countries returned to peacetime production. In 1921 the U.S. passed the Emergency Tariff, which raised duties on a few selected items. This signalled a change in behaviour, however, and heralded some of the tariff competition to follow. In 1922, the U.S. raised tariffs across the board, and for the first time raised *agricultural* tariffs to protect the domestic producers who had recently lost access to European markets.

These early tariff wrangles were symptomatic of the deeper problem faced in the 1920s—how could all these countries end their wartime production and return their economies to peacetime practices? This problem took on different dimensions in different places. In the U.S., the problem was that the Americans had done well in industry, services, and agriculture during the war because foreign competition had more or less disappeared. Once the war ended, the competition returned, and agriculture in particular had problems. The same sort of thing was happening in Latin America and the Pacific, where local industrialization had picked up or regional trade had increased in new and different ways. As international competition returned, it threatened to undo the recent changes and to push trade back to historical patterns. This was being pushed by those who wanted their old markets back but being resisted by those who now considered these markets their own.

The critical sector turned out to be agricultural. In the 1920s all the major trading countries raised their tariffs on agricultural goods. Overproduction would have occurred anyway, but the tariffs made the problem worse. Agricultural goods flooded the international markets and prices fell to lower and lower levels, until they were only at about 20 per cent of pre-war price levels. This obviously drove many farmers out of business. The United States, for instance, actually began to import agricultural goods in 1927, for the first time ever, because international prices fell so low. The political response was not surprising—farmers went to the government and demanded protection.

The stock market had crashed in 1929, financial crisis had spread everywhere, and demand was falling off in the U.S. and elsewhere. When the farmers asked for protection this time, there were potential allies. Other sectors were interested in protection, too, so the deal struck was broad and its impact forceful. Everyone else was willing to support the farmers' demands as long as they, too, received protective tariffs. This is an example of a legislative technique called "logrolling." In order to get one group's legislation through, many other groups' narrow conditions must be met; the various demands are wrapped up in one package and passed. The result, the Smoot-Hawley Tariff of 1930, moved American tariffs from among some of the lowest to among some of the highest. Whereas the U.S. had appeared to be one of the strongest proponents of trade liberalization in 1913, it now led the closure of the trade regime in the 1930s.

Systemic Theory: A Failed Hegemonic Transition?

For the realists, this episode creates a number of serious questions. If hegemonic stability theory is correct, the U.S. policy is difficult to understand. Since the U.S. emerged from World War 1 as the economic and financial centre of the international political economy, was its interest not in re-creating and then maintaining an open trading system? By leading the closure of the trade regime, the U.S. was certainly not stabilizing the regime. Why wasn't the U.S. acting more like a hegemonic power? More importantly for realists, could these questions be answered with the focus remaining on systemic variables?

One possible answer comes from David Lake,[1] whose argument hinges on how one identifies a hegemonic power. In short, he tries to make his own definition of hegemony more specific, while also identifying roles for other countries in the system. He argues that only states with significant involvement in the international economy and also high productivity relative to other states will have the interests and the capabilities to act as liberalizing hegemonic leaders. Productivity is used to gauge a country's economic competitiveness. States heavily involved in trade but with low productivity are more likely to act as "spoilers." That is, they would participate in the trade regime, yet resist opening up their own economies to foreign competition. States with a medium level of involvement in international trade and high relative productivity, on the other hand, have an interest in seeing the trade regime liberalized but may not have the capabilities to act as a leaders; thus, Lake termed such states "supporters."

The central question becomes where one draws the lines between medium and heavy involvement in the international economy, since that divides hegemonic powers from supporters.[2] Lake used the level of 15 per cent of world trade to mark where a state would hold hegemonic status. Britain's share of world trade had slumped below this level prior to World War 1, yet the American share would not rise above that line until after World War 1. In this interpretation, there were two "supporters" in the interwar years. It was a transition from one hegemonic leader to another, but one that was incomplete. While it was possible for these two countries to co-operate to provide stability and leadership, this co-operation was difficult to attain.

Rather than co-operation, a different sort of game took place. Each country knew the other was interested in maintaining freer trade in the international political economy—they were in head-to-head competition in several sectors and in many different regions of the world. Thus, each knew the other might take up some of the costs associated with providing leadership. The two engaged in a game of competitive irresponsibility (which we can model in game theory as "Chicken").[3] By acting irresponsibly, one state could hope to force the other to carry more of the burdens. This seems to capture the American attitudes in particular, since the U.S. government was doing its best to avoid any costly foreign policy activities. As the international economy became more unstable and concessions from the two supporters were less forthcoming, export markets were at risk. Without export markets, each of the two supporters had less and less to gain from leadership, until one—the U.S.—moved to defect from the regime first.

Domestic Level: The Logrolling of Sectoral Interests

While the system-level arguments of the realists provide a superficial fit with the evidence, questions remain. Why was the U.S. unwilling to carry more of the burdens of leadership? To answer that question, one must turn to the domestic level and consider politics within the country. Moreover, the domestic level theories may offer greater insight into the timing of the event. They may be able to tell us why the tariff was passed in 1930, as well as why the tariff took the shape that it did.

The Smoot-Hawley Tariff has long been the subject of political research. In some of the earliest analyses, the role of "pork-barrel politics" in the formation of the tariff took centre stage.[4] Pork-barrel politics refers to the traditional American practice where the members of Congress worry only about the impact of legislation in terms of their own constituency. The institutional structure of the American government encourages this pattern, leaving the President to worry about the impact on the country as a whole. The logroll of the tariff thus served many narrow interests, but taken overall its impact was negative for the country. In this analysis, the tariff is understood as the product of congressional practices.

Later analyses still rely on this sort of thinking to establish the conditions for such a logroll to take place but argue that the conditions existed long before the Smoot-Hawley Tariff was passed. The same institutional setting had produced the Underwood Tariff, which had been extremely low. What nudged Congress in the protectionist direction? According to Robert

Pastor, the answer can be found in party politics.[5] The Republicans had favoured protectionism for some time, while the Democrats had not. In the election of 1928 the Republicans won a majority in Congress and a Republican, Herbert Hoover, was elected President. Pastor argued that the Republicans placed faith in protectionism as an effective policy for remedying certain economic problems, so that when groups came and asked for help, the Republicans in Congress were more than willing to oblige with a tariff. Then the logroll took place and the tariff grew in size and scope.

One of the strongest insights to be raised more recently about the importance of the domestic-level factors in the passage of Smoot-Hawley comes from Barry Eichengreen. Eichengreen largely agrees with the earlier analyses of Schattschneider, in that interest groups pursuing pork-barrel politics brought about the logroll. As Eichengreen points out, if interest groups were to blame, along with Congressmen worried about narrow interests, then we would have expected the vote to be a landslide. After all, the pressures would have been the same for all Congressmen. Instead, the vote fell along party lines.[6] At first blush this seems to support Pastor's argument. In fact, Eichengreen disputes this and points out that both parties had supported protectionism (albeit at lower levels) at points in the recent past. Neither side in the debate could expect to support free trade by standing on principle. It wouldn't have been a credible position, and in fact the opponents of the tariff did not use ideological arguments as their centrepiece.

Eichengreen returns to the arguments about interest groups, but examines how their political power changed in the 1920s. Participation in World War 1 had profoundly altered the relationship between government and interest groups in two important ways. First, government had encouraged the organization of interests in order to promote economic activity as part of the war effort. The government encouraged both industry and agriculture to organize into large bodies to simplify the bureaucratic tasks of placing large contracts for goods and services. As a result, in the 1920s interest groups were more numerous than before, had more members, and were attuned to dealing with government. This increase in organized interest groups was reflected in the number presenting arguments in the debates surrounding the passage of the Smoot-Hawley Tariff.

That leads us to Eichengreen's other observation about the changes in the relationship between the government and interest groups. The interest groups had more extensive links to government than ever before. Prior to World War 1, interest groups stood apart from government, but by the late 1920s the same groups were right in the midst of political activities via numerous access points.[7] They were deeply involved in the legislative process and could be found on both sides of the debates. The strength of each coalition was therefore important for the tariff's passage. Prominent among the pro-protectionist groups were northern farmers (who grew grain) and labour-intensive industries. Labour organizations such as the American Federation of Labor (AFL) also turned protectionist. Farmers in particular were overrepresented, according to Eichengreen.

The main opponents to protectionism came from sectors using a lot of capital in the production of goods and services. Heavy industry and banking fall into this category. Southern farmers (who grew cotton and other competitive crops) tended to support freer trade. These groups could not rally the same support as the protectionist forces, however. If we were to return to our economic models of the distribution of the benefits of trade liberalization from the Stolper-Samuelson theorem, we would find that these alignments fit our expectations. The U.S. was moving from a relatively labour- and land-abundant economy to one where capital and land were relatively abundant. Yet these groups were unable to prevent the passage of a new higher tariff because they lacked the political power within Congress.

In a similar sort of analysis, Jeffry Frieden examines the two opposing coalitions. His argument is that the coalition of the domestically oriented sectors and that of the internationally oriented sectors were about the same strength.[8] Each side could control elements of the American political system, so a stalemate resulted. Policy therefore was driven first in one direction, then the other; on closer inspection, it is easy to see how American foreign economic policy in this period often contained contradictions. By moving to a broader picture (i.e., not simply looking at trade and tariffs) we can see how trade policy and monetary relations were not always headed in the same direction.

Bureaucratic Politics: The Fed's Attempts at International Leadership

Such arguments blend together the domestic politics arguments with those from bureaucratic politics. They are less useful for explaining the passage of the Smoot-Hawley Tariff, but shed light on how the U.S. was pursuing a mix of policies. The nationally oriented economic actors had strong organizations that gave them power in Congress (and hence the tariff was protectionist), but the anti-protectionist forces had their allies within the government, too. The banking community, for instance, had extensive connections with the Federal Reserve Banks. The banking community therefore tried to influence outcomes through the policy of the Federal Reserve Bank of New York. While this did not do them much good in trade policy, it did mean that in the 1920s the U.S. had exhibited some facets of leadership in the area of monetary policy. These efforts were not sanctioned by the President or Congress, however.

The governor of the New York Reserve Bank, Benjamin Strong, had urged the U.S. to hold an international conference to resolve the issue of debts after the war ended. Private firms in the U.S. had lent billions to allied governments before the U.S. officially entered the war. The allies didn't want to repay the debts, arguing that they had made more substantial sacrifices for the war in terms of their human losses. Strong proposed that all payments should be suspended for up to five years (or even longer if possible) and that the payments be reduced as much as possible, with the U.S. government extending credits to countries in difficulty.[9] Strong's views reflected those of the internationally oriented financial firms based in New York, which saw gains from the United States leading the reopening of the liberal international economic system. Instead, official policy (set by the executive branch) refused to take on any burdensome obligations. The U.S. funding commission set up in 1922 to renegotiate debt repayments refused any reduction of the amounts outstanding. This stand prompted the U.S. to refuse to send an official participant to the Geneva Conference held in 1922, thus leaving it without representation in crucial international monetary negotiations.[10]

Another example comes from 1927, when a surge of gold flowed out of Europe and into the United States. Other central bankers appealed to the Fed to ease its policies and reduce the amount of gold the U.S. was drawing in. Strong complied, so the Fed ran a counter-cyclical policy. (This was only the second time such a policy had been attempted; the first had been in 1924, when the goal had been to re-establish the international gold standard.) The aim was to establish an interest rate differential between New York and London that would divert international funds to Britain; rather than manage policy towards purely domestic goals, the Fed was trying to stabilize international flows.[11] Strong hoped that the policy would not only stabilize the two currencies but also help New York attract some of London's traditional business.[12]

These actions ended the strong flows of gold and stabilized the international financial system, but Strong's opponents pointed out how domestic economic goals had been subordinated to international needs. Worse still, because bank holdings were high, when extra reserves were released by the low interest rates in New York the banks engaged in risky loans, which in turn merely fuelled stock market speculation prior to the crash of October 1929.[13] Herbert Hoover (who served as President Coolidge's Secretary of Commerce prior to becoming President) clearly linked the Fed's international interests to its easy money policy and then to the stock market speculation and crash. Others have argued, however, that while Fed policy was slanted towards international goals in 1927, when sterling was under pressure in 1928-29, the Fed followed a policy guided by domestic concerns.[14] Since different Federal Reserve Banks were doing different things, both interpretations have an element of truth.

Policies outside of trade therefore looked somewhat different from trade policy. But the banking community did not have the connections to change trade policy itself. Instead, different facets of foreign policy ran in competition with each other. The result was failed leadership. This evidence supports the arguments made earlier; it also points out how, in foreign economic policy-making, bureaucracies have fairly clearly defined constituencies to which they respond. It makes it more difficult to use a bureaucratic politics analysis in the absence of a domestic politics argument.

Ideas and the Failure of Experts

Among the most poignant aspects of the debate leading up to the passage of the Smoot-Hawley Tariff were the numerous presentations made by the academic community. Professional economists seemed nearly unanimous in their opposition to the tariff. Many of the economists correctly predicted the disastrous results that would unfold if the tariff was passed. The tariff's passage led to retaliations by other countries and soon the economists' predictions came true. The Smoot-Hawley Tariff did not help American businesses, but rather did them great harm.

This poses several questions for those who would argue that ideas, by themselves, are powerful factors shaping foreign economic policy. Here the ideas were strongly supported by the relevant community of experts—there was a tremendous consensus among them. Moreover, this consensus had existed for some time. The economists' belief in the correctness of free trade had been held for decades. There was no surge of new ideologies or theoretical arguments to challenge that consensus, either. (Those rival ideas, such as socialism or even the pre-theories surrounding the utility of government intervention in the economy, could not command much support in the American political system yet.) As Eichengreen has pointed out, the ideological aspect of the debates was played out at the margins, not at the forefront.

Those who would have us see ideas as independently powerful factors need to elaborate the conditions under which ideas can play an important role and the conditions under which an epistemic community has power. Some analyses of American trade policy suggest that within a few years liberalism would become entrenched in institutions.[15] Why were the ideas supporting a policy of free trade so weak in 1929-30, yet so strong such a short time later? The interactions of ideas with other causal forces need to be further elaborated.

The Consequences of the Smoot-Hawley Tariff

When the American market was effectively closed off, it started a chain reaction—though it might be better to compare the reactions with a race. The producers of goods previously exported to the U.S. suddenly had to find new international markets; since Britain was the next most open economy for international trade, all the producers tried to shift their sales to Britain. Britain suffered a crisis as a flood of cheaply priced goods entered its market, so that British producers needed protection. The government felt compelled to close itself off as well. Other countries felt the same sorts of pressures, so they, too, raised tariffs.

These tariff strategies are referred to as "beggar thy neighbour" policies because whoever moves first gains in the short run but makes the impact worse for everyone else. (It fits the prisoners' dilemma game quite well.) So after 1930, and until 1933, tariffs on all sorts of goods were rising in all the major countries. Britain, which had resisted the temptation to close off the Empire and Dominions from international competition during its relative economic decline, reversed its stance. In 1931 Britain enacted the Imperial Preference System, focusing its trade and international investment almost totally on the Empire after that. For example, in 1913 Britain sent 22 per cent of its exports to the Empire, but by 1938 that had changed to 47 per cent. In 1913, 20 per cent of Britain's imports had come from the Empire, but by 1938 that figure had risen to 39 per cent. While this supported some of Britain's previous international economic interactions, Britain had lost the American market as well as many others.

Trade collapsed. Since the Great Depression was just beginning, these tariffs wrecked whatever possible positive role trade could have played in lifting countries out of their economic downturns. As exports decreased, exporting sectors also began to lay off workers, so that the impact was merely to accelerate the downward spiral of the economy. As more workers got laid off, they were unable to afford goods; demand fell lower, so that firms cut back production, and the cycle built on itself. Worse, the economic downturn and the collapse of trade encouraged several countries to create regional trade blocs. These trade blocs were aimed at economic self-sufficiency; if countries needed resources they could not get through trade, they used other policies to attain their needs. In places where unemployment was extremely high, fascist regimes took power. These countries saw conquest as the best way to do without trade. Soon Nazi Germany and Imperial Japan would use warfare as an element of their foreign economic policies. The collapse of trade, sparked by the Smoot-Hawley Tariff, helped lead to World War 11.

Suggested Readings

Colleen M. Callahan, Judith A. McDonald, and Anthony Patrick O'Brien, "Who Voted for Smoot-Hawley?" *Journal of Economic History* 54, 3 (September 1994), 683-90.

John Conybeare, "Trade Wars: A Comparative Study of Anglo-Hanse, Franco-Italian and Hawley-Smoot Conflicts," *World Politics* 38, 1 (October 1985), 147-72.

Barry Eichengreen, "The Political Economy of the Smoot-Hawley Tariff," *Research in Economic History* 12 (1989), 1-43.

Jeffry Frieden, "Sectoral Conflict and U.S. Foreign Economic Policy, 1914-1940," in John Ikenberry, David A. Lake, and Michael Mastanduno, eds., *The State and American Foreign Economic Policy*. Ithaca, NY: Cornell University Press, 1988, 59-90.

Peter Gourevitch, *Politics in Hard Times*. Ithaca, NY: Cornell University Press, 1986.

Marc Hayford and Carl Pasurka, "The Political Economy of the Fordney-McCumber and Smoot-Hawley Tariff Acts," *Explorations in Economic History* 29, 1 (January 1992), 30-50.

David Lake, "International Economic Structures and American Foreign Economic Policy, 1887-1934," *World Politics* 35, 4 (July 1983), 517-43.

David Lake, *Power, Protection and Free Trade*. Ithaca, NY: Cornell University Press, 1988.

Réal Lavergne, *The Political Economy of U.S. Tariffs: An Empirical Analysis*. Toronto: Academic Press, 1983.

Robert Pastor, *Congress and the Politics of US Foreign Economic Policy, 1929-1976*. Berkeley: University of California Press, 1980.

E.E. Schattschneider, *Politics, Pressures and the Tariff*. New York: Prentice-Hall, 1935.

Notes

1   David A. Lake, "International Economic Structures and American Foreign Economic Policy, 1887-1934," *World Politics* 35, 4 (July 1983), 517-43.

2   As for relative productivity, a country is either above average or below.

3   See Mark R. Brawley, *Liberal Leadership* (Ithaca, NY: Cornell University Press, 1993), ch. 5.

4   E.E. Schattschneider, *Politics, Pressures and the Tariff* (New York: Prentice-Hall, 1935).

5   Robert Pastor, *Congress and the Politics of U.S. Foreign Economic Policy, 1929-1976* (Berkeley: University of California Press, 1980).

6   Barry Eichengreen, "The Political Economy of the Smoot-Hawley Tariff," *Research in Economic History* 12 (1989), 1-43.

7   Ibid.

8   Jeffry Frieden, "Sectoral Conflict and U.S. Foreign Economic Policy, 1914-1940," in John Ikenberry, David A. Lake, and Michael Mastanduno, eds., *The State and American Foreign Economic Policy* (Ithaca, NY: Cornell University Press, 1988), 59-90.

9   Lester V. Chandler, *Benjamin Strong, Central Banker* (Washington: Brookings Institution, 1958), 143-45, 294-95; Stephen V.O. Clarke, "The Reconstruction of the International Monetary System: The Attempts of 1922 and 1933," *Princeton Studies in International Finance* No. 33 (November 1973), 15.

10 Clarke, "The Reconstruction of the International Monetary System," 7-8.

11 Elmus Wicker, *Federal Reserve Monetary Policy 1917-1933* (New York: Random House, 1966), 106, 114-15; Stephen V.O. Clarke, *Central Bank Cooperation 1924-1931* (New York: Federal Reserve Bank of New York, 1967), 125.

12 Clarke, *Central Bank Cooperation*, 72-73.

13 Donald F. Kettl, *Leadership at the Fed* (New Haven: Yale University Press, 1986), 33-34; William Grieder, *Secrets of the Temple* (New York: Simon & Schuster, 1987), 301-03; Albert Fishlow, "Lessons from the Past: Capital Markets during the Nineteenth Century and the Interwar Period," *International Organization* 39, 3 (Summer 1985), 80-81.

14 Clarke, *Central Bank Cooperation*, 42-43.

15 Judith Goldstein, *Ideas, Interests, and American Trade Policy* (Ithaca, NY: Cornell University Press, 1993).

Fifteen

THE CREATION OF THE BRETTON WOODS MONETARY REGIME

While the trade and monetary regimes were already largely closed off before World War II, the war itself naturally disrupted the relations that had been maintained. The war had another effect—it once again stimulated the economic growth of the United States. The American economy finally recovered from the Great Depression, thanks to the massive orders for war material. After the period of high unemployment, American policy-makers were especially concerned with avoiding postwar economic problems this time around. The U.S. and Britain knew that they wanted to re-establish international economic regimes around liberal principles. Leaders from the two countries held several meetings during the war to design these regimes.[1] Other nations also participated in some of these meetings, and that was considered essential by the Americans and British if these arrangements were to succeed since other states would have to participate.

One of the most important of these wartime discussions was held in Bretton Woods, New Hampshire, in 1944. Some forty-four allied nations sent representatives to these talks, which had the explicit aim of constructing the postwar monetary system. The results, however, were largely dominated by the need to construct a consensus among the most important financial powers.[2] The discussions culminated in the creation of the International Monetary Fund (IMF) and the International Bank for Reconstruction and Development (IBRD, better known as the World Bank). The IMF was created to assist countries with short-term balance-of-payments problems. The IBRD was to aid in recovery from the war and future economic development.[3]

These two institutions signalled a new approach to the construction of economic regimes. First, they embodied institutional support for liberal practices. They were, in that sense, a reflection of the new attitudes about the need for government action to stabilize or manage markets. There were three goals in the Bretton Woods system, as it came to be called: (1) to establish free capital flows; (2) to make currencies convertible into gold and/or other currencies; (3) to create stable exchange rates. These goals reflect the desire to reattain the benefits associated with the gold standard. They were also shaped by the needs of the trade and investment regimes being established. If international payments on trade are to be made, there must be some form of convertible payments. The investment regime, if based on liberal economic principles, would require free capital flows.

Within these three characteristics, though, many different arrangements are possible. For instance, the gold standard achieved similar ends by fixing all currencies in terms of gold. Because of the troubles in adjusting currencies to each other, this regime had been difficult to re-create after World War I. Gold had also been poorly distributed for return to such a system after 1918; in 1945, gold reserves were concentrated in the American vaults—it would have been impossible to base numerous countries' reserves entirely on gold. The gold-exchange standard set up briefly after World War I was intended to achieve the same three goals, but in a different way. The fixed exchange rate regime established under the Bretton Woods agreement would be geared to attain the same aims, but through different mechanisms and rules.

These new mechanisms and rules drew on lessons learned from the experiences of the 1930s. The most important lesson was that market forces created problems—governments needed to manage the international system, especially since all governments wished to pursue Keynesian programs domestically. Although this lesson was universal, that did not guarantee any agreement on how to establish an international regime congruent with new domestic practices. In fact, with an international monetary regime based on purely liberal principles new problems were anticipated, since no governments were following laissez-faire economics domestically. There was no consensus on the best way to resolve the tensions being created.

In the United States, the greatest fear was that there would be another recession after World War II. Production in the U.S. had risen dramatically in the war, and some American leaders feared overproduction in many economic sectors after Europe got back on its feet. Therefore, the economic nationalists in the U.S. wanted to make sure the U.S. could use Keynesian interventions in the economy to prop up demand if necessary. This group, led by Henry Morgenthau, the Secretary of the Treasury, and Harry Dexter White, the Assistant Secretary of the Treasury, wanted to make sure any international agreement on monetary affairs would not bind the American government's ability to act at home. Remember how the gold standard had forced inflation or deflation on governments? White and Morgenthau wanted to ensure that any future arrangements would allow the U.S. government the ability to pursue inflationary policies whenever necessary.

Morgenthau and White pushed to break the link between domestic inflationary policies and the impact of the balance of trade. There were domestic opponents to this perspective, especially among the representatives of the international business community. These had their own representatives in the U.S. government, led first by Cordell Hull, the Secretary of State, and then by his successor, Dean Acheson. While this side of the debate obviously agreed that the U.S. should do all that it could to avoid any postwar recession, they also thought the U.S. could do this without having to give up the possible restraints imposed by a fixed exchange rate system.

At first, the economic nationalists won out. This group convinced President Franklin Roosevelt of the correctness of their views, so he appointed some of them to draw up plans for the postwar monetary system. Harry Dexter White therefore had the greatest input into the design of the system, and then White was assigned the post of chief American negotiator in the international bargaining.

The White Plan versus the Keynes Plan

First, White's plan envisioned an International Monetary Fund with strong powers to advise governments on domestic macroeconomic policies. His real desire here was to give the IMF power to force or at least strongly encourage governments to pursue Keynesian full employment policies. More importantly, he wanted the IMF to get countries to pursue such policies together. Everything would work well if all the countries stimulated their economies at the same time and none engaged in competitive devaluation or protectionism. As White put it, when there was no economic cooperation between countries, relations would "inevitably result in economic warfare that will be but the prelude and instigator of military warfare on an even vaster scale."[4]

In accordance with this plan, the IMF would have veto powers over any country's decisions to change its exchange rate. This would give the IMF the power to prevent one problem from the 1930s: competitive devaluations. At the time of the negotiations (1944), the U.S. had to convince Britain to go along with this rule (which Britain wasn't very interested in). There were some forty-four other countries represented at these talks, but they were all so weak in financial and economic terms that their views only mattered to the extent that they coincided with either the American or British perspectives. The British representative was John Maynard Keynes himself. He actually took a position against White's; Keynes, too, was concerned with full employment, but the problems confronting Britain differed significantly from those the U.S. faced.

During World War II Britain was forced to sell off much of the remainder of British foreign investment to finance the war effort. Britain lost the ability to live off the returns on the earlier foreign investments. This meant British imports would in the future have to be paid for by British exports— Britain would have to learn to produce competitive exports again. Keynes knew this would take time to arrange (he had no idea just how long!). What Keynes wanted was an IMF that would serve British needs—an IMF that would give out credits and loans so that Britain could rebuild its economy.

Also important to Keynes was that any international monetary system constructed be outside of the sole control of the U.S. This, of course, was the opposite of White's view. Keynes didn't want Britain at the mercy of the United States and therefore proposed an alternative institution to monitor and co-ordinate international monetary relations: the International Clearing Union. As its name indicates, this would be a clearing-house for national currencies; currencies would not actually have to be convertible into other assets or each other, at least not in any public market. Countries could eliminate their outstanding balances with each other via transactions entirely within this Clearing Union. Moreover, as Keynes envisioned it, the International Clearing Union would have the ability to make loans to deficit countries. While this sounds like White's IMF, the financing of loans was to be quite different. Deficit countries (such as Britain) would be loaned money on easy terms, while the ICU would tax those countries with a surplus (though there would be only one surplus country in the near future, the U.S.).

The agreement reached at Bretton Woods set forth the IMF charter and reflected the U.S. arguments rather than the British.[5] (1) The system was designed to operate in a stable international environment; but the rules recognized the probability of problems with adjustments in the years immediately after the war, and therefore countries were allowed to exempt themselves from the rules for the first five years, while they recovered. (2) Members pledged to maintain fixed exchange rates. In other words they declared an exchange rate (a parity) and pledged to keep their exchange rates within plus or minus 1 per cent of this parity. The governments kept to this parity by intervening in exchange markets, that is, by buying or selling on the exchange markets. It was hoped that by intervening in this way to deal with pressures on exchange rates, domestic policies could be separated from exchange rate policy. Money required for intervention in exchange could be loaned to governments via the IMF. (3) The policy-makers didn't want to be stuck defending a parity indefinitely. They therefore created a loophole. If a country was in a condition of "fundamental disequilibrium," an official change of the exchange rate would be allowed; changes greater than 10 per cent would still have to be approved by the IMF first. "Fundamental disequilibrium" was left undefined.

As part of the agreement, each nation was assigned a quota to contribute to the IMF's funds, based on the size of the country's economic and financial resources. This assessment had to be paid one-quarter in gold and three-quarters in national currency. More importantly, voting within the IMF was directly proportional to the quotas—the U.S. had the largest quota, which made up more than one-third of the total. Not too surprisingly, the rules stated that the important decisions within the IMF required a two-thirds majority—in effect, the U.S. got veto power over critical decisions. And since any exchange rate changes of more than 10 per cent had to be approved by the IMF, the U.S. could exercise a veto over those judgements as well.

Borrowing from the IMF was to be done in multiples of a country's quota (or tranche, as these are also called). But with each tranche, the restrictions the IMF could place on the borrowing country went up. The conditions the IMF would impose on borrowing would spell out the adjustment policies a country would need to implement if it was to correct its balance-of-payments deficit. In effect, this places the entire burden of adjustment on countries in deficit. The rules of the regime basically punish countries with serious balance-of-payments deficits but do nothing to countries running large surpluses. (Compare this to the workings of the gold standard, which in theory forced both surplus and deficit countries to adjust.) This presumably reflected the interests of the U.S. in the late 1940s (as the single largest country running a surplus), and also reflected the desires of the American economic nationalists.[6] The U.S. did not want the international monetary regime to drive the country out of a surplus and force it to raise unemployment levels. It is clear that White's desires were largely met, rather than those of Keynes, at least in the way the rules were laid out.

The Bretton Woods Regime in Operation

The Bretton Woods system as it was designed in the late 1940s had been a victory for the American economic nationalists, led by Harry Dexter White. But as soon as the regime had to be put into practice, the American international business sector once again fought a battle over the IMF's role (as well as that of the IBRD). The rules established by the economic nationalists allowed the participating countries to follow Keynesian full-employment policies, and had broken the link between fixed exchange rates and balance-of-payments adjustment as a means of disciplining the domestic economy. Exactly this point, however, made the international sectors (bankers especially) uncomfortable. The internationalists were concerned that the IBRD and IMF rules would make borrowing too easy and therefore would stimulate not just growth but inflation—in other words, they feared the international system would have too much liquidity. (Bankers always oppose inflation since it devalues savings.)

What happened in practice turned out to be a compromise, because the IMF and IBRD had to be very conservative with their funds. There are two ways of looking at this outcome. On the one hand, Roosevelt died and the new President, Harry Truman, did not particularly like White and Morgenthau. Truman followed the advice of Acheson instead. Alternatively, a second explanation focuses on the pressures existing on the IMF and IBRD. For the IBRD to work, for instance, it had to raise money. The donations to the IBRD were small, and therefore the World Bank had to raise capital the only other way open to it—it floated bonds. The IBRD had to gain the confidence of the banking community to sell these bonds, and the result was that the IMF and IBRD both began to follow much more conservative policies. So the change in practice reflects the needs of the institutions (to appease the bankers).

In practice, then, things did not work as White had actually intended. Borrowing from the IMF could only be done with serious strings attached. Of course, another factor was that the devastation caused by the war was more than anyone had expected. Europe was in very bad shape, and the initial European harvests after the war were extremely low. These years also included some severe winters, which worsened conditions in Europe. Some of the initial policy responses the Europeans considered hinted at protectionism, so there was a threat that the open trading and monetary systems would never have a chance to operate. In fact, some would argue that the IMF and IBRD had already been made too conservative by the late 1940s to do the job White had hoped they would do!

Since the institutions were unable to carry out their obligations, and most countries weren't prepared to adhere to the rules yet anyway, the U.S. took action unilaterally to deal with the emerging problems by stepping forward to manage two parts of the international monetary system by itself: (1) to provide liquidity and (2) to aid in the adjustment of exchange rates. The way the system had been designed, gold was supposed to be the reserve asset— the backing for national currencies. But there were several problems with this plan. First, there was not enough gold in the international system, and what there was, was in the U.S. The United States had plenty of gold reserves (49.8 per cent of total world monetary reserves in 1950). The U.S. was also the only country consistently running a surplus in balance of payments, so no gold was leaving the country.

Just as important was the fact that holding dollars was preferred to holding gold at this time. It was clear that dollars could be turned in and exchanged for gold, but most actors would rather have the dollars because they could be deposited at a bank where they would earn interest—dollars were better than gold. But this still left the problem of a liquidity shortage. The U.S. had a payments surplus, meaning it was exporting goods and drawing in not only gold but other currencies, too. So, in practice, there was not so much a gold shortage as a dollar shortage. American policy-makers determined that this shortage was an obstacle to further economic growth and was especially an obstacle to the expansion of trade. The difficulty was in infusing the right amount of dollars into the international system so as to stimulate growth but not create real inflation, as well as how to achieve this when the U.S. economy had such an edge over all its economic competitors. These difficulties would continue even after the rules of the Bretton Woods regime came into full effect. Indeed, they would create some of the very pressures that would undermine the regime, as will be discussed in Chapter 16. The point to consider now, however, has to do with understanding how we should explain the design of the Bretton Woods monetary regime.

The Liberals' Explanation: The Liberal Principles at the Heart of Bretton Woods

From the liberal viewpoint, the regime's most important aspects were the ways in which it supported liberal trading and financial practices. The regime promised to tie national markets together and reduce the risks of undertaking international economic exchange. It aimed to remove barriers to international transactions, thereby allowing individuals and firms to pursue their economic interests. This was done in ways that reinstilled liberal practices in international economic relations.

Exchange rates would be fixed. This would provide economic predictability reminiscent of the gold standard. The fixed exchange rates were meant to be somewhat flexible, however. The IMF was supposed to approve of exchange rate changes when needed. The system was supposed to provide both stability and flexibility. Financial markets would be open to private individuals and firms to participate in. This would be necessary for capital to flow over borders as international investments took place. The monetary relations would be consistent with liberal economic regimes in other issue-areas.

Of course, there would be some tensions here—especially from the liberal perspective. For instance, private actors buying and selling currencies on exchange markets should have meant that currencies would fluctuate in value as supply and demand changed. Yet the regime had governments promising to intervene in these markets so that the outcome was always the same. This could be done with little effort if exchange markets were small; what the regime's designers failed to anticipate was the massive growth of international investments and capital flows. Nowadays, speculative capital flows are worth much more than the money that crosses borders to finance trade.

Ruggie notes about the liberal perspective in general that whenever it is put into practice, it tries very hard to "disembed" the economic system. In their models, liberals treat the economic system as something separate from the other aspects of society. They remove other factors so they can study the market as an abstraction. When liberals give policy prescriptions they argue that the market should be separated from other forces.[7] That can never be done in its entirety; more often, the policy as proposed founders on social forces that were unaccounted for.

But as Ruggie notes, Karl Polanyi has shown how the 1930s were a period when the market broke down in most of the industrialized countries. Certainly, there was widespread agreement that the international market and the international financial system failed to function properly. As Polanyi stresses, in most countries the politics of the 1930s are characterized by the efforts of social forces to control the market once again.[8] Nowhere was this clearer than in the domestic struggles over monetary policy in the 1930s. The discussion in the chapter on Britain's resumption of the gold standard illustrates one example of this conflict, but the struggle was played out along similar lines elsewhere.

In the Bretton Woods regime, the liberal practices at the international level had to be reconciled in some manner with interventionist policies within the domestic economy. Institutions to facilitate co-ordination would be required, giving credence to some aspects of the institutionalist perspective; because the particular way of balancing these domestic and international practices was largely consistent with White's views, realists argue that the liberals confuse their description of the regime with an explanation. The regime may have been based on liberal principles, but that may have been because liberal practices were in the interest of the strongest state that participated in the regime.

A Realist Explanation: A Regime to Protect American Interests

From the realist perspective, what is important is how the rules of the Bretton Woods regime reflected American interests. American views, after all, dominated the decision-making at the Bretton Woods conference. For realists, the regime is the product of the distribution of power. The United States emerged from World War II with the most powerful economy and the greatest financial resources, as well as the most military power among the Western democracies. The U.S. would exercise its resources in such a way that the monetary regime created after the war operated to its own benefit.

Evidence supporting the realist perspective comes in several forms. In the new institutions created, the U.S. would wield extensive power. Of all the post-World War II international organizations, these were the only ones to have such proportional voting (except, of course, for the UN's Security Council, where voting was not proportional but the U.S. exercises a veto). The U.S. ensured, even in the face of Britain's opposition, that it would have a dominant role to play within these institutions.

Moreover, the ways in which the IMF supported the fixed exchange rates reflected American interests. As the only country running a balance-of-payments surplus and the only one likely to run a surplus in the near future, the American negotiators wanted to ensure that surplus countries would not be punished. The set of rules proposed by Keynes, for instance, would have had the surplus countries bearing some of the brunt of adjustment, since surplus countries would have been taxed. Deficit countries would have drawn on these taxes to finance their adjustments. Instead, the American-backed rules placed the entire burden of adjustment on deficit countries.

The U.S. dollar became the true international currency, though that would have happened by default. The U.S. did have to take several steps in the 1950s to boost international liquidity. Payments for goods at American military bases, tax laws, and other policies were used to stimulate a flow of dollars out of the U.S. and into the international political economy. These actions weren't in the original plans for the Bretton Woods regime—the original rules of the regime spelled out the expectation that gold would be the primary reserve asset for participating countries. This would not come to pass, and the U.S. stepped up to provide its own currency as a reserve. The U.S. stabilized the regime, but also benefited from placing its currency in this role. The realists certainly argue that how the regime evolved in practice those first few years showed how American leadership mattered, both for the regime's functioning but also for garnering the U.S. benefits. The U.S. had to take direct, unilateral action to help countries with their balance-of-payments adjustments.

The Constructivists' Criticisms

Constructivists are critical of the realist arguments. On the surface, the realists have a powerful interpretation, especially if we were to examine how the regime operated over time. But if we stay focused on the rules of Bretton Woods as originally designed, the constructivists point out that the realists fail to explain the overarching thrust of the Bretton Woods monetary regime. As J.G. Ruggie put it, the regime's "social purpose" cannot be deduced from the distribution of power alone. The regime's purpose can only be understood by looking at the previous monetary regimes and the problems of the interwar period.[9]

Ruggie argues that the Bretton Woods monetary regime represents a compromise between the goal of having a regime based on liberal economic principles (i.e., one that supports the free flow of goods, services, and capital internationally) and that of having a regime based on domestic policy autonomy. While this served American interests, those interests were largely domestic aims, not international goals. According to Ruggie, the rules of the regime hardly represent those the United States could have installed if it was truly interested in the pursuit of international power. The realist approach is therefore useful, but limited, in Ruggie's point of view.[10] In short, the distribution of power tells us about which countries to focus on, but we cannot deduce those countries' interests merely from their position in the international structure.[11]

Also important in the constructivists' view is how the realist argument is supposed to work—it assumes that a hegemonic state will rationally create the system that maximizes its power. That implies that the hegemonic state can choose any set of rules it desires; the hegemonic power will construct the regime with the set of rules that benefits itself relatively the most. That is impossible, argue the constructivists. The rules always are embedded in some broader social setting, which cannot be evaded. In this particular instance, the choices were constrained by the experiences of the 1920s and 1930s. The regime's rules, constructivists argue, were designed to deal with the problems of the past, not with maximizing U.S. power.

One of Ruggie's important contributions, using this constructivist framework, is to point out that power and social purpose do not always change simultaneously, nor do they have to push change in the same direction. In terms of theory, the results expected from a realist type of analysis may clash with the results from an analysis based on an examination of social purposes. For political scientists, it may not always be clear which of these forces takes precedence, nor is it always clear how the clash of these forces is reconciled.

Another Rival View: Rationalist Institutionalism

Rationalist institutionalists also challenge the realists' interpretation of the creation of Bretton Woods. For rationalist institutionalists, the most important point is the role of all the participating countries. That is, the regime was not simply the product of U.S. designs. Representatives from forty-four other states took part at Bretton Woods, and ultimately the principles and rules adopted were a compromise between the main creditor country (the U.S.) and the numerous debtors (represented by Britain, which was still a financial power, but thanks to World War II was in debt to the U.S.).

The rationalist institutionalists argue that if power was the key determinant to who participated in the negotiations, the U.S. should have had its way completely. Why did Keynes even produce an alternative plan? Why was this alternative plan debated? Britain played a role in these negotiations, and this becomes even clearer when we look at the trade regime created at the same time. Parallel to the Bretton Woods monetary regime (with its international institutions), the World War II allies wanted to construct a trade regime based on liberal principles and led by a multilateral institution. The planned institution to govern trade, the International Trade Organization (ITO), was never actually established, however, due to difficulties in the negotiations. In these talks, held in Havana in 1948, the Soviet Union and Third World countries successfully included their own perspectives on nationalization of property in the final treaty. The U.S. wanted to protect creditors' interests, to ensure that investors were compensated if nationalizations took place. The U.S. was outvoted and therefore refused to ratify the final treaty.

Without the ITO and its supporting treaty in place, the U.S. had to fall back on to another agreement. Prior to the Havana conference, the U.S. had negotiated with Britain so that the two countries would present a unified position in the talks. The two countries had signed a General Agreement on Tariffs and Trade (GATT). The GATT represented a compromise between the two countries. On the one hand, the U.S. wanted Britain to dismantle the Imperial Preference System. The U.S. argued that any new trade regime should be based on non-discrimination—tariffs on goods should be based on the nature of the good, not on the country of origin. Britain countered with the argument that the new regime should aim to liberalize trade. In other words, Britain wanted the Smoot-Hawley Tariff lowered. The GATT represented a compromise, since both non-discrimination and liberalization became part of its basic goals.

The rationalist institutionalists point out two things about these negotiations. On the one hand, the U.S. could not completely force its own perspective on all other states. As powerful as the Americans may have been at the time, they could not create the trade regime they originally intended. Rather, they had to fall back on the GATT, which itself represented a compromise. Why would a hegemonic state have had such failures? Why the need to compromise? In addition, rationalist institutionalists argue that one of the chief lessons from the 1930s was the need to improve co-ordination and co-operation between states. No state could operate its economy in isolation; each country's policies had ramifications for others. If they wanted to practise liberalism internationally, they would also need to co-ordinate their interventionism, or at least restrain themselves from the temptation to use "beggar thy neighbour" policies. Institutions facilitate that sort of co-operation or co-ordination. In short, the rationalist institutionalists are arguing that hegemonic leadership is not enough.

Consequences:
An International Monetary Regime
Based on "Embedded Liberalism"

The rules set down in 1944 were not supposed to be implemented until five years after the war ended, but in fact they did not officially come into operation until 1961. By then the monetary and economic situation had changed. Gold had already been displaced by the dollar as the primary reserve asset in the system. American policies largely managed international liquidity, though this would lead to problems. These problems would grow to be major challenges in the late 1960s, and by the early 1970s the rules set down with so much foresight in 1944 would collapse. Yet, the institutions created, the IMF and the World Bank, continue to operate.

The U.S. maintains a strong say in the IMF to this day. The quota the U.S. paid into the IMF, and therefore its voting power, was 19 per cent in 1991.[12] As long as the U.S. can vote with other Western financial powers, it can still have its interests largely protected. However, the IMF's original mandate to assist in balance-of-payments adjustment under a fixed exchange rate regime no longer holds. While it and the World Bank remain important and powerful legacies from the Bretton Woods regime, the time may have come for serious reforms.

Ruggie concluded his analysis of the establishment of Bretton Woods with the recognition that the balance struck in these regimes, what he labelled "embedded liberalism," has largely endured. Not only have the Bretton Woods institutions themselves lasted, but more importantly, the reconciliation attempted between relatively free trade at the international level and domestic intervention in selected areas has also persisted.[13] The compromises have provided a stable foundation for a tremendous boom in international trade and international investment. While the specific aspects of the regime came unglued in the 1970s, as will be discussed in Chapter 17, the regime set down the broader practices of "embedded liberalism" with which we still live.

Suggested Readings

Alan P. Dobson, "Economic Diplomacy at the Atlantic Conference," *Review of International Studies* 10, 2 (April 1984), 143-63.

Eric Helleiner, "Chapter 2: Bretton Woods and the Endorsement of Capital Controls," in Helleiner, *States and the Reemergence of Global Finance*. Ithaca, NY: Cornell University Press, 1994.

John Ikenberry, "Creating Yesterday's New World Order: Keynesian 'New Thinking' and the Anglo-American Postwar Settlement," in Judith Goldstein and Robert O. Keohane, eds., *Ideas and Foreign Policy: Beliefs, Institutions and Political Change*. Ithaca, NY: Cornell University Press, 1993, 57-86.

Karl Polanyi, *The Great Transformation*. Boston: Beacon Press, 1957.

Notes

1   Perhaps the most important was the Atlantic Charter, signed in August 1941 by Roosevelt and Churchill. A reprint of the Atlantic Charter can be found in A.F.W. Plumptre, *Three Decades of Decision: Canada and the World Monetary System, 1944-75* (Toronto: McClelland & Stewart, 1977), 32.

2   Plumptre, who participated as a representative of Canada in these talks, gives a great description of the role these other states could play in these talks. As he put it, Canadians' "major contributions to postwar economic plans probably lay in helping to find acceptable compromises between British and American positions, which in some respects were wide apart." See ibid., 28-29.

3   This chapter will spend little time on the World Bank; for more information, see Robert Oliver, "Early Plans for a World Bank," *Princeton Studies in International Finance* No. 29 (1971).

4   As quoted in Joan E. Spero, *The Politics of International Economic Relations*, 4th ed. (New York: St. Martin's Press, 1990), 22.

5   In Plumptre's assessment, "the new international institutions, largely fashioned in Washington, were designed to serve the international interests of the U.S.," though he also notes how they were largely consistent with Canadian interests as well. See Plumptre, *Three Decades of Decision*, 31.

6   J.G. Ruggie, "International Regimes, Transactions, and Change: Embedded Liberalism in the Postwar Economic Order," *International Organization* 36, 2 (Spring 1982), 195-231.

7   Ibid.; Karl Polanyi, *The Great Transformation* (Boston: Beacon Press, 1957).

8   Ibid.

9   Ruggie, "International Regimes, Transactions, and Change."

10 Ibid., 197.

11 For more on this point, see Mark R. Brawley, "Political Leadership and Liberal Economic Sub-Systems: The Constraints of Structural Assumptions," *Canadian Journal of Political Science* 28, 1 (March 1995), 85-103.

12 See Melissa H. Bird, "The IMF," in Thomas J. Biersteker, ed., *Dealing with Debt* (Boulder, Colo.: Westview Press, 1993), 20. For more on how quotas have changed, and their impact, see Jacob S. Dreyer and Andrew Schotter, "Power Relationships in the IMF: The Consequences of Quota Changes," *Review of Economics and Statistics* 62, 1 (February 1980), 97-106.

13 Ruggie, "International Regimes, Transactions, and Change."

Sixteen

SOUTH KOREA OPTS FOR EXPORT-ORIENTED INDUSTRIALIZATION

Little happened in the post-World War II trade regime during the 1950s. The institutional framework for reciprocal trade liberalization was in place, but countries remained reluctant to offer real concessions. The Kennedy Round negotiations of the GATT (conducted between 1962 and 1967) introduced new bargaining techniques. This round marked the real beginning of a wave of tariff reductions by GATT members. The lower tariffs, plus the resulting expansion of trade, created the systemic environment where countries would have enormous opportunities to exploit trade.

It was in this setting that several economically less developed countries began to use trade as part of their economic strategy. The best known of these are South Korea, Taiwan, Hong Kong, and Singapore. This chapter focuses on the decision to pursue a development program based on trade, which was made by South Korea in the early 1960s. South Korea's strategy is often touted as an economic success story. In evaluating economic development, most people are actually referring to industrialization: the share of manufacturing in South Korea's GDP went from 14 per cent in 1960 to 30 per cent in 1983, and then still higher.[1]

Exports played an important role in the story. Between 1949 and 1960, South Korea's real export earnings grew 3.9 per cent (about the same rate as growth in its real GDP). While respectable, these figures are not very different from other industrializing countries, such as those in Latin America. But then, between 1963 (after the decision was made to concentrate on exports and to let exporting sectors lead the country's growth) and 1990, South Korea's merchandise exports grew by an average of 23 per cent per year.[2] In terms of per capita GDP, South Korea ranked 85th in 1962, but had risen to 44th by 1986.[3]

South Korea's Initial Trade and Industrialization Strategy: ISI

In the immediate post-World War 11 years, South Korea pursued the trade and development program popular with most other economically developing countries, adopting a development strategy based on blocking the import of industrial goods so that domestic demand would stimulate domestic production. This strategy is referred to as import substitution industrialization or ISI. In fact, South Korea is said to have pursued ISI in the years between 1950 and 1963 "with zeal."[4]

The typical liberal criticisms of ISI have been well documented.[5] By blocking foreign competition, ISI ensures that domestic manufacturers garner a profit. But this automatically means consumers are hurt by this lack of competition. ISI is a way of forcing a transfer of income from consumers to the industrial sector, which works through distorting prices in the market by eliminating cheaper-priced competition. These price shifts could create distortions in the ability of other sectors to use inputs—distortions introduce greater inefficiencies throughout the economy. Take the example of local steel production, which was supported through ISI; any other producers using steel as an input would have to pay more for steel, and this would make the price of their goods less competitive.

Along the same lines, though, there is no guarantee that greater profits accruing to the firm will be reinvested in the same industry. They might not be—instead, profits could be spent on many other things, including investment in unrelated sectors and conspicuous consumption (buying mansions and Rolls Royces), or they even could be taken out of the country and invested somewhere else. The industry might simply get comfortable behind the protective tariffs and manage its captive market without improving productivity or levels of production—but still receive a steady profit.

Sometimes ISI meant blocking imports that could not be fully replaced by domestic production in the short run. Say the import of steel was blocked to support higher prices for domestic steel producers. These steel producers would make more money, but it would take some time for that profit to be reinvested in new steel plants. In the meantime, steel demand might not be met. Other producers using steel as an input might have to slow down their production. So ISI could lead to bottlenecks.

In other areas, technology may be a barrier. ISI may not work very well if the country lacked the technical know-how or high-tech production facilities necessary for efficient production. For instance, many countries would like to make computers, but producing high-quality chips and assembling the components in dust-free labs are expensive and difficult. Even the Soviet Union had tremendous problems in this area. While Third World countries might possibly achieve production in certain high-tech areas, they may be expending a tremendous amount of resources that could be more effectively applied elsewhere.

In most cases, ISI was supposed to be a temporary policy, which would be dropped after the local industry got off its feet. Unfortunately, that has rarely happened because the local industry has no incentive to increase its competitiveness. This lack of competitiveness and distortions created in the domestic economy often lead to a slowdown in the pace of industrialization over time, even where ISI worked well in sparking or kicking off industrialization. It simply was difficult to sustain industrial growth through ISI. The reasons for this should be fairly easy to understand. The domestic market in many economically developing countries isn't that big (though there are some significant exceptions, such as India, Brazil, and perhaps Argentina and a few others), nor do consumers have much purchasing power. The larger the market, the more likely ISI will last longer and perform better. Small countries may not have the domestic base of demand to support industrial factories because of economies of scale. In this instance "economies of scale" refers to the optimal size of an efficient industrial plant. An efficient factory must maintain a high level of output per year to turn a profit. If a country bases its development strategy on ISI but the level of domestic demand does not meet the production level of a modern efficient plant, it makes little sense to build the plant and then underutilize its capacity.

All of these are simply the general liberal criticisms of protectionism, but addressed to the specifics of an ISI program. We can add to these the argument about the social losses associated with rent-seeking. In other words, individuals and groups will expend resources in the pursuit of the rights to participate in the ISI-protected sectors. Society as a whole loses because the individuals seeking the special privileges accruing to the protected firms are burning up the country's resources without adding to the country's ability to produce anything extra. This kind of consumption of resources can become quite high in some settings and represent a serious drain on the economy.[6]

Real problems may not have arisen with rent-seeking in South Korea at this time because of the external political pressures on the country. The government couldn't simply plunder the capital that came its way because the country's political survival was at stake. The South was locked in a political and economic competition with North Korea. It had to develop stronger political loyalties among its citizens, and that also meant improving the economy.[7] The government in South Korea certainly handed out privileges, and the entrepreneurs who benefited from ISI gave politicians kickbacks, yet the government was perhaps more self-restrained than it otherwise would have been.

Many of the problems associated with ISI that liberals identify did arise during South Korea's drive to industrialize in the 1950s. Production of critical basic materials lagged behind schedule. The production of many sectors remained well below standard. This had both economic and political consequences. On the one hand, the private business sector was not very well developed. Moreover, this community was not very powerful vis-à-vis the state. The business community could hardly argue that the state needed its support to survive—if anything, it was more the other way around. Economically, objective assessments recognized the need to modify policies. At the same time, in many ways the ISI period laid the economic foundation for South Korea's later success.[8] The country built up many of its basic industries (though they were not internationally competitive yet) and had identified some of its most pressing needs.

Export-Oriented Industrialization

The reverse of ISI is export-oriented industrialization (EOI). Instead of seeing international trade as a threat, EOI embraces trade. With EOI, a country builds industrial plants for efficiency, then produces for international demand. EOI does not require large size (indeed, for small countries it may be the only way to support industrial development without introducing too many distortions into the domestic economy).[9] EOI promises to avoid many of the problems associated with ISI. Also, a developing country need not have a high level of per capita income, since production is supported by consumption in the rich markets of the economically advanced states.

Being tied into the international market entails certain risks, however. Countries pursuing EOI are basing their future on forces beyond their control. If the world economy grows, then EOI is more likely to work well; if it does not, and the country has already invested in production, there is little an economically less developed country can do to stimulate international demand—presumably domestic demand was weak to begin with, which is why international markets had to be sought out, so compensating for a fall in international demand can be difficult. This means the timing of introducing production for trade (EOI) is critical.

EOI may be risky, too, in that it means entering a very competitive market system. If all states try to pursue the same markets at the same time, the chance of any of them being successful is lessened. In the steel sector, competition has been very high indeed. Since all countries wish to produce basic industrial products such as steel, many have entered this sector using an EOI strategy; but as many countries try to produce steel for the European and American markets, they saturate demand—prices fall and so do profits. So picking the right sectors to enter into, as well as doing so at the right time, is important for the success of EOI.

This is where strategic trade policy comes into play. Paul Krugman defines strategic trade policy as "government policy which can tilt the terms of oligopolistic competition to shift excess returns from foreign to domestic firms."[10] The state wishes to develop certain sectors that do not yet have the ability to compete. In essence, the state wishes to create a comparative advantage. That means government support for getting the necessary inputs, the technical know-how, or the human capital (in terms of skill and experience). But as Krugman also notes, strategic trade policy is far from perfect; there are problems with ISI, but a different range of dangers exist with EOI. What if international markets are suddenly cut off? After all, American and European producers don't appreciate foreign competition, so they have responded to increased imports by asking for protection. The whole strategy of EOI assumes relatively free trade in the international economy. This has led many of the developing countries that rely on EOI to make the transformation of the GATT into the new World Trade Organization a top priority.

Also, ISI works with very little capital in place to begin with—it is a way to transfer income from other sectors to industry, in lieu of savings. ISI, then, is a way to raise capital. EOI is not a way to raise capital domestically but can instead be a way to pay off foreign investments that have already been undertaken. But the capital has to be raised somewhere, either through forced savings domestically or by international borrowing.

There is a potential problem for both strategies. Both may have difficulty in achieving diversification. ISI can lead to distortions, and there may be a problem in directing the resources out of the protected industries and into other sectors. This sort of thing can also happen with EOI, since it may increase wealth or capital savings in one sector but not translate into wider changes. Wider changes are perhaps more likely to occur with EOI, however, since it can improve industrial efficiency and build up competitiveness in such a way as to stimulate other local producers rather than introducing distortions into the domestic market. EOI is also a way of producing an investable surplus in the longer run. Since a gain can be produced in trade, there may be more funds around after several years of EOI, while ISI is really based on redistributing domestic wealth.

All of these factors came into play in South Korea's eventual economic success. It is important to remember that the decision to adopt an export orientation did not guarantee that success—EOI does not always work so well. For South Korea, the timing happened to be right. The world's economy was booming in the 1960s, and the East Asian region in particular was growing. Strong economic expansion in Japan, plus heightened expenditures by the U.S. (as that country prosecuted the war in Vietnam) helped to stimulate growth in East Asia. South Korea's strategic importance to the U.S. also guaranteed that access to the American market was always available. As well, American funds, both public and private, were available to finance EOI. As one of the first countries to use EOI, South Korea also entered several markets when international competition was fairly low. Many of these same factors would not apply to countries attempting EOI in the 1990s.[11] Another important point to remember is that the EOI strategy South Korea adopted was not a blanket set of plans. Some sectors were left protected; EOI was pursued only in certain areas, while ISI was left in others. The decisions made were tailored to the specifics of South Korea's situation. ISI and EOI policies were integrated so that they reinforced each other.

The remainder of this chapter looks at the decision to adopt EOI. It does not address the reasons such a policy proved successful. Instead, it examines several explanations offered for why South Korea chose to adopt a new development program employing EOI at a time when most other states were still pursuing ISI. To begin with, we shall take a closer look at just what the decision itself entailed.

The Shift to EOI

In practice, the shift to EOI was merely the introduction of a new set of economic policies. During 1963-64 South Korea took a number of important steps, as well as several less obvious moves in support of the overall strategy.[12] First, exchange rate policy was changed. Until this time, South Korea had maintained a set of different exchange rates. Different international economic transactions were undertaken at different rates. In 1964, this practice was eliminated. All the different exchange rates were unified into a single rate.

Second, the currency was devalued in 1964. This is close to what several liberal economists have referred to as "getting the exchange rate right." The currency was set at a more realistic value. (One of the best ways to judge how realistic an official exchange rate is, is to compare it to rates on the black market.) Certainly by lowering the value of the currency, South Korea made its exports appear cheaper to foreign consumers. Previously, a high exchange rate supported the protectionism inherent in ISI.

Third, a set of domestic investment policies were intended to aid in the expansion of exports. The government made a concerted effort to invest in education. Infrastructural developments were also given priority. As well, interest rates were raised, partially in hopes of increasing domestic savings (which had been very low prior to 1963) and partially in hopes of drawing in foreign investment. When this was combined with the government's ability to offer cheaper credit to exports (thanks to its control over the financial sector), the policies created a split financial market. For most Koreans, interest rates were high, and therefore they chose to consume less and save more; for exporters, interest rates were low, and therefore they expanded their operations. Overall, the country imported less and exported more.

Fourth, trade relations were liberalized—though not completely. Tariffs were reduced on certain items to make it easier to import inputs the exporters could not otherwise attain. This was especially important for the importation of capital goods necessary for manufacturing exports (i.e., machinery). In this way the exporters found it cheaper to produce goods than before; under ISI, they had had to pay higher prices for goods, which were most often of inferior quality.

Fifth, a number of incentives were structured to entice businesses to engage in exporting. At one level this was by the most obvious route: some exports were subsidized. A special fund was created to help small firms enter the international market. But the state employed a wide range of techniques, including fostering the creation of exporter associations (so different firms could share information and experiences), the discounting of energy prices for exporters, and many different modifications of tax policies. Exporters were given breaks on their income tax. Credit necessary for foreign trade was especially subsidized by the government.

As an example, consider the treatment afforded South Korea's first auto assembly plant. This plant was set up in 1962. It received a variety of tax benefits. The government allowed components to be imported duty free and then placed stringent import controls on finished vehicles.[13] This allowed the firm to follow a pricing strategy similar to that used by Japanese firms: the home market becomes a reserved area, allowing the firm to charge high prices and offsetting any losses or small profit margins on products exported. It really represents a mix of EOI and ISI.

Overall, these policies marked the swing to EOI, which in turn is related to South Korea's sustained industrialization. Economists such as Jagdish Bhagwati and Anne Krueger have argued that South Korea's economic success came from its willingness to stop discriminating against exports and instead promote them.[14] Jung-en Woo credits the "back-and-forth dialectic between international and domestic realms" for the economic take-off that followed.[15] What drove the government to undertake this set of policy changes?

The Regional and Systemic Forces Conducive to EOI

As mentioned above, one of the systemic factors that may have shaped the Korean decision was the expansion of opportunities to export. The regional economy was especially healthy. Japanese economists use the analogy of the snow geese to illustrate the manner in which they believe regional factors helped pull South Korea into EOI. Geese fly long distances in a vee-formation; the first goose breaks air resistance, and those at each trailing wing-tip need less force to slice through the air. Economically, much the same can take place. Japanese firms had pioneered electronics markets; as they moved their product lines into more differentiated, high-end goods, South Korean (and Taiwanese) firms could start to export the basic models.[16]

This is somewhat against the understanding of North American political scientists. In fact, the decision to pursue ISI in the 1950s can be viewed in the opposite sense: South Korean policy-makers wanted to pursue ISI to get from under the shadow of Japan's industrialization.[17] Korean leaders were afraid that they would remain stuck in the position of exporting raw materials to Japan and in return purchasing Japanese manufactured goods. This point does not shed much light on the choice between EOI and ISI, however.

Neither policy was all that risky, thanks to systemic factors. Korean leaders in the 1950s had the opportunity to pursue ISI with few or no risks because of their relationship with another major power: the U.S. South Korea was important for American strategic interests in the Cold War. The massive inflows of American aid (as a recipient, South Korea ranked only behind South Vietnam and Israel during the Cold War[18]) allowed the South Korean state to play a mediating role between international capital and the domestic economy. The funds could be used to support either industrialization strategy.

American advisers were not in favour of ISI at the time. Instead, they were interested in seeing Japan develop economically and were ready to see South Korean interests and aspirations suppressed for the time being in order to achieve this broader goal. The Koreans, however, ignored the advice.[19] Instead, they pursued the whole range of policies in the typical ISI package. South Korea adopted numerous barriers to block international competition, namely licensing and tariffs, but also put in place a multiple exchange rate system and a host of other devices designed to shield parts of the domestic economy.

Cutbacks in American aid started in 1959, but the most severe cuts were to come in the early 1960s. Along with reduced aid during the Kennedy administration came new American advice: push for greater democratization and economic growth (around expansion of the light industries), and reduce military expenditures. The American advice looked like a textbook application of Rostow's take-off model, one form of modernization theory.[20] While this may at first glance appear to be what happened, we need to consider domestic politics to understand what exactly happened.

The systemic factors provide insight into some of the constraints and opportunities South Korea faced. They do not tell us about which way policy would move. Indeed, other countries in similar positions in the international political economy continued to pursue ISI. The systemic factors may have been important for the success of EOI, as discussed above, but domestic forces seem more important in South Korea's decision to adopt new policies. In May 1961 there had been a *coup d'état*, and a military government took over. While democratic institutions were restored in 1963, the military became firmly entrenched in society and government. Institutional arrangements were also altered in fundamental ways, thus changing how the government could interact with the economy.

Domestic-Level Theories: Strong State/Weak Society?

South Korea's adoption of EOI can perhaps best be explained by referring to the changes in the relationship between the South Korean state and other societal actors. The state became more powerful versus these other actors, as well as somewhat free to resist their demands. This was the result of changing institutional arrangements and political economic practices, which allowed the state to intervene in the economy in more effective and selective ways.

The new institutional arrangements made in 1961 after the *coup d'état* play an important role in the 1963-64 policy reforms. A new, key economic planning institution was created, the Economic Planning Board (EPB). The EPB was given authority over the setting of tariffs, administering direct subsidies to industries, and setting economic targets. It could carry out these functions without referring to the legislative branch. The EPB also had power over the government's budget.[21] In roughly the same period, KOTRA (the state's official trade promotion agency) and the Korean Development Institute were created. Many have argued that the EPB 's actions worked hand-in-hand with market forces. The EPB and other government institutions were able to eliminate some of the risk and uncertainty of the market by generating and disseminating critical information. They were also able to convince businesses to invest, thus bringing about an expansionist environment—a sort of self-fulfilling prophecy.[22]

In addition, the state stepped in and took over the banking sector at this time. According to Jung-en Woo, at the core of the state's strength vis-à-vis other actors is its ability to channel money into the economy. She characterizes the South Korean state as a prism, refracting international capital flows into different segments and sectors of the Korean economy. To understand the strength of the Korean state, one must therefore understand the working of the country's financial system.[23] Prior to 1961, the state had had funds at its disposal, thanks to American aid. After 1961, American aid declined, but the government began borrowing from private sources to make up the difference.

The state used the money in a variety of ways. Robert Wade is interested in the character of the state's intervention.[24] He goes so far as to argue that the public/private distinction is often blurred in South Korea because of government participation in ownership. The state also employed so-called "policy loans." These were special loans targeted for specific sectors of the economy the state had decided to favour. The loans were at very favourable rates, and banks were forced to issue the loans—the banks were given no say in the application of the loans (in either the rates or the level of participation).[25]

There is a bit of a false contrast suggested in this approach, however. The emphasis tends to be on the characteristics of the state, but that is only one side of the equation. After all, the limited success of ISI meant that the business class largely supported the shift to EOI. There were few powerful opponents to the use of EOI—in countries where ISI delivered more industrialization, it also created powerful, well-entrenched interests to oppose states trying to implement a similar policy shift. As it was, large firms were favoured by government policies encouraging exports because large firms were in the best position to exploit the opportunities the policies created. The largest firms were able to gather and handle the information necessary for engaging in international trade. They were more capable of ensuring the consistent quality of their products, a necessary ability for successful competition internationally. They had also often had previous experience in international trade, and therefore had connections and business relationships they could build on. Moreover, they had the collateral necessary for raising foreign loans.[26]

In regard to the state's relationship with business, the state's role in finance remains pivotal. South Korean firms became reliant on funds from government sources or government-controlled sources. The typical debt-equity ratio for Korean firms in the 1970s was between 300 per cent and 400 per cent. (Just to compare, the average Brazilian or Mexican firms in the 1970s probably had a debt-equity ratio of 100 to 120 per cent.)[27] Thus, the firms were quite sensitive to small changes in the interest rate. This gave the state additional leverage over firms, since it, rather than the financial community, determined interest rates.

Moreover, the state was relatively free from outside interference by other domestic forces. Not only was the business élite relatively weak compared to the state, but so was the agricultural élite. In many economically developing countries, traditional authority tends to rest with an élite based in the rural areas. These traditional élites have economic interests tied to the agricultural sector, which they seek to protect. In Korea, however, the landed interests had been broken years before. Land owned formerly by the Japanese had been redistributed by the American military government prior to 1950, and then after the Korean War the South Korean government itself had engaged in reforms. These reduced the power of the landed élite and also helped equalize wealth within the country.[28]

Some people argue that another basis for the state's power vis-à-vis other societal actors comes from Korea's corporatist political practices, which insulate the state (and bureaucracy) from particularistic interests.[29] This insulation definitely promotes stability in policy. While this may not tell us much about why one policy is selected over another, it does tell us that the bureaucracies are likely to stick with their choices over the long term. Ministries themselves are very centralized, but then so are businesses, thanks to the Korean conglomerates (called *chaebols*) and the business associations.[30] Korea's "hard state" has a centralized society to deal with, and the result is a situation where decisions can be made and implemented swiftly. Bruce Cumings developed a special term to refer to such strong states, calling them "Bureaucratic-Authoritarian Industrializing Regimes" (or BAIRS). He describes them as "penetrating, comprehensive, highly articulated, and relatively autonomous of particular groups and classes."[31]

Bureaucratic Politics: The Power of the Ministry of Technology and the EPB

All this emphasis on the state's capabilities could still be undone by bureaucratic politics. What allowed for the successful turn to EOI? Did all bureaucracies share a common vision? For one thing, the bureaucracies are not equally strong. For instance, South Korea lacks an independent, autonomous central bank.[32] Instead, the central bank is subordinate to the Finance Ministry. One potential source of independent policy, then, was exempt from the picture. Monetary policy could easily be co-ordinated with other economic plans.

One of the most important ministries in the formulation of economic policy has been the Ministry of Trade and Industry. In some ways, this body is modelled after Japan's Ministry of International Trade and Industry. It is an agency with the specific duty of co-ordinating industrial activity and engaging in long-range planning and technological development. The Ministry of Trade and Industry monitors exports and foreign markets.[33] It was the brains behind the development of a strategic trade policy. Because the central bank answers to the Ministry of Finance, and the Ministry of Finance has no clear authority over the other ministries, the others can actually have a greater say in monetary policy. The Ministry of Trade and Industry actually wields more influence than the central bank.[34]

Most important, however, was the Economic Planning Board (EPB). The new military government installed after 1961 had an immediate crisis to face: the reduction in U.S. economic aid. To respond to the impending fiscal crisis, the head of the government, Park Chung Hee, concentrated decision-making in a single agency. The EPB was formed by taking the old Ministry of Reconstruction and adding agencies taken from two other ministries. The Bureau of the Budget was transferred from the Ministry of Finance and the Bureau of Statistics was transferred from the Ministry of Home Affairs. The EPB took over the budgeting function and economic planning previously undertaken by other branches of the government.[35]

In short, policy-making powers were centralized in the EPB and the Ministry of Trade and Industry. Bureaucratic politics were circumvented by the concentration of power within these two agencies. The EPB produced the country's first development plan. While this first five-year plan (1962-66) wasn't really based on an overt plan to use exports as the engine for economic growth, it was intended to improve South Korea's balance of payments. The policy changes undertaken to stimulate exports in 1963-64 became the basis of a more conscious attempt to use exports to stimulate economic development.

Individuals and Ideas: The Role of Military Officers

While there were changes in the arrangement of political institutions, as well as between the institutions and other elements of society, it is impossible to separate these changes from simultaneous changes in personnel at the top of the government. The shift in policy is entirely intertwined with the changes in the government in 1961. In May of that year, a military coup put Park Chung Hee in power. While Park's government carried through the institutional reorganization, it also placed new people in the top posts, and drew on foreign experts to formulate policy.

The economic package came very much from the military government's American advisers.[36] Similar advice was coming to the Koreans from the IMF and other international organizations. Whether this advice was new or not, the relationship between the members of the military government and the American advisers was presumably closer than had been the relationship between the civilian government and other American counsellors.

It should also be remembered that the coup allowed the military to penetrate not only government bureaucracies but also the rest of society. Military officers were placed in key offices in the government, but more importantly, they were put in positions of authority within private firms.[37] This provided the organization and insulation necessary for the state to have strength versus other actors, but the individuals entrusted to make decisions also could rely on their personal linkages and shared experiences.

Whatever its source, the evidence over the decades since 1963 makes it apparent that the South Korean élite has shared an ideological commitment to unity. Despite turnover in the individuals at the top, the South Korean élite has maintained its focus on its primary goals and therefore has given economic development priority over other goals. Economic development has been seen as the means to other goals—enhanced defence, internal unity, ideological competition versus North Korea, and so on.

Consequences: South Korea's Trade-led Economic Success

South Korea's decisions translated into economic success. This has to be understood in terms of other questions and other answers than this chapter has considered. For instance, systemic factors were critical for South Korea's ability to use EOI successfully. The American market was largely open to Korean exporters. The growth of the Japanese economy in the 1960s and 1970s also fuelled demand for Korean exports. Though American aid was being slashed, the Vietnam War, which raged through the latter half of the 1960s and the early part of the 1970s, meant that regional demand for goods was being increased by American military purchases. (These included important new markets for South Korean exports, especially steel, chemicals, and machinery goods, as well as construction and engineering contracts.[38]) Without those external stimuli, the EOI strategy might not have succeeded.

In 1960, more than three-quarters of the population was still engaged in agricultural production. This changed rapidly as the manufacturing export sectors expanded. But with so many people in the agricultural sector, creating very little surplus, there was little domestic saving and slow growth continued in domestic demand. Foreign markets were much more attractive.[39] Labour used in the production of exports more than trebled in the 1960s. Between 1960 and 1970, income from exports rose 7.4 times, while income from domestic output rose only 2.4 times. Exports became the engine for South Korea's industrialization. South Korean conglomerates, *chaebols* such as Hyundai Samsung and Daewoo, now rank among the largest firms in the world.[40] South Korea has its own multinational corporations. Government policies have clearly benefited these firms, thus concentrating economic power in a relatively small number of executive posts. This has been especially true after 1970.[41]

There has also been a downside, namely that economic power remains in the hands of a select few. Labour has largely been excluded from decision-making, which naturally means that labour has not shared equally in all the benefits generated by industrialization. The greatest challenges for South Korea lie ahead. Can the country continue to diversify its production sufficiently that it no longer requires trade to maintain economic growth? Can wages be expanded in such a way that competitiveness is not hurt, but the domestic demand becomes the real engine of growth? Those are the ultimate goals of EOI, and South Korea has yet to reach them.

Suggested Readings

Frederic Deyo, ed., *The Political Economy of the New Asian Industrialism*. Ithaca, NY: Cornell University Press, 1987.

Aidan Foster-Carter, "Korea and Dependency Theory," *Monthly Review* 37, 5 (October 1985), 27-34.

Stephan Haggard, *Pathways from the Periphery*. Ithaca, NY: Cornell University Press, 1990.

Anne O. Kreuger, *Studies in the Modernization of the Republic of Korea, 1945-1975*. Cambridge. Mass.: Harvard University Press, 1979.

Robert Wade, *Governing the Market: Economic Theory and the Role of Government in East Asian Industrialization*. Princeton, NJ: Princeton University Press, 1990.

Jung-en Woo, *Race to the Swift: State and Finance in Korean Industrialization*. New York: Columbia University Press, 1991.

Notes

1 Robert Wade, *Governing the Market: Economic Theory and the Role of Government in East Asian Industrialization* (Princeton, NJ: Princeton University Press, 1990), 44.

2 Sebastian Edwards, *Crisis and Reform in Latin America: From Despair to Hope* (New York: Oxford University Press and World Bank, 1995), 49.

3 Wade, *Governing the Market*, 34.

4 Edwards, *Crisis and Reform in Latin America*, 49-50.

5 See, for instance, Bela Balassa, "The Process of Industrial Development and Alternative Development Strategies," *Princeton Essays in International Finance* No. 141 (December 1980); Wade, *Governing the Market*, 9.

6 This can best be seen in the development of certain African countries, such as Zaire, in those same years.

7 Wade, *Governing the Market*, 33.

8 This argument is made by Wade, *Governing the Market*, 84-87; see also Bruce Cumings, "The Origins and Development of the Northeast Asian Political Economy: Industrial Sectors, Product Cycles, and Political Consequences," in Frederic Deyo, ed., *The Political Economy of the New Asian Industrialism* (Ithaca, NY: Cornell University Press, 1987), 66-68.

9 In fact, the same sort of logic underpins the economic strategies of small industrialized states, such as Belgium and the Netherlands. See Peter Katzenstein, *Small States in World Markets* (Ithaca, NY: Cornell University Press, 1985).

10 See Paul R. Krugman, "Is Free Trade Passé?" in Philip King, ed., *International Economics and International Economic Policy: A Reader* (New York: McGraw-Hill, 1990), 91-107.

11 Robin Broad and John Cavanaugh, "No More NICs," *Foreign Policy* 72 (Fall 1988), 81-103.

12 The following paragraphs build on descriptions from a number of sources. The most important have been: Edwards, *Crisis and Reform in Latin America*, 49-50; Jung-en Woo, *Race to the Swift: State and Finance in Korean Industrialization* (New York: Columbia University Press, 1991), 102-03; Youngil Lim, *Government Policy and Private Enterprise: Korean Experience in Industrialization*, Korea Research Monograph 6 (Berkeley: Center for Korean Studies, Institute of East Asian Studies, University of California, 1981), 18-24, 31.

13 Wade, *Governing the Market*, 309.

14 See Jagdish N. Bhagwati and Anne O. Krueger, "Exchange Control, Liberalization and Economic Development," *American Economic Review* 63, 2 (May 1973), 419-27.

15 Woo, *Race to the Swift*, 116.

16 Wade, *Governing the Market*, 103.

17 Woo, *Race to the Swift*, 53-54.

18 Ibid., 45.

19 Ibid., 53-60, 63-64.

20 Ibid., 71-72, 75-80.

21 Lim, *Government Policy and Private Enterprise*, 2. The author's point in this monograph, how-
    ever, is that the private sector always played the major role in the country's economic perfor-
    mance; for instance, the country usually exceeded EPB targets in the 1960s, thereby suggesting
    that planning could be overemphasized.

22 Ibid., 4.

23 Woo, *Race to the Swift*, 2, 6-7.

24 Wade, *Governing the Market*, 157-58, 177-78, esp. n. 19.

25 Woo, *Race to the Swift*, 12.

26 Lim, *Government Policy and Private Enterprise*, 39.

27 Woo, *Race to the Swift*, 12.

28 Stephan Haggard, *Pathways from the Periphery* (Ithaca, NY: Cornell University Press, 1990), 51,
    55.

29 Wade, *Governing the Market*, 298. Also see Stephan Haggard and Tun-jen Cheng, "State and
    foreign capital in the East Asian NICs," in Deyo, ed., *The Political Economy of the New Asian
    Industrialism*, 111.

30. Wade, *Governing the Market*, 322-24, 337-39.

31 Cumings, "The Origins and Development of the Northeast Asian Political Economy," 71.

32 Woo, *Race to the Swift*, 51-52.

33 For a description of its activities, see Lim, *Government Policy and Private Enterprise*, 15.

34 Wade, *Governing the Market*, 323.

35 Cumings, "The Origins and Development of the Northeast Asian Political Economy," 72-73;
    Haggard and Tun-jen Cheng, "State and Foreign Capital in the East Asian NICs," 111;
    Chalmers Johnson, "Political Institutions and Economic Performance: the Government-
    Business Relationship in Japan, South Korea and Taiwan," in Deyo, ed., *The Political Economy
    of the New Asian Industrialism*, 154.

36 Cumings, "The Origins and Development of the Northeast Asian Political Economy," 70. Also
    see Haggard and Tun-jen Cheng, "State and Foreign Capital in the East Asian NICs," 111.

37 Johnson, "Political Institutions and Economic Performance," 153-55.

38 Woo, *Race to the Swift*, 85, 95-97.

39 Lim, *Government Policy and Private Enterprise*, 81, 84, 86-87.

40 Woo, *Race to the Swift*, 15.

41 Wade, *Governing the Market*, 309.

Seventeen

THE COLLAPSE OF
THE BRETTON WOODS
MONETARY REGIME

Bretton Woods in Operation

The goals of the Bretton Woods system, as it was designed under the guidance of officials from the U.S. Treasury, were to achieve an orderly balance-of-payments adjustment system, provide adequate liquidity for international trade, facilitate private international investment, and stabilize financial markets (by limiting speculative flows), while maximizing the effectiveness of domestic monetary and fiscal policies.[1] The monetary system was intended to be subordinate to and supportive of the open international trading system, while governments would be allowed to intervene in the domestic economy.

The dollar assumed the chief functions of an international money under the Bretton Woods rules, even though this was perhaps not the intention. Supported by U.S. economic and political strength, the dollar became the primary medium of international payment, the primary reserve asset (serving along with gold and several other currencies), and the primary currency used by governments to intervene in exchange markets to stabilize the value of their own currencies.[2] But since the U.S. dollar remained a national currency, American monetary authorities were given two separate sets of goals to decide between: their own domestic goals versus the system's requirements.[3] During the early years of the Bretton Woods regime, these goals were not necessarily in conflict.

The U.S. allowed foreigners to increase their holdings of dollars not only because they wanted foreigners to be able to pay for American exports, but also because they did not necessarily want gold to flow out of the United States. Since confidence in the dollar was so high, with the pound being the only possible alternative, and with the American market the largest open market in the world, demand for dollars soared. American firms could use dollars to purchase assets abroad. This situation also made it possible for the government to wield dollars as an international policy instrument in various ways. Through these channels, American policy provided enough international liquidity to support the resurrection of commerce and actually support the expansion of international trade and investment to new levels. The accumulation of dollar balances abroad accounted for approximately half of the increase in world liquidity between 1949 and 1958.[4]

The Emergence of the Dollar Overhang

The dollar shortage of the 1950s meant there had to be a conscious policy implemented to get dollars into the world economy despite the underlying economic conditions driving the U.S. to a certain balance-of-payments surplus. This was done in three ways: (1) foreign aid, the largest single chunk being the Marshall Plan; (2) increased military expenditures outside the U.S.—this dovetailed nicely with American strategic concerns over Soviet power, and the outbreak of the Korean War further stimulated U.S. expenditures in Asia; and (3) American foreign direct investment—American corporations took dollars abroad and spent them buying up foreign companies, foreign property, and so on. So the end result of these policies was that the dollar became the principal reserve asset held by others, meaning that the U.S. Federal Reserve Banks could control not only U.S. domestic monetary supply but the international supply as well.

The U.S. also controlled exchange rate adjustment, but this was done through the auspices of the International Monetary Fund. Because the U.S. dominated voting within the IMF at this time, the U.S. basically ran things differently from how the rules dictated. The convertibility of the European currencies was suspended from 1947 to 1958. Non-IMF policies got linked to exchange rate adjustments—for instance, Marshall Plan money was linked to currency devaluations in 1949. The U.S. took several measures such as pushing for these devaluations to get other countries to discriminate against American goods so that other countries might gain more dollars through foreign exchange.

All these unilateral American actions worked, slowly, so that by 1958 convertibility could be reinstituted among the economically advanced countries and these countries could earn enough dollars through regular channels that the U.S. didn't have to run things by itself any more. The other countries were able to defend their parities on their own. So the IMF as originally designed finally came into force in 1958.

Unfortunately some inherent instabilities were built into the system. Most importantly, some of the American policies of running a balance-of-payments deficit continued (the U.S. learned to like them). The Cold War, American military aid, and foreign expenditures continued, and so the dollar shortage of the early 1950s was by the early 1960s rapidly becoming a dollar glut. As the Vietnam War began to heat up, American deficits and foreign expenditures increased even more.

One way of dealing with this monetary situation would have been to back out of the Cold War, which wasn't very likely. Another would have been to redress the American balance-of-payments deficit and turn it into a surplus again. This, of course, is easier said than done, since it would have required deflating the American economy; moreover, much of the European growth in the 1960s was being driven by American demand, so a slowing down of the American market would have slowed the growth of America's largest export market, too, meaning the balance would most likely have stayed in a deficit.

The third possibility for fixing the situation would have been devaluing the dollar but this was problematic because so many countries held dollars as their primary reserve asset. Devaluation of the dollar would automatically affect all the other currencies' values. And as in Britain in the 1920s, there was fear that a devaluation would appear as a sign of weakness and would be bad psychologically for investors. These factors meant the U.S. did nothing for several years and simply continued to run deficits, making the problem worse. It became obvious that there were more dollars in circulation than could ever be converted into gold.

A related problem was the increasing amount of speculation in foreign exchange markets after the return of convertibility in 1958. This was tied to individual countries' balance-of-payments problems. Think of the dollar glut as a market problem; there were more dollars out there than people wanted. People began to expect the dollar to be devalued in the later 1960s, and the IMF system of fixed exchange rates gave speculators a great deal. The IMF system, after all, committed governments to keep their currencies within 1 per cent of their pledged parities. If the dollar was expected to be devalued in the near future, then dollars would be ditched for something else, say Deutschmarks (DMs). If the dollar is in fact devalued, then the DMs can be sold and one can get back more dollars than one started with! If nothing happens and the dollar is not devalued, you simply sell back your DMs and get the same amount of dollars you started off with. That's why this type of speculation was known as a "one-way bet," as well as why speculation became such a problem—patient speculators never lost money!

The obvious problem was that everybody would have the same fears of a devaluation, so everyone would try to sell the same currency. And who would buy? The governments committed to maintaining their parities. So if enough people feared a devaluation and therefore bailed out of a currency, they could actually so drain government reserves that the government might actually be forced to devalue. This kind of large-scale market pressure first happened to the dollar in 1960; in 1961, when the British pound came under market pressures, the Bank of England's reserves were depleted and the pound had to be devalued in just this fashion.

The designers of the IMF had not thought about what the situation would eventually become, with billions of dollars floating across international lines transmitted electronically wherever the markets are highest. IMF reserves simply weren't large enough, so the U.S. had to begin several stopgap measures to deal with the dollar glut and the speculation problem.

The first of these was the Gold Pool. The central banks agreed to pool their reserves of gold in order to centralize and co-ordinate interventions in the gold market and to defend the dollar's value at $35/ounce. This was an attempt to end speculation of the dollar being devalued versus gold. The second was the construction of the General Agreements to Borrow (GAB) in 1961. This was in response to the run on the pound and the realization that the IMF did not have reserves large enough to deal with immediate crises. The ten members of the IMF with the largest financial holdings (G10) agreed to lend up to $6 billion overnight whenever the whole group agreed to do so. The G10 also sought to augment IMF reserves. The third response was to establish swap agreements. Central banks agreed to make swaps of currencies (interest-free loans) on a quick basis so that each could intervene in markets without having to dip into their reserves. In other words, if there's a problem in the parity of the dollar versus the DM because everyone expects the dollar to be devalued, the central bank in the U.S. will need DMs to sell in order to prop up the value of the dollar. The swaps are ways of sharing currencies in order to intervene in markets. The fourth was the establishment of Roosa Bonds, named after the American Assistant Secretary of the Treasury, Robert Roosa, who designed these devices. These are bonds denominated in foreign currencies that the U.S. government sold for dollars—in order to draw some of the dollars back into the U.S.

But all of these actions were just Band-Aid solutions, and they failed to solve the problem. Ultimately, these temporary measures could not stem the market forces driving change. The rules would have to be changed because countries were increasingly unhappy with the existing state of affairs. By the late 1960s the U.S. wasn't particularly happy about several things, even though it also had some advantages in the existing state of affairs. The political problem was that the U.S. wanted to improve its position, just as the other countries had decided the U.S. already had too many privileges. In addition, other countries felt their own monetary policies were being adversely affected by U.S. policy; under the Bretton Woods rules, they were continually having to maintain exchange rate parities by buying up dollars. This forced their own money supplies up, with inflation as a consequence.[5] Negotiations stalled and the response—at least in the late 1960s and the early 1970s—was for the U.S. to go its own way.

This period of tinkering with the rules (the beginning of the end of Bretton Woods) started in 1968. In that year, the U.S. acted to undercut market speculation between the dollar and gold. It had become clear to everyone that there were many more dollars floating around than there was gold in Fort Knox, and the official ratio of dollars to gold would have to be changed. The Gold Pool deal still didn't provide central banks with the strength to dissuade speculation (if anything, their efforts simply fuelled speculation). So the U.S. unilaterally declared there would be two markets for gold—one for private citizens and the other for governments. The U.S. government would deal directly with other governments concerning the dollar's ratio to gold but would no longer defend the ratio in private markets. In a sense, this broke the dollar's connection to gold, though the real break was yet to come.

The split of the gold market into two tiers really signalled that the U.S. would no longer solve its balance-of-payments deficit problems. The United States had taken the first step towards adjusting the rules to fit the situation rather than adjusting its policy to fit into the rules. The U.S. then adopted the policy of "benign neglect" by ceasing to do its share of intervening in exchange markets to defend the parity of the dollar. If other countries wanted to keep the parities fixed, let them use their own resources. This was an easy way for the U.S. to act unilaterally to force the costs of maintaining fixed exchange rates on the other countries. By the summer of 1971, the other countries could no longer sustain the system.

The Nixon Shocks

In the summer of 1971 the U.S. had inflation (from the Vietnam War build-up), had the beginnings of high unemployment, and was running a large trade deficit. But because of the practices followed in the previous two decades, there were lots of dollars out there internationally—perhaps as much as eight times as many foreign-held dollars as could be supported by the gold reserve. So any actions by the U.S. would affect the value of other countries' reserves. What the Nixon administration wanted to do was devalue the dollar, but without bearing any of the costs of adjustment. This was the only way to remove the immediate problem of speculation against the dollar. Because the Nixon administration didn't want to look weak (that is, didn't want to admit to a devaluation), the government tried to pressure all the other major countries to revalue their currencies. The result is exactly the same—the ratio is changed—but the psychological impact is smaller. In the words of Nixon's advisers, "devaluations are what small backward countries do, not the United States." The other countries wouldn't go for this, so in August 1971 there was more unilateral American action, known as the "Nixon shocks," which effectively ended the Bretton Woods system.

On 15 August 1971 the Americans announced two actions that caught everyone off guard and fatally wounded Bretton Woods. First, the U.S. broke the convertibility of the dollar into gold. No longer could foreign governments show up and expect to change their dollars into gold. Second, the U.S. imposed a 10 per cent surcharge (or tax) on all imports. This was not done to protect American industry from competition but instead was punishment to other countries for not revaluing their currencies. It was an attempt to use the American market as a lever in bargaining, because the U.S. made it clear that if other countries would revalue, it would drop the surcharge. These actions are important because they were done unilaterally. The U.S. did not warn other countries, nor did officials consult other countries. That is why they're known as the "Nixon shocks." The decision was made by members of the Nixon administration over a weekend at Camp David, where the U.S. position was deemed unsustainable and foreign co-operation missing.

The domestic economic situation and the dollar's role as a reserve asset were no longer compatible. By breaking the link between the dollar and gold, the U.S. was severing more links between the domestic economy and the balance-of-payments situation. The U.S. could only maintain a balance-of-payments deficit as long as other countries were willing to accept dollars. The U.S. was simply admitting that these dollars could only be returned and exchanged for American goods and services. Thus gold disappears from the picture. The U.S. was now free to run a deficit without risking any loss of gold. Instead, it was argued, these dollars floating around internationally would have to come back to the States and be spent on American products or services—and stimulate American business. (Inflation still lurked in the background as a problem.) Suddenly the deficit was no longer such a problem.

What this really added up to was that the U.S. liked having the powers that went to a reserve asset currency but didn't like the costs associated with that same role. The American decision-makers were trying to cut the best possible deal here, wanting to continue running a deficit but not wanting to have to deal with the speculation that had accompanied those deficits in the Bretton Woods system. The Nixon shocks pretty much achieved those goals in the short run.

In his examination of the Nixon shocks, John Odell explores five possible explanations for the policy of the United States: the balance-of-payments situation, the international military-political situation, the domestic political situation, organization and internal bargaining, and the policy or ideological beliefs of key decision-makers. These five run the gamut of the levels of analysis, making Odell's work an important reference for our consideration of the possible explanations.

Systemic Theory:
The U.S. as a Declining Hegemonic Power

Two of Odell's five competing possible explanations work at the system level. One is purely political: the consideration of the military and political environment. The other is purely economic: the balance-of-payments situation.

The balance-of-payments argument is essentially an argument about markets. That is, under the Bretton Woods arrangements, exchange markets were open for all buyers and sellers to come and purchase or sell their currencies. Yet at the end of the day, the governments had promised to "fix" the prices. Prices in these markets would not be allowed to stray very far from announced parity rates. This meant that prices could not vary, as they should have, when demand and supply varied.

When governments are forced to intervene to fix the market price, they must expend resources. Getting the market price to match the pledged parity only works if the government is buying up excess supply, or meeting excess demand. In the case of the U.S. dollar, there already was excess supply, thanks to the dollar overhang already described. But the overhang also identifies the lack of resources in the coffers of the U.S. By definition, an overhang involves too much currency for reserves. If the holders of the currency doubt that they can get the nominal (or face) value for the currency, they are likely to offload it. Moreover, in a fixed exchange rate system, if one currency is grossly overvalued, some other currency or currencies are going to be undervalued. Thus a wise currency trader would have recognized that the dollar was no longer backed by much reserves; if the overhang was corrected, then each dollar would be worth less in terms of gold and therefore in terms of other currencies. Other currencies would be worth the same amount of gold, but worth more dollars. (So you should sell dollars and buy Deutschmarks; once the dollar is devalued, you can sell your Deutschmarks and buy more dollars.)

The dollar overhang was not an overwhelming problem. Smart intervention by American authorities could move the currency market in one direction or another. But as more people became convinced of the need (or impending inevitability) of a devaluation, it became harder to convince them through minor intervention. This entailed ever greater expenditure of resources by the government. And Odell's point here was that in such a situation, the market will eventually win. As long as authorities were willing to allow an open market in currencies, the market would reflect the underlying laws of supply and demand. No amount of marginal intervention would change that pattern. According to this argument, the U.S. would have to devalue the dollar at some point.

But we should remember what this argument is missing. The overhang had persisted for several years before the Nixon shocks. Why did the U.S. have to react to this problem in 1971 and not before? Several possible solutions existed as well—the U.S. could have devalued the dollar to an appropriate level (i.e., fixed the new value of the dollar to existing reserves). Yet it sought one solution. The balance-of-payments situation suggests that the U.S. could not hope to ignore this problem, but it also does not give us much insight into why one policy response was selected over another. The international military-political setting was key to why some of the theoretically possible solutions were not attempted. In the monetary realm, the U.S. did not have any particular challengers.[6] At the same time, the American government was acutely aware of the fact that it was stretched in terms of commitments. The war in Vietnam was not going well, and America was just beginning to feel the pinch of economic competition from its allies.

The international setting must also be taken into account in the sense that the leading monetary challengers (primarily West Germany and Japan, but also Switzerland) were beholden to the U.S. in security terms. The West Germans were in the best position to challenge the Americans' predominant position in monetary affairs. Yet they proved to be quite co-operative, all things considered, largely because they did not want to antagonize their most important ally.

Domestic Level: The Changing U.S. Economy?

Instead of submitting domestic economic performance to the needs of the international monetary regime, the United States chose to pull Bretton Woods down with the Nixon shocks of August 1971. In her analysis in *Closing the Gold Window*, Joanne Gowa clearly stresses the Nixon administration's emphasis on the domestic economy and the need for autonomy in the domestic realm as reasoning behind the shocks.[7] Rather than supporting the continuance of the international monetary regime it created, the U.S. destroyed the regime in order to throw off the constraints the international regime placed on its own domestic policy.

The new economic policy Nixon announced in conjunction with the decision to take the dollar off gold also froze wages and prices in order to slow inflation, while seeking to stimulate employment by reducing taxes and spending.[8] Nixon presented these policy decisions as an effort to make the international economic competition a "fair game" for the United States. Trade statistics issued in the summer of 1971 showed that the U.S. would have a yearly trade deficit for the first time in almost eighty years. As Nixon put it, "The time has come for exchange rates to be set straight and for the major nations to compete as equals. There is no longer any need for the United States to compete with one hand tied behind her back."[9]

Included in Gowa's assessment of these decisions is an examination of the sectoral explanation. She argues that the U.S. economy, because of its low reliance on international trade, lacked a powerful constituency that would support Bretton Woods at the expense of the domestic economy's performance. Saving Bretton Woods would require suppressing the U.S. economy to end the balance-of-payments deficit; as Gowa puts it, "The idea of increasing domestic unemployment in order to preserve the monetary regime commanded no political following either within or outside the executive branch…. As a consequence, domestic economic policy was considered virtually sacrosanct, very largely immune from the conduct of U.S. balance-of-payments or international monetary policy."[10]

The primary actors that might be expected to support the hegemon-led international monetary regime, even at the cost of the domestic economy's performance, would be those sectors that derived much of their income from international interactions. One obvious group would be New York bankers, who had been so prominent in the creation of the Federal Reserve and the rise of the U.S. dollar as an international currency. Yet the internationally oriented banking community, multinational corporations, and other likely supporters of the Bretton Woods regime remained silent. It seems that they either had enough interests in the domestic economic performance of the U.S. to cancel out their international interests or at least perceived rising protectionism to be a bigger threat than the loss of the Bretton Woods regime. Even they were unwilling to trade off the health of the domestic economy to save Bretton Woods.[11]

While no sectoral voices defended the Bretton Woods regime, it is not apparent that any groups lobbied strongly for the downfall of Bretton Woods, either. Instead, Gowa argues that the executive branch decision-makers saw electoral repercussions if the economy's performance sagged, and were therefore indirectly constrained in evaluating the policy trade-offs.[12] On the other hand, John Odell challenges this interpretation, for he sees no such pressure building up; as he puts it, "an analyst monitoring only public opinion, electoral struggles, and group pressures would have had virtually no clue that a change in international monetary policy was imminent. Instead this analyst would have anticipated a shift in trade policy that did not occur." Thus, Odell puts little faith in the notion that domestic pressure was the source of the changes in monetary policy.[13]

Evidence confirms Odell's suggestion that instead of targeting international monetary policy, the domestic groups adversely affected by the dollar's overvaluation were interested in achieving more traditional, sector-specific forms of protection. Some in the Nixon administration (advisers such as Gottfried Haberler and Hendrik S. Houthakker) saw the rising pressures for protectionism as a much more dangerous threat to the open international economy than any depreciation of the U.S. dollar. Since depreciation was the lesser evil, these advisers saw changes in monetary policy as a substitute for protectionism.[14]

Bureaucratic Politics: The Volcker Group, the Treasury, and the Fed

Given the weakness in the sectoral argument, it is important to turn to any bureaucratic factors that might have come into play, especially if we think about how similar problems were resolved in Britain in the 1920s. In that case, the Treasury and the Bank of England experienced different pressures and expressed somewhat different policy goals. In the case of the U.S. response to its own currency overhang, Gowa claims the Treasury had the greatest say in international monetary affairs and that the Treasury opposed reform within Bretton Woods, preferring to abandon the monetary regime instead. The Federal Reserve Board was less interested in international monetary policy—the Fed consistently placed higher priority on domestic economic concerns. The exception to this pattern was the New York Federal Reserve Bank, which was concerned with international finance more than any other part of the Fed, and which was also responsible for the execution of international monetary policy.[15]

This bureaucratic politics argument is subtle and can be best appreciated when this case is placed in comparison with the British case. During Britain's currency overhang in the 1920s, when there were too many pounds held abroad and there was also the threat of foreigners cashing them in for gold in order to transfer their holdings into a rival currency based on a rival financial centre, the Bank of England had wanted to defend the pound with ever higher interest rates—even if that meant depressing national economic performance (an example of "hegemonic afterglow"). The Treasury increasingly resisted the Bank of England's position, and in the early 1930s finally took the opportunity afforded by the creation of special financial accounts under its own control to influence international monetary policy and divorce it from domestic policy as much as possible. In the U.S. case, faced with a choice between supporting the role of the dollar at the cost of domestic economic performance or letting the international monetary regime crash, the U.S. quickly moved to the position we would expect to be supported by the Treasury but perhaps opposed by the Fed—protect the domestic economy. Yet the Fed accepted the decision to end the

Bretton Woods regime, including eliminating the commitment linking gold to the dollar. Perhaps systemic factors still come into play, for the Fed could take this stand because there was no strong currency rivalling the dollar.

It would be wrong, however, to imply that international monetary policy was formulated by the Treasury alone. Instead, during the early years of the Nixon administration international monetary policy flowed from an inter-agency team, known as the "Volcker group," after Paul Volcker, the Undersecretary of the Treasury for Monetary Affairs. The group consisted of members of the Council of Economic Advisers, the State Department, the staff of the Assistant for National Security Affairs, the Treasury, and the Fed. Despite the broad composition of this group, all shared a common belief that national interest should be defined in terms of the domestic economy rather than preservation of the international monetary regime.[16] The conclusion this evidence suggests, which the work of other scholars supports, is that there was no disagreement along bureaucratic lines.

Other policy-making elements of the executive branch that discussed international monetary affairs were the Cabinet Committee on Economic Policy and the cabinet-level Council on International Economic Policy. Similar to the Volcker group, the Council on International Economic Policy included a broad representation of different agencies (in fact, even broader).[17] Perhaps none of this matters, and in the end Nixon selected policies on the advice of John Connally (the Secretary of the Treasury) and chose to ignore the others, as Odell claims. But it is surprising to see how much consistency there was in the views of officials from different agencies; at first glance, this consensus suggests bureaucratic concerns did not factor into the decision.

The Fed, however, put up the most significant opposition to Connally's decision to suspend the dollar's convertibility to gold. The Fed knew something had to change, but rather than see the Bretton Woods system undermined in one fell swoop, it argued for a more effective devaluation of the dollar. The Federal Reserve chairman argued that devaluation was the most sensible policy because the dollar would still be difficult to defend on international markets at the existing rate.[18] Thus the Fed may have valued the Bretton Woods system more than the Treasury, but it, too, wanted to see international monetary policy brought into line with domestic needs one way or another.

The end result of these discussions was a partial adjustment of the dollar's value, which more accurately reflected the supply of the currency in circulation. The U.S. was reducing the gap between resources and commitments by dropping commitments. This is precisely the response to a currency overhang we would expect, if the central bank was not yet concerned about rival foreign currencies while the Treasury was increasingly concerned with fiscal deficits.

Individual Level: Nixon, Kissinger, and Connally

In Odell's analysis, a shift in personnel was more significant than bureaucratic politics. Whenever an American administration changes after a presidential election, a large number of top government officials are replaced. While the offices and positions remain largely the same (so bureaucratic interests do not change), the individuals filling those roles are different. Odell argues that when officials of the Nixon administration took office, the key players had very new ideas compared to members of the previous administration. In monetary affairs, we have already identified the key institutions: the Fed and the Treasury.

The Secretary of the Treasury under Lyndon Johnson had been Henry H. Fowler. Fowler was in that office from 1965 until 1969, so the entire time he was Secretary there had been a currency overhang. Fowler resisted any discussion of taking the dollar off gold. To him, a switch to floating exchange rates would be a step towards the chaos of the 1930s. Reflecting back on the problems of the interwar period, Fowler wanted to prevent any return to those sorts of policies. He saw a breakdown of the monetary regime as the first step to increased trade competition, the development of trading blocs, and perhaps then even another war between major powers. Also, Fowler had plenty of faith in the wisdom and capability of central bank intervention. He strongly believed that monetary authorities could move markets in such a way as to stabilize them and keep the fixed exchange rate system going.[19]

In late 1970 Nixon filled the post of Secretary of Treasury with John Connally. Connally, a former governor of Texas, was given a high-profile post in hopes of bolstering the popularity of the Nixon administration in that large, populous state. Connally's ideas on monetary policy were apparently not very fixed; he had little experience in this area and probably hadn't spent much time or invested much energy in formulating any fixed beliefs. The same could be said of Nixon himself; both Nixon and Connally were more interested in the administration's popularity at home than in any particular ideological position.

The Undersecretary of the Treasury for Monetary Affairs, Paul Volcker, had much experience within both the Treasury and the Fed; he held beliefs like those of most others in those two bureaucracies, in line with Fowler's ideas. He was prepared to defend the Bretton Woods rules. By coincidence, a new Chairman of the Federal Reserve was named in 1970. Arthur Burns had experience as a banker and central banker, and thus was a strong believer in the fixed exchange rate system. The other important player on the scene, according to Odell, was George Shultz. As Director of the Office of Management and the Budget (OMB), Shultz was involved in planning and policy discussions, although he did not have the policy instruments at his disposal to shift policy in the directions he desired. Shultz's role is important, because he did not believe in government intervention in the marketplace; he did not fear the consequences of "closing the gold window." He would argue for free market solutions and would downplay the dangers of economic repercussions or a repeat of the 1930s.[20]

Thus, among the individuals making monetary policy in the early 1970s were several who lacked any fixed ideological positions on monetary issues. Nixon, Connally, and Secretary of State Henry Kissinger were prepared to throw Bretton Woods and the fixed exchange rate system out the window for domestic political gains. Moreover, the frustrations in arriving at a multilateral solution to questions about the dollar's value had merely prompted Connally to turn his back on multilateral efforts. Connally and Nixon found the idea of striking out boldly more attractive, and would then seek diplomatic solutions later.

Would the same policies have been followed if different people had held these key positions? Why is it that some of those with entrenched beliefs, such as Burns or Volcker, were unable to prevent "the shocks"? Structural systemic factors shaped the problem and may have largely outlined the only possible responses, providing us with insight into how to think about the different arguments coming together; individuals mattered, for they played a role in selecting and implementing the policies. The dollar–gold relationship was unsustainable; the only real question was how would that relationship be broken.

The Consequences of the End of Bretton Woods

Of course, the end of the regime did not terminate the dollar's role as the primary instrument for international payment because there were no readily available substitutes to serve as an international medium of exchange. Indeed, Nixon wanted to throw off the constraints of the Bretton Woods system yet maintain the dollar's status as the main reserve currency for two reasons: prestige, but also the leverage this brought the U.S. over other states.[21] The end of Bretton Woods meant the end of the promise to redeem foreign central banks' dollars into gold, but this merely underlined the lack of confidence in the dollar. When the dollar was devalued further after discussions with the Western Europeans and Japanese later in 1971, confidence was still waning, and the dollar could no longer be supported via interventions by the spring of 1973. The failure to re-establish any sort of binding international monetary regime in the 1970s can be traced right back to the unilateral decision that the American domestic economy's performance was of paramount importance. In discussions concerning the creation of a new international monetary regime held in the fall of 1975, French and American officials agreed that domestic economic stability was more important than exchange rate stability.[22] Yet large numbers of dollars continued to be held abroad and the dollar's role as international medium of exchange remained largely unchallenged.

Other countries did not appreciate the U.S. actions, however. The period from August 1971 to 1976 represented a search for a new set of international rules to cover international monetary affairs. Before 1971 had ended, the U.S., the Western Europeans, and the Japanese had gotten together and reached an agreement on meeting some of the U.S. desires. This is known as the Smithsonian Agreement. The Americans did not get everything they wanted. The U.S. wound up changing the value of the dollar by a little less than 10 per cent, and the West Germans, Japanese, and Swiss (all the countries that provided rival reserve assets) agreed to revalue their currencies by more than 10 per cent. Nixon was able to declare this an American victory because the others moved their currency values more than the U.S. did. Consequently, he dropped the import surcharge.

At the same time, it was agreed that the Bretton Woods fixed exchange rate rules would be maintained, but the band of fluctuation would be increased. The bands around the parities were widened to plus or minus 2.50 per cent. It was hoped that this would give the markets a little more room for manoeuvre and give the governments a respite from intervening in currency markets so often. So this wasn't a real reform of Bretton Woods, but was instead a sort of crisis control (or better yet, damage control) operation.

Speculators, of course, got a totally different message out of this. The U.S. had withstood attacks on the dollar in exchange markets for more than a decade—in other words, speculators thought the dollar should have been devalued way back in 1960. Now the dollar actually had been devalued, though not very much. The likelihood of future devaluations suddenly seemed much greater. So after the Smithsonian Agreement, speculation increased.

By June of 1972, the British pound was under speculative pressure and Britain decided it could no longer defend its parity (even with the wider bands), so Britain became the first major country truly to float its currency (i.e., let the market totally decide the currency's parity). Speculative pressures on the dollar continued, and in February 1973 the U.S. devalued the dollar another 10 per cent—but again, this was an insufficient amount to calm the speculation in exchange markets. Exchange markets had to be closed. When they reopened the pressures were so strong that on 1 March 1973 the Bundesbank was forced to buy up $2.6 billion in a single day.[23] At that point, central banks everywhere gave up on defending parities, and all currencies were allowed to float.[24]

Suggested Readings

Fred Block, *The Origins of International Economic Disorder: A Study of U.S. International Monetary Policy from World War II to the Present*. Berkeley: University of California Press, 1977.

Joanne Gowa, *Closing the Gold Window*. Ithaca, NY: Cornell University Press, 1983.

Joanne Gowa, "State Power, State Policy: Explaining the Decision to Close the Gold Window," *Politics and Society* 13, 1 (1984), 91-117.

Stephen Krasner, "U.S. Commercial and Monetary Policy: Unravelling the Paradox of External Strength and Internal Weakness," in Peter Katzenstein, ed., *Between Power and Plenty*. Madison: University of Wisconsin Press, 1978, 51-87.

John Odell, "The U.S. and the Emergence of Flexible Exchange Rates: An Analysis of Foreign Policy Change," *International Organization* 33, 1 (Winter 1979), 57-81.

John Odell, *U.S. International Monetary Policy: Markets, Power and Ideas as Sources of Change*. Princeton, NJ: Princeton University Press, 1982.

Notes

1   Edward L. Morse, "Political Choice and Alternative Monetary Regimes," in Michael Schwarz, ed., *Alternatives to Monetary Disorder* (New York: McGraw-Hill, 1977), 81, 83.

2   John S. Odell, *U.S. International Monetary Policy: Markets, Power and Ideas as Sources of Change* (Princeton, NJ: Princeton University Press, 1982), 84.

3   Morse, "Political Choice and Alternative Monetary Regimes," 85.

4   Barry Eichengreen, "Hegemonic Stability Theories of the International Monetary System," in *Can Nations Agree? Issues in International Economic Cooperation* (Washington: Brookings Institution, 1989), 275.

5   For an examination of whether these charges that the U.S. exported inflation have merit, see Edgar Feige and James M. Johannes, "Was the U.S. Responsible for Worldwide Inflation under the Regime of Fixed Exchange Rates?" *Kyklos* 35, 2 (1982), 263-77.

6   The one exception would be France, which, under De Gaulle, was mounting a systemic disruption to stress the need for independence from American leadership. See the discussion in Jonathan Kirshner, *Currency and Coercion* (Princeton, NJ: Princeton University Press, 1995), 192-203.

7   Joanne Gowa, *Closing the Gold Window: Domestic Politics and the End of Bretton Woods* (Ithaca, NY: Cornell University Press, 1983), 14.

8   Odell, *U.S. International Monetary Policy*, 165.

9   Ibid., 166, 202.

10 Gowa, *Closing the Gold Window*, 25.

11 Ibid., 67; Odell, *U.S. International Monetary Policy*, 238-39.

12 Gowa, *Closing the Gold Window*, 151.

13 Odell, *U.S. International Monetary Policy*, 233.

14 Ibid., 192, 346-47.

15 Gowa, *Closing the Gold Window*, 31, 107-08, 115.

16 Ibid., 62.

17 Odell, *U.S. International Monetary Policy*, 268-69.

18 Ibid., 270.

19 John S. Odell, "The U.S. and the Emergence of Flexible Exchange Rates," *International Organization* 33, 1 (Winter 1979), 65-66.

20 Ibid., 68.

21 Gowa, *Closing the Gold Window*, 132.

22 Kenneth W. Dam, *The Rules of the Game* (Chicago: University of Chicago Press, 1982), 256; Tom de Vries, "Jamaica, or the Non-Reform of the IMF," *Foreign Affairs* 54, 3 (April 1976), 577-605.

23 The rapidity of the collapse certainly reflects another factor in modern international monetary relations: the advent of technology. It was possible even then, some twenty-five years ago, to undertake massive international transactions electronically.

24 There were possible advantages to flexible exchange rates—especially after the oil crisis hit, which created strains in international payments. See Otmar Emminger, "International Financial Markets and the Recycling of Petrodollars," *The World Today* 31, 3 (March 1975), 95-102.

Eighteen

BRAZIL'S RESPONSES
TO THE DEBT CRISIS

The debt crisis began when Mexico announced in August 1982 it could no longer pay the interest on its international debts. Soon thereafter, the leading lenders to Brazil began to scale back their loans, anticipating similar problems with that country's finances. In October, Brazil declared that it would not need debt rescheduling; perhaps this was because Brazil had already arranged a $1.2 billion loan from the U.S. Treasury. None the less, by the middle of December 1982, Brazil was unable to meet its financial obligations, and by the end of the month it had stopped payment on the principal of its foreign debt.

Background:
Sources of the Debt Crisis

According to Ethan Kapstein, three prominent theories explain why debt crises occur.[1] The first emphasizes the role of external shocks, which upset the calculations of both borrower and lender. The second is overlending— banks err in loaning out more money than they should. The third explanation looks at the borrowers and stresses how they fail to use their loans effectively.[2] Kapstein also points out the flaws with each of these explanations when applied to the debt crisis of the 1980s. For instance, the argument that an external shock hit the borrowers and lenders, and therefore made it impossible for borrowers to meet their obligations, can only be partially true. While there were shocks (discussed below), these hit all borrowers evenly, yet not all borrowers failed to meet their obligations. East Asian debtors (such as South Korea) were able to meet the increased interest payments because they had high enough export earnings.[3] Exports gained them U.S. dollars, so when the value of the dollar rose their incomes rose as well. They were therefore in a much better position to make their payments on or near schedule.

It is perhaps also worth noting that the suddenness of the crisis caught the markets off guard. The interest rate spread (defined below) is the banks' measure of a borrower's riskiness. The spreads charged on Mexican and Brazilian bonds did not start moving up until the last few weeks before the crisis broke.[4] As for overlending, Kapstein points out that banks are supposedly prevented from overlending by regulations. The domestic authorities that are supposed to ensure that overlending does not occur were circumvented, at least partially, by the emergence of the Euromarket.[5] None the less, this points out that governmental authorities shared part of the responsibility if overlending is to blame.

Finally, Kapstein does not believe that the third explanation, which underscores the importance of how the borrowers used the funds, can fully account for the debt crisis. After all, debtors used their borrowings for a wide variety of uses. Some of these were guaranteed not to earn much of an economic profit (in certain cases, some of the money went to providing government services, rather than being invested in a directly profit-generating endeavour). Others appeared to be wise investments. Once again, the example of the East Asian countries illustrates that some of the transactions made perfect economic sense.

Most observers agree that the dynamics of the early 1980s upset the calculations of borrowers and lenders alike. The biggest movements came in interest rates. The interest charged on a loan is intended to earn the bank a profit; if the bank judges the loan to be a higher risk, it charges the borrower a higher price. This is reflected in the two parts of an interest charge: there is a base rate plus a "spread." The base rate is the rate the bank gives its best customers, what is called the prime rate in the U.S. (i.e., the rate given to the bank's prime customers). Internationally, the base is the rate at which banks loan money to each other in London, known as the London Inter-Bank Offer Rate (LIBOR). The spread is then added to the base, with the size of the spread reflecting the riskiness of the particular loan.

Interest rates in earlier days were almost always fixed at some nominal rate. That is, at the time the debt was undertaken, the interest rate for the entire term was established by taking the base and adding the spread. Inflation had made banks change their practices. Inflation rates had risen to such levels in the 1970s that fixed rate loans were losing money. Let's say a bank made a loan and charged the borrower 10 per cent per year. If inflation was rising at 10 per cent per year over that same period, the real value of the principal plus interest would only equal the real value of the original loan—the bank would earn no profit. When inflation was soaring in a period when most loans were at fixed rates, real interest rates were very, very low. It didn't take long for the banks to figure this out; they began to issue most loans on the basis of variable interest rates, so that the interest charge moved as the underlying base rate changed. Almost all of Brazil's borrowing after 1979 (something like 95 per cent between 1979 and 1981) was at variable interest rates.[6] Any increases in the LIBOR would be passed along to Brazil as higher interest charges.

The base rate would rise, but so, too, would the spread. Developing countries in the early 1970s may only have been paying about 1 per cent spreads; from 1975 to 1977 the spreads climbed slightly, but then they fell off again, only to climb back up to 1.7 per cent on average by 1983.[7] The riskier borrowers were paying even higher spreads. For Brazil, the spread charged by banks in 1980 was 1.5 per cent. It took an initial jump in late 1982 to average 2.25 per cent, but then stabilized after February 1983, when Brazil made its first deal with the IMF, settling in at 2.5 per cent.[8]

While the spreads paid by developing countries were higher than other borrowers might have faced, this had been true for some time. The major source of the rising interest charge came from movements in the LIBOR and the American prime rate. The U.S. Federal Reserve had decided to combat inflation by restricting the American money supply. This goal was pursued through higher interest rates, which pulled the LIBOR up as well. In 1978, the LIBOR was 8.7 per cent; by 1981 this rate had risen to 17 per cent. This was a much higher interest rate than the borrowers had ever thought about paying. As part of debt servicing, interest payments went from 38 per cent in 1978 to 61 per cent in 1984.[9] (The real interest rate paid by Brazil on foreign debt went from an average of 4.236 per cent in 1979 to 9.232 per cent in 1981 and then 14.245 per cent in 1982.[10])

These higher interest rates, plus the downturn in global markets caused by the same pressures on credit, made Brazil's ability to service its debt nearly impossible: the debt service ratio (i.e., the ratio of debt payments to exports) for 1982 hit 98.5 per cent—and Brazil also had to pay for necessary imports, such as oil.[11] As Frieden illustrates in *Debt, Development, and Democracy*, the climbing interest rate after 1979 upset Brazil's domestic political and economic relations. In his words, "A political economy that had come to rely on foreign finance was driven into political and economic crisis by so major a reversal in its international financial position."[12]

The Role of Debt in Brazil's Development Strategy

Since the 1940s, Brazil had employed a development strategy based mostly on ISI. This was pursued even more aggressively after 1967, a few years after a military government took power. Shortly thereafter, European and American banks were expanding their international lending. The military government took advantage of these new opportunities for borrowing.

As access to foreign loans increased, so did the government's role in the economy.[13] As an example of the increased foreign borrowing by the government, Frieden gives statistics on the distribution of private versus government components of the debt. In 1974, more than half of the country's medium- and long-term foreign debt was owed by the private sector; by 1979, the private sector owed only a third of this type of debt.[14]

From the late 1960s until the debt crisis hit, the military ruled with the support of a political coalition oriented around ISI.[15] This coalition had four major components: (1) the modern industrial sector, (2) the domestic financial sector, (3) agricultural businesses (especially the largest farms, which produced commodities for both domestic and international markets), and (4) state-owned enterprises (SOEs). These four elements of the economy received the lion's share of the funds raised via international borrowing.

The government took some of its borrowing and, in good fashion with the ISI strategy, invested it in SOEs producing basic inputs. By increasing domestic production of basic goods such as steel, electricity, etc., it was hoped the overall economy would be stimulated. As it turned out, SOEs were part of the problem. For instance, at the end of 1985 Siderbrás, the national holding company that ran the steel industry, held $15.6 billion in foreign debt. That amounted to roughly 14 per cent of the country's foreign debts. And while these debts had been incurred by the individual companies, it was possible for the SOEs to transfer these debts to the federal government.[16] The government invested elsewhere, too. Rudiger Dornbusch has used examples from Brazil to show just how deeply the government of an economically developing country could get involved in its economy, in ways that had little to do with industrialization; the Brazilian government owned such diverse businesses as motels and perfume stores![17]

Meanwhile, the government adapted to its own inflation by introducing indexation.[18] Just as the banks had adjusted to inflation by using variable rate loans, other actors were building rising costs into their charges. In Brazil (and elsewhere) the government introduced policies to ensure that workers' wages would rise with inflation as well. Wages were indexed so they could be raised as inflation went up. Indexation kept workers from being hurt by inflation in the short-run, but the practice made inflation a permanent fixture of the Brazilian economy.

None of these problems meant Brazil's strategy was necessarily headed towards failure. Brazil's merchandise exports grew by an average of 9.4 per cent per year between 1965 and 1980. That outpaced Singapore over those same years and was just behind Hong Kong's rate.[19] Yet the political economy created would be vulnerable to rising interest charges; obstacles to adjustment would be difficult to overcome.

Brazil's Situation Leading up to 1982

Brazil had already introduced austerity measures before Mexico announced its inability to meet its external debt obligations. As early as the year before, Brazil had struggled with its debt burden—largely because of the expenses of importing oil after the second oil price shock.[20] In 1981, oil imports cost Brazil the equivalent of 43 per cent of the country's export earnings. Brazil was already borrowing from abroad simply to pay the interest on previous debts.[21]

The military government spent the initial period of the debt crisis trying to keep its domestic support satisfied, which meant maintaining future capital inflows. This in turn required Brazil to prove its creditworthiness. This was difficult, since the government was unable to increase taxes. The public sector would have to reduce its expenditures so additional funds could be spent on interest charges. To ensure that local investors would not take their money to another country (such as the U.S.) where interest rates were higher in what is known as capital flight, and perhaps to entice foreign money to come in, Brazil would have to have a high domestic interest rate. Finally, in order to raise and to conserve hard currency for debt repayment, Brazil would have to export more and spend less on imports. This policy could be enhanced by devaluing the currency.[22]

Debt service would be difficult, however. Thanks to the banks' higher interest rates, the debt service ratio was profoundly affected. In 1977, debt service payments equalled 51 per cent of Brazil's merchandise exports. In 1982, debt service payments equalled 91 per cent.[23] Interestingly, the response by the military government was to pursue a set of policies much like those the IMF would advocate: it struggled to reduce its budget deficit and to limit growth of the domestic money supply. And this was in 1981 before Brazil had negotiated with the IMF! The result was a fall in gross output (by 1.6 per cent in 1980-81) while inflation climbed from 94 to 121 per cent.[24] This set the stage for the later problems Brazil would confront.

Inflation grew to 211 per cent by 1983, causing widespread problems. Domestic product fell 3.2 per cent that year, per capita income dropped 5.5 per cent, and real wages fell even further (16 per cent). The most modern industrialized sectors of the economy had to lay off workers. As a result, these sectors would no longer support the government. Meanwhile, the statistics on Brazil's international economic relations were not very encouraging. Gross foreign debt in 1983 grew by 17 per cent. The dollar total of that debt amounted to more than $81 billion. The only positive sign was that Brazil had earned a trade surplus in 1983 of $6.4 billion. The external accounts seemed headed in the proper directions. From 1982 to 1984, export earnings increased by 35 per cent, while imports fell by 30 per cent.[25] With an upsurge in this trade surplus, Brazil alone among the largest debtors in Latin America appeared to be able to finance its debt through trade.

The Initial International
Responses to the Debt Crisis

At first glance, one might have expected the debtors to default on their loans; they were sovereign actors, after all, so how could the banks hope to collect? Both sides understood, however, that default would carry long-term repercussions. If borrowers defaulted, causing the collapse of several large banks, then other banks would not be willing to extend these countries new loans in the future. Also, default would open them up to possible retaliations by the creditor countries. The U.S. and the Europeans might simply put up barriers to trade against the debtors' exports. This would punish defaulting debtors and reward other countries still trying to meet their debt obligations.

The banks were similarly constrained in that they could not simply write off the loans as mistakes or losses because they were simply too large. To have written off these debts in the early 1980s would have been tantamount to a default, since the result would have been the same—the banks going out of business. As it was the value of the banks' stock dropped precipitously once it was clear they would not meet projected earnings after 1982.

The other actors with so much at stake were the creditor governments. Since the major banks threatened by the debt crisis were American and European, these governments might have to bail out some very large banks. This encouraged the U.S. in particular to take action. Likewise at the international level, the U.S. did not want to see any of its neighbours experience too much internal turmoil, nor did the U.S. government wish to have to pay off any other country's debts. No one would really benefit from a default (some would simply lose less than others). The response was for the U.S. to ask both sides to make every effort to ease repayment; the U.S. also made its own efforts to prevent the politicization of the debt crisis. American goals were short-term crisis management (i.e., preventing a collapse of the financial system) and long-term stabilization—the U.S. pursued both.[26]

The first stage of the debt crisis, then, was to pretend that it was manageable: with enough work the Third World borrowers would be able to repay their entire debts. The U.S. government and the banks also made efforts to keep the borrowers bargaining individually rather than as a debtor cartel.[27] The banks organized on their own and picked lead banks to deal with each of the major borrowers, so that negotiations were simplified to one country dealing with one bank; all the other banks would go along with the agreement made. The Third World borrowers, on the other hand, did not use their collective power. And prior to 1985, the U.S. government eschewed any direct responsibility in the debt crisis, though it had already issued loans to several debtors.

From the American perspective, the only possible long-term solution within the existing relationships (and maintaining existing economic principles) was for the debtors to expand their economies, earn more money through exports, and pay off the debts.[28] This left the debt crisis to be settled by individual debtor's policies. The most popular program initially used in Latin America was to refinance the debts, which meant getting new cheaper loans to pay off the original debts. These new loans were available from the IMF and the U.S. government, as well as from renegotiating the terms on old commercial debts.

The IMF Finds a New Role

After the fall of the Bretton Woods monetary regime, the IMF's major responsibility disappeared. The IMF had been created to help deficit countries maintain their pledged parity on the fixed exchange rate system. Without a fixed exchange rate regime, the IMF's duty was less important. Now if a country had a balance-of-payments deficit, it could simply allow its currency to float. Yet by 1992 the IMF had some sort of lending operation in effect with fifty-six countries.[29] The debt crisis had created a new opportunity for the IMF to employ its expertise and financial resources. The debtors needed cash to meet obligations, and they were unable to raise more funds from private sources. The IMF continued its policy of only making loans with conditions attached, but now private actors would look to the IMF to help evaluate whether debtors were making the proper economic adjustments to earn the hard currencies needed to pay off debts.[30]

The orthodox IMF stabilization plan consisted of three elements, which actually reflect its earlier responsibilities under the fixed exchange rate regime. First, it recommended devaluing the debtor country's currency. This was intended to affect the country's balance of payments in order to help the debtor adjust its debt service ratio. Second, the IMF advocated methods to control domestic inflation. These entailed reducing domestic demand, which would also reduce demand for imports. Third, and for many of the same reasons, the IMF worked to reduce government spending, contracting the money supply and reducing wage demands. In application, the policies looked consistent from one country to the next: control the money supply, put in place controls on domestic credit, reduce real wages, and liberalize markets. Most importantly, the IMF began to stretch out the timeframe of its adjustment packages; prior to the 1980s, they had all been short-term. It was only through the experience of the early 1980s that the IMF began to engineer medium-term packages.[31]

The IMF's typical package has been criticized on a number of counts. For one, such adjustment schemes tend to create large trade surpluses so that

external debts can be paid, but they lead to higher rates of domestic inflation. They also cut back on domestic investment—suggesting that as long-
term economic plans they reduce growth and the ability to pay back debts.[32]
Other economists have noted that these policy recommendations are based
largely on models developed for analysing industrialized countries; the
assumptions behind such models may simply be inappropriate for less economically developed countries.[33] Along the same lines, many have argued
that the IMF packages all look alike. Notably, in the early years of the debt
crisis more than 80 per cent of IMF adjustment packages included devaluation. As one finance minister is said to have lamented, "The IMF uses devaluation like a man with a hammer who believes that everything is a nail."[34]

The orthodox structural adjustment loans (SALs) from the World Bank
were conditional on a similar set of policies. In effect, the longer term of the
SALs gave the World Bank the opportunity to stress the need to institutionalize the practices emphasized by the IMF's conditions. In the words of John
Loxley, the emphasis on "structural" adjustment "simply makes more
explicit the fact that contemporary programs frequently imply substantial
changes in the direction of the economy, in its sectoral priorities, and in its
institutional make-up."[35] The term SAL was only used after September 1979.
SALs were intended to give debtors a period of five to ten years in which
they could restructure their economies. IMF conditionality was a precondi-
tion to getting an SAL from the World Bank, but the SAL offered lower interest rates and longer terms than IMF loans.[36]

There were often four separate elements to an SAL. First was the elimination or reduction of macroeconomic imbalances, or what is usually
referred to as "stabilization" (along the lines of the IMF policies). Second
were policies aimed at shifting resources into the production of goods for
the market, especially away from consumption and into the production of
exports. This is also referred to as "switching." Third was improvement of
economic efficiency through support for rationalization and deregulation.
The fourth element was mobilization and co-ordination of the application
of resources (especially those coming from outside the country). The SALs
were conditional on establishment of a longer-term plan for making such
changes. On an issue such as currency devaluation, instead of asking for a
one-shot adjustment the World Bank's SAL would ask the country to adopt
a longer-term pattern of small adjustments. These changes were intended to
have a deeper, more lasting impact: they would include reforming taxes,
tariffs, price controls or subsidization of parts of the economy, privatizing
state-owned enterprises, and so on.[37]

The largest debtors had the most power to upset the international financial system. In due course, they have received the most attention from both
international organizations and the industrialized countries. These debtors
(Brazil, but also Mexico and Argentina) were given lower interest rates,

longer maturities on their debts, and longer grace periods in their debt reschedulings.[38] Brazil was the single largest Third World debtor at this time,[39] and certainly received its share of breaks compared to smaller debtors.

Brazil's First Interactions with the IMF

Brazil initially negotiated with the IMF in December 1982, signing a letter of intent in early January 1983. Since Brazil was unable to uphold its end of the deal, the conditions were renegotiated over the next few months. Some economists have been critical of this initial plan, because they believe the IMF rushed into the agreement without taking Brazil's position into account— apparently the IMF was more interested in showing that the crisis was solvable and that it could play a positive role in resolving the crisis.[40] In the deal struck in January 1983, the IMF made $5.9 billion available over 1983, 1984, and 1985, which Brazil could use in its negotiations with commercial lenders.[41] The commercial banks were to make fresh funds available and maintain Brazil's trade credits.

In 1983, some relief came as the LIBOR fell back to 9.8 per cent.[42] Yet by May 1983 Brazil was no longer meeting the conditions as specified. Renegotiations were undertaken, but since Brazil was not heeding to the earlier promises, the IMF would not release planned disbursements and the commercial banks would not make new loans. Finally, a revised letter of intent was signed in September 1983, for which Brazil received new IMF funds. Unfortunately, this did not convince private creditors that Brazil was committed to reforms. Since no new private funds were forthcoming, yet another deal with the IMF was negotiated before the end of 1983.[43]

One of the reasons for the difficulties was a disagreement over how to measure particular facets of the economy and the government's macroeconomic policies. For instance, the IMF used the "credit-based" approach to measure Brazil's fiscal deficit. This tracked the deficit in terms of overall flows of revenues and expenditures. The Brazilian government preferred to use an "operational" measure that took indexation as a given, and therefore increasing costs were built into the calculations. The two systems produced different numbers. But the biggest reason for problems was that the IMF's targets on defeating inflation were never hit.[44]

The conditions imposed by the IMF had a positive impact on Brazil's balance of trade. The policies Brazil adopted in 1983 resulted in a $12 billion trade surplus. At the same time, Brazil had difficulty meeting the terms of its agreements because it could not limit internal inflation. The IMF asked that any wage increases via indexation be limited to 80 per cent of any increase in the consumer price index—at a time when inflation was roaring along at 200 per cent. Fresh loan disbursements from the IMF had to be put on hold while the government struggled with budget deficit reductions as well. For these reasons, Brazil wound up signing four letters of intent with the IMF in 1983, then three more in 1984.[45] The letters signed in 1984 stressed the IMF's desire to see Brazil pursue higher exports, continue the policy of small but regular devaluations of the currency, and liberalize trade. In the end, Brazil received a new "jumbo" loan of $6.5 billion and had another $5 billion in debts rescheduled.[46]

Brazil's exports did increase, hitting levels well above the targets set by the IMF in the letters of intent. The 1984 surplus was $13.1 billion, and the 1985 surplus $12.4 billion. That was the positive part of the story. Brazil was able to reduce its needs for imports in dramatic fashion. Domestic production of aluminum and energy in several forms were all increased. Production for domestic markets was also reoriented to exports with remarkable success.[47] None the less, Brazil was once again unable to meet the austerity targets established by the IMF, so the IMF suspended credit to Brazil in February 1985. Since the two sides were unable to reach an agreement that year, Brazil introduced its own adjustment package early in 1986.

On the downside, many of the domestic adjustments were difficult to implement. The IMF would have preferred an outright end to wage indexation.[48] Brazil had had indexation since 1964, which explains why the IMF would target it as a source of problems, but this also tells us why it would be so difficult for the government to dismantle the policy. Indexation enforced expectations of wage and price increases. At the same time, indexation is intended to ensure that wages grow as fast as price increases and therefore ending indexation would hurt wage-earners, at least in the short run. (In the long run Brazil's inflation was perhaps more detrimental to the poor than anything else.[49]) One of the conclusions reached by some economists was that the IMF approach had simply hit its limits. While Brazil's external accounts had been adjusted in the ways the IMF urged and Brazil's export earnings increased, internal stabilization did not follow suit. Without the internal adjustment, the debt problem remained.[50] It illustrates how poorly equipped the IMF was to deal with these sorts of problems.

Brazil's Turn to Unorthodox Responses: From the Cruzado Plan to the Moratorium

Having first followed the recommendations from the IMF and others, Brazil then tried its own unorthodox responses to the debt crisis. This is marked by the Cruzado Plan, which was presented by President Jose Sarney on 28 February 1986. The government's plan was to implement a sophisticated set of policies geared to achieve domestic adjustments without suffering the recessionary side-effects of traditional stabilization packages. The main goals were to eliminate inflation and raise revenues for the government by stimulating domestic demand, making it similar to the Austral Plan introduced in Argentina at about the same time. The measures that kept inflation going were supposed to be torn down.[51]

It included several tough measures that had been avoided up to that point. First, indexation was finally to be ended, at least for short-term contracts. Second, there was an immediate and indefinite freeze on more than 80 per cent of goods and services. Third, the money was to be altered—in hopes of changing the way people thought about the currency. In reality, this was only a redenomination of the currency, with a slight change in the name of the unit. One thousand cruzeiros would now be worth one cruzado. (Hence the name of the scheme: the Cruzado Plan.) Fourth, wages were controlled. The minimum wage was increased by one-third, and other wage-earners were given an 8 per cent bonus; future wage adjustments would only be triggered when the inflation rate hit 20 per cent (and then would be adjusted with every following 20 per cent increment in the inflation rate).[52] Another important aspect was the elimination of indexed government bonds, which were a popular method for holding savings. The indexed government bonds were replaced by a non-indexed version, again with the aim of destroying the inertia-propelling inflation.[53]

Each of these measures was intended to disrupt inflation. The greatest political difficulty was to implement the policies in a way that would be perceived as fair, as well as actually convincing everyone that inflation would in fact stop. Typical wage contracts in Brazil ran for six months. Rent contracts were sometimes for six months, but more often ran for a year. Since contracts were constantly turning over, if the government had merely picked a day and decided to enforce a freeze instantly, those individuals who had just renegotiated their wage contracts would be far ahead of those who were just days away from renegotiating their contracts. To make the freeze fairer, the Cruzado Plan contained augmentations for some, plus rollbacks in some rent contracts (with the amount of adjustment based on the rent's average real value during the previous year).[54]

The Cruzado Plan seemed at first to have stopped inflation "cold," according to one assessment.[55] The inflation rate remained low for about six months, but within a year inflation returned. From March 1986 until the end of the year, total consumption increased by 10.9 per cent in real terms, while GDP in real terms only rose by 7.6 per cent.[56] The inflation rate hit 20 per cent by January 1987, triggering the first wage adjustments. This brought on a whole number of other small policy changes. To counteract the impact of inflation on trade, small devaluations of the currency were reintroduced. Indexation of the economy was brought back. Soon inflation was running at an even higher rate than before.

These policies unleashed a splurge in consumer spending. The boom in consumption created shortages of many items, including foodstuffs. There had been a severe drought in late 1985, so the 1986 harvest turned out to be small. To meet increased demand, the import of food items was liberalized, with the results that Brazil's positive trade balance was reduced and precious monetary reserves were spent. Brazil's trade surplus, which had averaged $12.8 billion in 1984-85, fell back to $8.4 billion in 1986. Even worse, the increasing demand and resultant shortages pushed inflation back into the economy. By the end of 1986, Brazilian interest rates hit 400 per cent; various elements of indexation were brought back. Even the savings bonds were indexed again. By February 1987 the price freezes were lifted and the price of many goods immediately jumped 30-40 per cent. By the end of 1987, consumer prices in urban centres such as Rio de Janeiro hit an annual increase of 230 per cent or more.[57]

The Cruzado Plan failed on at least two major counts. First, it failed to increase government revenues. The indirect taxes introduced as part of the overall plan were simply too small to generate large amounts of funds. What Brazil needed to do was something politically difficult in any country whenever the economy is in a downturn: reduce government expenditures while increasing taxes. Tax hikes were unpopular, further expenditure cuts were next to impossible, and now investments were being slashed.[58] Second, the Brazilian government had done little to prevent the expansion of domestic credit. This was intended to allow the government to raise funds to pay off debts, but it had other consequences. Inflation was one, capital flight another.[59]

Rather than drop the Cruzado Plan, the government introduced some minor adjustments. These modifications came too late. Instead of enacting them when needed, the government postponed them until after congressional and gubernatorial elections in the fall of 1986.[60] The policies in this plan were intended to raise new revenues. Compulsory deposits were required for the purchase of many consumer durables, such as automobiles. New taxes, aimed at the upper class, were put in place. Also, sales taxes were put into effect.[61] Other adjustments included price increases on many goods, an altered inflation index, a wage adjustment scheme, a series of minor currency devaluations, and some efforts to boost domestic savings. Naturally, the newly elected government's popularity dropped.[62]

The Moratorium

Brazil's inflation had already returned. Monetary reserves were shrinking. Brazil now had $110.5 billion in long- and medium-term debt. This amounted to more than a third of Brazil's GDP. The country was completing a full 180-degree swing in policies; in the first years of the debt crisis, the military government had tried to retain Brazil's creditworthiness by increasing export earnings just as the international organizations would have urged. But now, in 1987, Brazil was going to do what every one of the international monetary organizations had been arguing against. Brazil was no longer a well-behaved success; instead, it would challenge the debt regime.[63]

Brazil declared a moratorium on interest payments to commercial banks on 20 February 1987. The government expected this action to earn it greater popularity at home; perhaps, too, the government thought this would enable it to find other debtors willing to pursue a similar course. It was also hoped that the sheer size of Brazil's debt, backed now by a refusal to pay, would force the banks to make concessions.[64] The Brazilian government would be disappointed. Domestic popularity was not boosted by the moratorium, nor did other debtors rally to Brazil's side.[65] Instead, the other countries with heavy debt burdens were rescheduling their repayments. Brazil stood alone.[66] Moreover, the banks were preparing themselves for losses—they were ready to call Brazil's bluff.[67]

In May 1987, Citicorp moved to bolster its loan loss reserves. This was an amazing turnaround. In 1983, Citicorp had earned a quarter of its gross profits from the interest paid by Brazil on its jumbo loan. Citicorp was the largest commercial bank in the U.S.; while it had engaged in foreign lending, it also had other streams of income, most notably the interest Americans paid on credit cards. Citicorp was able to set aside earnings from these other areas to cover losses on international loans. In short, Citicorp was positioning itself to say it could afford not to collect the debts. Citicorp's stock immediately rallied.[68] Other banks were pressured to take similar actions, though not all had the diversified income stream of Citicorp.

As a result of Brazil's moratorium, the U.S. took punitive action. In order to force the Brazilians into some sort of repayment on interest charges, the U.S. imposed trade sanctions worth $100 million in November 1987. This jousting did not last long. After further negotiations, Brazil resumed full interest payments in January 1988.[69] The moratorium strategy simply could not last long without inviting retaliation. In September 1988 Brazil was able to renegotiate its debts. A little more than $62 billion in debts were refinanced at lower interest rates and the principal repayments were stretched out for several extra years. Brazil also received $5.2 billion to meet future interest payments.[70]

None the less, Brazil was able to increase its exports. The 1988 trade surplus ran at $19.1 billion, and in that year $10 billion in external debt was cut via debt-equity conversions. The country also easily met the IMF's goals for foreign exchange reserves. Yet GDP failed to grow, and the inflation rate neared 1,000 per cent.[71] Brazil's experiment with unorthodox policies had failed.

The System-Level Explanations for Brazil's Policies

The debt crisis erupted as a problem for many countries at once. The increases in the LIBOR and the downturn of the global economy presented economic problems for many developing countries that had relied on international borrowing to finance development. The similarity of the crisis is perhaps especially true across Latin America.[72] Yet these countries, despite the similarity of their position in the international political economy, responded to these systemic stimuli with different policies. This stands out most clearly with Brazil's moratorium, when the country stood alone.

Despite the fact that many of the same international organizations have been involved in the development of responses to the debt crisis and the obvious similarity in the problem each country faces in paying back debts, the responses debtors have used have been quite varied.[73] Such observations naturally turn us to domestic-level explanations. As Thomas Biersteker argues, any understanding of the responses adopted by the various debtor countries requires a two-level approach, bringing in both domestic and systemic actors.[74]

Domestic Politics: The Military Government Falls

The military government in power when the crisis first broke was discredited by its handling of the issue. The developmental coalition that had been so solid for nearly twenty years came unglued. The debt crisis created a political opening for democratization, which, in the words of Frieden, was "overtaken and accelerated" by the continuing evolution of the issue.[75] The military government relented to demands for greater participation by holding indirect elections in 1984, which the military intended to swing to its own favour.

As noted above, the economic slow-down in 1982 and 1983 hit hard at some of the core groups in the military government's support. The modern industrial sectors, both businessmen and organized labour, opposed the government now. In July 1983, business leaders had issued a policy paper urging the government to rethink its debt strategy. The paper argued that the government needed to renegotiate its deal with the IMF and that part of this renegotiation should include an end to austerity programs.[76] By 1985 the opposition groups—strengthened by defections from the military's support—were in position to have their own leader, Tancredo Neves, elected President. Neves, however, fell ill and died before taking office. Jose Sarney, who took his place, would institute the Cruzado Plan.

The Plan therefore reflects the bases of Sarney's support. The unorthodox approach taken was an attempt to make the necessary adjustments to pay off the debt while maintaining the government's central role in the overall development strategy.[77] Organized labour did not support the Cruzado Plan.[78] At the same time, we should note that labour organizations are fragmented in Brazil. Unions are divided along sectoral and regional lines, and there are also important urban-rural splits.[79] Thus, labour would not voice a united opposition to any adjustment policies, though it had much at stake. Labour's opposition was important for creating the political stand-off over how to distribute the costs associated with defeating inflation.[80]

The political stand-off was worsened by the new constitution put in place when the military government ended. The new constitution gave the Congress and the President shared responsibility for approving the federal budget, prioritizing expenditures, and dealing with wage policies (such as indexation), privatizations, etc. Any redistribution of the costs of adjustment would require broad public support.[81] During the period 1984-90, the budget was gradually unified with the different elements being tied into a single package. But Congress and the various governmental agencies have worked to upset any attempts to control expenditures.[82] The adjustment policies have therefore been hamstrung by the need to ensure their popularity.

The Overlap between Bureaucratic Politics and Domestic Politics

Kurt Weyland relies on a bureaucratic politics approach to explain, at least partially, the incoherence of Brazil's adjustment efforts.[83] Weyland makes the point that the Brazilian government is very fragmented. This allows for the typical factors in bureaucratic politics to come into play. But Weyland also tries to tie together the fragmentation of the state with pluralist models. He cites the arguments of Theodore Lowi, who claimed that where the state is fragmented, policy-making gets driven towards distributive policies. In other words, each group can achieve access and capture a small part of the government, which it uses for its own purposes.

There is some support for this argument in the later policies implemented by the Brazilian government itself. President Fernando Collor's administration (1990-92) tried to combat this problem by introducing measures to centralize the federal agencies. The reorganization of ministries may have lessened the problems but certainly did not eliminate them. The next government, the administration of Itamar Franco, reversed many of these reforms.[84] The most important point to draw from this analysis is that bureaucratic politics probably mirrored the domestic politics discussed above.

Did Individuals Matter Most?

Weyland also notes that political parties fail to serve their traditional purpose in Brazil. Parties do not aggregate interests well. Instead, politics is along very personalistic and narrow interest lines.[85] This suggests that the personalities of individual leaders may hold key evidence for understanding policy decisions. Many observers have noted differences in the personalities of the various presidents who have led Brazil since the military government left power in 1985.[86] For instance, Jose Sarney took office as a result of Neves's death; Sarney was not seen as a strong figure, able to stand above specific interest groups. Instead, he was seen to yield to sectoral pressures.

President Collor, on the other hand, ran on his own. He was considered by many to stand apart from particular groups. His ability to hold off the pressures of narrow interest groups illustrates how an individual can make a difference. At the same time, we should recognize that the president shares powers with other institutions and therefore has little room to manoeuvre. While journalistic impressions make it appear that personalities matter, the evidence is much less clear.

Consequences: The Far-Ranging Impact of the Debt Crisis

The evidence suggests that while systemic pressures presented opportunities and constraints, the responses tried out in Brazil are best explained by considering the ways in which systemic factors were filtered through domestic politics. The pressures generated by the debt crisis hit groups within each country differently; each country had a particular domestic political economy that the pressures upset. Past practices created serious constraints on any adjustment policies, the most important in Brazil's case being indexation.

Brazil attempted to make its adjustments in ways that were not quite consistent with the recommendations of the international organizations such as the IMF and World Bank. Brazil hoped that a set of unorthodox policies would deliver it from the debt crisis with less pain and sacrifice than the orthodox strategies recommended by the international financial institutions. These rival strategies never lived up to their promise, however. Their failure helped consolidate the dominance of orthodox economic policies, not just in the international organizations (such as the IMF and World Bank) but also among the debtors themselves.[87] This may have been the most important consequence of Brazil's decisions.

For the borrowers, the 1980s were the lost decade in the sense that for most, growth was problematic, and investment difficult. This has not been purely the case, however; Brazil's real GDP grew by 16 per cent between 1984 and 1986, in the heart of the crisis. Overall, for Latin America, capital flowed out of the region. In 1982, the year the crisis started, the Latin American countries had $23 billion in new lending. By 1985, new lending to the region fell to $3.5 billion, while the interest being paid out amounted to $22 billion![88]

The commercial banks swallowed some of the losses and negotiated new loans with the debtors. Over time, the U.S. and other creditor governments would have to take more direct action in the crisis, however reluctantly. As a consequence, the creditor governments would take steps to co-ordinate their regulatory efforts. They wished to force banks to be more prudent in their lending, as well as to lessen the competitive pressures associated with international lending. Their actions represent a remarkable example of international co-operation.[89]

Meanwhile, the IMF and World Bank found new roles for themselves. By 1988, the World Bank had issued more than 150 different loans as part of adjustment programs in fifty-five countries.[90] The two agencies were much more active than in the preceding years—though this brought them more criticism than ever before. Also, serious questions have been raised about just what their mandates entail and the appropriateness of the policy instruments and resources they have to deal with their evolving responsibilities.[91] These matters will certainly be on the agenda of future reform efforts in the monetary sphere. In the meantime, the institutions continue to try to prove their value in a changing international political economic environment.

Suggested Readings

Vinod Aggarwal, *Debt Games: Strategic Inter-action in International Debt Rescheduling.* New York: Cambridge University Press, 1996.

Thomas J. Biersteker, ed., *Dealing with Debt.* Boulder, Colo.: Westview Press, 1993.

Richard N. Cooper, *Economic Stabilization and Debt in Developing Countries.* Cambridge, Mass.: MIT Press, 1992.

Jeffry Frieden, "Third World Indebted Industrialization: International Finance and State Capitalism in Mexico, Brazil, Algeria and South Korea," *International Organization* 35, 3 (Summer 1981), 407-31.

Jeffry Frieden, *Debt, Development, and Democracy.* Princeton, NJ: Princeton University Press, 1991.

Miles Kahler, "Politics and International Debt: Explaining the Crisis," *International Organization* 39, 3 (Summer 1985), 357-82.

Notes

1   Also see Miles Kahler, "Politics and International Debt: Explaining the Crisis," *International Organization* 39, 3 (Summer 1985), 357-82.

2   This and the next few paragraphs draw on Ethan B. Kapstein, *Governing the Global Economy* (Cambridge, Mass: Harvard University Press, 1994), 84-85.

3   See Jeffrey Sachs, "External Debt and Macroeconomic Performance in Latin America and East Asia," *Brookings Papers on Economic Activity* 2 (1985), 523-64.

4   Sebastian Edwards, *Crisis and Reform in Latin America: From Despair to Hope* (New York: Oxford University Press and World Bank, 1995), 19-21.

5   For more on the development of the Euromarket and its connections to the debt crisis, see John Loxley, *Debt and Disorder: External Financing for Development* (Boulder, Colo.: Westview Press, 1986), 65-71; James P. Hawley, "Protecting Capital From Itself: U.S. Attempts to Regulate the Eurocurrency System," *International Organization* 38, 1 (Winter 1984), 131-65.

6   James Dinsmoor, *Brazil: Responses to the Debt Crisis* (Washington: Inter-American Development Bank and Johns Hopkins University Press, 1990), 31.

7   Jeffry Frieden, *Debt, Development, and Democracy: Modern Political Economy and Latin America, 1965-1985* (Princeton, NJ: Princeton University Press, 1991), 61-64.

8   Edwards, *Crisis and Reform in Latin America*, 21; Loxley, *Debt and Disorder*, 78; Dinsmoor, *Brazil: Responses to the Debt Crisis*, 31.

9   Loxley, *Debt and Disorder*, 64.

10 These figures are from Table A.33 in Eliana Cardoso and Albert Fishlow, "The Macroeconomics of the Brazilian External Debt," in Jeffrey Sachs, ed., *Developing Country Debt and Economic Performance*, Volume 2, Country Studies—Argentina, Bolivia, Brazil, Mexico (Chicago: University of Chicago Press, 1990), 385.

11 Dinsmoor, *Brazil: Responses to the Debt Crisis*, 33.

12 Frieden, *Debt, Development, and Democracy*, 126.

13 Ibid., 74-75; Cardoso and Fishlow, "The Macroeconomics of the Brazilian External Debt," 274.

14 Frieden, *Debt, Development, and Democracy*, 120.

15 This paragraph draws on Frieden's excellent analysis, ibid., ch. 4.

16 Dinsmoor, *Brazil: Responses to the Debt Crisis*, 65.

17 Rudiger Dornbusch, "From Adjustment with Recession to Adjustment with Growth," in John F. Weeks, ed., *Debt Disaster?: Banks, Governments, and Multilaterals Confront the Crisis* (New York: New York University Press, 1989), 209.

18 Cardoso and Fishlow, "The Macroeconomics of the Brazilian External Debt," 274.

19 Ibid., 335.

20 The first oil shock had been caused by OPEC's Arab members' embargo on oil sales after the Arab-Israeli conflict in 1973; the revolution in Iran in 1979 and the subsequent war between Iran and Iraq sparked the second oil price shock.

21 Cardoso and Fishlow, "The Macroeconomics of the Brazilian External Debt," 275; Dinsmoor, *Brazil: Responses to the Debt Crisis*, 31.

22 Frieden, *Debt, Development, and Democracy*, 126-27.

23 Ibid., 128.

24 Cardoso and Fishlow, "The Macroeconomics of the Brazilian External Debt," 295.

25 The statistics are drawn from Hugo Pregrave de A. Faria, "Brazil, 1985-1987: Pursuing Heterodoxy to a Moratorium," in Thomas J. Biersteker, ed., *Dealing with Debt* (Boulder, Colo.: Westview Press, 1993), 176; Cardoso and Fishlow, "The Macroeconomics of the Brazilian External Debt," 275-76.

26 Kapstein, *Governing the Global Economy*, 89.

27 For more on how the creditors were able to maintain a united front and achieve co-operation to overcome the danger of free-riding, see Vinod K. Aggarwal, *International Debt Threat* (Berkeley: Institute of International Studies, Policy Papers in International Affairs, No. 29, 1987); Charles Lipson, "Bankers' Dilemma: Private Cooperation in Rescheduling Sovereign Debts," *World Politics* 38, 1(October 1985), 200-25.

28 Kapstein, *Governing the Global Economy*, 96.

29 Thomas J. Biersteker, "Introduction," in Biersteker, ed., *Dealing with Debt*, 1. Interestingly, twenty-eight of these countries were in Africa.

30 See Charles Lipson, "International Debt and International Institutions," in Miles Kahler, ed., *The Politics of International Debt* (Ithaca, NY: Cornell University Press, 1986), 219-43.

31 See Robin A. King and Michael D. Robinson, "Assessing Structural Adjustment Programs: A Summary of Country Experience," in Weeks, ed., *Debt Disaster?* 105-06.

32 Cardoso and Fishlow, "The Macroeconomics of the Brazilian External Debt," 302.

33 King and Robinson, "Assessing Structural Adjustment Programs," 106-08.

34 The quote is from Carl Greenidge, finance minister of Guyana in January 1988; Richard D. Fletcher, "Undervaluation, Adjustment and Growth," in Weeks, ed., *Debt Disaster?* 125.

35 Loxley, *Debt and Disorder*, 26.

36 Ibid., 125, 141.

37 Biersteker, "Introduction," 5-6; see also Kapstein, Governing the Global Economy, 96; Loxley, *Debt and Disorder*, 26; Robert Liebenthal and Peter Nicholas, "World Bank-Supported Adjustment Programs," in Weeks, ed., *Debt Disaster?* 94.

38 Biersteker, "Introduction," 7.

39 Frieden, *Debt, Development, and Democracy*, 95.

40 See Cardoso and Fishlow, "The Macroeconomics of the Brazilian External Debt," 297-300.

41 Dinsmoor, *Brazil: Responses to the Debt Crisis*, 35.

42 Ibid., 36.

43 Pregrave de A. Faria, "Brazil, 1985-1987," 176-77; Dinsmoor, *Brazil: Responses to the Debt Crisis*, 36.

44 Dinsmoor, *Brazil: Responses to the Debt Crisis*, 75-78. These sorts of disagreements should sound familiar to any who have followed the budgetary debates within the U.S. government, where different accounting rules also exist.

45 Cardoso and Fishlow, "The Macroeconomics of the Brazilian External Debt," 300.

46 Dinsmoor, *Brazil: Responses to the Debt Crisis*, 36-37.

47 Ibid., 36-37, 41-49.

48 Ibid., 83-85.

49 Kurt Weyland, *Democracy without Equity: Failures of Reform in Brazil* (Pittsburgh: University of Pittsburgh Press, 1996), 25-26.

50 This point is stressed by Cardoso and Fishlow, among others; see "The Macroeconomics of the Brazilian External Debt," esp. 301.

51 Ibid., 276.

52 Pregrave de A. Faria, "Brazil, 1985-1987," 186; Edwards, *Crisis and Reform in Latin America*, 36-37; Dinsmoor, *Brazil: Responses to the Debt Crisis*, 96-97.

53 Dinsmoor, *Brazil: Responses to the Debt Crisis*, 9.

54 Cardoso and Fishlow, "The Macroeconomics of the Brazilian External Debt," 311-13.

55 Ibid., 319; Edwards, *Crisis and Reform in Latin America*, 37.

56 Dinsmoor, *Brazil: Responses to the Debt Crisis*, 97.

57 Pregrave de A. Faria, "Brazil, 1985-1987," 189; Dinsmoor, *Brazil: Responses to the Debt Crisis*, 9, 98-102.

58 Cardoso and Fishlow, "The Macroeconomics of the Brazilian External Debt," 353. See also Dornbusch, "From Adjustment with Recession to Adjustment with Growth," 212-13.

59 Dornbusch, "From Adjustment with Recession to Adjustment with Growth," 213. Also see Edwards, *Crisis and Reform in Latin America*, 36-37.

60 Weyland, *Democracy without Equity*, 63.

61 Pregrave de A. Faria, "Brazil, 1985-1987," 187.

62 Ibid., 189-90; Dinsmoor, *Brazil: Responses to the Debt Crisis*, 99.

63 This characterization comes from Cardoso and Fishlow, "The Macroeconomics of the Brazilian External Debt," 277, 318.

64 Joan E. Spero, *The Politics of International Economic Relations*, 4th ed. (New York: St. Martin's Press, 1990), 191.

65 Pregrave de A. Faria, "Brazil, 1985-1987," 192; Kapstein, *Governing the Global Economy*, 99.

66 Pregrave de A. Faria, "Brazil, 1985-1987," 193.

67 "Bluff" is Spero's term; see *The Politics of International Economic Relations*, 191.

68 Kapstein, *Governing the Global Economy*, 99; Paul M. Sacks and Chris Canavan, "Safe Passage through Dire Straits: Managing an Orderly Exit from the Debt Crisis," in Weeks, ed., *Debt Disaster?* 81; Aggarwal, *International Debt Threat*, 16-17.

69 Pregrave de A. Faria, "Brazil, 1985-1987," 194.

70 Dinsmoor, *Brazil: Responses to the Debt Crisis*, 104.

71 Ibid., 105.

72 Ibid., 1.

73 Biersteker, "Introduction," 4.

74 Ibid., 2.

75 Frieden, *Debt, Development, and Democracy*, 87.

76 Ibid., 131-33.

77 Edwards, *Crisis and Reform in Latin America*, 33.

78 Ibid., 36-37, 40.

79 Weyland, *Democracy without Equity*, 55-56, 68.

80 Edwards, *Crisis and Reform in Latin America*, 71.

81 Dinsmoor, *Brazil: Responses to the Debt Crisis*, 112; Weyland, *Democracy without Equity*, 8.

82 Weyland, *Democracy without Equity*, 74.

83 Ibid., 4-5, 184-85.

84 Ibid., 75.

85 Ibid., 78.

86 Ibid., 187-89.

87 Edwards, *Crisis and Reform in Latin America*, 42.

88 Kapstein, *Governing the Global Economy*, 97; Dinsmoor, *Brazil: Responses to the Debt Crisis*, 3.

89 Ethan B. Kapstein, "Resolving the Regulators' Dilemma: International Coordination of Banking Regulations," *International Organization* 43, 2 (Spring 1989), 323-47; Kapstein, "Between Power and Purpose: Central Bankers and the Politics of Regulatory Convergence," *International Organization* 46, 1 (1992), 256-87.

90 Liebenthal and Nicholas, "World Bank-Supported Adjustment Programs," 97.

91 See Richard E. Feinberg and Edward L. Bacha, "When Supply and Demand Don't Intersect: Latin America and the Bretton Woods Institutions in the 1980s," *Development and Change* 19, 3 (July 1988), 371-99.

Nineteen

....

CANADA AND THE
FREE TRADE AGREEMENT
WITH THE U.S.

Background: The Historical Parameters of the U.S.-Canada Relationship

Historically, Canada and the United States had explored freer trade on several occasions. After the disastrous effects of the Smoot-Hawley Tariff had exacerbated the Great Depression, Canada and the U.S. struck several deals to liberalize their trade. These bilateral agreements (1935, 1938) were fuelled by the need to stimulate production and employment any way possible. These were enhanced over time, most notably in the Auto Pact signed in 1965. Canada's high tariffs had attracted investment by American producers who wanted to sell in the Canadian market. The pact introduced waivers on the duty for original equipment parts and automobiles, allowing the American firms to integrate their production in the two countries. In return, the U.S. manufacturers had to produce a certain percentage in Canada, with the amount relative to the level of their sales in that country. The target was to make sure that 60 per cent of the content of the vehicles sold in Canada was produced there. As Casper Garos points out, this is managed trade,[1] though it was liberalized compared to simply having tariff barriers. Much about these agreements went against Canada's longer tradition of protectionism, especially those signed in the 1930s. Since Sir John A. Macdonald's National Policy (1879), higher tariffs had been seen as part of a policy package helping Canada to industrialize and supporting Canadian unity.

These same goals of national unity and industrialization had been put forth as the reasons to reject an American offer to negotiate freer trade in 1911. Now, some seventy years later, it was the Canadians who initiated the talks to liberalize trade. The central question for this chapter, then, is why Canada chose to initiate such an agreement at this time.[2] The impact of an economic downturn was perhaps once again one of the driving forces behind the decision to explore new economic relations. It was hoped that improvements in trade could be used as an engine to stimulate the economy.

By the mid-1980s some of Canada's political leaders were also beginning to worry about ensuring access to the American market. Industrial leaders and businessmen were increasingly concerned that if Canadian firms were to remain competitive, they would have to achieve higher economies of scale. That meant ensuring that a greater volume of goods produced could be sold—and the Canadian market itself wasn't large enough to support those economies of scale. At Canada's initiative, negotiations with the U.S. on a free trade agreement were requested in late 1985.

Fears of the New Protectionism

Another issue, of course, was to provide insurance against several forms of potential problems in international trade. Of course, the GATT had provided enormous benefits to countries such as Canada that rely heavily on trade. In the early 1980s, however, there were worries that the GATT was in trouble. On the one hand, the GATT's principles and practices appeared to be under attack. As more and more countries entered international trade, including those such as South Korea that were using EOI as a development strategy, and the economically advanced countries were racked with economic downturns coupled with rising interest rates, it was small wonder that protectionist pressures rose everywhere. These pressures were somewhat controlled by the GATT rules—if a country actually raised tariffs, other states were allowed to retaliate with tariff hikes. The GATT rules therefore prevented tariffs from rising but sparked an increase in non-tariff barriers (NTBs).

NTBs lie in the grey area of the GATT rules; they are clearly against GATT's underlying principles, but they are difficult to control with explicit rules or codes of behaviour. NTBs are easily disguised as the exercise of a state's regulatory powers in the areas of the environment, safety, or health. If a state passes a law banning a particular form of fishing or requiring products to include special features, this can effectively block imports from other countries. Yet no international agreements would prevent a country from exercising its sovereignty, regulating its own internal affairs—though in the GATT's Tokyo Round negotiations the GATT members had tried. Their efforts were not entirely successful. A new form of protectionism was on the rise.

There was a second fear among Canadians, associated with the GATT. The GATT's future hinged on the progress of multilateral negotiations. The Uruguay Round was dragging on to ever greater lengths. Particular issues such as trade in services and in agricultural goods threatened to upset the talks. Without forward movement in these negotiations, many feared that

GATT would no longer be a source of stability in economic relations but would instead begin a steady erosion and decline.[3] As insurance against the possible decline of the GATT regime, in either a failure of the Uruguay Round talks or the rise of NTBs, Canadians sought a bilateral trade agreement with the U.S. The Free Trade Agreement was not intended to circumvent or replace the GATT, but rather to supplement the existing regime.

Canada's Attitudes towards the U.S.

Since 1972, Canada's official perspective on trade relations with the U.S. had been dominated by views set out by Mitchell Sharp, at that time the Minister of External Affairs in the federal government. Sharp's essay, "Canada-U.S. Relations: Options for the Future," had underlined Canada's vulnerability to American threats. Written just after the Nixon shocks, when Canada had been hurt by the import surcharge Nixon had created, the essay stressed the need for Canada to pursue multilateral trade strategies. It was intended that Canada could lessen its economic dependence on the U.S., or at least find better safeguards for its trade via multilateral institutions.[4]

In step with this attitude, the Canadian government established several policies and agencies designed to carry out this distancing from the United States. In 1974, the Foreign Investment Review Agency (FIRA) was created to monitor and regulate foreign investments entering Canada. In 1980, the National Energy Program (NEP) was introduced to promote Canadian ownership of the energy sector. (This would automatically require reducing and limiting the percentage of American ownership in that sector.) In 1982-83, the Canadian government had reviewed its stand on trade policies. The Trudeau government chose to re-emphasize a sectoral trade approach.[5]

In the 1980s, the combination of monetary and fiscal policies in the U.S. were increasing capital flows into that country. Moreover, with the threat of rising American protectionism, investors were beginning to calculate ways to avoid potential barriers. Even Canadian investors were looking to put their new investments in the U.S. rather than relying on continued access to the American market.[6] Previous tariff reductions by Canada had increased trade levels, and this in turn had influenced decisions made by investors from other countries. Whenever Canada had liberalized its trade relations (either bilaterally or multilaterally) foreign investors had responded by increasing their holdings in Canada. Thus it was clear to Canadian decision-makers that investment levels were being (and could be) affected by trade policy.

Despite the Canadian attempts to create some distance between the American economy and their own, the two countries' economies remained quite intertwined. The extensive economic ties go beyond simply having the largest trading relationship of any two countries. Canada supplies raw materials and energy to the U.S., is a very important market for American manufactured goods, and receives large amounts of American investments. Not many people know it, but Canada is one of the top foreign investors in the U.S., so the relationship works in both directions.[7] While the two countries have far-reaching economic connections, the relationship is asymmetric—the U.S. clearly dominates.

There were also other sources providing the Canadian government the momentum to engage in talks at this time. The previous Liberal government had explored the possibility of a deal with the U.S. in the Royal Commission on the Economic Union and Development Prospects for Canada. When the Macdonald Commission, as it is better known, reported in 1985, it endorsed the idea that free trade with the U.S. would promote increased efficiency and productivity in Canadian firms by exposing them to greater competition. The report would be used by the Conservatives to promote their own goal of reducing the role of government in the economy—they could make such an outcome persist after their departure from government by signing a treaty from which Canada would have difficulty withdrawing. Another source for change came from the Canadian business community itself. Prominent lobbying groups such as the Business Council on National Issues and the Canadian Manufacturers' Association pronounced their support of an exploration of a broad trade liberalization with the U.S. The Conservative government of Brian Mulroney would capitalize on these forces to promote the deal.[8]

Canada Initiates Talks

Canada's goals in initiating the talks included securing access to the U.S. market, opening up parts of the American market previously blocked to Canadian exporters, and establishing special rules for some sectors (especially agriculture, wine and spirits, energy, and autos). These talks were also seen as a way to create precedents for other talks elsewhere—especially for introducing service sector and investment issues and for establishing patterns that could be replicated at the multilateral level.[9] Since any deal would supplement the GATT, the talks provided the opportunity to establish examples that could be referred to in multilateral trade negotiations.

Canada's first probing discussions in 1984 were aimed at replicating the Auto Pact in other sectors. It was hoped that trade in other selected sectors could be handled in similar ways as the trade in autos and auto parts. Unfortunately, the symmetry of such deals was missing, which undermined the ability to reach an agreement. It was simply too difficult to see where each side would win or lose; without knowing where the benefits would accrue it was impossible to create reciprocity. Rather than let this issue extinguish the talks, it was decided that any deal would have to be much broader—and both sides seemed interested in this possibility.[10] Interestingly, public support within Canada for some sort of free trade agreement with the U.S. had existed for many years prior to the Canadian government taking any action.[11] It appeared there was an opportunity to make a far-reaching economic arrangement.

American Priorities

In responding to Canada's offer to negotiate, the U.S. wanted to take this opportunity not only for immediate potential economic gains but also as a way to establish important precedents. For Canada, access to the American market was an obvious priority; Canada's trade and investments are concentrated in the U.S. For the U.S., Canada is very important, but the U.S. has several other large trading partners. The broader U.S. aims were to get issues such as the liberalization of trade in services on the world's agenda, as well as open up investment opportunities and put in place controls on intellectual property.[12] The U.S. therefore saw these negotiations much more as a single facet in a much larger game.

This did not mean the U.S. provided the most momentum in these talks. Canada initiated the negotiations, not the U.S.—in fact, the U.S. wasn't well prepared for the talks once they started. Instead, in 1985, thanks in large part to the rising value of the U.S. dollar, Congress was feeling all sorts of protectionist pressures. Among the strongest then being expressed came from the American lumber industry, which was specifically aimed at competition from Canadian firms.[13] Senator Robert Packwood from Oregon happened to be chair of the Senate Finance Committee, which gave him the vantage point to make the lumber industry's points a major issue in the passage of the Free Trade Agreement (FTA), since treaties have to be ratified in the Senate and the Finance Committee is charged with reviewing treaties' impact.[14]

In short, the U.S. was interested in responding to Canada's offers, but the U.S. was unready to initiate the talks itself. It took some time for the Canadians to convince decision-makers in the United States that the issues at stake were significant. The talks remained low on the list of American priorities for quite some time, and therefore the American negotiators expended few resources in preparing their positions. The talks would seem one-sided in their first few years. The onus for completing the talks would rest heavily on the shoulders of the Canadian negotiating team. This poses another question for us—why did the Canadians place such importance on the FTA, given the somewhat indifferent attitude coming from the Americans?

Canada's Systemic Concerns: Ensuring a Future with Free Trade

As suggested above, one of the possible factors shaping the position of Canadian decision-makers was the systemic environment. As the Uruguay Round negotiations dragged on, some doubts began to emerge about the long-term viability of the GATT regime. As a nation that relies on exports, Canada needed some sort of insurance that it would have access to foreign markets in the future. The insurance aspect also helps us understand how the FTA relates to other multilateral agreements. The FTA was not meant to supplant the GATT but to reinforce and supplement the broader trade regime. Thus this bilateral effort reflected Canada's fears about the collapse of the larger trade regime.

Moreover, there were signs that the U.S. itself might start to practise more protectionism. The U.S. had already deployed some of its own NTBs, and more were possible. Tariffs were also possible, especially where the U.S. felt Canadian producers benefited from government support. Friction with Canada had occurred already, and the possibility that a new, tighter relationship could be constructed was apparent. One of the primary goals for Canada would be to ensure that explicit rules governed more of the trade relationship. Within the set of goals about legal codes governing trade, there was naturally a set of issues concerning how disputes would be settled. This was very important for Canada, because in many disputes in the past the U.S. had taken unilateral action. Canada wanted a clear set of rules for how disputes would be handled in the future. With clear adjudication, trade disputes could be settled with minimal risk of their spiralling out of control as each side retaliated.

Canadian leaders would stress that since more than three-quarters of Canadian trade is with the U.S., Canada had to act.[15] There was too much potentially at stake. If the GATT talks foundered, or if American protectionism surged, Canada's economy would be seriously hurt. These broad calculations about the future systemic environment helped Canadian policy-makers decide to initiate the negotiations with the U.S.

Problems with the Systemic Arguments

One of the problems with the systemic arguments just presented has to do with the timing of Canada's initiatives. After all, fears about the breakdown of the GATT regime had existed since the mid-1970s. The Tokyo Round negotiations were just as difficult as the Uruguay Round negotiations, though the number of states involved were fewer. The Tokyo Round was supposed to prevent the spread of NTBs, but it was quickly apparent that NTBS were going to be more numerous in the future. None the less, systemic goals were stressed in public explanations by the administration of Canadian Prime Minister Brian Mulroney.

Mulroney and the Progressive Conservatives also mentioned other reasons for pursuing the FTA. Prominent among these were the needs of Canadian businesses to improve their competitiveness. The economic arguments often centred on the need for new investment and investment in plants so that they could be as efficient as possible. Yet, the need for economies of scale had been present for a long time. The Conservatives still stressed the need for Canadian businesses to become more competitive, and that meant facing up to American competition.[16] Perhaps the Conservatives were simply more sensitive to these needs than were previous governments.

Critics pointed out that Canadian firms had largely achieved whatever economies of scale were possible. The U.S. market was already largely open to manufacturers, according to Riel Miller. Certainly in terms of tariffs, this point was true; in terms of other issues, there was dissatisfaction with the existing relationship. By giving up its tariffs, Miller and other critics contended that Canada would be pushed to specialize along the lines of the country's comparative advantage in resource production, not manufacturing.[17] They predicted a decline in Canadian manufacturing if the FTA was signed.

Along similar lines, critics argued that the "New Protectionism" was no longer so new by the mid-1980s. Tariffs were already fairly low—as Duncan Cameron wondered, what would their elimination bring? No more than a marginal impact on the final price of the goods.[18] However, there were other issues at stake. The Conservatives were arguing that Canadians needed to remove their trade disputes from the American courts. Too many of the disputes were ending up in the U.S. legal system; Canadian interests would be better served by the binational adjudication panels created by the FTA.[19]

All of these points remain legitimate concerns for any Canadian government. Yet these issues had been present for some time. As for the timing of Canada's initiative, the systemic arguments are simply too vague. They point out why such an effort may have seemed unnecessary prior to the early 1970s, but they cannot distinguish between time periods after that. Once again, we need to turn to the domestic-level arguments to get a better understanding of just what was motivating the Canadian decision-makers.

Domestic Politics: The Electoral Strategy of the Conservatives

As Cameron, one of the more vocal academic critics of the agreement, argued, it was easier to identify those sectors likely to suffer losses in the

agreement than it was to identify winners.[20] As with other free trade agreements, the big winners should be consumers—but consumers are notori-
ously difficult to mobilize as a political group. There is little evidence that
consumers somehow pressured for this outcome. This begs the question:
Why then did the Conservatives follow this policy? Shouldn't the opposition have been too costly?

One such easily identifiable group likely to oppose the FTA, for instance,
would have been comprised of the workers and owners of the large number of small American-owned branch plants. These tended to be in Ontario;
their operations often mirrored those of their American parents, but they
were less efficient and had higher labour costs. They existed because
American firms wanted to leap behind Canada's tariff barriers. Once there
was a free trade agreement, the American firms could simply concentrate
their production at the more efficient American home plant—or so the
Canadian employees feared.[21]

One of the domestic splits likely to emerge in Canada's domestic politics
surrounding the FTA would have to do with differing provincial interests.
On the one hand, the provincial governments themselves wanted a hand in
the talks—which wasn't allowed, though there were regular consultations
between the federal government and the provinces. Yet as we might expect,
in the end support for the talks fell largely along provincial lines. The West
and Quebec were largely in favour of free trade, while opposition was centred in Ontario.[22] These splits set the stage for electoral political strategies by
the federal parties.

As Michael Lusztig argues, the regional variation in support for free trade
allowed the issue to become a pivotal question in federal elections.[23] In his
analysis, the Conservatives pursued free trade as a conscious campaign strategy to retain office. The Conservatives had traditionally had strength in the
western provinces; the pursuit of free trade with the U.S. would allow them
to unite these established bases of support with popularity in Quebec. Free
trade was a national issue that could give the Conservatives broad support.
The Conservatives' main rivals, the Liberals, were divided over whether
they should oppose the FTA.[24] Thus the very same strategy that would boost
the Conservatives promised to split their opponents.

The Conservatives also had one thing going in their favour in 1988,
when Canada was on the verge of ratifying the agreement with the U.S. and
a federal election was called: they had largely delivered on their economic
policy promises from their last campaign. In 1984, the Conservatives had
promised to deal with unemployment without spurring inflation—and this
they had largely done, though the costs were in a rising deficit.[25] The electorate may have been persuaded by the Conservatives' campaign statements,
given the Mulroney government's record in economic policy. In the 1988
election, where the FTA was the dominant issue, the Conservatives won 43

per cent of the vote and 170 seats (out of 295). The Liberals came second, with 32 per cent and 82 seats. The most vehement critics of the agreement, the New Democratic Party (NDP), won 20 per cent of the vote and 43 seats.

Bureaucratic Politics: Canada's Trade Negotiator's Office

Besides the domestic politics, there were bureaucratic divisions within the Canadian government concerning the wisdom of free trade with the U.S. For instance, the Department of Regional Industrial Expansion (DRIE) was one source of opposition to any free trade deal.[26] This department's job, after all, was to assist industrial sectors in trouble. Foreign competition was often the source of their trouble; certainly the DRIE was unlikely to welcome the elimination of tariffs. The department was deeply suspicious of any free trade agreement with the Americans. Within other departments opposition could also be found.

The Mulroney government perhaps circumvented much of the potential bureaucratic opposition, however, by setting up a new agency to undertake these negotiations: the Trade Negotiator's Office (TNO), which drew most of its staff from the Department of External Affairs. Since other agencies were wary of this new body, Simon Reisman, the head of the Canadian negotiating team, made a point of establishing a narrow agenda and laying out a limited scope of action.[27] His team also coalesced into a tightly knit group, whereas the American team lacked a real mandate and suffered from weaker leadership.

On the American side, the U.S. Trade Representative (USTR) office was responsible for the American team. The USTR was understaffed; also, the FTA talks were merely one job the USTR people were concerned with, and not even the most important one. Most of the USTR staff were concentrating their energy in the formulation of strategies and policies for the Uruguay Round talks. Moreover, the USTR was more tightly constrained in its mandate. The American team had to keep in touch with the other relevant agencies in the U.S., and most importantly, the executive branch agencies in general had to work with Congress if there was any hope of getting the agreement through to final ratification. It could hardly have been more different on the Canadian side. Given the parliamentary and political party practices in Canadian government, decision-making has become centralized in the cabinet. When the cabinet moves forcefully in one direction, the Parliament and the bureaucracy follow.[28] The Canadian negotiating team was much more insulated from these other pressures because it had strong backing from the cabinet.

Political Leaders and the Ideas They Shared

Journalists have focused on another angle in explaining Canada's decision to pursue free trade with the United States. This is hardly surprising, given that the political leaders of the two countries themselves have stressed how close their co-operation was. As conservative politicians, it is no surprise that Brian Mulroney and Ronald Reagan (and later George Bush) held similar ideological convictions. In the public's perceptions of the Free Trade Agreement, the ideological affinity of the two governments was paramount. The March 1985 Quebec City meeting, for instance, allowed Mulroney and Reagan to lay out their similar visions for free trade—and, as both are of Irish descent, sing "When Irish Eyes are Smiling" from the stage at a public gala.

One of the points raised in the previous section, however, was that bureaucrats actually formulated and executed the negotiations themselves. The top political leadership only stepped in at a few points along the way, and then again at the end of the whole process. As Michael Hart described the early months of the talks, the Canadians supplied the vision, the American politicians enthusiastically endorsed this vision, but then American bureaucrats would put the brakes on.[29] The bureaucrats, as well as the politicians, were critical for reaching successful negotiations.

Even the ideological affinity of the two governments may not explain as much as one might think. The Reagan administration's support for the ideology of free trade did not necessarily mean they would take action to back up their verbal convictions. In fact, some have compared the Reagan administration's position on the FTA with its stand on budget deficits: "long on ideology and rhetoric but very short on policy and execution." What was more worrisome to Canadians was that the gap between rhetoric and reality seemed to expand as the administration was in office.[30]

In Canada, the Conservatives were ideologically behind liberalization, and they argued that they were simply following a longer-term trend in Canadian policy.[31] As for the negotiators themselves, on the Canadian side they were all "true believers" in the benefits of freer trade. That was part of the way the TNO team was assembled. As one, Michael Hart, explains the switch in Canadian policy, "it had become clear that the resource base could no longer finance the maintenance of an inefficient manufacturing economy sheltered behind high tariff walls."[32] On the American side, chief negotiator Peter Murphy was described as having "no vision and no compelling philosophy."[33] His experience had been in negotiations concerning the textile trade—the greatest area of managed trade in the post-war Western economy. Ideology may have been a motivating factor for the Canadians, but that point doesn't carry over to the American negotiators.

Consequences: The Impact of the FTA

On 2 January 1988, Mulroney and Reagan signed the Free Trade Agreement. The preliminary agreement had been reached just before midnight on 3 October 1987, only after an erratic set of negotiations that spanned sixteen months. The FTA was intended to be a comprehensive and sweeping arrangement. All tariffs were to be eliminated over a span of ten years. Goods were separated into three categories, with some having their tariffs eliminated right away, others in a period of five years, and the last group phased out in the ten-year period. The rules of origin (i.e., assessment of the content of a final product) refer to the value of the goods involved, with the limit being at least 50 per cent of the value of the good. This is one part of the modification of the Auto Pact, since the rules of origin replace the previous Canadian content rules. (And, of course, the duties on car components would be phased out along with other tariffs.) Investment and the service sector were also liberalized, though some areas were kept apart.[34] Also, Canada made the cultural industry (e.g., television, radio, newspapers, etc.) exempt, though there has since been pressure by the U.S. to alter practices in this area.

While the two countries signed as part of the FTA a deal to co-ordinate technical standards (a common form of NTB), these rules are largely set by state/provincial governments, and therefore the agreement is not as binding as either federal government might have wished. Government procurement was also liberalized beyond the codes set in the GATT. Agriculture was largely left in the hands of the GATT talks, though some Canadian special requests were maintained in the FTA. While there were promises made on the liberalization of trade in alcoholic beverages, these, too, remain largely in the hands of Canadian provincial governments and little change has occurred so far.

Paul Wonnacott defends the agreement as the best possible deal Canada could expect.[35] The greatest success for Canada may well have been the institutionalization of new dispute settlement mechanisms. These have been expanded in the North American Free Trade Agreement (NAFTA). They serve to protect the FTA from coercive uses of economic power, which obviously pose a greater threat to Canada than the U.S. The dispute settlement mechanisms also set up specific time limits for resolving cases, which was an improvement over the GATT's rules and the mechanisms used in other free trade zones (which allowed cases to drag on indefinitely).[36]

Of course, within a few years the FTA was superseded by NAFTA, which included Mexico; those negotiations were concluded on 12 August 1992.[37] NAFTA included several items the FTA did not, but in most ways NAFTA was built on the base of the FTA.[38] Moreover, the Uruguay Round was completed, and this, too, borrowed certain features from the FTA. While the FTA wasn't needed by Canada as insurance in the end, the FTA was a powerful precedent for these other negotiations.

In assessing the economic impact of the FTA on Canada (the initiator of the treaty), one must try to separate the impact of trade from the broader factors affecting the economy of Canada.[39] The critics claimed that Canadian manufacturing jobs would be lost in large numbers and that Canada would slip into the role of a resource exporter. In fact, the preferred jobs seem to have been retained (with adjustments in some sectors and job losses that can be accounted for by other facets of economic policy). Canadian exports to the U.S. have grown at a faster rate than Canadian exports to other markets, suggesting that liberalization did have an impact.[40]

A major question remains, however. Are regional arrangements such as the FTA or NAFTA a positive omen for the future of the trade regime? In this case, the regional trade agreement was intended to work alongside the GATT. Fears that this sort of regional arrangement would undermine the GATT appear to be unfounded, though the same cannot be said about some of the other regional trade deals struck in recent years. Free trade blocs are not necessarily a problem for a broader regime based on similar principles, and there are those who even argue that momentum for further liberalization might best come from regional agreements. Certainly in this example, the FTA did not upset liberal trade relations elsewhere and may have helped expand free trade by establishing a base for an agreement involving the U.S., Canada, and Mexico.

Suggested Readings

Bruce Doern, Les Pal, and Brian Tomlin, *Border Crossings*. New York: Oxford University Press, 1996.

Richard G. Lipsey, "Unsettled Issues in the Great Free Trade Debate," *Canadian Journal of Economics* 22, 1 (February 1989), 1–21.

Richard G. Lipsey, Daniel Schwanen, and Ronald Wonnacott, *The NAFTA: What's In, What's Out, What's Next*. Toronto: C.D. Howe Institute, 1994.

William G. Watson, "Canada-U.S. Free Trade: Why Now?" *Canadian Public Policy* 13, 3 (September 1987), 337–49.

Notes

1 Casper Garos, *Canada-U.S. Free Trade* (Amsterdam: VU University Press, 1990), 8-9.

2 The fact that the U.S. was caught unprepared by the Canadian initiative is best captured by Michael Hart's title for the chapter covering the starting position of the U.S.: "No Anchor, No Rudder, No Compass." See Michael Hart (with Bill Dymond and Colin Robertson), *Decision at Midnight: Inside the Canada-U.S. Free-Trade Negotiations* (Vancouver: University of British Columbia Press, 1994), ch. 3.

3 Stephen D. Cohen, Joel R. Paul, and Robert A. Blecker, *Fundamentals of U.S. Foreign Trade Policy* (Boulder, Colo.: Westview Press, 1996), 239. Also see "Editor's Introduction," in Murray G. Smith and Frank Stone, eds., *Assessing the Canada-U.S. Free Trade Agreement* (Halifax: Institute for Research on Public Policy, 1987), 3-17, esp. 5-6.

4 Hart, *Decision at Midnight*, 14. For a brief discussion of these ideas, see Garos, *Canada-U.S. Free Trade*, 9-11.

5 Hart, *Decision at Midnight*, 17-22.

6 Ibid., 6.

7 Garos, *Canada-U.S. Free Trade*, 4-6. Also see David Leyton-Brown, "The Political Economy of North American Free Trade," in Richard Stubbs and Geoffrey Underhill, eds., *Political Economy and the Changing Global Order* (Toronto: McClelland & Stewart, 1994), 353-54.

8 Leyton-Brown, "The Political Economy of North American Free Trade," 358; Maureen Appel Molot, "The Canadian State in the International Economy," in Stubbs and Underhill, eds., *Political Economy and the Changing Global Order*, 516-17.

9 Simon Reisman, "The Nature of the Canada-U.S. Trade Agreement," in Smith and Stone, eds., *Assessing the Canada-U.S. Free Trade Agreement*, 42-48.

10 Hart, *Decision at Midnight*, 57-62.

11 Hart presents polling statistics in several places. See ibid., esp. 71-73.

12 Ibid., 96.

13 Ibid., 114-19, 161-63.

14 Ibid., 142-52.

15 Duncan Cameron, "Introduction," in Cameron, ed., *The Free Trade Deal* (Toronto: James Lorimer, 1988), iv-vi; see also Richard G. Lipsey, Daniel Schwanen, and Ronald J. Wonnacott, *The NAFTA: What's In, What's Out, What's Next* (Ottawa: C.D. Howe Institute, Policy Study No. 21, 1994), 19-21.

16 Cameron, "Introduction," iv-vi; also Lipsey, Schwanen, and Wonnacott, *The NAFTA: What's In, What's Out, What's Next*, 19-21.

17 Riel Miller, "Assessing Economic Benefits," in Cameron, ed., *The Free Trade Deal*, 62-65.

18 Duncan Cameron, "Striking a Deal," in Cameron, ed., *The Free Trade Deal*, 19.

19 Cameron, "Introduction," iv-vi; see also Lipsey, Schwanen, and Wonnacott, *The NAFTA: What's In, What's Out, What's Next*, 19-21.

20 Duncan Cameron and Hugh Mackenzie, "Manufacturing," in Cameron, ed., *The Free Trade Deal*, 118.

21 Hart, *Decision at Midnight*, 76–82.

22 Ibid., 128–29, 138–40.

23 Michael Lusztig, *Risking Free Trade* (Pittsburgh: University of Pittsburgh Press, 1996).

24 Hart, *Decision at Midnight*, 122–24.

25 Cameron, "Introduction," iv–vi.

26 Hart, *Decision at Midnight*, 65.

27 Ibid., 124–25.

28 Ibid., 312–14.

29 Ibid., 68–71.

30 Ibid., 313.

31 Cameron, "Introduction," iv–vi.

32 Hart, *Decision at Midnight*, 5.

33 Ibid., 239.

34 For a brief overview of the FTA, see Garos, *Canada-U.S. Free Trade*, 42–47; for a more extensive assessment (and naturally a favourable one), see Hart, *Decision at Midnight*, ch. 17; also Smith and Stone, "Editor's Introduction," 7–13.

35 Paul Wonnacott, "The Automotive Sector in the U.S.-Canada Free Trade Agreement," in Smith and Stone, eds., *Assessing the Canada-U.S. Free Trade Agreement*, 73–77.

36 Debra Steger, "Analysis of the Dispute Settlement Provisions: A Canadian Perspective," in Smith and Stone, eds., *Assessing the Canada-U.S. Free Trade Agreement*, 91–98.

37 Cohen, Paul, and Blecker, *Fundamentals of U.S. Foreign Trade Policy*, 240. For a comparison between the FTA and NAFTA, see Lipsey, Schwanen, and Wonnacott, *The NAFTA: What's In, What's Out, What's Next*, 31–38.

38 For a description of the ways in which NAFTA builds off the FTA and tries to improve on the latter, see Lipsey, Schwanen, and Wonnacott, *The NAFTA: What's In, What's Out, What's Next*, 26–27.

39 For an overview of some of the literature on the subject, see Kenneth Woodside, "The Canada-U.S. FTA," *Canadian Journal of Political Science* 22, 1 (March 1989), 155–70.

40 Lipsey, Schwanen, and Wonnacott, *The NAFTA: What's In, What's Out, What's Next*, 149–53.

Twenty

GERMANY'S ROLE IN
EUROPEAN MONETARY UNION

With the potential for economic and financial disruptions associated with floating exchange rates, some countries have sought to re-create stability through regional arrangements. This has been most apparent in Western Europe where the members of the European Common Market have strong incentives to ensure that exchange rate movements do not undercut their efforts to construct a free trade zone. Detailed plans for European monetary unification as part of a broader political economic co-operation were first made in 1969, with the Werner Report. When the Bretton Woods system of fixed exchange rates collapsed within a couple of years, the Werner Report's conclusions were no longer applicable. The six original members of the European Common Market decided to maintain some sort of stable exchange rates after 1972. They agreed to maintain their currencies within a band of plus or minus 2.25 per cent. This system was referred to as the "Snake."[1] As other states joined the European Community in 1973 (Denmark, Britain, and Ireland), they, too, joined the Snake. Yet they found it difficult to maintain their commitments, given their very different economic circumstances.[2]

By 1976, the Snake consisted only of Germany and those countries able to match Germany's tight monetary policies: the Netherlands, Belgium, Luxembourg, and Denmark. Yet talks with the other European Community states about closer monetary links were continued. The European Monetary System (EMS) was constructed out of the Snake. In March 1979 the EMS was enacted with its exchange rate mechanism (ERM), though Britain did not join at this time. Once again states pledged to maintain their currencies in a ± 2.25 per cent band, but this time the currencies were anchored to a basket composed of the participating currencies. (In other words, each currency had to fix its value versus a single "basket" of currencies rather than against each other individually; yet each currency involved accounted for part of the basket itself.) The Italian lira was given special treatment—a 6 per cent band.[3] The EMS was to avoid some of the problems of earlier fixed exchange rate systems by having more frequent realignments of currency values. There were also special arrangements made to assist countries that needed help in maintaining their commitments in the face of balance-of-payments shocks.

The Performance of the European Monetary System

In the first few years of the EMS (1979-83) there were seven currency realignments. In the next few years (1983-87) the number of realignments fell to four; then in the years 1987-92 there were no major realignments at all. The arrangement became more rigid than intended. Between 1979 and 1983, the Deutschmark (DM) was revalued while the French franc and the lira were devalued. The higher rates of inflation in France and Italy continually drove down the value of the latter two currencies. The result of the realignments in those first four years of the EMS was downward shifts of 27 per cent and 25 per cent, respectively, for those two currencies.[4]

Despite some of these movements, or perhaps because of them, the EMS seemed to be a set of rules that all the participants could live with. In general, the European countries were pleased with the performance of the EMS in the 1980s. The system seemed to offer the stability of exchange rates they wanted, without locking countries in permanently. It allowed countries with traditionally disparate domestic monetary practices to create some sort of exchange rate stability. Adjustments were made when necessary, but in normal times exchange rates were firm.[5]

The next step was to create a single currency that represented in practice the basket to which each of the individual currencies was fixed. The creation of the (ECU) European currency unit was supposed to help make the impact of monetary factors become more equal across the EMS participants. Because the ECU was never issued as an actual currency, it has not had its intended impact.[6] Moreover, as a basket currency, it is comprised of parts of each of the member's currencies; asymmetries within the system persist due to this connection. Since the single largest component of the ECU is the DM, many observers have concluded that the EMS is little more than a Deutschmark-zone.[7] Wherever the DM moves, the basket must follow—it is practically impossible for the Deutschmark ever to be out of alignment with the ECU. In other words, Germany's central bank, the Bundesbank, could set an independent policy while the other central banks could not. They had to follow the basket's trends, and hence the Bundesbank's lead. At the same time, the realignments of exchange rates and the existence of capital controls allowed countries such as France, Italy, and later Spain some room for independent policy manoeuvres.[8]

The EMS seemed to satisfy the needs of the European Community members for exchange rate stability yet allow them to exercise freedom in their own macroeconomic policy. Why, then, would these countries give up that room for manoeuvre? Why would Germany, in particular, push to modify this regional regime?

Deciding on the Next Step: Monetary Union

In 1989, the Delors Committee recommended making the exchange rate rules the basis for even tighter monetary co-ordination—monetary union would be the long-term goal.[9] The report recommended that the European Union, as the European Community would now be called, should have a single currency. Unification of currencies should be the next step forward; it would be an improvement on stable exchange rates, for all the risk in currency instability would be eliminated and transaction costs associated with economic activity among the member states would be reduced. The move should be made in three phases, according to the committee.

First, there should be a period in which the last national capital controls were removed. This would allow for the complete integration of financial markets. Member countries would all join the EMS and hold to the ERM at this stage. Second, the members would co-ordinate their macroeconomic policies. Monetary policies would be synchronized by having each country's central bank become a member of the European System of Central Banks. Third, an EC-wide central bank (the European Central Bank, or ECB) would be created, a new common currency introduced, and co-ordinated fiscal policies followed.[10] As with many other phased integration plans developed in the EC, the easiest steps come first and then each progressive stage becomes more and more difficult.

Since the EMS appeared to be working smoothly, these recommendations were accepted and soon acted on. In December 1991, the members of the EC signed the Maastricht Treaty,[11] which spelled out the obligations of the members in the various steps to monetary union, as well as establishing a timetable for the entire project.

The Goals of Monetary Union

There are two strands of economic arguments in support of monetary unification. Most are usually extensions of those made concerning the benefits of a monetary regime based on liberal principles, such as stable exchange rates and open capital flows. The first strand of economic arguments emphasizes how monetary unification could eliminate the costs of currency conversion. To illustrate the point about the costs of currency conversion, the typical example looks at a tourist moving from each of the member countries and converting his/her currency each time he/she crosses a border. Since commissions must be paid with each conversion, the cost of converting currency can add up. Moreover, there is also the risk that the values of the currencies will move, since the exchange rates are not fixed.

Some analysts, such as Barry Eichengreen and Jeffry Frieden, argue that the overall benefits of unification for eliminating the costs of currency conversion would most likely be small. Though the example of a tourist paying fees to convert funds as he/she moves from one country to the next may resonate with many individuals' experiences, it is not typical of international economic transactions. Large firms and banks have developed several techniques to accommodate the instabilities of floating or flexible exchange rates. Because the currency markets work fairly efficiently, and with great speed, it is easy for large businesses and other economic actors to hedge their interests; that is, they can cover their assets so that exchange rate changes do little damage to them.[12]

The second strand of economic arguments takes German leadership of the new monetary union as a given. These arguments emphasize the benefits other states would receive by joining a monetary system where Germany served as the anchor. Since it would be very difficult to opt out of monetary union once it went into effect, individual countries would in effect be forced to follow the group's monetary and macroeconomic policies. Germany is in fact working hard to ensure that the ECB will be independent of political pressure, and historically this has been a good indicator of a central bank's stand against inflation. Many also assume the ECB will institutionally be a reconstruction of the Bundesbank. This assumes that Germany would indeed be the anchor, or that the system as set up would emulate German practices. As Eichengreen and Frieden point out, the reasons for making such assumptions are not entirely clear.[13]

There are, of course, important political goals behind monetary unification. Many Europeans believe that economic integration requires steady progress. If forward movement is halted, the entire process is put in jeopardy. Many also believe that the EMS has been too costly to maintain precisely because it is a compromise between fixed and floating exchange rates—and rather than go to a system of floating exchange rates, they would push the whole arrangement to the ultimate fixed exchange rate system: union. Paramount among the political concerns driving European integration has been the desire of the member states to control German ambitions and lessen friction between the major European powers. Monetary union can be seen as an important element in the process of economically binding the European states together to achieve these broader aims.

Germany's Bargaining Position, and the Process of EMU

Perhaps the single most problematic point in the negotiations concerning the EMU (European Monetary Union) revolves around the process to be employed. Some states see the act of union as a way to force monetary policy convergence; others see policy convergence as a necessary ingredient in the process leading up to monetary union. The two views distribute the costs of policy convergence differently and also create different projections as to what the policies of the ECB would be like. Germany has very hard and fast positions on these issues, which it wanted included in the Maastricht Treaty.

Germany wanted to force policy convergence before union. In other words, Germany wanted states to prove their ability and willingness to adhere to the union's stated goals before getting in.[14] Since the policy goals after monetary union are largely those that Germany has long held—and successfully attained for some time—Germany does not want to jeopardize its own policy success by participating in monetary union. German policy-makers hold that countries must make the commitment to the policy goals of low inflation and tight monetary supplies first; if they cannot or will not make such commitments on their own, the new institutional arrangements will not be able to force them to do so. Costly efforts would have to be made to keep them within the monetary union, but in the end these would probably fail.

A second sticking point centred on questions about how new members would be admitted to the monetary union. There were two formulas proposed. One would require the existing members to vote unanimously in favour of admission; the other required only that a qualified majority of the existing members vote in favour. Germany supported unanimity voting on membership because it wanted to ensure that it held a veto over new entrants to the monetary union.

A third point of debate concerned the methods for disciplining members of the union. Germany wanted automatic fines to be built into the system. That is, any countries violating the system's performance criteria would automatically be penalized. This would force countries whose policies were disrupting the union's performance to bear additional costs so long as they continued to be a source of disturbance. Moreover, such punishments would serve as a deterrent to poor behaviour on the part of other members.

The poorer states in the EC asked for compensation as part of their fee for their entrance. As Lisa Martin has pointed out, their demands for compensation were made very explicitly.[15] As one of the richest members, and the one with the most to lose if monetary union went in a different direction than it intended, Germany would be expected to pay for these compensations. This followed in the longer tradition of bargaining in European monetary affairs, for Germany has often made side-payments to persuade other states to participate in monetary arrangements.

Germany's preferences make it clear that foremost among its aims were to balance out the achievement of monetary unification with the desire to keep the maintenance costs down. Germany wishes to exercise some sort of leadership in this issue-area in Europe, yet keep the price of leadership to a minimum. Also high among Germany's priorities were monetary relations with non-European states. Germany undoubtedly wanted to see the impacts of third party relations softened. There were always problems with the DM's relationship to the dollar, as there had been under the Bretton Woods monetary regime.[16] Whenever confidence in the dollar was shaken, people would transfer out of their dollar holdings and into Deutschemarks. As soon as confidence in the dollar was restored, DM holdings might be lowered. These were the risks of having a strong currency that foreigners would wish to possess. Such actions would drive the Deutschemark up or down in value, against the wishes of the monetary authorities. By having the rest of Europe behind the DM, Germany hoped that the increases in the money supply caused by international flows would be spread out among the other members of the union as well.[17]

Systemic Changes: The Impact of the Long Decline of the Dollar

Since the fall of Bretton Woods, experts have predicted the downfall of the dollar out of the "top" or "key" currency role. Yet the dollar continues to hold on. For the most part, the dollar remains the preferred currency for international transactions. As asset-holders move out of the dollar, they switch to other currencies. This has had a different impact on the various European countries because some currencies are more attractive than others. Due to the relative independence of the Bundesbank and that institution's historically embedded commitment to resist inflation, the DM is a good long-term bet to retain its value.[18] The DM is a good substitute for the dollar in many ways.[19] Moreover, Germany is the most open to capital flows and has the largest domestic financial base (though London has an important role as an international financial centre).[20]

German thinking has therefore been keen to spread the pressures created by the dollar's decline. Instead of letting the dollar's decline lead to increased usage of the DM internationally, the Germans (and the Bundesbank in particular) wanted to have people switch dollars for Deutschmarks and other currencies. This meant finding a way to make these other currencies just as attractive as the DM. In return, the other European countries are hoping to have Germany's credibility transferred to them, but without all the policy repercussions that go with earning that credibility. Costs will have to go up for these other members, however, if that credibility is to be maintained.[21]

The chief obstacle in getting others to agree to go along with the Germans in any zone of monetary stability was that stabilization takes resources. If the others were to use Deutschmarks in their stabilization efforts, the Germans would fail to achieve their goal as well. Handing over loans of Deutschmarks for intervention purposes would simply put more DMs in circulation anyway. So the main challenge for the Germans has been to devise a way to create a zone of monetary stability in Europe, diffuse pressures created by the decline of the dollar, but still maintain independence in domestic monetary affairs (i.e., don't let foreign holdings of DMs increase substantially).[22]

The Domestic Pressures for and against EMU

By most accounts, the strongest supporters of the EMU are large corporations. These large firms and large financial institutions have holdings among the many different members of the EC and do business across borders. They stand to gain from the elimination of costs associated with converting currencies with each cross-border transaction.[23] At the same time, these same firms are in the best position to deal with the costs of converting currencies. In fact, the banks should be the ones making profits from handling currency conversion!

Of course, banks have another interest in seeing monetary union: the anti-inflationary results expected. Bankers always oppose inflation, because inflation makes money (the banks' primary asset and source of income) worth less and less over time. Thus financial firms might very well be pushing for monetary union, but perhaps as a second-best outcome.

The domestic opposition to monetary union comes largely from those economic actors who do their business almost entirely within their national borders. These actors do not stand to gain much from monetary union; when one throws in other factors, such as the anti-inflationary results expected from monetary union, we can easily find groups who would be strongly opposed to the EMU. Actors who earn their incomes largely from domestic business, and who also benefit from inflationary policies, see little to gain and a lot to lose. Moreover, the real appreciation of their national currencies is likely to invite imports, meaning greater competition for their products within their own market. The best examples of such actors would be workers in sectors such as steel or auto manufacturing in countries such as France or Italy (in the early 1980s).[24]

There are also two other sorts of opposition to monetary union, which in fact highlight that the Maastricht agreement covers much more than monetary relations.[25] Some oppose any sort of political union, especially since they see it as a loss of national sovereignty. Nowhere, perhaps, is this sentiment stronger than in Britain. This undoubtedly also played a role in the Danish public's initial rejection of the Maastricht Treaty. The same feeling shows up in Germany, where the DM has become a symbol of Germany's success in the postwar period. Giving up the DM for a new currency would require the sacrifice of one of Germany's most potent national symbols.

There are also those who oppose the transfer of so much decision-making power to European-wide institutions that do not seem to have to answer to any particular electorate. Journalists refer to this situation as the "democratic deficit." Those who dislike the concentration of decision-making in EU institutions are hardly likely to favour the creation of a new, independent supranational central bank.

As for the policies this European central bank is likely to pursue, there is greater support within Germany. Germans have long expressed a consensus around support for domestic price stability. Pursuit of this goal has assured that the DM stayed strong—the policy translates into a higher value for the DM. At the same time, Germany relies extensively on trade, which means the country should be interested in seeing a lower value of the DM so as to enhance the competitiveness of its exports. This goal has clearly been subordinated to the domestic goal of price stability, however.[26] (Perhaps this is because many of Germany's exports are sold on the basis of quality, not price; Germany has long been a major exporter of machinery and other products where reliability is more important than price.) Since Germany is likely to dominate the ECB, Germans should be satisfied with the ECB's policies.

These points having been made, Bundesbank officials do not seem to have been altogether pleased with the results of the Maastricht negotiations.[27] The German government got the treaty it was after, but that did not mean the Bundesbank was completely happy. The central bank stands independent from the government; the federal government carried the day in this dispute, since it is responsible for international negotiations, yet it must rely on the Bundesbank to execute policy decisions.[28] Hence we need to examine bureaucratic politics.

Bureaucratic Politics: Bundesbank Independence

In a comparison of the array of institutions in charge of monetary policy in the U.S., Germany, and Japan, C. Randall Henning concluded that Germany has the most independent central bank.[29] This is consistent with most assessments of central banks. At the same time, Henning would argue that policy outcomes can best be understood by analysing both the structure of domestic institutions and their connections to groups within the private sector.[30]

Technically, the Bundesbank's autonomy derives from its statutory basis (the Bundesbank Act of 1957). This legislation not only establishes the Bundesbank's independence from direct political authority, it also establishes the institution's policy goal: stability. However, as Henning points out, its real power stems from the broad political consensus behind its independence (and behind the goal of stability) in Germany. This broad political support for independence prevents the federal government from "packing" the Bundesbank's upper ranks with appointees sharing a particular slant.[31]

The Bundesbank's independence sets the stage for bureaucratic politics, for its bureaucratic turf overlaps that of other agencies. Frictions are most likely between the two chief institutions in Germany in charge of monetary policy simply because they have different goals and experience different political pressures. The Bundesbank is in charge of domestic policy and relies primarily on interest rates as the tool for executing policy. The Foreign Ministry, on the other hand, is in charge of exchange rate policy. The Foreign Ministry negotiates the commitments, for instance, and also handles decisions about foreign exchange intervention, though the execution of policy remains in the Bundesbank's jurisdiction.

On the EMU, the Bundesbank was always distrustful of what the Foreign Ministry was doing. The Bundesbank's power comes from its independence; it would essentially be giving up its position in the EMU, so one would expect the institutional imperatives to be to resist the changes. As Henning remarks, the Bundesbank's views on the EMU were "publicly cool and privately hostile."[32] But as discussions on the EMU proceeded, the Bundesbank position evolved; since it could hardly veto such a step, it decided to go along with the process but used its participation to push for stricter conditions on membership. The Bundesbank stressed the need for strict conditions to be met before a country could participate. This was perhaps meant to dissuade others from joining the project; if that was the plan, it didn't work, and the Bundesbank officials may well have been surprised by other European countries gladly signing on to the strict conditions.[33] The Bundesbank then had to fight to have the criteria for membership established as a condition to be met *before* membership.[34] Thus the Bundesbank's positioning, which was influenced by domestic bureaucratic conflicts, had a dramatic impact on the way the entire negotiations unfolded. Bureaucratic politics generated Germany's policy stance, which in turn shaped the results of the international agreement.

Consequences: What Went Wrong?

A variety of changes in the international system threw these plans askew. Most importantly, the end of the Cold War gave Germany the opportunity to push for national unification. By bringing together East and West Germany, the West German government took an extremely popular and long dreamed of step—but also a step that proved to be quite costly. The economic adjustments and investments necessary to modify the East totalled into a hefty bill. As a result, Germany's central government budget deficit went from 0.5 per cent of GDP in 1989 to 5 per cent in 1991.[35]

Some countries were having trouble meeting the criteria for convergence in the first place, even without any extraordinary circumstances. Britain and Italy were not meeting the performance criteria. Then came the real shocker: Danish voters, asked in a referendum to support Maastricht, rejected the treaty in June 1992. The EMS was thrown into turmoil.[36] Speculators did not believe that the countries could maintain their exchange rate commitments and thus began heavy trading on currency markets.

The Germans were forced to carry out extensive and heavy interventions in 1992. In September alone, the Bundesbank spent 92.7 billion DMs buying up the British pound and the Italian lira. The single largest intervention was on 16 September, when 36 billion DMs were spent on propping up those two currencies before they fell out of the ERM. While the purchases of currency were sterilized (i.e., kept separate from the domestic money supply), a tight monetary policy had to be initiated, which brought on an economic recession. This in turn led to negotiations between various levels of government and the financial sector; a widespread solidarity pact on public-sector borrowing was eventually reached.[37]

In some ways, these crises within the ERM represent a victory for the Bundesbank over its opponents within and outside Germany. First, as noted above, realignments in the EMS had been fewer and fewer. The Bundesbank had argued that other states needed to alter their exchange rate commitments to fit more closely with their domestic policies. The Bundesbank was pleased to see realignments used again, though this was a costly way to reach this conclusion. Second, the failure of several countries to stay within the EMS effectively meant that the preferred process for the EMU would move ahead in the way the Germans wished; only those already seriously committed to the target policies remained in. Policy convergence would have to come before union. Third, the explicit timetable laid out in the Maastricht Treaty was placed in serious doubt.[38]

As a result of these speculative attacks and the ensuing crises on the currency markets, the EMS band had to be widened to 15 per cent in August of 1993. This would give the members relief from speculative attacks by making their commitments extremely loose. Critics wondered aloud whether a band so wide was really a band at all.[39] One economist, Paul Krugman, notes the irony of current discussions about the politics of monetary policy co-ordination. In his view, they have come full circle. In the early 1970s, fixed exchange rates were dropped because countries needed their independence. Then it proved that the independence gained was much less than expected. Now countries seem to realize a need to co-ordinate their monetary policies, and thus monetary union is proposed as a mechanism for co-ordination.[40]

Despite these problems in the early 1990s, monetary union remains a central goal of the EU. The timetable will have to be adjusted, and the process of implementing the new union-wide currency remains unclear, but the determination and the will to pursue this goal are still strong. The design of the new currency, the Euro, has been unveiled. Despite the apparent progress, the obstacles to the EMU are significant. We will all have to wait to see if Europe's plans for monetary union will come to full fruition.

Suggested Readings

David Cobham, "Strategies for Monetary Integration Revisited," *Journal of Common Market Studies* 27, 3 (March 1989), 203-18.

Barry Eichengreen and Jeffry Frieden, eds., *The Political Economy of European Monetary Unification.* Boulder, Colo.: Westview Press, 1994.

Michele Fratianni, Jürgen von Hagen, and Christopher Waller, "The Maastricht Way to EMU," *Princeton Essays in International Finance* No. 187 (June 1992).

Daniel Gros, "Paradigms for the Monetary Union of Europe," *Journal of Common Market Studies* 27, 3 (March 1989), 219-30.

Patrick Minford, "The Path to Monetary Union in Europe," *The World Economy* 16, 1 (January 1993), 17-28.

Notes

1   John B. Goodman, *Monetary Sovereignty* (Ithaca, NY: Cornell University Press, 1992), 186-87.

2   Barry Eichengreen and Jeffry Frieden, "The Political Economy of European Monetary Unification: An Analytical Introduction," in Eichengreen and Frieden, eds., *The Political Economy of European Monetary Unification* (Boulder, Colo.: Westview Press, 1994), 2-3.

3   Goodman, *Monetary Sovereignty*, 191-93.

4   Eichengreen and Frieden, "The Political Economy of European Monetary Unification," 2-3; Jeffry Frieden, "Making Commitments: France and Italy in the EMS, 1979-1985," in Eichengreen and Frieden, eds., *The Political Economy of European Monetary Unification*, 33.

5   Jose Vinals, "The EMS, Spain and Macroeconomic Policy," in Paul de Grauwe and Lucas Papademos, eds., *The EMS in the 1990s* (New York: Longman, 1990), 202; Niels Thygesen, "Institutional Developments in the Evolution from EMS Towards EMU," in de Grauwe and Papademos, eds., *The EMS in the 1990s*, 19.

6   Rainer Stefano Masera, "An Increasing Role for the ECU: A Character in Search of a Script," *Princeton Essays in International Finance* No. 167 (June 1987).

7   Patrick Honohan and Paul McNelis, "Is the EMS a DM Zone?—Evidence from the Realignments?" *The Economic and Social Review* 20, 2 (January 1989), 97-110.

8   Paul de Grauwe and Lucas Papademos, "Introduction," in de Grauwe and Papademos, eds., *The EMS in the 1990s*, xiii.

9   Niels Thygesen, "The Delors Report and European Economic and Monetary Union," *International Affairs* 65, 4 (Autumn 1989), 637-52.

10 Eichengreen and Frieden, "The Political Economy of European Monetary Unification," 4.

11 Ibid.

12 Ibid., 4-8.

13 Ibid., 5-8. Also see Geoffrey Garrett, "The Politics of Maastricht," in Eichengreen and Frieden, eds., *The Political Economy of European Monetary Unification*, esp. 47-50.

14 This and the next sections build off Garrett, "The Politics of Maastricht," esp. 55.

15 Lisa Martin, "International and Domestic Institutions in the EMU Process," in Eichengreen and Frieden, eds., *The Political Economy of European Monetary Unification*, 90.

16 Elke Thiel, "Die D-Mark zwischen dem Dollar und dem EWS," *Aussenpolitik* 33, 1 (1982), 37-46.

17 Garrett, "The Politics of Maastricht," 54.

18 For more on the Bundesbank's independence and the connection between this and the DM's performance, see Ellen Kennedy, *The Bundesbank: Germany's Central Bank in the International Monetary System* (London: Pinter, 1991); Goodman, *Monetary Sovereignty*, ch. 3.

19 See C. Randall Henning, *Currencies and Politics in the United States, Germany and Japan* (Washington: Institute for International Economics, 1994), 317, Table 7.2, for international use of DM. Also see George Tavlas, "On the International Use of Currencies: The Case of the Deutsche Mark," *Princeton Essays in International Finance* No. 181 (1991).

20 Niels Thygesen, "Institutional developments in the evolution from EMS towards EMU," 17.

21 Paul Krugman, "Policy problems of a monetary union," in de Grauwe and Papademos, eds., *The EMS in the 1990s*, 57.

22 Henning, *Currencies and Politics in the United States, Germany and Japan*, 185-86.

23 Eichengreen and Frieden, "The Political Economy of European Monetary Unification," 13.

24 Ibid.

25 The following paragraphs draw on Wolfgang Rieke, "Alternative views on the EMS in the 1990s," in de Grauwe and Papademos, eds., *The EMS in the 1990s*, 31.

26 Henning, *Currencies and Politics in the United States, Germany and Japan*, 178.

27 Garrett, "The Politics of Maastricht," 64.

28 Henning, *Currencies and Politics in the United States, Germany and Japan*, 178.

29 Ibid., 84-85.

30 Ibid., 177.

31 This is similar to the sort of obstacles formed by public opinion in the U.S. that restrained Roosevelt from changing the number of justices on the Supreme Court. For the points on the Bundesbank's independence, see ibid., 90-93.

32 Ibid., 230.

33 Ibid., 230-31.

34 Ibid., 231-32.

35 Garrett, "The Politics of Maastricht," 58.

36 Eichengreen and Frieden, "The Political Economy of European Monetary Unification," 4.

37 Henning, *Currencies and Politics in the United States, Germany and Japan*, 241.

38 Ibid., 243-44.

39 Eichengreen and Frieden, "The Political Economy of European Monetary Unification," 5.

40 Krugman, "Policy problems of a monetary union," 56.

Twenty-One

JAPAN, INTERNATIONAL
MONETARY RESPONSIBILITIES,
AND POLICY CO-ORDINATION:
THE LOUVRE AND PLAZA ACCORDS

U.S. Monetary Policy in the 1980s

Several prominent specialists in international political economy, including Susan Strange and David Calleo, describe United States monetary policy in the 1980s as the actions of a leader, but a leader behaving irresponsibly.[1] The U.S. moved to resolve its own problems with inflation, but these same policies had serious international repercussions. One we have already covered— the tight monetary policy pursued in the early 1980s—drove up interest rates and sparked the debt crisis. Since these same policies successfully raised the value of the dollar compared to other currencies in a very short amount of time, the financial and trade positions of the U.S. were affected. The U.S. soon was drawing in money from elsewhere (as foreign investors sought high returns), shifting the country into the position of a net international debtor. The American trade balance went into a large deficit, largely due to the dollar's overvaluation.[2]

Responding to Dollar Overliquidity Again

Due to the combination of policies pursued in the early 1980s, the American GNP grew, as did total employment, while inflation and unemployment rates fell. Inflation was to be fought with high interest rates, while spending would be maintained even though taxes would be reduced. But a new problem emerged, as a large and consistent current account deficit appeared and a massive foreign debt arose. Foreign financial centres were also on the rise, most notably in Japan. The positive American economic performance (defeating stagflation) was financed by foreign capital. The combination of tight monetary policy and loose fiscal policy was arrived at more by accident than by plan.[3] In any case, the U.S. now faced a situation conducive to maladjustment—the central bank pushed for a higher exchange rate as it sought to reassert the dollar's international role, while the Treasury had to worry about a growing fiscal deficit.

During the first Reagan administration, official intervention in the exchange markets was avoided for ideological reasons. The Treasury's foreign activities instead focused on pressuring other countries to liberalize their capital markets. This was aimed at letting American service-sector businesses enter foreign markets that had previously been closed; particular attention was paid to Japan. The net effect of agreements (such as the one reached with Japan in May 1984) was to encourage the flow of foreign funds to the United States. The Treasury also began to woo foreign capital more directly that same year by altering tax laws on foreign holders of U.S. government and corporate bonds and by introducing new bond issues of its own aimed at the foreign market.

Several actors became concerned about the rising value of the dollar. Paul Volcker, now chairman of the Fed, was still interested in defeating inflation, so he was unwilling to change domestic policy to reduce the dollar's international value. Instead, Volcker spoke out against the consequences of the administration's lack of a coherent foreign exchange policy.[4] Not only were foreign governments increasingly asking the Treasury to intervene in currency markets, so was the Fed.[5]

Who was in charge of international monetary policy? The Fed always guaranteed the Treasury that it would never intervene in exchange markets without Treasury approval, but at the same time it never recognized the Treasury's right to veto any planned Fed actions. In the early 1970s, the Treasury had blocked Fed interventions on several occasions.[6] The Treasury and the Fed co-ordinated foreign exchange intervention through regular consultation (the Fed chairman and the Secretary of the Treasury have had the regular practice of meeting weekly for breakfast on Thursdays since the late 1930s), institutional bonding (through policies such as constant exchange of personnel), equal participation in operations (each agency contributing around half the funds for intervention and splitting the proceeds), and having all intervention for either agency handled by the New York Federal Reserve Bank. But each bureaucracy was pulling monetary policy in its own direction: the Fed was tightening the domestic money supply while the Treasury was running a loose fiscal policy. Combined with the facts that other currencies were emerging as clear rivals to the dollar, other financial centres were developing to rival New York, and the Treasury had already begun borrowing heavily from abroad, all the elements of maladjustment came together. The Treasury and the Fed shared responsibility in the 1980s, with the peripheral actors such as interest groups, Congress, and other executive branch agencies entering only after monetary issues became politicized by the mid-1980s. The fact that one of these other actors—Congress—posed a common threat helped drive the Fed and Treasury together, so that this example of maladjustment did not have the vitriolic public atmosphere one might expect.[7]

Although some sectors of the economy were clearly hurt by the rising value of the dollar, such as several large manufacturing sectors and parts of agriculture, the sectoral influence argument is again not very persuasive because these groups failed to take political action on monetary policy prior to 1985.[8] It was only after the split between the Fed and the Treasury became apparent that such groups focused attention on monetary policy. At that point, business leaders like Lee Iacocca of Chrysler and Lee Morgan of Caterpillar Tractor began to campaign for a lower dollar, especially as the way to regain a competitive stance against Japanese firms.

Of course, some other actors also benefited from the higher dollar. Yet there is little evidence that such groups had ever actually lobbied to support the dollar's rise in value. The most obvious candidates to engage in such lobbying activities in terms of both interests and access to the Treasury and Federal Reserve would be the large money-centre banks, which had the most to gain internationally. These actors' interests in the domestic economy, however, cut across their international interests; their portfolios were sufficiently mixed that they had no clear interest in supporting specific movements of the exchange rate. The large money-centre banks have also learned how to turn exchange rate fluctuations into profits, so foreign exchange trading is increasingly important as a source of revenue. The rise and fall of the dollar in the 1980s did not elicit a strong reaction from the banking community until 1987, when the subsequent fall in the dollar's value made bankers concerned about a possible return of inflation.[9]

Despite these weak and varied signals from different economic sectors, a broad consensus among both political parties arose in Congress that blamed the high dollar for the burgeoning trade imbalance.[10] In July 1985, Democrats in Congress, led by Lloyd Bentsen, Dan Rostenkowski, and Richard Gephardt, introduced a bill to impose a 25 per cent duty on imports from countries running large trade surpluses with the U.S. At the same time, other Democrats such as Bill Bradley, Daniel Patrick Moynihan, and M.S. Baucus submitted bills in various banking committees to legislate specific foreign exchange market interventions when the U.S. was running large current account deficits. Similar pieces of legislation would later be included as provisions of the 1988 Trade Act.[11] When Senator Robert Byrd threatened to order the Fed to ease its policies via legislation in a confrontation with Volcker on 18 December 1982, he reminded Volcker who was ultimately responsible by asking, "To whom are you accountable?" Volcker responded by noting that "the Congress created us and the Congress can uncreate us," although it would be hard to imagine that there would be popular approval for a radical change in the Fed's mandate.[12] Still, the threat of congressional action was made clear.

Within the executive branch, some decision-makers whose offices were under pressure also fought to get a change in policy. Secretary of Commerce Malcolm Baldrige, Special Trade Representative William Brock, and Secretary of Agriculture John Block all argued in cabinet meetings in 1984 that the dollar's international value was too high. Secretary of State George Shultz identified the high value of the dollar as the main source of the trade imbalance (and thus international friction) with Japan. But none of these actors had any way to control monetary policy.[13]

In *Secrets of the Temple*, William Grieder titles his chapter summarizing the Fed's monetary policies of the late 1970s and early 1980s "The Triumph of Money," because the Fed achieved its objective of restoring confidence in the dollar. Inflation was reduced significantly, and the public's expectations of future inflation were altered. The Fed pursued its objective of strengthening the dollar regardless of the short-run economic repercussions on the dollar's international value, the trade balance, growth, or employment.[14]

Co-ordination to Bring the Dollar Down

The threat of congressional activity to mandate Treasury policy convinced the Treasury to respond to some of the problems related to the rising value of the dollar.[15] Once the Treasury decided to take action on the exchange rate, it had to abandon its earlier position of unilateral inaction in terms of the exchange markets and seek to establish a policy based on multilateralism.[16] The multilateral approach was necessary in order to deal with the trade imbalance directly while convincing other countries it could pre-empt the threat of protectionism.[17] In the second Reagan administration, the Secretary of the Treasury, James A. Baker, led the efforts to co-ordinate the decline in the dollar's value.[18] During the 1985-86 negotiations the same split could be seen in almost all the major economic powers' negotiating teams. Finance ministers promoted currency co-ordination, while central bankers resisted. As a group, the central bankers placed institutional independence ahead of other goals, including price stability and economic growth, during these discussions.[19]

For the Treasury and the Fed, the goals of policy were largely the same— ease monetary policy and get the value of the dollar down, but without setting the dollar's market value into a downward spiral. At first glance bureaucratic politics do not seem to be a major factor because each side agreed on the goals; but there is still debate about the degree of co-ordination of their activities. The result was that the Treasury acted to push the dollar down, while occasionally Volcker used the Fed's policies to put the brakes on.[20] At the same time, co-ordination with the IMF's most powerful members, the G-5, tended to reassert the Treasury's control over international monetary policy.[21] While the Fed and Treasury were interested in dealing with their own policy objectives, they seemed able to co-ordinate their actions in a satisfactory manner. As long as the two worked together, the domestic politicization of monetary policy subsided.[22]

This co-ordination of Fed and Treasury policies also required additional international co-ordination to be effective. In the Plaza Accord of September 1985, Baker found the other G-5 countries willing to agree to help bring the dollar down in order to thwart the growth of protectionism in the United States. Fears of inflation had also subsided by then.[23] In the Baker-Miyazawa Accord of late 1986, the Japanese agreed to lower their discount rate significantly, to proceed with tax reform, and to submit a supplemental budget to the Diet in order to increase government spending. The U.S., in return, agreed to take actions to stabilize the exchange rate between the dollar and the yen. In fact, by January 1987, the dollar was falling in value so rapidly that the Fed began to threaten to use interest rates to stabilize its value once again.[24]

The Plaza Accord: Japan's Rising Role in Monetary Affairs

As mentioned above, in September 1985 a secret meeting was held at the Plaza Hotel in New York. The U.S. agreed to take action, but only in co-ordination with Japan, Britain, West Germany, and France. While co-ordination in intervention in the exchange markets was agreed upon, countries pledged to make further commitments to ensure that monetary co-operation would work. The U.S. was asked to lower its budget deficit by reducing spending, while the other powers would increase their spending (thereby accepting a low rate of inflation). This was aimed at bringing the exchange rates of the dollar, yen, and Deutschmark back into more reasonable patterns. The Plaza Accord ushered in a period of co-ordination among the major powers, at least in monetary affairs. Finance ministers began to meet regularly, co-ordinating their intervention in exchange markets but also trying to co-ordinate other aspects of economic policy.

What we are most interested in for this chapter is how the Plaza Accord denotes Japan's entry into a position of greater responsibility in managing the international monetary system. Japan clearly had reasons to take on a greater responsibility, due to its rise into the position of the foremost international financial creditor. The U.S. had been borrowing abroad, and in 1985 the U.S. became a net debtor for the first time since World War I.

While the U.S. still had very much invested abroad, its borrowings now outweighed its lending. Japan, meanwhile, had used its large export earnings to build up its financial position (rising from $7 billion in external credits in 1976 to $241 billion in 1987). As Joan Spero points out, "Any efforts to stabilize the system and to co-ordinate economic policies would be meaningless without Japan."[25]

In May 1986, the major powers made an effort to institutionalize the spirit of the Plaza agreement via the G-7 economic summit in Tokyo. In particular, the leaders of the G-7 countries stressed the need to co-ordinate their *domestic* economic policies to achieve their individual goals and stabilize the international monetary and trading systems.[26] They all wanted the same thing: steady growth with low inflation. The problem was how to attain this goal.

In accordance with these negotiations, the U.S. did take some steps to reduce its budget, while West Germany and Japan lowered their interest rates. The idea was to reverse the earlier trends set in motion. Now it was necessary to weaken the yen and Deutschmark while strengthening the dollar in order to stop the dollar's descent in value versus rival currencies. But because each country was also worried about its trade balances, each wound up not going as far as it could—and then accused the others of doing too little. This necessitated another meeting to reaffirm the major powers' commitment to co-ordinated action.

The Louvre Accord

In the Louvre Accord of February 1987, the G-5 (plus Canada) secretly agreed to stabilize the exchange values of the dollar, yen, and DM (Italy also co-operated with the policies decided on). By and large, these countries did not live up to their commitments under the Louvre negotiations.[27] The U.S. could not reach a domestic consensus on how much to reduce the budget deficit; since it took both Congress and the President to agree on the budget, the U.S. simply never got the budget reductions the Reagan administration had committed to in the Louvre Accord. The other countries were reluctant to introduce the economic stimulations they had committed to as their part of the Accord. The one exception was Japan; Japan introduced a more expansionary fiscal policy in an effort to raise domestic demand (and therefore reduce Japan's overall trade deficit with the U.S., among others).[28]

In lieu of macroeconomic co-ordination, foreign central banks were forced to intervene in currency markets. They aimed to keep their currencies from rising in value too fast, as the dollar continued to fall in value. Soon the dollar not only stabilized on exchange markets but began to appreciate. This result brought about the need to renegotiate the dollar-yen exchange rate. Also, the flow of private capital into the U.S. fell back to lower levels.[29]

On the American side, domestic concerns continued to shape attitudes about foreign monetary policy and the need to co-ordinate policies with other financial powers, in particular. The stock market collapse in late 1987 sparked renewed interest in monetary policy—many were critical of the Fed's policies. Scrutiny over monetary policy remained high in 1988. That year the Fed began to tighten monetary policy to restrain domestic demand in order to ensure that improvements in trade did not ignite domestic inflation.[30] The Federal Reserve was more concerned with domestic policy considerations than with the exchange rate, particularly given the upcoming elections and the apparent weakness of the U.S. economy. Monetary policy was aimed at stimulating the economy, while pressure was placed on other countries to change their policies and manage the dollar's international value for the Fed.[31]

Because the Treasury's actions had lessened the problems with exchange rates, domestic political activity aimed at monetary policy was reduced. Policy had deflated protectionist pressures, even as the legal aspects of earlier actions were coming into effect. The 1988 Trade Act gave Congress the power to review the Treasury's exchange rate policy every six months.[32] Under the present arrangements, senior Fed officials come before congressional committees (or subcommittees) around forty times per year, with the chairman himself called on to testify approximately twenty times a year.[33]

While the protectionist demands within the U.S. subsided and the value of the dollar was eventually stabilized at a level American policy-makers were satisfied with, we need to turn our attention to the other side in the negotiations. Most importantly, we wish to examine how Japan's policies were selected. Why did Japan choose to co-operate so fully in these accords?

Systemic Explanations: Japan as Rival Leader?

Traditionally in the postwar period, Japanese international monetary policy had been to remain fairly passive, which meant that the undervalued yen remained undervalued. This helped make Japanese exports competitive. The Plaza Accord marked a change in Japanese policy. Japan would become more active, and would also begin to support the appreciation of the yen relative to other currencies.[34]

In the early 1980s, Japan had done nothing to alter its previous policies in monetary affairs. Between 1980 and 1985, Japanese interventions never included any significant purchases of the dollar. The U.S. was running its policy of "benign neglect" and Japan was also pursuing a form of unilateralism. The yen remained weak compared to the U.S. dollar. But by 1983, the governor of the Bank of Japan, Haruo Maekawa, was calling for some sort of "international concerted action." He added that the floating exchange rate regime "hasn't come up to our expectations." The main thrust of his position was that the yen needed to increase in value.[35]

The U.S. was hardly ready to encourage the rise of the yen to the same international status as the dollar. The distribution of power within financial relations had shifted, but the dollar remained the most popular currency to use in international transactions. The defeat of inflation had helped to maintain the attractiveness of the dollar. Now the U.S. merely wanted to counteract some of the side-effects associated with the higher dollar—the U.S. probably would have resisted attempts to see the yen replace the dollar internationally; then again, that was not something that would have been popular within Japan. In short, there were those within Japan who felt that the country's changing financial status required new policies. These individuals were few in number, however. Most Japanese were interested in continuing to support those international economic policies that had built up the country's financial reserves—and that meant expanding exports. Exports would be helped by a lower-valued yen, not a higher-valued yen. Such disagreements naturally make us turn to the domestic level.

The Domestic Sources of International Monetary Co-operation

The traditional undervaluation of the yen and the rising value of the U.S. dollar in the early 1980s combined to create the demands for policy actions from the sphere of domestic politics. The currency trends accentuated the trade imbalance between the U.S. and Japan. The higher interest rates in the U.S. pushed the value of the dollar up but also brought on a serious recession. Japan was able to expand exports, and while Japan's growth rate slowed down from previous years, it was the only G-7 country not to drop into a recession.[36]

As noted earlier, protectionist threats were on the rise in the U.S. American businesses losing ground to Japanese imports, including such important manufacturing sectors as machinery and automobiles, called for some sort of action. Sector-specific trade protection was one possibility raised, as these firms lobbied Congress. Changes in monetary policy were another. To head off demands for tariff barriers, the Reagan administration sought to use monetary co-operation to resolve the trade imbalance with Japan.

The first measure of co-ordination between the U.S. and Japan, the Yen-Dollar Agreement struck between Secretary of the Treasury Donald Regan and Finance Minister Noboru Takeshita, occurred in April 1984. The central effort was to liberalize Japan's domestic financial markets. This was meant as a counter to any pressures for protectionism beginning in the U.S.—American service sector businesses would presumably have new opportunities in Japan, which the American government could rely on as allies to counter any demands for protectionist policies against Japan. The end result of the international agreement, however, was not to change the relative values of the two currencies. Instead, as Japan continued to run a loose monetary policy, even more capital flowed from Japan to the U.S.[37]

The protectionist threat in the U.S. hit a new high the following year. Japanese businesses became more concerned in 1985, as American businessmen began testifying before Congress about the need to take legislative action in trade policy. As Japanese businesses started to worry, so did Japanese bureaucrats and policy-makers. Domestic politics in one country would soon influence domestic politics in the other. At the same time, members of the Reagan administration also decided that changes needed to be made. Secret negotiations were carried out in the summer of 1985 by Finance Minister Takeshita's team and the U.S. Treasury, now headed by James Baker.[38]

If the Japanese had hoped to defuse the protectionist threat in the U.S., as many analysts think, they probably underestimated how much the yen would have to move to affect trade flows. Henning argues that the Japanese misjudged the amount of correction needed by a wide margin. The relevant Japanese decision-makers made a private assessment at the beginning of the process (1985) that the value of the yen would probably have to rise to 210¥ to the dollar. (Readers should remember that when a currency rises in value compared to another, it takes less of the currency to buy the same amount of the other.) This target was further adjusted to 200 ¥ to the dollar.[39] At the Plaza meeting of 22 September 1985, when the yen stood at 242 to the dollar, Japan agreed to intervene to alter the value of the dollar and the yen. Over the next month and a half, Japan spent $3 billion in interventions.

Japan also agreed to other policy changes, committing itself to further liberalizations of the domestic financial markets and to reduce the government's budget deficit. There were also promises to allow greater use of the yen internationally—and the U.S. extracted similar promises from the Germans, though most observers agree that the Japanese respected their commitments in these areas more than the Germans did.[40]

When the yen had risen to 200 ¥ to the dollar and then continued to rise (February-March 1986), Japanese businesses began to become concerned about the currency's value. They now wanted the currency's rise to stop. The policy-makers shared the business community's concerns, though there was some disagreement between the Bank of Japan and the Finance Ministry (see below) over where the levelling off of the currency's value should be.

In the following months (April-August), the business sector's concerns
about the yen's value solidified and broadened, thus bringing greater pressure to bear on the politicians and bureaucrats. In response, the Bank of
Japan wound up taking unilateral action to strengthen the dollar versus the
yen by purchasing $12.4 billion.[41] What was necessary was some sort of con-
certed action with the U.S., and the necessary agreement was elusive. Only
in February 1987 were the correct ingredients present within both countries
for a new agreement, the Louvre Accord.

Bureaucratic Politics: The Cabinet's Relations with the Bank of Japan

In this particular instance, we once again have the ingredients for a bureaucratic struggle between a central bank and a finance ministry. The relationship between the Bank of Japan and the Japanese government is a little
different from the same sort of institutional arrangements we have considered in other countries. One might be misled by impressions formed by
journalistic coverage, too. The governor of the Bank of Japan holds the
spotlight in relations with the press. The governor announces policy on
exchange rates and other areas, though, in fact, the governor is not entirely
responsible for making such policy. Unlike the Federal Reserve in the U.S.,
the central bank is actually under the supervision and authority of the
Ministry of Finance. Any decisions about intervention in exchange markets
or international agreements are made by the Minister of Finance (though the
Prime Minister can become more involved as well, of course) rather than by
the central bank's governor.[42]

In 1983, when the Bank of Japan's top official was encouraging some sort
of co-ordination to increase the value of the yen, the Ministry of Finance
seemed on a different policy direction altogether. The Prime Minister and
cabinet simply did not want a tighter monetary policy.[43] Because the Bank
of Japan is responsible to the Finance Ministry, the cabinet had the final say
in policy. Though the institutional arrangement is straightforward, there is
still room for disagreements to surface, as they did soon after the Plaza
Accord was reached.

The Bank of Japan was quite willing to increase the value of the yen as
required under the agreement. In fact, the Bank's targets were perhaps even
above those of the cabinet. The Ministry of Finance and the cabinet anticipated less of an increase in the yen's value. The Bank's governor, Satoshi
Sumita, and the Finance Minister, Takeshita, publicly differed over the goals
of Japan's international monetary policies in February 1986. The value of the
yen went past the initial targets, right past 200 ¥; as the value rose higher,
however, even the Bank of Japan thought the yen had risen in value as far

as it should. Bureaucratic splits subsided. From March 1986 the Japanese again presented a united front, this time to stop the further appreciation of the yen. (The U.S., on the other hand, continued to urge the Japanese to push the yen higher, though the U.S. agreed the pace of the increase should be slowed.)[44] The yen continued to rise in value, however. In about a year, by February 1987, even the U.S. policy-makers agreed that the yen had risen enough, which provided the basis for the Louvre Accord.

How Miyazawa's Background Played a Role

In late 1986 and early 1987, Japanese officials sought to slow down the rise of the yen, but they needed co-operation from the U.S. to achieve this goal. Many people argue that joint action as taken in the Louvre Accord was only possible because of a change in personnel. Kiichi Miyazawa took over the post of Finance Minister; Miyazawa was a former official in the Ministry of Finance who had developed extensive relationships with his American counterparts over the years. He spoke English well, which also enhanced his ability to reach out to American negotiators. Moreover, Miyazawa's personal beliefs about Japan's proper policies were reflected in his approaches to the Americans.

In September 1986, Miyazawa met with Treasury Secretary Baker and reached rough agreement on several subjects. Miyazawa's personal beliefs in the importance of a more expansive role for the Ministry of Finance (and therefore of Japan internationally) meant that he was willing to strike an agreement with Baker on the need for Japan to have a more expansive fiscal policy.[45] In return, Baker agreed that the U.S. would help stabilize the yen-dollar rate at 153-163 ¥.

These ranges would be adjusted slightly in the Louvre Accord. The Accord included similar negotiations with Germany; the yen's rate was now set at 153.5 ¥ ± 5 per cent. These ranges were secret. The levels were too high for Miyazawa, however. Psychologically, the rate of 150 ¥ to the dollar was an important barrier. Miyazawa did not want the rate to go up to that barrier, let alone go beyond it. Unfortunately, he had already staked out some of his positions before coming to the meeting; when the agreements forced him to make greater concessions, he was left dissatisfied.[46] Even with the agreement and the massive interventions carried out as part of the Accord, the yen continued to rise in value. The targets soon had to be adjusted, so that the yen was to be stabilized at 146 ¥ to the dollar—still too high for Miyazawa, but he had to accept the rate if he was to get foreign assistance in achieving those targets.

By April 1987 the yen was at 137 ¥ to the dollar, and it would go even higher by the end of the year. All told, Japan carried out massive interventions in 1987. If we look at the combined amounts the Bank of Japan and the Ministry of Finance spent over the course of the year in interventions in the exchange markets, it comes to the staggering total of $35 billion (greater than 1 per cent of Japan's GNP that year).[47]

Summary and Consequences: Currencies and Trade

The potential problem of dollar overliquidity remains, though it is a manageable issue, at least until a rival currency emerges. Japan now accepts the higher value of the yen, as well as the need for further international co-ordination in international monetary affairs.[48] Japan is prepared to accept a greater, more active role in international monetary affairs. While Japan plays a greater role, it has not sought to displace the U.S.—the framework for successful co-operation is in place.

In the early 1980s, Japan and the U.S. pursued almost opposite policies. The U.S. had a loose fiscal policy while tightening monetary policy; Japan had a loose monetary policy with a tight fiscal policy. In Japan this caused a surge in asset prices.[49] Real estate became massively overvalued, for instance. The resulting bubble burst at the end of the decade, when the value of real estate came crashing down. This became a serious problem for Japanese financial actors when international capitalization accords were struck. In most other countries, banks are not allowed to count real estate as an asset in their portfolios in the same way the Japanese banks had been allowed to value it. The portfolios of Japanese banks had been massively inflated by their valuation of property holdings. International agreements on how to value real estate would use an Anglo-American standard, forcing the Japanese banks to lower the value of their assets considerably. While Japan can still boast of some of the world's most powerful financial actors, their relative strengths have receded.

The trade imbalance between the U.S. and Japan continues. The tensions and struggle between the two countries over how to resolve this issue also continue. The relationship between the dollar and the yen will remain a point of concern for businesses, policy-makers, and politicians in both countries for some years to come. Fortunately, the agreements of the 1980s have provided the basis for some sort of bilateral management of the two countries' relationship, which we can expect to grow in the future.

Suggested Readings

Yoichi Funabashi, *Managing the Dollar: From the Plaza to the Louvre*. Washington: Institute for International Economics, 1988.

Takatoshi Ito, "The Yen and the International Monetary System," in C. Fred Bergsten and Marcus Noland, eds., *Pacific Dynamism and the International Economic System*. Washington: Institute for International Economics, 1993.

Yoshikazu Miyazaki, "Debtor America and Creditor Japan: Will There Be a Hegemony Change?" *Japanese Economic Studies* 15, 3 (Spring 1987), 58-96.

Tanaka Naoki, "The Dollar's Fin de Siècle, the Yen's Debut," *Japan Quarterly* (April-June 1989), 120-26.

Frances McCall Rosenbluth, *Financial Politics in Contemporary Japan*. Ithaca, NY: Cornell University Press, 1989.

Jeffrey Sachs, "The Uneasy Case for Greater Exchange Rate Coordination," *American Economic Review* 76, 2 (May 1986), 336-41.

Notes

1   Susan Strange, *Casino Capitalism* (London: Basil Blackwell, 1986); David P. Calleo, *Beyond American Hegemony* (New York: Basic Books, 1987).

2   See Jeffrey Frankel, "Six Possible Meanings of 'Overvaluation': The 1981-85 Dollar," *Princeton Essays in International Finance* No. 159 (December 1985).

3   I.M. Destler and C. Randall Henning, *Dollar Politics: Exchange Rate Policymaking in the United States* (Washington: Institute for International Economics, 1989), 2, 28.

4   Ibid., 31.

5   Yoichi Funabashi, *Managing the Dollar: From the Plaza to the Louvre* (Washington: Institute for International Economics, 1988), 68; Destler and Henning, *Dollar Politics*, 2-3, 29.

6   Destler and Henning, *Dollar Politics*, 88.

7   Ibid., 12, 89; David M. Jones, *The Politics of Money: The Fed Under Alan Greenspan* (New York: New York Institute of Finance, 1991), 119.

8   Funabashi, *Managing the Dollar*, 69-74.

9   Destler and Henning, *Dollar Politics*, 132-33.

10 I.M. Destler and C. Randall Henning, "From Neglect to Activism: American Politics and the 1985 Plaza Accord," *Journal of Public Policy* 8, 3/4 (June 1988), 323.

11 Destler and Henning, *Dollar Politics*, 39.

12 William Grieder, *Secrets of the Temple* (New York: Simon & Schuster, 1987), 473-74.

13 Destler and Henning, *Dollar Politics*, 40.

14 Grieder, *Secrets of the Temple*.

15 Destler and Henning, *Dollar Politics*, 43-44.

16 Destler and Henning, "From Neglect to Activism," 317.

17 Ibid., 326-27.

18 Destler and Henning, *Dollar Politics*, 2-3.

19 Funabashi, *Managing the Dollar*, 46.

20 Destler and Henning, *Dollar Politics*, 53.

21 Destler and Henning, "From Neglect to Activism," 326-27.

22 In short, I am arguing that domestic interests are reluctant to try to alter monetary policy unless there is an overt bureaucratic split between the agencies responsible for monetary policy that they could possibly exploit. Otherwise, it makes more sense for such groups to focus their efforts on changing trade policy, which is more easily broken down into discrete elements.

23 Destler and Henning, *Dollar Politics*, 43-44.

24 Ibid., 58-59.

25 Joan E. Spero, *The Politics of International Economic Relations*, 4th ed. (New York: St. Martin's Press, 1990), 60-61.

26 Ibid., 61.

27 Ibid., 62.

28 Ibid.

29 Destler and Henning, *Dollar Politics*, 60-61.

30 Ibid., 67-68.

31 Funabashi, *Managing the Dollar*, 57.

32 Destler and Henning, *Dollar Politics*, 74-75.

33 Jones, *The Politics of Money*, 113.

34 C. Randall Henning, *Currencies and Politics in the United States, Germany, and Japan* (Washington:5Institute for International Economics, 1994), 134.

35 Ibid., 137-39

36 Ibid., 135.

37 Ibid., 140-41.

38 Ibid., 144-45.

39 Ibid., 145.

40 Ibid., 145-46.

41 Ibid., 147-48.

42 Ibid., 80.

43 Ibid., 137-39.

44 Ibid., 146-47.

45 Ibid., 149-50.

46 Ibid., 152.

47 Ibid., 154.

48 Hirohisa Kohoma and Shujiro Urata, "The Impact of the Recent Yen Appreciation on the Japanese Economy," *The Developing Economies* 26, 4 (December 1988), 323-40.

49 Henning, *Currencies and Politics in the United States, Germany, and Japan*, 158.

Part Four

CONCLUSION

Twenty-Two

THEORIES, EVIDENCE, AND THE EVOLUTION OF THE INTERNATIONAL POLITICAL ECONOMY

Having considered theories that seek to explain international outcomes, examined particular descriptions of issues and problems within the different areas of international political economic relations, and reviewed a number of cases illustrating how critical foreign economic policy decisions were made, we must now pull this material together. What do the cases, taken together, tell us about the evolution of the international political economy? How can the cases help us understand the application of theories, so that we may refine the theories or at least apply them more effectively in the future?

The Evolution of Regimes Governing the International Political Economy

Let us begin by seeing what the historical examples have illustrated in terms of how the international regimes in the issue-areas of trade, investment, and monetary affairs changed over time. The story of the evolution of the trade regime began with Britain's repeal of the Corn Laws in the 1840s. This signalled Britain's desire to lead the liberalization of the international economy, although such unilateral action had only a limited impact on the behaviour of other states. Direct negotiations with another country, France, resulted in the Cobden-Chevalier Treaty in 1860, which sparked a chain reaction among European states, thereby creating a relatively open trading system. This regime was built out of numerous bilateral relations—it was a regime built in an ad hoc fashion. It only lasted for a brief time, for by the 1880s and 1890s several countries were again raising barriers to trade. Just as the regime had been created in an ad hoc manner, so it fell apart. Most notable among the defectors from this regime was Germany, where the proponents of free trade were unable to install and maintain their preferred policy.

World War I disrupted trade relations. After the war, the victorious powers attempted to rebuild a trade regime around liberal economic principles, but this attempt soon fell victim to protectionist pressures. The U.S. Smoot-Hawley Tariff led the closure of international trade. After World War II, an open international system was established around the GATT; in contrast to the earlier trade regimes, the GATT regime is much more explicit and much more institutionalized. These characteristics may make the GATT regime less susceptible to erosion, though the rise of non-tariff barriers has presented a serious challenge to the GATT principles. This open trading system has remained intact, although there are some signs of the threat of closure emerging. Regional trading blocs have been added to the picture in recent years, as has the further institutionalization of the GATT as it evolves into the World Trade Organization. Whether the WTO and regional trading blocs can function alongside one another remains to be seen.

In the issue-area of international investment, the story is a bit simpler. In the nineteenth century there were increased levels of international investment. These investments took the form primarily of portfolio investment. The gold standard facilitated such flows. Britain was the centre of these flows, though other European countries also invested capital internationally. These interests in international investment shaped Britain's attitudes about trade and monetary relations, as was evident in Britain's attitudes towards German protectionism prior to World War I and the need to resume the gold standard in the 1920s. After World Wars I and II, the U.S. emerged as the primary source of international investments, and American investments were dominated by foreign direct investment by multinational corporations. In the 1970s, the expansion of Eurodollar holdings laid the basis for a massive expansion in international lending. When American monetary policy was tightened in the early 1980s, these international loans created an enormous debt crisis. The debt crisis engendered a clash among private international actors, international agencies, and the creditor states, as well as the debtor states. As a result, new patterns and rules governing international banking and international investment have been developed.

In international monetary relations, a much more diverse pattern can be observed. There have been periods with very strict rules, as well as periods when the regime exerted little constraint on monetary policies. When trade was finally opened in the mid-nineteenth century, the gold standard was adopted to regulate international monetary affairs and facilitate the free trade and investment regimes. The gold standard operated on a strict model— though practice often diverged from theory. The outbreak of World War I effectively destroyed the gold standard; it was not successfully rebuilt in the interwar period, despite the tremendous efforts Britain made. After World War II, a new monetary regime was created around the U.S. dollar and the institutions of the IMF and the World Bank. The Bretton Woods regime, however, had inherent weaknesses in balancing liquidity with confidence in the dollar. The system collapsed under these pressures in the early 1970s and has not been replaced by a new set of real regulations. Instead, rules have been written to allow countries to do whatever they wish. This has required greater co-operation among the major financial powers, and ignited desires among the Europeans to tie their currencies more strongly together.

Explaining Regime Change: The Development of Theoretical Paradigms

By taking a broader perspective of the evolution of international regimes, we may appreciate the reasons for the popularity of particular paradigms in international political economy. A more comprehensive consideration of the ways in which we explain regime change may also shed light on the directions in which more recent research in international political economy has been headed. The popularity of realism springs from its ability to provide insight into numerous cases across issue-areas and over time. Structural realists have centred their explanations on the role of hegemonic leaders in the international system. Remember how realists base their arguments on states and power (and the pursuit of power)? Realists associate periods of stable economic relations with stable political power; regimes reflect the distribution of power. Realists face several tough questions, however. Why do hegemonic states follow these policies of maintaining an open trading system, with high levels of international investment and so on? In the cases we've taken a closer look at, the trade and investment regimes supported first by Britain and then by the United States have ultimately led to the relative decline of the hegemonic country. Given that the U.S. remains a dominant military power while its relative economic position is in doubt, how should we expect international regimes to develop in the future? The realists must look at issues such as the creation of regional trading blocs as signs of the future demise of the trade regime; examples of co-ordinated adjustment, such as in monetary affairs in the 1980s, raise questions as to how well the realist theories can explain current outcomes.

These questions also provide insight into some of the reasons variations in realism have arisen. Neo-realism, in particular, has attempted to compensate for some of the apparent weaknesses in realist explanations by opening up assumptions about the goals of states. If states are doing other things besides maximizing power, such as maximizing wealth, then some of these questions disappear—though we are left with new questions, about the ways in which we as theorists should make assumptions about states' goals.

In contrast, classical liberals relate changes in the international political economy to how individuals pursue their interests (usually material interests).

For classical liberals and their modern descendants, the swings of the international political economy from more open relations to closure and back again are evidence of the overpoliticization of the international political economy. What liberals tend to ignore is the need for political order to underwrite or support international economic relations. Politics are always a force in the international political economy, but all political orders do not support markets. Classical liberals tend to spend time now thinking about how to get politics out of international economic relations. By examining the role of individuals and firms, liberals provide insight into the connections between domestic politics and foreign economic policy; as a paradigm, liberalism has failed to present a coherent set of arguments for the explanation of foreign economic policy, even though liberal assumptions are the starting point for many—if not most—analyses from the domestic level (as will be examined below).[1] As a paradigm for explaining regime change, liberalism's apparent weakness has led its proponents to create two new paradigms: institutionalism and constructivism.

Institutionalists have observed the difficulties realists have in explaining why regimes persist after hegemonic powers decline. Where does continued co-operation come from? The institutionalists have focused their efforts on explaining these anomalies and then used these theories to illuminate how co-operation can be created without relying on the expression of international power. The institutionalists offer a much more optimistic picture of the future as compared to the realists. Co-operative management of existing regimes is not only possible, it is likely.

Constructivists have picked up on a different set of anomalies in the realists' analyses. The realists have been unable to explain much of the content of the regimes hegemonic states played a role in creating. Constructivists use the formation of identities as a starting point to develop a better understanding of how all states, including hegemonic powers, have formulated their interests. Since constructivists see outcomes flowing from the formation of interests as well as the exertion of power, they, too, offer more optimistic projections of the future of the international political economy. As long as states understand their interests lie in co-operation within existing regimes, states will not only adhere to those regimes' rules but will even be prepared to enhance these international arrangements. One of the challenges confronting the proponents of constructivism is to go back and illustrate in several cases how their analyses would provide a better understanding of past events. Ruggie's analysis of the creation of the Bretton Woods regimes is an excellent exemplar of the manner in which this can be done, but as a young paradigm more such interpretations need to be constructed.

Other, older paradigms have provided contrasting analyses of past events, as we saw in some of the chapters in Part III. Marxists see politics at the heart of the international political economy, but relate changes in the international political economy to changing economic bases (which are filtered through politics). They see the rise of capitalism and markets as an economic activity that results in political manifestations of exploitation by capitalists—such as imperialism. These analyses in turn spawned newer paradigms, such as the modern world-system approach, which shares both strengths and weaknesses with some of the realist models.

If there is one thing we have learned from the examination of the cases presented here, it is that these paradigms are simple ways of approaching some rather complex phenomena. No single paradigm provides correct interpretations of each and every event; none works well for all the questions we have posed about the international political economy. The exercise of academic inquiry is to engage in debates, appreciate what is right and what is wrong with each approach, and use those lessons to learn how to improve existing theories. Only by appreciating a paradigm's deficiencies, and knowing the strengths of alternatives, can we hope to refine and adapt our theories in ways that overcome their current weaknesses.

State Behaviour and the Levels of Analysis

These same points hold for the theories when we group them together by the levels of analysis. By seeing what realism or other system-level theories can do—and what they cannot do—we can appreciate the value of other approaches. Consider the value of domestic-level theories—the ones that used models of domestic politics to explain how state policies were developed. For traditional questions in international political economy, such as tariff changes or agreements to fix exchange rates at particular levels, economic models provide excellent material for constructing theories about the domestic political basis of foreign economic policies.

In the cases, we also reflected on the impact of specific decision-makers. Decision-makers may get locked into roles, with the roles determining how the decision-makers formulate and execute foreign economic policy. In such cases, we can understand policy as a result of bureaucratic politics and/or organizational process. Policy may be formulated to achieve bureaucratic goals as much as (or more than) for national interest. Policy may not make sense as a comprehensive package because the different bureaucracies formulate different policies, putting their own institutional twist on the interpretation of foreign policy so that overall policy may not appear to be rational. Below the level of bureaucratic politics, we examined individuals and their idiosyncratic characteristics to try to come to grips with state behaviour. How do individuals differ, and how do their differences show up in foreign economic policy? How would policy have differed if different individuals were in power?

At the outset of this book, I stressed that one of the key tasks we face as theorists in international relations is the simplification of reality. We know that the world is a complicated place, and that coming up with persuasive explanations for past events is difficult; accurate prediction is even harder. Yet, if we want to get some sort of control over the future—to prevent wars, ensure smoother handling of international crises, conduct more satisfactory economic negotiations, whatever—if we want to gain some leverage over tomorrow's events, we have to have some notions about the consequences of our own actions and form expectations about how others are likely to act, react to our deeds, or otherwise interact with us. Which of these various theoretical approaches should we rely on? First, let us reflect on the strengths and weaknesses of each of the levels of analysis in turn (remembering that each level of analysis represents a whole array of theories that share common assumptions—but are not necessarily saying the same thing).

System-level theories explain state behaviour by looking at characteristics of the system. For Waltz (and most other realists), a key characteristic of the system is its anarchic nature. That forces all states to become concerned with preserving their own interests, and allows states to choose to use force to resolve disputes. Realists wind up focusing on the role of power in international relations. But what can we say about arguments made around the causal weight of systemic characteristics? Well, first, they are generalizable—that is, they can be used to talk about the foreign policy or behaviour of many different states, in different issue-areas, and across long spans of time.

System-level theories also tend to be parsimonious. Whether or not the theory is accurate depends on the specific theory examined out of this grouping, and indeed we can picture two different system-level arguments that make opposite predictions (such as balancing and bandwagoning). Both may operate with similar assumptions about actors and actors' goals, and thus exhibit similar strengths and weaknesses as theories. On the whole, these theories are generalizable and parsimonious, so if they are accurate as well, they may be doing well across the board—hence, the popularity of systemic theories.

By focusing on specific factors that characterize nation-states, national or state-level theories are naturally limiting their generalizability. By saying some states are not like others, and therefore are likely to behave differently, these theories are saying we cannot apply the same logic to predict the actions of all states. We know specific theories drawn from this group of theories are not as generalizable as system-level theories. They may be just as parsimonious as system-level theories, since they may only need small amounts of information, but they can also become much more complicated and require greater detail. To counterbalance the lack of generalizability, however, we often see that these theories are more accurate—more accurate in the sense that they integrate more details into their analysis. These theories are often more descriptive.

When we come to the next kind of argument, bureaucratic politics, the picture gets even more complicated. What do we need to make such theories work? We need information about the decision-making structure, the bureaucracy. That should tell us two things—these theories are likely to be less parsimonious, since the information required is more detailed, and certainly they are going to be specific to particular countries, so these theories are not likely to be very generalizable (across cases or, for that matter, across time, because bureaucracies change over time, too). Though generalizability is sacrificed, as is parsimony, supporters of this approach would argue that accuracy is gained.

When we drop down to the lowest-level theories, the individual level with the emphasis on idiosyncratic features, we need even more specific, detailed information to apply the theory. We need to know who is making decisions, we need to know background information on the personal level. So again we see some sort of trade-off between generalizability, parsimony, and accuracy. Again, the sorts of trade-offs become clear—if we want generalizability, often we have to give up some detail.

These trade-offs matter when we remember the tasks of theories— describing, explaining, and predicting foreign policy. The more detail-oriented theories are great for describing, and might be very useful when we go back and gather all the evidence needed for supporting the theory. They may be weaker when used to formulate predictions. The more generalizable and parsimonious theories are better at prediction, for they allow for faster theorizing and reaching conclusions with less information. If we were to predict Russian foreign economic policy five years from now, what kind of information would we need to employ theories from each level of analysis? A prediction based on the individual level would have to start by predicting who would be in charge of foreign economic policy in five years. Will Yeltsin's government still be in power? Who will be in charge of particular ministerial portfolios? If we turn to the next level of analysis and consider domestic politics, what would the Russian government look like? How will different interest groups compete? What will the role of political parties be in the future? Will the country keep its democratic institutions, or will these be modified? This brief example illustrates how these issues of parsimony, generalizability, and accuracy interact to influence the qualities of theories.

Combining Theories for a More Complex and Comprehensive Understanding of Events

With a few exceptions, the analyses in the cases have primarily presented these theories as rivals. That is not the only way they are used—sometimes specific theories drawn from different levels of analysis can be used in combination to make a better theory than either level alone could produce.[2] While this is a topic for more advanced study in international relations, it should be evident that each of the types of theories can potentially give us part of the bigger picture, part of the larger answers we seek. Moreover, combining analyses from different levels may be the most effective way to extract the best from each level of analysis. The challenge is to understand when to use particular theories, to figure out which types of theories are best for what sorts of question, and to determine how they might be used together to derive theories that are better in all characteristics: more accurate, more generalizable, and more parsimonious. Having completed this book, the reader should not only appreciate how particular decisions shaped the evolution of the international political economy, but also have a better understanding of how theories of the international political economy (and political science more generally) are formed, how to go about testing them, and how they could be refined and improved. Those are the tasks for the next generation of theorists.

Notes

1　See Andrew Moravscik's insightful discussion, "Liberalism and International Relations Theory," Harvard University Working Paper No. 92-6.

2　A good example of how this can be done can be found in the concluding chapter of Deborah Larson's *The Origins of Containment* (Princeton. NJ: Princeton University Press, 1985).

References

Achen, Christopher, and Duncan Snidal. "Rational Deterrence Theory and Comparative Case Studies," *World Politics* 41 (January 1989), 143-69.

Aggarwal, Vinod K. *International Debt Threat.* Berkeley: Institute of International Studies, *Policy Papers in International Affairs* No. 29 (1987).

Allison, Graham. "Conceptual Models and the Cuban Missile Crisis," *American Political Science Review* 63 (September 1969), 689-718.

Allison, Graham. *The Essence of Decision.* Boston: Little, Brown, 1971.

Andriole, S.J. "The Levels of Analysis Problems and the Study of Foreign, International and Global Affairs: A Review Critique, and Another Final Solution," *International Interactions* 5, 2/3 (1978), 113-33.

Angell, Norman. *The Great Illusion.* New York: Putnam's, 1910.

Art, Robert. "Bureaucratic Politics and American Foreign Policy—A Critique," *Policy Sciences* 4 (1973), 467-90.

Axelrod, Robert. *The Evolution of Cooperation.* New York: Basic Books, 1984.

Baker, Ray S., ed. *Woodrow Wilson and World Settlement.* Garden City, NJ: Doubleday, Page, 1922.

Balassa, Bela. "The Process of Industrial Development and Alternative Development Strategies," *Princeton Essays in International Finance* No. 141 (December 1980).

Baldwin, David A. "Security Studies and the End of the Cold War," *World Politics* 48, 1 (October 1995), 117-41.

Bergsten, C. Fred. *The Dilemmas of the Dollar.* New York: New York University Press, 1975.

Bhagwati, Jagdish N., and Anne O. Krueger. "Exchange Control, Liberalization and Economic Development," *American Economic Review* 63, 2 (May 1973), 419-27.

Biersteker, Thomas J. "Introduction," in Biersteker, ed., *Dealing with Debt.* Boulder, Colo.: Westview Press, 1993, 1-15.

Bird, Melissa H. "The IMF," in Biersteker, ed., *Dealing with Debt.* Boulder, Colo.: Westview Press, 1993, 19-36.

Boulding, Kenneth. *Conflict and Defense.* New York: Harper & Row, 1963.

Braudel, Fernand. *The Structures of Everyday Life: Civilization and Capitalism, 15th-18th Century,* Volume 1. New York: Harper & Row, 1979.

Braudel, Fernand. *The Wheels of Commerce: Civilization and Capitalism, 15th-18th Century,* Volume 11. New York: Harper & Row, 1982.

Braudel, Fernand. *The Perspective of the World: Civilization and Capitalism, 15th-18th Century*, Volume III. New York: Harper & Row, 1984.

Brawley, Mark R. "Factoral or Sectoral Conflict? Partially Mobile Factors and the Politics of Trade in Imperial Germany," *International Studies Quarterly* 41, 4 (December 1997), 633-53.

Brawley, Mark R. *Liberal Leadership: Great Powers and Their Challengers in Peace and War*. Ithaca, NY: Cornell University Press, 1993.

Brawley, Mark R. "Political Leadership and Liberal Economic Sub-Systems: The Constraints of Structural Assumptions," *Canadian Journal of Political Science* 28, 1 (March 1995), 85-103.

Brawley, Mark R. *Afterglow or Adjustment?* (forthcoming).

Brecher, Michael. "State Behavior in International Crisis," *Journal of Conflict Resolution* 23, 3 (September 1979), 446-80.

Brenner, Robert. "The Origins of Capitalist Development: A Critique of Neo-Smithian Marxism," *New Left Review* (1977).

Broad, Robin, and John Cavanaugh. "No More NICs," *Foreign Policy* 72 (Fall 1988), 81-103.

Bull, Hedley. *The Anarchical Society*. London: Macmillan, 1977.

Bullock, Alan. *Hitler: A Study in Tyranny*. New York: Harper & Row, 1964.

Cain, Peter. "Capitalism, War and Internationalism in the Thought of Richard Cobden," *British Journal of International Studies* 5, 3 (October 1979), 229-47.

Cairncross, Alec, and Barry Eichengreen. *Sterling in Decline*. Oxford: Basil Blackwell, 1983.

Calleo, David P. *The German Problem Reconsidered*. New York: Cambridge University Press, 1978.

Calleo, David P. *Beyond American Hegemony*. New York: Basic Books, 1987.

Cameron, Duncan. "Introduction," in Cameron, ed., *The Free Trade Deal*. Toronto: James Lorimer, 1988, i-xviii.

Cameron, Duncan. "Striking a Deal," in Cameron, ed., *The Free Trade Deal*. Toronto: James Lorimer, 1988, 16-25.

Cameron, Duncan, and Hugh Mackenzie. "Manufacturing," in Cameron, ed., *The Free Trade Deal*. Toronto: James Lorimer, 1988, 117-24.

Cardoso, Eliana, and Albert Fishlow. "The Macroeconomics of the Brazilian External Debt," in Jeffrey Sachs, ed., *Developing Country Debt and Economic Performance*, Volume 2, Country Studies—Argentina, Bolivia, Brazil, Mexico. Chicago: University of Chicago Press, 1990, 269-391.

Carr, E.H. *The Twenty Years' Crisis, 1919-1939*. New York: Harper, 1964 (originally published in 1939).

Caves, Richard. *Multinational Enterprise and Economic Growth*. New York: Cambridge University Press, 1982.

de Cecco, Marcello. *Money and Empire*. Totowa, NJ: Rowman & Littlefield, 1975.

Chan, Steve. "Mirror, Mirror on the Wall ... Are the Freer Countries More Pacific?" *Journal of Conflict Resolution* 28, 4 (1984), 617-48.

Chan, Steve. "In Search of the Democratic Peace: Problems and Promise," *Mershon International Studies Review* 41, 1 (May 1997), 59-91.

Chandler, Lester V. *Benjamin Strong, Central Banker*. Washington: Brookings Institution, 1958.

Chase-Dunn, Christopher. "Comparative Research on World-System Characteristics," *International Studies Quarterly* 23, 4 (December 1979), 601-23.

Chase-Dunn, Christopher. "Interstate System and Capitalist World-Economy: One Logic or Two?" *International Studies Quarterly* 25 (March 1981), 19-42.

Clarke, Stephen V.O. *Central Bank Cooperation 1924-1931*. New York: Federal Reserve Bank of New York, 1967.

Clarke, Stephen V.O. "The Reconstruction of the International Monetary System: The Attempts of 1922 and 1933," *Princeton Studies in International Finance* No. 33 (November 1973).

Cline, Ray. *World Power Assessment.* Boulder, Colo.: Westview Press, 1977.

Cohen, Benjamin J. *In Whose Interest?* New Haven: Yale University Press, 1986.

Cohen, Stephen D., Joel R. Paul, and Robert A. Blecker. *Fundamentals of U.S. Foreign Trade Policy.* Boulder, Colo.: Westview Press, 1996.

Cooper, Richard N. "Prolegomena to the Choice of an International Monetary System," *International Organization* 29, 1 (1975), 63-97.

Cumings, Bruce. "The Origins and Development of the Northeast Asian Political Economy: Industrial Sectors, Product Cycles, and Political Consequences," in Frederic Deyo, ed., *The Political Economy of the New Asian Industrialism.* Ithaca, NY: Cornell University Press, 1987, 44-83.

Dahl, Robert. "The Concept of Power," *Behavioral Science* 2, 3 (July 1957), 201-15.

Dam, Kenneth W. *The Rules of the Game.* Chicago: University of Chicago Press, 1982.

Denemark, Robert A. and Kenneth P. Thomas. "The Brenner-Wallerstein Debate," *International Studies Quarterly* 32, 1 (March 1988), 47-65.

Dessler, David. "What's at Stake in the Agent-Structure Debate?" *International Organization* 43, 3 (Summer 1989), 441-73.

Destler, I.M. *Making Foreign Economic Policy.* Washington: Brookings Institution, 1980.

Destler, I.M., and C. Randall Henning. "From Neglect to Activism: American Politics and the 1985 Plaza Accord," *Journal of Public Policy* 8, 3/4 (June 1988), 317-33.

Destler, I.M., and C. Randall Henning. *Dollar Politics: Exchange Rate Policymaking in the United States.* Washington: Institute for International Economics, 1989.

Dinsmoor, James. *Brazil: Responses to the Debt Crisis.* Washington: Inter-American Development Bank and Johns Hopkins University Press, 1990.

Doran, Charles. *The Politics of Assimilation: Hegemony and Its Aftermath.* Baltimore: Johns Hopkins University Press, 1971.

Dornbusch, Rudiger. "From Adjustment with Recession to Adjustment with Growth," in John F. Weeks, ed., *Debt Disaster?: Banks, Governments, and Multilaterals Confront the Crisis.* New York: New York University Press, 1989, 207-21.

Dos Santos, Theotonio. "The Structure of Dependence," *American Economic Review* 60, 2 (May 1970), 231-36.

Doyle, Michael. "Liberalism and World Politics," *American Political Science Review* 80, 4 (1986), 1151-61.

Doyle, Michael. "Thucydidean Realism," *Review of International Studies* 16 (July 1990), 223-37.

Dreyer, Jacob S., and Andrew Schotter. "Power Relationships in the IMF: The Consequences of Quota Changes," *Review of Economics and Statistics* 62, 1 (February 1980), 97-106.

Dunham, Arthur Lewis. *The Anglo-French Treaty of Commerce of 1860.* Ann Arbor: University of Michigan Press, 1930.

Dunn, Robert M., Jr. "The Many Disappointments of Flexible Exchange Rates," *Princeton Essays in International Finance* No. 154 (December 1983).

Edelstein, Michael. "Rigidity and Bias in the British Capital Market, 1870-1913," in Donald N. McCloskey, ed., *Essays on a Mature Economy: Britain after 1840.* Princeton, NJ: Princeton University Press, 1971, 83-105.

Edwards, Sebastian. *Crisis and Reform in Latin America: From Despair to Hope.* New York: Oxford University Press and World Bank, 1995.

Eichengreen, Barry. "Hegemonic Stability Theories of the International Monetary System," in *Can Nations Agree? Issues in International Economic Cooperation.* Washington: Brookings Institution, 1989, 255-98.

Eichengreen, Barry. "The Political Economy of the Smoot-Hawley Tariff," *Research in Economic History* 12 (1989), 1-43.

Eichengreen, Barry, and Jeffry Frieden. "The Political Economy of European Monetary Unification: An Analytical Introduction," in Barry Eichengreen and Jeffry Frieden, eds., *The Political Economy of European Monetary Unification*. Boulder, Colo.: Westview Press, 1994, 1-23.

Eichengreen, Barry, and Jeffrey Sachs. "Exchange Rates and Economic Recovery in the 1930s," *Journal of Economic History* 45, 4 (December 1985), 925-46.

Elbaum, Bernard, and William Lazonick. "The Decline of the British Economy: An Institutional Perspective," *Journal of Economic History* 44, 2 (June 1984), 567-83.

Emminger, Otmar. "International Financial Markets and the Recycling of Petro-dollars," *The World Today* 31, 3 (March 1975), 95-102.

Evangelista, Matthew. *Innovation and Arms Races: How the United States and the Soviet Union Develop New Military Technologies*. Ithaca, NY: Cornell University Press, 1988.

Falkus, M.E. "U.S. Economic Policy and the Dollar Gap of the 1920s," *Economic History Review* (Second Series) 24, 4, (November 1971), 599-623

Feierabend, Ivo K. "Expansionist and Isolationist Tendencies of Totalitarian Political Systems: A Theoretical Note," *Journal of Politics* 24 (November 1962), 733-42.

Feige, Edgar, and James M. Johannes. "Was the U.S. Responsible for Worldwide Inflation under the Regime of Fixed Exchange Rates?" *Kyklos* 35, 2 (1982), 263-77.

Feinberg, Richard E., and Edward L. Bacha. "When Supply and Demand Don't Intersect: Latin America and the Bretton Woods Institutions in the 1980s," *Development and Change* 19, 3 (July 1988), 371-39.

Finlayson, Jock A., and Mark W. Zacher. "The GATT and the Regulation of Trade Barriers: Regime Dynamics and Functions," *International Organization* 35, 4 (Autumn 1981), 561-602.

Fishlow, Albert. "Lessons from the Past: Capital Markets during the Nineteenth Century and the Interwar Period," *International Organization* 39, 3 (Summer 1985), 37-93.

Flanders, M. June. *International Monetary Economics: Between the Classical and the New Classical*. New York: Cambridge University Press, 1989.

Fletcher, Richard D. "Undervaluation, Adjustment and Growth," in John F. Weeks, ed., *Debt Disaster?: Banks, Governments, and Multilaterals Confront the Crisis*. New York: New York University Press, 1989, 125-30.

Frank, Andre Gunder. *World Accumulation, 1492-1789*. New York: Monthly Review Press, 1978.

Frankel, Jeffrey. "Six Possible Meanings of 'Overvaluation': The 1981-85 Dollar," *Princeton Essays in International Finance* No. 159 (December 1985).

Frieden, Jeffry. "Capital Politics: Creditors and the International Political Economy," *Journal of Public Policy* 8, 3/4 (July-December 1988), 265-86.

Frieden, Jeffry. "Sectoral Conflict and U.S. Foreign Economic Policy, 1914-1940," in John Ikenberry, David A. Lake, and Michael Mastanduno, eds., *The State and American Foreign Economic Policy*. Ithaca, NY: Cornell University Press, 1988, 59-90.

Frieden, Jeffry. "The Economics of Inter-vention: American Overseas Investments and Relations with Underdeveloped Areas, 1890-1950," *Comparative Studies in Society and History* 31, 1 (1989), 55-80.

Frieden, Jeffry. *Debt, Development, and Democracy: Modern Political Economy and Latin America, 1965-1985*. Princeton, NJ: Princeton University Press, 1991.

Frieden, Jeffry. "Invested Interests: The Politics of National Economic Policies in a World of Global Finance," *International Organization* 45, 4 (Autumn 1991), 425-51.

Frieden, Jeffry. "Making Commitments: France and Italy in the EMS, 1979-1985," in Barry Eichengreen and Jeffry Frieden, eds., *The Political Economy of European Monetary Unification*. Boulder, Colo.: Westview Press, 1994, 25-46.

Fukuyama, Francis. "The End of History?" *National Interest* (Summer 1989), 3-18.

Funabashi, Yoichi. *Managing the Dollar: From the Plaza to the Louvre*. Washington: Institute for International Economics, 1988.

Garos, Casper. *Canada-U.S. Free Trade*. Amsterdam: VU University Press, 1990.

Garrett, Geoffrey. "The Politics of Maastricht," in Barry Eichengreen and Jeffry Frieden, eds., *The Political Economy of European Monetary Unification*. Boulder, Colo.: Westview Press, 1994, 47-65.

Garrett, Geoffrey, and Peter Lange. "Internationalization, Institutions and Political Change," *International Organization* 49, 4 (Autumn 1995), 627-55.

Garrett, Geoffrey, and Barry Weingast. "Ideas, Interests, and Institutions: Constructing the European Community's Internal Market," in Judith Goldstein and Robert Keohane, eds., *Ideas and Foreign Policy*. Ithaca, NY: Cornell University Press, 1993, 173-206.

George, Alexander. "The 'Operational Code': A Neglected Approach to the Study of Political Leaders and Decision-Making," *International Studies Quarterly* 13 (June 1969), 190-222.

George, Alexander. "The Causal Nexus between Cognitive Beliefs and Decision-Making Behavior: The 'Operational Code' Belief System," in Lawrence S. Falkowski, ed., *Psychological Models in International Politics*. Boulder, Colo.: Westview Press, 1979, 95-124.

George, Alexander, and Juliette L. George. *Woodrow Wilson and Colonel House*. New York: John Day, 1956.

George, Alexander, and Juliette L. George. "Woodrow Wilson and Colonel House: A Reply to Weinstein, Anderson, and Link," *Political Science Quarterly* 96 (Winter 1981-82), 641-65.

Gilpin, Robert. *U.S. Power and the Multinational Corporation*. New York: Basic Books, 1975.

Gilpin, Robert. *War and Change in World Politics*. Cambridge: Cambridge University Press, 1981.

Gilpin, Robert. *The Political Economy of International Relations*. Princeton, NJ: Princeton University Press, 1987.

Goldstein, Judith. *Ideas, Interests and American Trade Policy*. Ithaca, NY: Cornell University Press, 1993.

Goldstein, Judith, and Robert Keohane, eds. *Ideas and Foreign Policy*. Ithaca, NY: Cornell University Press, 1993.

Goldstein, Judith, and Robert Keohane. "Ideas and Foreign Policy: An Analytical Framework," in Goldstein and Keohane, eds., *Ideas and Foreign Policy*. Ithaca, NY: Cornell University Press, 1993, 3-30.

Goodman, John B. *Monetary Sovereignty*. Ithaca, NY: Cornell University Press, 1992.

Gourevitch, Peter. "International Trade, Domestic Coalitions, and Liberty: Comparative Responses to the Crisis of 1873-1896," *Journal of Interdisciplinary History* 7 (1977), 281-313.

Gowa, Joanne. *Closing the Gold Window: Domestic Politics and the End of Bretton Woods*. Ithaca, NY: Cornell University Press, 1983.

Gowa, Joanne. *Allies, Adversaries, and International Trade*. Princeton, NJ: Princeton University Press, 1994.

de Grauwe, Paul. *International Money: Postwar Trends and Theories*. Oxford: Clarendon Press, 1989.

de Grauwe, Paul, and Lucas Papademos. "Introduction," in de Grauwe and Papademos, eds., *The EMS in the 1990s*. New York: Longman, 1990, xi-xvi.

Grieco, Joseph. *Cooperation Among Nations*. Ithaca, NY: Cornell University Press, 1990.

Grieder, William. *Secrets of the Temple*. New York: Simon & Schuster, 1987.

Griffiths, Martin. *Realism, Idealism, and International Politics: A Reinterpretation*. New York: Routledge, 1992.

Guiseppi, John. *The Bank of England*. Chicago: Henry Regnery, 1966.

Haas, Peter M. "Epistemic Communities and International Policy Coordination," *International Organization* 46, 1 (1992), 1-36.

Haggard, Stephan. *Pathways from the Periphery*. Ithaca, NY: Cornell University Press, 1990.

Haggard, Stephan, and Tun-jen Cheng. "State and foreign capital in the East Asian NICs," in Frederic Deyo, ed., *The Political Economy of the New Asian Industrialism*. Ithaca, NY: Cornell University Press, 1987, 84-135.

Hall, John A. "Ideas and the Social Sciences," in Judith Goldstein and Robert Keohane, eds., *Ideas and Foreign Policy*. Ithaca, NY: Cornell University Press, 1993, 31-54.

Hall, Peter. "The Movement from Keynesianism to Monetarism: Institutional Analysis and British Economic Policy in the 1970s," in Sven Steinmo, Kathleen Thelen, and Frank Longstreth, eds., *Structuring Politics*. New York: Cambridge University Press, 1992, 90-113.

Halperin, Morton H. "The Decision to Deploy the ABM: Bureaucratic and Domestic Politics in the Johnson Administration," *World Politics* 25, 1 (October 1975), 62-95.

Halperin, Morton H., and Arnold Kanter. *Readings in Foreign Policy: A Bureaucratic Perspective*. Boston: Little, Brown, 1973.

Harris, Richard G., "Why Voluntary Export Restraints are 'Voluntary,'" *Canadian Journal of Economics* 18, 4 (November 1985), 799-809

Harris, Richard G. "The New Protectionism Revisited," *Canadian Journal of Economics* 22, 4 (November 1989), 751-78.

Hart, Jeffrey. "Three Approaches to the Measurement of Power in International Relations," *International Organization* 30, 2 (Spring 1976), 289-305.

Hart, Michael (with Bill Dymond and Colin Robertson). *Decision at Midnight: Inside the Canada-U.S. Free-Trade Negotiations*. Vancouver: University of British Columbia Press, 1994.

Hawley, James P. "Protecting Capital From Itself: U.S. Attempts to Regulate the Eurocurrency System," *International Organization* 38, 1 (Winter 1984), 131-65.

Heckscher, Eli. *Mercantilism*, 2 vols. London: George Allen & Unwin, 1934.

Henning, C. Randall. *Currencies and Politics in the United States, Germany and Japan*. Washington: Institute for International Economics, 1994.

Henning, Friedrich-Wilhelm. "Vom Agrarliberalismus zum Agrarprotektionismus," in Hans Pohl, ed., *Die Auswirkungen von Zöllen und anderen Handelshemmnissen auf Wirtschaft und Gesellschaft von Mittelalter bis zur Gegenwart*. Stuttgart: Franz Steiner Verlag, 1987 (Vierteljahrschrift für Sozial- und Wirtschaftsgeschichte, Beiheft 80), 252-74.

Hobson, J.A. "Imperialism: A Study, 1902," in D.K. Fieldhouse, ed., *The Theory of Capitalist Imperialism*. London: Longmans, 1967, 65-72.

Hobson, J.A. "The Theory of Underconsumption, 1894," in D.K. Fieldhouse, ed., *The Theory of Capitalist Imperialism*. London: Longmans, 1967, 54-59.

Holborn, Hajo. *A History of Modern Germany 1840-1945*. Princeton, NJ: Princeton University Press, 1982.

Honohan, Patrick, and Paul McNelis. "Is the EMS a DM Zone?—Evidence from the Realignments?" *Economic and Social Review* 20, 2 (January 1989), 97-110.

Howson, Susan. *Domestic Monetary Management in Britain 1919-1938.* New York: Cambridge University Press, 1975.

Huntington, Sam. "Transnational Organizations in World Politics," *World Politics* 25 (April 1973).

Jaeger, Hans. *Unternehmer in der deutschen Politik (1890-1918).* Bonn: Ludwig Röhrscheid Verlag, 1967.

James, Scott, and David Lake. "The Second Face of Hegemony: Britain's Repeal of the Corn Laws and the American Walker Tariff of 1846," *International Organization* 43, 1 (Winter 1989), 1-29.

Jervis, Robert. "Cooperation under the Security Dilemma," *World Politics* 30 (January 1978), 167-214.

Johnson, Chalmers. "Political Institutions and Economic Performance: The Government-Business Relationship in Japan, South Korea and Taiwan," in Frederic Deyo, ed., *The Political Economy of the New Asian Industrialism.* Ithaca, NY: Cornell University Press, 1987, 136-64.

Jones, David M. *The Politics of Money: The Fed Under Alan Greenspan.* New York: New York Institute of Finance, 1991.

Jones, Kent. "The Political Economy of VER Agreements," *Kyklos* 37, 1 (1984), 82-101.

Kahler, Miles. "Politics and International Debt: Explaining the Crisis," *International Organization* 39, 3 (Summer 1985), 357-82.

Kant, Immanuel. *Perpetual Peace.* New York: Columbia University Press, 1939.

Kaplan, Morton A. *System and Process in International Politics.* Huntington, NY: Robert Krieger, 1975 (originally published in 1957).

Kaplan, Morton A. "The New Great Debate: Traditionalism versus Science in International Relations," *World Politics* 19, 1 (1966), 1-20.

Kapstein, Ethan B. "Resolving the Regulators' Dilemma: International Coordination of Banking Regulations," *International Organization* 43, 2 (Spring 1989), 323-47.

Kapstein, Ethan B. "Between Power and Purpose: Central Bankers and the Politics of Regulatory Convergence," *International Organization* 46, 1 (1992), 256-87.

Kapstein, Ethan B. *Governing the Global Economy.* Cambridge, Mass.: Harvard University Press, 1994.

Katzenstein, Peter, ed. *Between Power and Plenty.* Madison: University of Wisconsin Press, 1978.

Katzenstein, Peter. *Small States in World Markets.* Ithaca, NY: Cornell University Press, 1985.

Katzenstein, Peter. "The Role of Theory in Comparative Politics: A Symposium," *World Politics* 48, 1 (October 1995), 1-49.

Kehr, Eckhart. *Economic Interest, Militarism and Foreign Policy,* Craig Gordon, ed. Los Angeles: University of California Press, 1977.

Kennedy, Ellen. *The Bundesbank: Germany's Central Bank in the International Monetary System.* London: Pinter, 1991.

Keohane, Robert. "The Theory of Hegemonic Stability and Changes in International Economic Regimes, 1967-1977," in Ole R. Holsti, R.M. Siverson, and Alexander L. George, eds., *Changes in the International System.* Boulder, Colo.: Westview Press, 1980, 131-62.

Keohane, Robert. "The Demand for International Regimes," *International Organization* 36, 2 (Spring 1982), 141-71.

Keohane, Robert. *After Hegemony.* Princeton, NJ: Princeton University Press, 1984.

Keohane, Robert, ed. *Neorealism and Its Critics.* New York: Columbia University Press, 1986.

Keohane, Robert. "International Institutions: Two Approaches," *International Studies Quarterly* 32 (December 1988), 379-96.

Keohane, Robert, Gary King, and Sidney Verba. *Designing Social Inquiry.* Princeton, NJ: Princeton University Press, 1994.

Keohane, Robert, and Joseph Nye. "The Role of Transnational Forces," *International Organization* 25 (Summer 1971), 721-48.

Keohane, Robert, and Joseph Nye. *Power and Interdependence*. Boston: Little, Brown, 1977.

Kettl, Donald F. *Leadership at the Fed*. New Haven: Yale University Press, 1986.

Kindleberger, Charles P. *The World in Depression, 1929-1939*. Berkeley: University of California Press, 1973.

Kindleberger, Charles P. "The Rise of Free Trade in Western Europe," *Journal of Economic History* 35, 1 (March 1975), 20-55.

Kindleberger, Charles P. "Dominance and Leadership in the International Economy," *International Studies Quarterly* 25, 2 (June 1981), 242-54.

Kindleberger, Charles P. "The Functioning of Financial Centers: Britain in the Nineteenth Century, the United States since 1945," *Princeton Essays in International Finance* No. 157 (September 1985), 7-18.

Kindleberger, Charles P. "International Public Goods without International Government," *American Economic Review* 76, 1 (March 1986), 1-13.

King, Robin A., and Michael D. Robinson. "Assessing Structural Adjustment Programs: A Summary of Country Experience," in John F. Weeks, ed., *Debt Disaster?: Banks, Governments, and Multilaterals Confront the Crisis*. New York: New York University Press, 1989, 103-23.

Kirshner, Jonathan. *Currency and Coercion*. Princeton, NJ: Princeton University Press, 1995.

Kissinger, Henry. *American Foreign Policy*. New York: W.W. Norton, 1969.

Kohoma, Hirohisa, and Shujiro Urata. "The Impact of the Recent Yen Appreciation on the Japanese Economy," *The Developing Economies* 26, 4 (December 1988), 323-40.

Krasner, Stephen. "State Power and the Structure of International Trade," *World Politics* 28, 3 (April 1976), 317-47.

Krasner, Stephen. *Defending the National Interest*. Princeton, NJ: Princeton University Press, 1978.

Krasner, Stephen, ed. *International Regimes*. Ithaca, NY: Cornell University Press, 1983.

Krasner, Stephen. *Structural Conflict: The Third World Against Global Liberalism*. Berkeley: University of Califonia Press, 1985.

Krasner, Stephen. "Westphalia and All That," in Judith Goldstein and Robert Keohane, eds., *Ideas and Foreign Policy*. Ithaca, NY: Cornell University Press, 1993, 235-64.

Krugman, Paul R., ed. *Strategic Trade Policy and the New International Economics*. Cambridge, Mass.: MIT Press, 1986.

Krugman, Paul R. "Is Free Trade Passé?" in *International Economics and International Economic Policy: A Reader*. New York: McGraw-Hill, 1990, 91-107.

Krugman, Paul R. "Policy problems of a monetary union," in Paul de Grauwe and Lucas Papademos, eds., *The EMS in the 1990s*. New York: Longman, 1990, 48-64.

Kuhn, Thomas. *The Structure of Scientific Revolutions*. Chicago: University of Chicago Press, 1962.

Kuhn, Thomas. "Reflections on my Critics," in Imre Lakatos and Alan Musgrave, eds., *Criticism and the Growth of Knowledge*. New York: Cambridge University Press, 1970, 231-78.

Lakatos, Imre. "Falsification and the Methodology of Scientific Research Programmes," in Imre Lakatos and Alan Musgrave, eds., *Criticism and the Growth of Knowledge*. New York: Cambridge University Press, 1970, 91-196.

Lake, David. "International Economic Structures and American Foreign Economic Policy, 1887-1934," *World Politics* 35, 4 (July 1983), 517-43.

Lairson, Thomas D., and David Skidmore. *International Political Economy: The Struggle for Power and Wealth*. New York: Harcourt Brace, 1993.

Lambi, Ivo. *Free Trade and Protection in Germany 1868-1879*. Weisbaden: Frantz Steiner Verlag, 1963.

Larson, Deborah. *The Origins of Containment*. Princeton, NJ: Princeton University Press, 1985.

Lebow, Richard Ned. *Between Peace and War*. Baltimore: Johns Hopkins University Press, 1981.

Lebow, Richard Ned. "Generational Learning and Conflict Management," *International Journal* 40, 4 (Autumn 1985), 555-85.

Lenin, V.I. "The Mature Marxist Theory, 1916," in D.K. Fieldhouse, ed., *The Theory of Capitalist Imperialism*. London: Longmans, 1967, 99-109.

Leyton-Brown, David. "The Political Economy of North American Free Trade," in Richard Stubbs and Geoffrey R.D. Underhill, eds., *Political Economy and the Changing Global Order*. Toronto: McClelland & Stewart, 1994, 352-65.

Liebenthal, Robert, and Peter Nicholas. "World Bank-Supported Adjustment Programs," in John F. Weeks, ed., *Debt Disaster?: Banks, Governments, and Multilaterals Confront the Crisis*. New York: New York University Press, 1989, 91-102.

Lim, Youngil. *Government Policy and Private Enterprise: Korean Experience in Industrialization*. Korea Research Monograph 6, Center for Korean Studies, Institute of East Asian Studies (Berkeley), 1981.

Lindert, Peter. "Key Currencies and Gold, 1900-1913," *Princeton Studies in International Finance* No. 24 (August 1969).

Lipsey, Richard G., Daniel Schwanen, and Ronald J. Wonnacott. *The NAFTA: What's In, What's Out, What's Next*. Ottawa: C.D. Howe Institute, Policy Study No. 21, 1994.

Lipson, Charles. "Bankers' Dilemma: Private Cooperation in Rescheduling Sovereign Debts," *World Politics* 38, 1 (October 1985), 200-25.

Lipson, Charles. "International Debt and International Institutions," in Miles Kahler, ed., *The Politics of International Debt*. Ithaca, NY: Cornell University Press, 1986, 219-43.

List, Friedrich. *The National System of Political Economy*. New York: Augustus M. Kelley, 1966 (originally published between 1841 and 1844).

Lowi, Theodore. "Making Democracy Safe for the World: National Politics and Foreign Policy," in James N. Rosenau, ed., *Domestic Sources of Foreign Policy*. New York: Free Press, 1967, 295-331.

Loxley, John. *Debt and Disorder: External Financing for Development*. Boulder, Colo.: Westview Press, 1986.

Lusztig, Michael. "Solving Peel's Puzzle: Repeal of the Corn Laws and Institutional Preservation," *Comparative Politics* 27, 4 (July 1995), 393-408.

Lusztig, Michael. *Risking Free Trade*. Pittsburgh: University of Pittsburgh Press, 1996.

Mackinder, Halford. "The Geographical Pivot of History," *Geographical Journal* 23 (April 1904).

Mackinder, Halford. *Democratic Ideals and Reality*. New York: Norton, 1962.

Magee, Stephen. "Three Simple Tests of the Stolper-Samuelson Theorem," in P. Oppenheimer, ed., *Issues in International Economics*. London: Oriel Press, 1978, 138-53.

Magee, Stephen. "The Political Economy of Protectionism: Comment," in J.N. Bhagwati, ed., *Import Competition and Response*. Chicago: University of Chicago Press, 1982.

Mahan, Alfred T. *The Influence of Seapower on History, 1660-1783*. Boston: Little, Brown, 1897.

Mansfield, Edward D. *Power, Trade and War*. Princeton, NJ: Princeton University Press, 1994.

Martin, Lisa. "International and Domestic Institutions in the EMU Process," in Barry Eichengreen and Jeffry Frieden, eds., *The Political Economy of European Monetary Unification*. Boulder, Colo.: Westview Press, 1994, 87-106.

Martin, Lisa. "An Institutionalist View: International Institutions and State Strategies," in John A. Hall and T.V. Paul, eds., *International Order in the Twenty-first Century* (forthcoming).

Masera, Rainer Stefano. "An Increasing Role for the ECU: A Character in Search of a Script," *Princeton Essays in International Finance* No. 167 (June 1987).

May, Trevor. *An Economic and Social History of Britain, 1760-1970*. New York: Longman, 1987.

Mayer, Arno. "Internal Causes and Purposes of War in Europe, 1870-1956," *Journal of Modern History* 41 (September 1969), 291-303.

McCloskey, Donald N., and Richard J. Zecher. "How the Gold Standard Worked, 1880-1913," in Jacob A. Frenkel and Harry G. Johnson, eds., *The Monetary Approach to the Balance of Payments*. London: Allen & Unwin, 1976, 184-208.

McKeown, Timothy. "Hegemonic Stability Theory and Nineteenth Century Tariff Levels in Europe," *International Organization* 37, 1 (Winter 1983), 73-92.

Mearsheimer, John. "Back to the Future: Instability in Europe after the Cold War," *International Security* 15 (1990), 5-56.

Mielke, Siegfried. *Der Hansa-Bund für Gewerbe, Handel und Industrie 1909-1914, Der gescheiterterte Versuch einer antifeudalen Sammlungspolitik,* Kritische Studien zur Geschichtswissenschaft (Band 17). Göttingen: Vandenhoek & Ruprecht, 1976.

Miller, Riel, "Assessing Economic Benefits," in Duncan Cameron, ed., *The Free Trade Deal*. Toronto: James Lorimer, 1988, 59-70.

Milner, Helen. "A Critique of Anarchy," in Robert Art and Robert Jervis, eds., *International Politics: Enduring Concepts and Contemporary Issues*. New York: Harper-Collins, 1996, 70-80.

Modelski, George. *Long Cycles in World Politics*. Seattle: University of Washington Press, 1987.

Moggridge, D.E. *The Return to Gold, 1925: The Formulation of Economic Policy and its Critics*. London: Cambridge University Press, 1969.

Moggridge, D.E. *British Monetary Policy 1924-1931*. New York: Cambridge University Press, 1972.

Molot, Maureen Appel. "The Canadian State in the International Economy," in Richard Stubbs and Geoffrey R.D. Underhill, eds., *Political Economy and the Changing Global Order*. Toronto: McClelland & Stewart, 1994, 511-23.

Moravscik, Andrew. "Liberalism and International Relations Theory," Harvard University Working Paper No. 92-6.

Morgenthau, Hans. *Scientific Man vs. Power Politics*. Chicago: University of Chicago Press, 1946.

Morse, Edward L. "Political Choice and Alternative Monetary Regimes," in Michael Schwarz, ed., *Alternatives to Monetary Disorder*. New York: McGraw-Hill, 1977, 65-139.

Nipperdey, Thomas. "Interessenverbände und Parteien in Deutschland vor dem Ersten Weltkrieg," in H.-U. Wehler, ed., *Moderne deutsche Sozialgeschichte*. Berlin: Kiepenheuer & Witsch, 1966.

Nipperdey, Thomas. *Deutsche Geschichte 1866-1918, Zweiter Band, Machtstaat vor der Demokratie*. München: Verlag C.H. Beck, 1992.

North, Robert C. "Towards a Framework for the Analysis of Scarcity and Conflict," *International Studies Quarterly* 21 (December 1977), 569-91.

Nye, John Vincent. "The Myth of Free-Trade Britain and Fortress France: Tariffs and Trade in the Nineteenth Century," *Journal of Economic History* 51, 1 (March 1991), 23-46.

O'Brien, Patrick K., and Geoffrey Pigman. "Free Trade, British Hegemony, and the International Economic Order in the Nineteenth Century," *Review of International Studies* 18 (April 1992), 89-113.

Odell, John S. "The U.S. and the Emergence of Flexible Exchange Rates," *International Organization* 33, 1 (Winter 1979), 57-81.

Odell, John. *U.S. International Monetary Policy*. Princeton, NJ: Princeton University Press, 1982.

Odell, John. "From London to Bretton Woods: Sources of Change in Bargaining Strategies and Outcomes," *Journal of Public Policy* 8, 3/4 (1988), 287-315.

Oliver, Robert. "Early Plans for a World Bank," *Princeton Studies in International Finance* No. 29 (1971).

Organski, A.F.K. "The Power Transition," in *World Politics*. New York: Knopf, 1958.

Pastor, Robert. *Congress and the Politics of U.S. Foreign Economic Policy, 1929-1976*. Berkeley: University of California Press, 1980.

Paul, T.V. *Asymmetric Conflicts: War Initiation by Weaker Powers*. Cambridge: Cambridge University Press, 1994.

Plumptre, A.F.W. *Three Decades of Decision: Canada and the World Monetary System, 1944-75*. Toronto: McClelland & Stewart, 1977.

Polanyi, Karl. *The Great Transformation*. Boston: Beacon Press, 1957.

Popper, Karl. *The Logic of Scientific Discovery*. New York: Basic Books, 1959.

Pregrave de A. Faria, Hugo. "Brazil, 1985-1987: Pursuing Heterodoxy to a Moratorium," in Thomas J. Biersteker, ed., *Dealing with Debt*. Boulder, Colo.: Westview Press, 1993, 175-97.

Preussen, Ronald W. *John Foster Dulles: The Road to Power*. New York, 1982.

Puhle, Hans-Jürgen. "Parlament, Parteien und Interessenverbaende 1890-1914," in Michael Stürmer, ed., *Das kaiserliche Deutschland, Politik und Gesellschaft 1870-1918*. Düsseldorf: Droste Verlag, 1970, 340-77.

Pzerworski, Adam, and Henry Teune. *The Logic of Comparative Social Inquiry*. New York: Wiley, 1970.

Quester, George. *Offense and Defense in the International System*. New York: John Wiley & Sons, 1977.

Rees, J.F. *A Short Fiscal and Financial History of England*. London: Methuen, 1921.

Reisman, Simon. "The Nature of the Canada-U.S. Trade Agreement," in Murray G. Smith and Frank Stone, eds., *Assessing the Canada-U.S. Free Trade Agreement*. Halifax: Institute for Research on Public Policy, 1987, 41-50.

Ricardo, David. *Principles of Political Economy and Taxation*. London: Dent, 1965 (originally published in 1817).

Richardson, J. David. "The Political Economy of Strategic Trade Policy," *International Organization* 44, 1 (Winter 1990), 107-35.

Rieke, Wolfgang. "Alternative views on the EMS in the 1990s," in Paul de Grauwe and Lucas Papademos, eds., *The EMS in the 1990s*. New York: Longman, 1990, 29-39.

Rogowski, Ronald. *Commerce and Coalitions*. Princeton, NJ: Princeton University Press, 1989.

Röhl, John C.G. "Beamtenpolitik im Wilhelminischen Deutschland," in Michael Stürmer, ed., *Das kaiserliche Deutschland, Politik und Gesellschaft 1870-1918*. Düsseldorf: Droste Verlag, 1970, 287-311.

Rosecrance, Richard. *Action and Reaction in World Politics*. Boston: Little, Brown, 1963.

Rosecrance, Richard. *The Rise of the Trading State*. New York: Basic Books, 1986.

Rosenau, James R., and Mary Durfee. *Thinking Theory Thoroughly*. Boulder, Colo.: Westview Press, 1995.

Roskin, Michael. "From Pearl Harbor to Vietnam: Shifting Generational Paradigms," *Political Science Quarterly* 89, 3 (Fall 1974), 563-88.

Ruggie, J.G. "International Regimes, Transactions, and Change: Embedded Liberalism in the Postwar Economic Order," *International Organization* 36, 2 (Spring 1982).

Russett, Bruce. *Grasping the Democratic Peace*. Princeton, NJ: Princeton University Press, 1993.

Russett, Bruce, and Harvey Starr. *World Politics: The Menu for Choice,* 4th ed. New York: Freeman, 1992.

Sachs, Jeffrey. "External Debt and Macroeconomic Performance in Latin America and East Asia," *Brookings Papers on Economic Activity* 2 (1985), 523-64.

Sacks, Paul M., and Chris Canavan. "Safe Passage through Dire Straits: Managing an Orderly Exit from the Debt Crisis," in John F. Weeks, ed., *Debt Disaster?: Banks, Governments, and Multilaterals Confront the Crisis*. New York: New York University Press, 1989, 75-87.

Scammell, W.M. *The Stability of the International Monetary System*. Totowa, NJ: Rowman & Littlefield, 1987.

Schattschneider, E.E. *Politics, Pressures and the Tariff*. New York: Prentice-Hall, 1935.

Schneider, Jürgen. "Die Auswirkungen von Zöllen und Handelsvertrgen sowie Handelshemmnissen auf Staat, Wirtschaft und Gesellschaft zwischen 1890 und 1914," in Hans Pohl, ed., *Die Auswirkungen von Zöllen und anderen Handelshemmnissen auf Wirtschaft und Gesellschaft von Mittelalter bis zur Gegenwart*. Stuttgart: Franz Steiner Verlag, 1987 (Vierteljahrschrift für Sozial- und Wirtschaftsgeschichte, Beiheft 80), 293-327.

Schonhardt-Bailey, Cheryl. "Specific Factors, Capital Markets, Portfolio Diversification and Free Trade: Domestic Determinants of the Repeal of the Corn Laws," *World Politics* 43 (1991), 345-69.

Simmons, Beth. *Who Adjusts?* Princeton, NJ: Princeton University Press, 1994.

Singer, John David. "The Level-of-Analysis Problem in International Relations," in Klaus Knorr and Sidney Verba, eds., *The International System: Theoretical Essays*. Princeton, NJ: Princeton University Press, 1961, 77-92.

Smith, Adam. *The Wealth of Nations*. Oxford: Clarendon Press, 1976 (originally published in 1776).

Smith, Murray, and Frank Stone. "Editor's Introduction," in Smith and Stone, eds., *Assessing the Canada-U.S. Free Trade Agreement*. Halifax: Institute for Research on Public Policy, 1987, 3-17.

Snyder, Glenn H. "'Prisoner's Dilemma' and 'Chicken' Models in International Politics," *International Studies Quarterly* 15 (March 1971), 66-103.

Snyder, Glenn, and Paul Diesin. *Conflict Among Nations*. Princeton, NJ: Princeton University Press, 1977.

Snyder, Jack. *Myths of Empire*. Ithaca, NY: Cornell University Press, 1991.

Spero, Joan E. *The Politics of International Economic Relations*, 4th ed. New York: St. Martin's Press, 1990.

Spykman, Nicholas. "Geography and Foreign Policy, 1," *American Political Science Review* 32 (February 1938), 213-36.

Spykman, Nicholas. *America's Strategy in World Politics*. New York: Harcourt Brace Jovanovich, 1942.

Steger, Debra. "Analysis of the Dispute Settlement Provisions: A Canadian Perspective," in Murray G. Smith and Frank Stone, eds., *Assessing the Canada-U.S. Free Trade Agreement*. Halifax: Institute for Research on Public Policy, 1987, 91-98.

Stein, Arthur A. "The Hegemon's Dilemma: Great Britain, the United States, and Economic Order," *International Organization* 38, 2 (Spring 1984), 355-86.

Stein, Arthur A. *Why Nations Cooperate*. Ithaca, NY: Cornell University Press, 1990.

Steinberg, Blema. *Shame and Humiliation*. Montreal: McGill-Queen's University Press, 1996.

Stoessinger, John. *Crusaders and Pragmatists*. New York: W.W. Norton, 1979.

Strange, Susan. *Sterling and British Policy: A Political Study of an International Currency in Decline*. New York: Oxford University Press, 1971.

Strange, Susan. "The Politics of International Currencies," *World Politics* 23, 2 (January 1971), 215-31.

Strange, Susan. *Casino Capitalism*. London: Basil Blackwell, 1986.

Tavlas, George. "On the International Use of Currencies: The Case of the Deutsche Mark," *Princeton Essays in International Finance* No. 181 (1991).

Thiel, Elke. "Die D-Mark zwischen dem Dollar und dem EWS," *Aussenpolitik* 33, 1 (1982), 37-46.

Thygesen, Niels. "The Delors Report and European Economic and Monetary Union," *International Affairs* 65, 4 (Autumn 1989), 637-52.

Thygesen, Niels. "Institutional developments in the evolution from EMS towards EMU," in Paul de Grauwe and Lucas Papademos, eds., *The EMS in the 1990s*. New York: Longman, 1990, 3-26.

Ullmann, Hans-Peter. *Der Bund der Industriellen*. Göttingen: Vandenhoek & Ruprecht, 1976 (Kritische Studien zur Geschichtswissenschaft, Band 21).

Vasquez, John A. *The Power of Power Politics: A Critique*. New Brunswick, NJ: Rutgers University Press, 1983.

Vernon, Raymond. "International Investment and International Trade in the Product Cycle," *Quarterly Journal of Economics* 80, 2 (1966), 190-207.

Vinals, Jose. "The EMS, Spain and macroeconomic policy," in Paul de Grauwe and Lucas Papademos, eds., *The EMS in the 1990s*. New York: Longman, 1990, 201-26.

Viner, Jacob. "Power versus Plenty as Objectives of Foreign Policy in the Seventeenth and Eighteenth Centuries," *World Politics* 1, 1 (October 1948), 1-29.

de Vries, Tom. "Jamaica, or the Non-Reform of the IMF," *Foreign Affairs* 54, 3 (April 1976), 577-605.

Wade, Robert. *Governing the Market: Economic Theory and the Role of Government in East Asian Industrialization*. Princeton, NJ: Princeton University Press, 1990.

Wallerstein, Immanuel. *The Modern World-System*, 3 vols. New York: Academic Press, 1974, 1980, 1989.

Walt, Stephen M. *The Origins of Alliances*. Ithaca, NY: Cornell University Press, 1987.

Walter, Andrew. *World Power and World Money*. Hertfordshire: Harvester Wheatsheaf, 1991.

Waltz, Kenneth. *Man, the State, and War*. New York: Columbia University Press, 1954.

Waltz, Kenneth. "The Stability of a Bipolar World," *Daedalus* 93 (Summer 1964), 881-909.

Waltz, Kenneth. *Theory of International Politics*. Reading, Mass.: Addison-Wesley, 1979.

Weede, Erich. "Democracy and War Involvement," *Journal of Conflict Resolution* 28, 4 (1984), 649-64.

Wehler, Hans-Ulrich. *The German Empire 1871-1918*. Dover, NH: Berg, 1985.

Weinstein, Edwin A., James William Anderson, and Arthur S. Link. "Woodrow Wilson's Political Personality: A Reappraisal," *Political Science Quarterly* 93 (Winter 1978), 585-98.

Weitowitz, Rolf. *Deutsche Politik und Handelspolitik unter Reichskanzler Leo von Caprivi 1890-1894*. Düsseldorf: Droste Verlag, 1978.

Wendt, Alexander. "Anarchy is What States Make of It," *International Organization* 46, 2 (Spring 1992), 391-425.

Weyland, Kurt. *Democracy without Equity: Failures of Reform in Brazil*. Pittsburgh: University of Pittsburgh Press, 1996.

Wicker, Elmus. *Federal Reserve Monetary Policy 1917-1933*. New York: Random House, 1966.

Wolfers, Arnold. "National Interest as an Ambiguous Symbol," in *Discord and Collaboration*. Baltimore: Johns Hopkins University Press, 1962, 147-65.

Wonnacott, Paul. "The Automotive Sector in the U.S.-Canada Free Trade Agreement," in Murray G. Smith and Frank Stone, eds., *Assessing the Canada-U.S. Free Trade Agreement*. Halifax: Institute for Research on Public Policy, 1987, 73-77.

Woo, Jung-en. *Race to the Swift: State and Finance in Korean Industrialization*. New York: Columbia University Press, 1991.

Woodside, Kenneth. "The Canada-U.S. FTA," *Canadian Journal of Political Science* 22, 1 (March 1989), 155-70.

Yee, Albert S. "The Causal Effects of Ideas on Policies," *International Organization* 50, 1 (Winter 1996), 69-108.

Glossary

....

This glossary does not refer to the general definition of these terms, or even to their general usage in political science, but rather refers merely to their common usage within the subfield of international political economy. Some frequently used political economic terms are also provided.

absolute advantage → An actor has an absolute advantage in the production of a good or service if it can produce that good or service with fewer resources than other actors.

accuracy → One of the qualities we can use in evaluating and comparing theories, referring to the probability that the theory will provide the correct answer.

adjustable peg → A type of exchange rate regime where rates are fixed, but countries retain the right to change rates whenever they see fit. See *exchange rate*.

assumption → The basic starting point for a causal theory. Something assumed to be true; a simplification, used to bring clarity to a complex situation or relationship.

autarky → A situation where there are no international economic transactions taking place.

balance of payments → A nation's accounting records, which track its international economic transactions.

balance-of-payments adjustment → This refers to the way in which states settle their bills.

balance of power → A term with many meanings, it usually refers to either any distribution of power (it doesn't matter if power is evenly distributed or not) or a perfectly even distribution of power.

beggar-thy-neighbour policy → A policy intended to transfer unemployment problems from one country to another via protectionism.

behaviouralists → Those who believe that the proper way to construct and to test theories involves making many observations of variables, aggregating the information, and applying methods of data analysis (statistics) to interpret the evidence. This view is contrasted with that of the *traditionalists*.

belief system → A set of beliefs about how the world works, and/or how it ought to work. See *ideology*.

bipolar → One of several different possible distributions of power; in this case, a distribution where two states or alliances have power concentrated in their control.

bolstering → Bolstering occurs when a decision-maker stops engaging in the broad search for information and, instead of exploring the full range of policy options, merely searches for information that supports the choice he or she has already made.

bureaucratic politics → One of the commonly used levels of analysis; theories in this group concentrate their explanations for state policy on divisions within the state itself, which pit one bureaucracy against another.

capital account → A subset of the balance of payments, which records the borrowing, selling, or purchasing of assets.

classical liberalism → The earliest form of liberalism, which promised that national wealth would be increased if individuals were free to compete against each other (pursuing their own narrow self-interest), as opposed to having the state interfere with the market

classical Marxism → The earlist form of Marxism, which emphasized that social classes are the most important actors in domestic or international politics. See *Marxism*.

classical realism → The earliest version of *realism*, which, in order to counter the arguments of idealists, assumed human nature to be selfish and driven by a desire for power.

Coase theorem → An argument describing possible situations where problems with externalities can be overcome, even in the absence of government. The Coase theorem states that if (1) there is a legal framework to establish liabilities, (2) there is perfect information (and also everyone understands their own preferences), and (3) there are zero negotiating costs, actors can resolve problems arising from externalities through deal-making.

commercial liberalism → An early version of liberalism, which argued that free trade was not only beneficial to individuals in an economic sense, and therefore economically beneficial to states (since states are merely agglomerations of individuals), but would also provide the basis for a harmony of interests in the international system. See *liberalism*.

comparative advantage → If two actors have different opportunity costs for producing a good or service, the one with the lower opportunity cost has a comparative advantage in that good or service.

competitive devaluation → A reduction in the value of a currency in order to gain a competitive advantage in trade.

complex interdependence → An approach developed by Keohane and Nye in the 1970s to open up the realms of theorizing away from the narrow assumptions of realism.

Concert of the Great Powers → The management of the European state system after the defeat of Napoleon in 1815, through a conscious co-ordinated effort by the most powerful states.

confidence → A characteristic of a currency, referring to the faith people place in it as a store of value.

constructivism → A commonly used paradigm in international relations. It poses questions that come prior to the analysis undertaken in most paradigms. Key concepts such as interests have no meaning without establishing actors' identities and placing actors and interests in social context, argue the Constructivists.

convertibility → The ability to switch from a currency to another currency or asset.

crawling peg → A type of exchange rate regime where rates are fixed only for the very short run, with many frequent small changes in rates. The intention is to prevent any large changes. See *exchange rate*.

crisis → Most definitions of an international crisis include (1) a high threat to something valued very highly, (2) surprise, and (3) the need for a quick response.

culture → A set of characteristics shared by a group of individuals or a nation; this has been used as a causal factor for explaining international outcomes.

current account → A subset of the balance of payments denoting net changes in a country's claims on foreigners.

deductive theorizing → One method of reasoning, which involves first postulating a logical relationship between cause and effect, then making repeated observations to evaluate and refine the relationship. See *inductive theorizing*.

defensive procrastination → Defensive procrastination occurs when someone refuses to deal with a problem in the hope that the problem will resolve itself.

deflation → A decline in the average level of prices.

dependent variable → The term used to identify the outcome one is attempting to predict or explain. Its variation depends on the variations of the independent variables.

description → One of the basic tasks of a causal theory; the act of forming a representation.

dirty float → On a floating exchange rate, a situation where a state has intervened in the market to set its exchange rate at a level it desires. See *exchange rate*.

division of labour → The breaking up of the stages of production into different tasks. See *specialization*.

domestic level → One of the commonly used levels of analysis; theories in this group concentrate their explanations for state policy on domestic characteristics of countries, or on the politics that takes place within their borders. See *societal level*.

dumping → Selling a good in foreign markets at a price lower than the price charged in the home market.

epistemic communities → A group of experts whose consensus on what constitutes knowledge creates a shared view of an issue.

Eurodollars → U.S. dollars held by banks outside the U.S. government's jurisdiction.

exchange rate → The price of one national currency in terms of another. Systems of exchange rates are either fixed (i.e., the prices are set and not allowed to vary very much) or floating (i.e., the prices fluctuate as in most other markets).

export-oriented industrialization (EOI) → A strategy for developing a country's industrial sector by selling its output abroad, rather than relying on domestic demand. See *import-substitution industrialization* (ISI).

externality → Situations where the market fails to cover the entire set of costs and benefits associated with a particular transaction.

externalization → Externalization occurs when a society is becoming unstable, and in order to reconsolidate their control, élite policymakers instigate an international incident, crisis, or conflict to divert the population from domestic problems or domestic differences.

extraterritoriality → Extraterritoriality is the extension of national jurisdiction beyond a nation's own borders.

factor mobility → The ease with which a factor of production can be moved form one application to another.

factors of production → The inputs necessary for producing a good or service. In the most simple models, the factors are capital and labour.

falsifiability → One of the qualities we can use in evaluating and comparing theories. It refers to our ability to test a theory; if a theory is falsifiable, there are explicit terms under which the theory could be said to fail.

foreign direct investment (FDI) → International investment involving the direct ownership and operation of the venture. See *portfolio investment*.

generalizability → One of the qualities we can use in evaluating and comparing theories, referring to how widely the theory can be applied.

Gresham's law → The observation that bad money will drive good money out of circulation.

Heartland → A geopolitical notion developed by Mackinder to describe the centre of the Eurasian land mass, which he considered to be the most important strategic terrain in the world. See *Rimland*.

Heckscher-Ohlin (H-O) *model* → A model intended to explain the content and direction of trade flows. It expects each country to export goods that intensively use the locally most abundant factor(s) and to import goods whose production required intensive use of the locally scarce factor(s) of production.

hegemonic → See *unipolar*.

hegemonic stability theory → A realist explanation for the creation and maintenance of international regimes; according to this view, regimes are an outcome of the exercise of power. Therefore, regimes are only strong and stable when international power is concentrated in the hands of one state (a hegemonic power) that supports the international regime in question.

horizontal integration → One strategy for expansion of a firm; it entails monopolization of one step in the production process.

idea → A thought or belief; recently being used as a causal factor in theories in international relations.

idealism → A commonly used paradigm in international relations. It was the first dominant paradigm to emerge (after World War 1). Idealism stresses the possibility of perfecting the behaviour of man (usually through the creation of institutions or laws) and thus perfecting the actions of states, thereby making possible the attainment of international peace and harmony.

ideology → A set of beliefs about how the world works, and/or how it ought to work. See *belief system*.

import-substitution industrialization (ISI) → A strategy for developing a country's industrial sector by blocking imports of industrial goods, forcing domestic demand to support national industries. See *export-oriented industrialization* (EOI).

independent variable → The causal factor in a theory.

indifference curve → A diagram showing the possible mix of two goods, which then depicts on a curve all the points between which an actor is indifferent.

individual level → One of the commonly used levels of analysis; theories in this group concentrate their explanations for state policy on idiosyncratic characteristics of individuals.

inductive theorizing → One method of reasoning, which involves first making repeated observations, then inferring the logical relationship between cause and effect. See *deductive theorizing*.

inflation → A rise in the average level of prices.

institutionalism → A recently developed paradigm that was originally postulated to explain the persistence of regimes outside of hegemonic stability theory. Institutionalists argue that if regimes deliver benefits to the participants, the participants would have reasons to maintain or even create international regimes. Also referred to as *rationalist institutionalism*.

instrumental Marxism → A version of Marxism, made popular by Lenin, that focuses on explaining the actions of states but views states as instruments of the interests of each country's capitalists. See *Marxism*.

interdependence → Interdependence can be defined as a situation where changes or events in any single part produce some reaction or have a significant consequence in other parts of the system, or more simply, as the mutual contingency of policies.

international political economy → The analysis of the interaction of power and the processes of wealth creation at the international level.

international regime → According to Krasner, an international regime is a set of "principles, rules, norms and decision-making procedures around which actors' expectations converge."

international relations → The study of politics involving an international dimension; relations between states and external actors (states and non-state actors), as well as between non-state actors and other external actors (states and non-state actors), or involving the formulation of a policy with repercussions for actors outside the country.

key currency → A national currency that plays the role of international money.

Keynesianism → A view of macroeconomics that prescribes an active, positive role of government in managing the economy through manipulation of fiscal and monetary policy.

law → Laws are connections between variables of which we have repeated observations, of such strength and number that we can safely expect the relations to continue into the future.

Leontief paradox → paradoxical results produced in empirical analysis of the imports and exports of U.S., which seem to disconfirm the *Heckscher-Ohlin model*.

levels of analysis → A method for grouping theories together, based on the types of assumptions made about the most important actors.

leverage → One of the qualities we can use in evaluating and comparing theories. The ability to explain as much as possible with as little as possible.

liberalism → A commonly used paradigm in international relations that bases its arguments on the actions of rational utility-maximizing individuals.

liquidity → A characteristic of a currency, referring to its availability, which in turn determines how well it can serve as a medium of exchange.

Marxism → A commonly used paradigm in international relations that bases its explanations of politics on the relationships between social classes.

mercantilism → A practice in foreign economic policies of the seventeenth and eighteenth centuries that entailed a set of policies designed to maintain an inward flow of money, but these policies were barriers to trade and international investment.

modern world-systems → A set of works that blends history, sociology, and political science to develop a deeper understanding of the historical development of the international political economy. It is rooted within Marxist traditions and looks at actors at several levels of analysis.

monopoly → A market in which there is only one seller.

most-favoured-nation (MFN) *clause* → A clause in a trade treaty that commits a country to impose no greater barriers to imports of the signatory than it imposes on imports from any other country.

multinational corporation (MNC) → A corporation that carries on business operations in several countries.

multipolar → One of several different possible distributions of power; in this case, a distribution where more than three states or alliances have power concentrated in their control.

national level → One of the commonly used levels of analysis; theories in this group concentrate their explanations for state policy on characteristics of the country or on internal political economic activities. See *societal level*.

neo-realism → A recent version of realism, recognizing the importance of other goals that states might have by modifying the assumption that states seek to maximize power.

non-tariff barrier (NTB) → A broad concept, used to denote impediments to trade (excepting tariffs).

normative goal → One of the basic tasks of a causal theory. A vision of the way things ought to be.

oligopoly → A market in which there are only a few sellers.

opportunity cost → The amount an input could earn in its next best possible application; the alternative forgone when something is produced.

organizational processes → Here, the argument is that bureaucratic organizations are entirely flexible, and thus may affect the implementation of policy; policy may be rationally formulated, but then bureaucracies and organizations may not be able to carry them out as originally intended, making policy appear irrational.

paradigm → An example that others copy and employ as well, or a set of core assumptions (often established in a single example that theorists draw on) shared by many similar theories. The set of core assumptions defines a grouping of theories, and separates one paradigm from another.

parsimony → One of the qualities we can use in evaluating and comparing theories. It refers to the degree of simplicity and reflects the ability to explain much of the variation in the dependent variable with as little information or theory as possible.

Phillips curve → A diagram used to portray the relationship between inflation and unemployment.

policy paradigm → A concept developed by Peter Hall, which he defines as an overarching set of ideas that specify how the problems facing them are to be perceived, which goals might be attained through policy, and what sorts of techniques can be used to reach those goals.

portfolio investment → An indirect investment—one where ownership or investment does not entail direct management of the economic activity resulting from the investment.

power → In political science, power is usually defined as control over actors, especially their actions (i.e., the ability to get an actor to do something which he/she otherwise wouldn't do).

power transition → A term originated by A.F.K. Organski to identify a period when internally driven changes rapidly alter a country's strength, thereby altering the systemic distribution of power.

prediction → One of the basic tasks of a causal theory, referring to the act of foretelling an event.

prescription → One of the basic tasks of a causal theory, referring to the act of providing advice or direction.

prisoners' dilemma → An example from game theory, which illustrates a situation where two egoistic actors interact yet fail to attain their harmony of interests.

product cycle → An argument developed by Vernon to explain when FDI takes place; it is based on the notion that products go through a characteristic life cycle, reflecting the varying ability of firms to produce the good over time.

production possibility frontier → A curve illustrating the limits of output that can be produced with various combinations of inputs.

public good → A good characterized by both non-excludability and non-rival consumption.

quota → A typical barrier to trade, which limits the volume of goods coming into a country.

rally-round-the-flag effect → A concept used to identify the tendency for domestic differences to be set aside in a foreign policy crisis.

rate of transformation → The rate at which production can be shifted from one product to another.

rationality → A common assumption made about actors in our theories, which states that actors will try to attain their highest preferences at the least cost. The assumption of rationality contains three conditions: first, the actor is assumed to have perfect information—it is assumed the actor knows all its options and all the costs and benefits (the ramifications) associated with each option; second, the actor must understand the causal effect of each possible choice; third, the actor must be able to rank its choices, which requires that it be able to relate what it values into some sort of schedule of preferences.

rationalist institutionalism → See *institutionalism*.

realism → A commonly used paradigm in international relations. Realism emerged as the dominant paradigm in the 1940s and has remained so until recent years. It has stressed the importance of power in international relations and the continuity in states' behaviour. It also emphasizes the anarchic nature of the international system, which allows states to use power to resolve differences.

reflectivist institutionalism → A very recent version of institutional-ism, which argues that existing institutions and norms shape the ways in which actors' preferences are defined. The institutionalists using a reflectivist approach stress that international regimes are rarely the product of purely rational design, but instead are shaped by existing norms and institutions.

republican liberalism → A version of liberalism emphasizing the polit-ical aspects of liberalism by arguing that republics behave differently; where individuals have a say in the formulation of national policy, national policy will be peaceful and pursue the creation of wealth. See *liberalism*.

reserves → Commodities or assets held as backing for a currency.

Rimland → A geopolitical notion developed by Nicholas Spykman to describe the outer edge of the Eurasian land mass, which he consid-ered to be the most important strategic terrain in the world due to the concentration of economic and industrial power in these regions. See *Heartland*.

role level → See *bureaucratic politics*.

security dilemma → A concept used to describe relations between sovereign states in the context of international anarchy, where each state treats its neighbours as the potential source of threats; as each increases its power, it makes the other insecure. The overall results are competitions for power and insecurity.

specialization → The act of concentrating production on one type of good, or even one stage in the production of a good, to exploit *com-parative advantage*.

societal level → One of the commonly used levels of analysis; theories in this group concentrate their explanations for state policy on char-acteristics of the country's society or on internal political economic activities. See *national level*.

sovereignty → Sovereignty refers to the ability to exercise the ultimate legitimate political authority.

stagflation → A situation where an economy suffers both high inflation and high unemployment.

standard operating procedures → In order to function smoothly, large organizations such as government bureaucracies must practise routine operations; the range of manoeuvres a bureaucracy can perform may constrain policy choice or affect the way policy is actually implemented. See *organizational processes*.

state level → One of the commonly used levels of analysis; theories in this group concentrate their explanations for state policy on characteristics of the country overall, such as the type of governing institutions it has.

status inconsistency → A concept borrowed from sociology that denotes differences in the status an actor is accorded in the various facets of interactions with other actors. Inconsistency in the levels of status may be the root of frustrations and aggressive behaviour.

Stolper-Samuelson theorem → A theorem developed to understand the distribution of gains and losses from international trade. The relatively scarce factor of production will lose real earnings when trade levels rise, while the relatively abundant factor of production will gain real earnings.

strategic trade policy → A policy intended to change the benefits from trade, either by altering the position of particular firms or by changing the position of their economies in the international division of labour.

structural Marxism → A version of Marxism that explains the actions of states by arguing that states act politically to maintain the overall political economic structure of capitalism.

structural realism → A version of realism laid out by Kenneth Waltz in *Theory of International Politics* (1979). It stresses the characteristics of the structure of the international system in its explanations of state behaviour.

structure → Structure is a way of depicting the relations of the units or the composition of a system.

systemic level → One of the commonly used levels of analysis; theories in this group concentrate their explanations for state policy on characteristics of the international system.

tariff → A typical barrier to trade, which is a tax on goods as they cross a border.

theory → A speculative process for explaining observed relationships between variables.

traditionalists → Those who believe that the best way to construct theories is to make detailed observations of a few cases, relying more on historical analysis and seeing the uniqueness of each event. This view is contrasted with that of the *behaviouralists*.

tripolar → One of several different possible distributions of power; in this case, a distribution where three states or alliances have power concentrated in their control.

unipolar → One of several different possible distributions of power; in this case, a distribution where one state or alliance has power concentrated in its control. Also possibly described as *hegemonic*.

Utopianism → See *idealism*.

value-complexity → A term created by Alexander George to describe situtations where policies may entail trade-offs in values that a decision-maker would rather not face.

variable → A term used in our construction of theories that can refer to the forces or factors of both cause and effect.

vertical integration → One strategy for forming a large firm; it entails capturing the various stages of production within one firm.

wealth → A central concept in economics, referring to affluence and/or abundance.

Index